KINGSLEY JUNIOR HIGH SCHOOL

Cancer information for teens :

Cancer Information for Teens

TEEN HEALTH SERIES

First Edition

Cancer Information for Teens

Health Tips about Cancer Awareness, Prevention, Diagnosis, and Treatment

Including Facts about Frequently Occurring Cancers, Cancer Risk Factors, and Coping Strategies for Teens Fighting Cancer or Dealing with Cancer in Friends or Family Members

◆

Edited by Wilma R. Caldwell

Omnigraphics

615 Griswold Street • Detroit, MI 48226

McLean County Unit #5
204-Kingsley

Bibliographic Note

Because this page cannot legibly accommodate all the copyright notices, the Bibliographic Note portion of the Preface constitutes an extension of the copyright notice.

Edited by Wilma R. Caldwell

Teen Health Series

Karen Bellenir, *Managing Editor*
David A. Cooke, M.D., *Medical Consultant*
Elizabeth Barbour, *Permissions Associate*
Dawn Matthews, *Verification Assistant*
Laura Pleva Nielsen, *Index Editor*
EdIndex, Services for Publishers, *Indexers*

* * *

Omnigraphics, Inc.

Matthew P. Barbour, *Senior Vice President*
Kay Gill, *Vice President—Directories*
Kevin Hayes, *Operations Manager*
Leif Gruenberg, *Development Manager*
David P. Bianco, *Marketing Director*

* * *

Peter E. Ruffner, *Publisher*

Frederick G. Ruffner, Jr., *Chairman*

Copyright © 2004 Omnigraphics, Inc.

ISBN 0-7808-0678-6

Library of Congress Cataloging-in-Publication Data

Cancer information for teens : health tips about cancer awareness, prevention, diagnosis, and treatment ; including facts about frequently occurring cancers, cancer risk factors, and coping strategies for teens fighting cancer or dealing with cancer in friends or family members / edited by Wilma R. Caldwell.
    p. cm. -- (Teen health series)
Includes index.
ISBN 0-7808-0678-6 (hardcover : alk. paper)
1. Cancer--Juvenile literature. I. Caldwell, Wilma. II. Series.
RC264.C36 2004
616.99'4--dc22

2004006115

Electronic or mechanical reproduction, including photography, recording, or any other information storage and retrieval system for the purpose of resale is strictly prohibited without permission in writing from the publisher.

The information in this publication was compiled from the sources cited and from other sources considered reliable. While every possible effort has been made to ensure reliability, the publisher will not assume liability for damages caused by inaccuracies in the data, and makes no warranty, express or implied, on the accuracy of the information contained herein.

∞

This book is printed on acid-free paper meeting the ANSI Z39.48 Standard. The infinity symbol that appears above indicates that the paper in this book meets that standard.

Printed in the United States

Table of Contents

Preface ix

Part I—Introduction To Cancer

Chapter 1—What Is Cancer: Cancer's History, Nature, Causes, And Symptoms 3

Chapter 2—Types Of Cancer Teens Get 11

Chapter 3—Cancer Among Adolescents: Understanding The Statistics 17

Chapter 4—Leukemia In Teens 23

Chapter 5—Lymphoma In Teens 31

Chapter 6—Bone Cancer In Teens: Ewing's Sarcoma And Osteosarcoma 37

Chapter 7—Germ Cell Tumors In Teens 43

Chapter 8—Skin Cancer: Facts, Figures, And Questions 45

Chapter 9—What You Should Know About Common Cancers In Older Family Members 49

Part II—Risks, Rumors, And Controversies

Chapter 10—Tobacco And Cancer Risk 67

Chapter 11—Sun Exposure And Cancer Risk 87

Chapter 12—Cervical Cancer Risks Linked To
            Unprotected Sex 99

Chapter 13—Cancer Risks Associated With Heterocyclic
            Amines In Cooked Meats 105

Chapter 14—Studying A Possible Link Between Obesity
            And Cancer Risk 109

Chapter 15—Oral Contraceptives: Risks Are Difficult
            To Evaluate 117

Chapter 16—Cancer Risk Controversies About Cell Phones
            And Other Electronics 125

Chapter 17—Are There Any Cancer Risks Associated
            With Artificial Sweeteners And Fluoridated
            Water? 133

Chapter 18—Cancer Myths And Rumors 139

Part III—Cancer Detection, Diagnosis, And Treatment

Chapter 19—Screening Tests For Various Cancers 157

Chapter 20—How To Perform A Breast Self-Examination 169

Chapter 21—Testicular Cancer And The Importance Of
            Self-Examination 175

Chapter 22—How Cancer Is Diagnosed 181

Chapter 23—Who's Who In The Health Care System 195

Chapter 24—Hospitalization And Surgery For Cancer
            Treatment 201

Chapter 25—Chemotherapy, Radiation Therapy, And
            Immunotherapy 205

Chapter 26—Bone Marrow Transplants: Treatment, Side
    Effects, And Possible Complications 213

Chapter 27—Supportive Care During Cancer Treatment:
    Blood Transfusions, Antibiotics, And
    Supplemental Nutrition 219

Chapter 28—Complementary And Alternative Treatments
    In Cancer Care 227

Chapter 29—What Is Standard Therapy Versus A
    Clinical Trial? 237

Chapter 30—Uses And Side Effects Of Cancer Drugs 241

Chapter 31—Managing Side Effects Of Cancer Treatments 253

Chapter 32—Long-Term Side Effects Of Childhood
    Cancer Therapy 267

Part IV—Coping Strategies For Adolescents With Cancer

Chapter 33—School And Cancer: Advice On Staying Current,
    Getting In The Swing, And Finding Help If
    You Need It 275

Chapter 34—Counseling For Psychological Issues:
    Depression, Anxiety, And Post-Traumatic Stress 283

Chapter 35—Coping With Cancer's Affect On Appearance 287

Chapter 36—Sexuality And Dating: Special Concerns For
    Teens With Cancer 297

Chapter 37—When Friends Don't Call: Coping With
    Isolation and Loneliness 303

Chapter 38—What If The Cancer Comes Back? 307

Chapter 39—Follow-Up Care For Childhood Cancer Survivors 323

Part V—When A Family Member Or Friend Has Cancer

Chapter 40—If Someone You Know Has Cancer 331

Chapter 41—Helping Family Members Cope With Cancer 349

Chapter 42—Coping With Death, Traumatic Events,
            And Feelings 359

Part VI—If You Need More Information

Chapter 43—Sources Of Cancer Information, Advocacy,
            And Support 373

Chapter 44—Finding Cancer Information On The Internet 393

Chapter 45—Additional Reading On Cancer 403

Index 411

Preface

About This Book

Although cancer is rare in teens, it remains the leading cause of death by disease among young people between the ages of 10 and 19 in the United States, and during the past 20 years an increase in the incidence of some childhood cancers has been noted. Additionally, many of the lifestyle choices that are associated with increased cancer risk in later years—such as tobacco use, sun exposure, sexual practices, and diet—are linked to decisions made during the teen years. Adolescents also may encounter cancer in the people they care about and have questions regarding its causes, symptoms, and effects.

Cancer Information For Teens provides answers. It offers basic information about cancer, including the types of cancer that are most frequently diagnosed in adolescents, such as leukemia, lymphoma, osteosarcoma, Ewing's sarcoma, and testicular cancer, and common types of cancer that occur more frequently in older people. Known cancer risk factors are explained and differentiated from commonly circulated myths and rumors. A section on coping strategies offers suggestions for adolescents undergoing cancer treatment. Those whose lives are touched by cancer in a family member or friend will also find suggestions for handling their feelings and helping others. An end section includes directories that list resources for additional information and support.

How To Use This Book

This book is divided into parts and chapters. Parts focus on broad areas of interest; chapters are devoted to single topics within a part.

Part I: Introduction To Cancer provides basic information about the history of cancer, its symptoms, and the types of cancer most likely to affect teens or their family members or friends.

Part II: Risks, Rumors, And Controversies examines some known risk factors for cancer and describes how teens can take action to reduce those risks. It also includes information about suspected or controversial links to cancer, and it reports on cancer myths and rumors that continue to circulate despite evidence that they are unfounded.

Part III: Cancer Detection, Diagnosis, And Treatment describes the screening tests and self-examination procedures used to help identify cancer in its early stages. Facts about medical tests and who's who in the hospital help sort through the confusing maze of people and procedures involved in diagnosing cancer. Various forms of treatment—including radiation, surgery, immunotherapy, chemotherapy, bone marrow transplants, and complementary and alternative options—are explained, along with information about and the short-term and long-term side effects of cancer treatments.

Part IV: Coping Strategies For Adolescents With Cancer deals with areas that are of special concern to many teens: school, peer relationships, appearance, the emotional consequences of cancer, and handling the reactions of others. Issues related to long-term follow-up and the fear of cancer recurrence are also addressed.

Part V: When A Family Member Or Friend Has Cancer explains many of the issues that arise when a family member, friend, or other acquaintance has cancer. Topics include talking about cancer, coping with loss, and handling such feelings as anger and sadness.

Part VI: If You Need More Information provides information about resources for more information, support groups, and advocacy organizations. It also offers suggestions for distinguishing between valid and unreliable medical information.

Bibliographic Note

This volume contains documents and excerpts from publications issued by the following government agencies: Centers for Disease Control and

Prevention, Environmental Protection Agency, Food and Drug Administration, and the National Cancer Institute.

In addition, this volume contains copyrighted documents and articles produced by the following organizations and publications: American Cancer Society; Atlantic Health System; CancerSource; Children's Oncology Group; Columbia University Health Education Program; ERIC Counseling and Student Services Clearinghouse; Gale Group; Gillette Company; Melissa's Living Legacy Foundation; National Children's Cancer Society, Inc.; National Mental Health Association; National Pesticide Telecommunications Network; Nemours Foundation; Planned Parenthood Federation of America; *Prevention Magazine* (Rodale, Inc.); *Science News* (SCI Service, Inc.); TeenGrowth.com; and the University of Iowa Virtual Hospital.

Full citation information is provided on the first page of each chapter. Every effort has been made to secure all necessary rights to reprint the copyrighted material. If any omissions have been made, please contact Omnigraphics to make corrections for future editions.

Acknowledgements

The editor wishes to thank permissions associate Liz Barbour for her invaluable assistance and Karen Bellenir for her patience and guidance.

Note From The Editor

This book is part of Omnigraphics' *Teen Health Series*. The series provides basic information about a broad range of medical concerns. It is not intended to serve as a tool for diagnosing illness, in prescribing treatments, or as a substitute for the physician-patient relationship. All persons concerned about medical symptoms or the possibility of disease are encouraged to seek professional care from an appropriate health care provider.

At the request of librarians serving today's young adults, the *Teen Health Series* was developed as a specially focused set of volumes within Omnigraphics' *Health Reference Series*. Each volume deals comprehensively with a topic selected according to the needs and interests of people in middle school and high school. If there is a topic you would like to see addressed in a future volume of the *Teen Health Series*, please write to:

Editor
Teen Health Series
Omnigraphics, Inc.
615 Griswold Street
Detroit, MI 48226

Our Advisory Board

The *Teen Health Series* is reviewed by an Advisory Board comprised of librarians from public, academic, and medical libraries. We would like to thank the following board members for providing guidance to the development of this series:

> Dr. Lynda Baker, Associate Professor of Library and Information Science, Wayne State University, Detroit, MI
>
> Nancy Bulgarelli, William Beaumont Hospital Library, Royal Oak, MI
>
> Karen Imarisio, Bloomfield Township Public Library, Bloomfield Township, MI
>
> Karen Morgan, Mardigian Library, University of Michigan-Dearborn, Dearborn, MI
>
> Rosemary Orlando, St. Clair Shores Public Library, St. Clair Shores, MI

Medical Consultant

Medical consultation services are provided to the *Teen Health Series* editors by David A. Cooke, M.D. Dr. Cooke is a graduate of Brandeis University, and he received his M.D. degree from the University of Michigan. He completed residency training at the University of Wisconsin Hospital and Clinics. He is board-certified in internal medicine. Dr. Cooke currently works as part of the University of Michigan Health System and practices in Brighton, MI. In his free time, he enjoys writing, science fiction, and spending time with his family.

Part 1
Introduction To Cancer

Chapter 1

What Is Cancer: Cancer's History, Nature, Causes, And Symptoms

Cancer is a scary word. Even grown-ups get scared when someone has cancer. Why is cancer so scary? Because most people don't know a lot about cancer—like how few people get it, what it really is, and how it can be treated. Plus, almost everyone knows someone who got very sick or died from cancer. That makes it very scary. Read on to find out more about cancer in kids.

What Is Cancer?

Cancer is actually a group of many related diseases that all have to do with cells. Cells are the very small units that make up all living things, including the human body. There are billions of cells in each person's body.

Cancer happens when cells that are not normal grow and spread very fast. Normal body cells grow and divide and know to stop growing. Over time, they also die. Unlike these normal cells, cancer cells just continue to

---

About This Chapter: This information was provided by KidsHealth, one of the largest resources online for medically reviewed health information written for parents, kids, and teens. For more articles like this one, visit www.KidsHealth.org, or www.TeensHealth.org. © 2001 The Nemours Center for Children's Health Media, a division of the Nemours Foundation. Text beginning at "Causes And Symptoms Of Cancer" is from *GALE ENCYCLOPEDIA OF MEDICINE, 1ST EDITION*, by Lata Cherath, 2, Gale Group, © 1999, Gale Group. Reprinted by permission of The Gale Group. Reviewed by David A. Cooke, M.D., on January 24, 2004.

grow and divide out of control and don't die. Cancer cells usually group or clump together to form tumors (say: **too**-mers).

A growing tumor becomes a lump of cancer cells that can destroy the normal cells around the tumor and damage the body's healthy tissues. This can make someone very sick.

Sometimes cancer cells break away from the original tumor and travel to other areas of the body, where they keep growing and can go on to form new tumors. This is how cancer spreads. The spread of a tumor to a new place in the body is called metastasis (say: meh-**tas**-tuh-sis).

People with cancer may feel pretty sick at times—but can usually still do lots of normal things. Unless they are very sick, kids and teens with cancer may still be able to go to school. They may be tired or bruise easily, but they can sometimes go to camp, movies, and sleepover parties. People with cancer still like the same things they did before they got sick.

Cancer in kids is rare—but today, many kids who do get cancer go on live normal lives. The number of kids who beat cancer goes up every year because of new cancer treatments. So a lot of kids with cancer will some day drive cars, go to college, have careers, and even get married and have families of their own.

Causes Of Cancer

Cancer is a rare illness in children. Most kids will not know another kid who has cancer. If you had

> ♣ **It's A Fact!!**
> **Origin Of The Word Cancer**
>
> The origin of the word *cancer* is credited to the Greek physician Hippocrates (460–370 B.C.), considered the "Father of Medicine." Hippocrates used the terms *carcinos* and *carcinoma* to describe non-ulcer forming and ulcer-forming tumors. In Greek these words refer to a crab, most likely applied to the disease because the finger-like spreading projections from a cancer called to mind the shape of a crab. Carcinoma is the most common type of cancer.
>
> Source: Reprinted by permission of the American Cancer Society, Inc. Full text available at http://www.cancer.org/docroot/CRI/content/CRI_2_6x_the_history_of_cancer_72.asp.

What Is Cancer 5

a large football stadium packed with kids, probably **only one** child in that stadium would have cancer.

Doctors aren't sure why some people get cancer and others don't. They do know that cancer is **not** contagious. You can't catch cancer from someone else who has it. Cancer isn't caused by germs, like colds or the flu are. So don't be afraid of other kids—or anyone else—with cancer. You can talk to, play with, and even hug someone with cancer.

Kids can't get cancer from anything they do either. Some kids think that a bump on the head causes brain cancer or that bad people get cancer. This isn't true! Kids don't do anything wrong to get cancer. But some unhealthy habits, especially cigarette smoking or drinking too much alcohol every day, can make you a lot more likely to get cancer when you become an adult.

Finding Out About Cancer

Usually, a patient's symptoms (clues that tell your doctor what's wrong with you) do not tell the doctor right away that a kid has cancer. Most of the time cancer causes things like weight loss, fevers, swollen glands, or feeling overly tired or sick for a while. Symptoms like these are also seen in many other common illnesses, especially during infections. So, at first, doctors and parents often think another illness like an infection—not cancer—is to blame for the symptoms (and this is often true). Medical tests are needed to make sure a kid has cancer.

If someone is very sick, a doctor might order x-rays and blood tests. If it is then suspected that the problem is cancer, the doctor will usually recommend seeing an oncologist (say: on-**kol**-ah-jist). An oncologist is a doctor who takes care of and treats cancer patients. The oncologist will likely run other tests to find out if someone really has cancer—including exactly what kind of cancer it is, if it has spread to other parts of the body, and the best way to treat it.

One test that an oncologist (or a surgeon) may perform is a biopsy (say: **by**-op-see). During a biopsy, a piece of tissue is removed from a tumor or a place in the body where cancer is suspected, like the bone marrow. The tissue will be put under a microscope to look for cancer cells. The sooner cancer is found and treatment begins, the better someone's chances are for a full recovery and cure.

Treating Cancer Carefully

Cancer is treated with surgery, chemotherapy, or radiation—or sometimes a combination of these treatments. The choice of treatment depends on:

- the type of cancer someone has (the kind of abnormal cells causing the cancer)

- the stage of the tumor (meaning how much the cancer has spread within the body, if at all)

❧ Weird Words

Malignant: Cancerous; a growth with a tendency to invade and destroy nearby tissue and spread to other parts of the body.

Metastasis: The spread of cancer from one part of the body to another. Tumors formed from cells that have spread are called "secondary tumors" and contain cells that are like those in the original (primary) tumor. The plural is metastases.

Remission: A decrease in or disappearance of signs and symptoms of cancer. In partial remission, some, but not all, signs and symptoms of cancer have disappeared. In complete remission, all signs and symptoms of cancer have disappeared, although there still may be cancer in the body.

Staging: Performing exams and tests to learn the extent of the cancer within the body, especially whether the disease has spread from the original site to other parts of the body. It is important to know the stage of the disease in order to plan the best treatment.

Tumor: An abnormal mass of tissue that results from excessive cell division. Tumors perform no useful body function. They may be benign (not cancerous) or malignant (cancerous).

Source: Excerpted from "Cancer.gov Dictionary," National Cancer Institute, December 2003. The full text of this dictionary is available online at http://www.cancer.gov/dictionary.

What Is Cancer

Surgery is the oldest form of treatment for cancer. Three out of every five people with cancer will have an operation to remove the cancer. During surgery, the doctor tries to take out as many cancer cells as possible. Some healthy cells or tissue may also be removed to make sure that all the cancer is gone.

Chemotherapy (say: **kee-moe-ther**-ah-pee) is the use of anti-cancer medicines (drugs) to treat cancer. These medicines are sometimes taken as a pill, but are usually given through a special intravenous (say: in-truh-**vee**-nus) line, also called an IV. An IV is a tiny catheter (straw-like tube) that is put into a vein through someone's skin, usually on the arm. The catheter is attached to a bag that holds the medicine. The medicine flows from the bag into the kid's vein, which puts the medicine into her blood, where it can travel throughout the body and attack cancer cells.

Many kids with cancer will need more than one dose of chemotherapy—sometimes given over weeks to months—as they are being treated for cancer. Often, a permanent catheter is placed under the skin into a larger blood vessel of the upper chest. This way, a kid can easily get several courses of chemotherapy and other medicines through this catheter without having to always use a vein on the arm. The catheter remains under the skin until all the cancer treatment is completed.

Chemotherapy is often used for cancer that has spread from where it started as a tumor to other areas of the body.

Anti-cancer drugs are made to kill cancer cells. But many of these drugs can affect normal, healthy cells, too. Damage to healthy cells causes side effects. The most common side effects of chemotherapy are nausea and vomiting, hair loss, and tiredness. Other common side effects include an increased chance of bleeding, getting an infection, or anemia (a low blood count). Kids with cancer may lose their hair, get thin, or be really pale because of their chemotherapy.

Radiation therapy (say: ray-dee-**ay**-shun **ther**-ah-pee) uses high-energy waves, such as x-rays (invisible waves that can pass through most parts of the body), to damage and destroy cancer cells. It can cause tumors to shrink and even go away completely. Radiation therapy is one of the most common treatments for cancer. Many people with cancer find it goes away after receiving radiation treatments.

Radiation treatment destroys cancer cells, but it can also hurt normal cells. This causes side effects. Many people have no side effects at all, but some will. Although unpleasant, most side effects from radiation are not serious and can be controlled. The most common side effects are tiredness, skin changes (like redness and burns), and loss of appetite (not feeling hungry). Some side effects happen in the area where the radiation was given. For example, after radiation treatment to the head, a kid might lose his hair.

Side effects depend mostly on the amount of radiation and the part of the body that is treated. Kids should tell their doctor, nurse, or radiation therapist how they are feeling and about any side effects. There are some medicines that can be given to help with side effects so kids can feel better.

When Kids Get Better

Remission (say: ree-**mih**-shun) is when all the signs of cancer are gone from someone's body. After surgery or treatment with radiation or chemotherapy, a doctor will then do tests to see if the cancer is still there. If there are no signs of cancer, then that kid is in remission.

Remission is the goal when any kid with cancer goes to the hospital for treatment. Sometimes, additional chemotherapy might be needed for a while to keep someone in remission—to keep cancer cells from coming back. And luckily, for many kids who have cancer, continued remission is the end of the story.

Causes And Symptoms Of Cancer

The major risk factors for cancer are: tobacco, alcohol, diet, sexual and reproductive behavior, infectious agents, family history, occupation, environment and pollution.

Tobacco

Eighty to ninety percent of the lung cancer cases occur in smokers. Smoking has also been shown to be a contributory factor in cancers of upper respiratory tract, esophagus, larynx, bladder, pancreas, and probably liver, stomach, and kidney as well. Recently, scientists have also shown that second-hand smoke (or passive smoking) can increase one's risk of developing cancer.

What Is Cancer

Alcohol

Excessive consumption of alcohol is a risk factor in certain cancers, such as liver cancer. Alcohol, in combination with tobacco, significantly increases the chances that an individual will develop mouth, pharynx, larynx and esophageal cancers.

Diet

Thirty five percent of all cancers are due to dietary causes. Excessive intake of fat leading to obesity has been associated with cancers of the breast, colon, rectum, pancreas, prostate, gall bladder, ovaries, and uterus.

Sexual And Reproductive Behavior

The human papilloma virus, which is sexually transmitted has been shown to cause cancer of the cervix. Having too many sex partners and becoming sexually active early has been shown to increase one's chances of contracting this disease. In addition, it has also been shown that women who don't have children or have children late in life, have an increased risk for both ovarian and breast cancer.

Infectious Agents

In the last 20 years, scientists have obtained evidence to show that approximately 15% of the world's cancer deaths can be traced to viruses, bacteria, or parasites.

Family History

Certain cancers like breast, colon, ovarian and uterine cancer, recur generation after generation in some families. A few cancers, such as the eye cancer "retinoblastoma," a type of colon cancer, and a type of breast cancer known as "early-onset breast cancer," have been shown to be linked to certain genes that can be tracked within a family. It is therefore possible that inheriting particular genes makes a person susceptible to certain cancers.

Occupational Hazards

There is evidence to prove that certain occupational hazards account for 4% of all cancer deaths. For example, asbestos workers have an increased incidence of lung cancer. Similarly, a higher likelihood of getting bladder cancer is associated with dye, rubber and gas workers; skin and lung cancer with smelters, gold miners and arsenic workers; leukemia with glue and varnish workers; liver cancer with PVC manufacturers; and lung, bone and bone marrow cancer with radiologists and uranium miners.

Environment

Radiation is believed to cause 1–2% of all cancer deaths. Ultra-violet radiation from the sun accounts for a majority of melanoma deaths. Other sources of radiation are x-rays, radon gas, and ionizing radiation from nuclear material.

Pollution

Several studies have shown that there is a well-established link between asbestos and cancer. Chlorination of water may account for a small rise in cancer risk. However, the main danger from pollution occurs when dangerous chemicals from the industries escape into the surrounding environment. It has been estimated that 1% of cancer deaths are due to air, land, and water pollution.

♣ **It's A Fact!!**
Oldest Descriptions Of Cancer

Cancer has afflicted humans throughout recorded history. It is no surprise that from the dawn of history doctors have written about cancer. Some of the earliest evidence of cancer is found among fossilized bone tumors, human mummies in ancient Egypt, and ancient manuscripts. Bone remains of mummies have revealed growths suggestive of the bone cancer, osteosarcoma. In other cases, bony skull destruction as seen in cancer of the head and neck has been found.

Our oldest description of cancer (although the term cancer was not used) was discovered in Egypt and dates back to approximately 1600 B.C. The Edwin Smith Papyrus, or writing, describes 8 cases of tumors or ulcers of the breast that were treated by cauterization, with a tool called "the fire drill." The writing says about the disease, "There is no treatment."

Source: Reprinted by permission of the American Cancer Society, Inc. Full text available at http://www.cancer.org/docroot/CRI/content/CRI_2_6x_the_history_of_cancer_72.asp.

Chapter 2

Types Of Cancer Teens Get

There are some types of cancer that teens are more likely to get. What these cancers have in common are cells, the basic components or "building blocks" of the human body. Cancer occurs when cells develop abnormally and grow in an uncontrolled way. Read on to learn information about types of cancer that teens may get, including warning signs and symptoms and how these cancers can be treated.

Osteosarcoma

Osteosarcoma (pronounced: **os-tee-oh-sar-koh**-ma) is the most common type of bone cancer. It usually appears in teen guys, often during their growth spurt. Osteosarcoma affects twice as many guys as girls, and tends to show up in people who are taller than average. Certain medical problems that may be caused by genes, such as retinoblastoma (pronounced: reh-tin-oh-blas-toe-muh), a tumor that develops in the retina of the eye, may predispose some teens to develop osteosarcoma. The same is true if a teen has received bone radiation treatments for other cancers.

About This Chapter: This information was provided by TeensHealth, one of the largest resources online for medically reviewed health information written for parents, kids, and teens. For more articles like this one, visit www.TeensHealth.org, or www.KidsHealth.org. © 2001 The Nemours Center for Children's Health, a division of The Nemours Foundation. Reviewed June 2002 by Robin Miller, MD. Available online at http://kidshealth.org/teen/diseases_conditions/cancer/types_of_cancer.html.

The most common symptoms of osteosarcoma are pain and swelling in an arm or leg that is sometimes accompanied by a lump. Some people have more pain at night or when they exercise. Osteosarcoma is most often found in the bones around the knee but can occur in other bones as well.

Treatment usually involves chemotherapy (intravenous, or IV, medication that kills cancer cells) as well as surgery to remove the tumor.

A doctor may perform limb-salvage surgery, where the bone that has cancer is removed and the limb (usually an arm or leg) is saved from amputation by filling the gap with a bone graft or special metal rod. But if the tumor has spread or metastasized (when cells from a tumor break away from the original cancer site and travel to a different tissue or organ) beyond the bone to nerves and blood vessels of the limb, the doctor may need to amputate (remove) part or all of the limb along with the cancer.

✎ Weird Words

Amputate: Remove part or all of a limb.

Anemia: Low numbers of red blood cells.

Leukocytes: Abnormal white blood cells.

Limb-Salvage Surgery: Surgery that saves the limb (usually an arm or leg) from amputation. A bone graft or special metal rod is used to fill the gap created when cancerous bone is removed.

Lymphatic System: Body system that includes the lymph nodes, thymus, spleen, adenoids, tonsils, and bone marrow. The lymph system functions in the body by fighting off germs that cause infection and illness.

Lymphocytes: White blood cells found in lymph nodes.

Metastasize: When cells from a tumor break away from the original cancer site and travel to a different tissue or organ.

Platelets: Cells in the bloodstream which help blood to clot.

Prosthesis: An artificial limb.

Red Blood Cells: Cells in the bloodstream which carry oxygen.

Losing a limb can be devastating, especially for teens who already may have problems related to their body images. Counseling and physical rehabilitation, also called physical therapy, can both be helpful in this situation. Teens who undergo amputations are usually fitted with a prosthesis (pronounced: pros-**thee**-sis), or artificial limb, which can help them adapt. Most teens are able to return to normal activities—even sports.

Most teens develop side effects, such as hair loss, bleeding, infections, and heart or skin problems, from medicines used in chemotherapy treatment for osteosarcoma. Chemotherapy may also increase the person's risk of developing other cancers in the future. The good news is that most teens with osteosarcoma do recover.

Ewing's Sarcoma

Another type of cancer that affects the bone is Ewing's sarcoma. It is similar to osteosarcoma in that it also affects teens and young adults and is usually located in the leg or pelvis.

Most teens with Ewing's sarcoma receive chemotherapy as well as surgery. Some patients will also need radiation in addition to or instead of surgery to make sure that remaining cancer cells have been destroyed. Ewing's sarcoma generally responds well to chemotherapy and radiation.

Osteosarcoma and Ewing's sarcoma share common risk factors and side effects from treatment. Chances for recovery depend upon where the tumor is located, its size, and whether it has spread. But both types of bone cancer respond well to treatment and are curable in many cases.

Leukemia

Leukemia is one of the most common childhood cancers. It occurs when large numbers of abnormal white blood cells called leukocytes (pronounced: **loo**-koh-sites) fill the bone marrow and sometimes enter the bloodstream.

Because these abnormal blood cells are defective, they don't help protect the body against infection the way normal white blood cells do. And because they grow uncontrollably, they take over the bone marrow and interfere with the body's production of other important types of cells in the bloodstream, like red blood cells (which carry oxygen) and platelets (which help blood to clot).

Leukemia causes problems like bleeding, anemia (low numbers of red blood cells), and infections. It can also spread to other places like the lymph nodes, liver, spleen, and brain.

The types of leukemia most likely to occur in teens are acute lymphocytic (pronounced: lim-foe-**sih**-tick) leukemia (ALL) and acute myelogenous (pronounced: my-uh-**lah**-juh-nus) leukemia (AML). ALL, the most common form, is seen more frequently in Caucasians and affects guys more often than girls.

Virtually all people with ALL and AML are treated with chemotherapy, and some also receive stem cell transplants, in which they are given new stem cells from another person. Bone marrow transplants are a common form of stem cell transplantation. Some people also receive radiation. The length of treatment and types of medicine given will vary depending on the type of leukemia.

The chances for a cure are very good with certain kinds of leukemia. With treatment, most patients with ALL and many patients with AML are free of the disease without recurrence.

Lymphoma

Lymphoma refers to cancer that develops in the lymphatic system, which includes the lymph nodes, thymus, spleen, adenoids, tonsils, and bone marrow. The lymph system functions in the body by fighting off germs that cause infection and illness. Most teens with lymphoma have either Hodgkin's disease (cancer of the lymph tissue) or non-Hodgkin's lymphoma (cancer of the cells of the immune system that circulate throughout the body).

Hodgkin's disease usually occurs in adolescents and young adults. It can show up in lymph nodes in the neck, armpits, or chest that are enlarged but are usually not painful. Hodgkin's disease is identified by large, unusual cells called Reed-Sternberg cells that are detected under a microscope after a biopsy, a procedure in which a doctor removes a small tissue sample to examine it for cancer cells. Radiation and chemotherapy are generally used to treat Hodgkin's disease.

Non-Hodgkin's lymphoma (NHL) is similar to leukemia (ALL) because both involve malignant lymphocytes (pronounced: **lim**-foe-sites), white blood cells found in lymph nodes, and because many of the symptoms of these diseases are the same. NHL is usually treated with chemotherapy.

The majority of teens with Hodgkin's disease who have completed their treatment achieve a complete remission with no signs of the disease. The outlook for those with NHL is similar.

Brain Tumors

Brain tumors are not common in teens. Primary cancers of the brain (cancers that arise from brain cells), such as ependymomas (tumors that usually begin in the lining of brain ventricles) and astrocytomas (tumors that begin in cells called astrocytes), don't usually spread outside the brain and spinal cord and don't usually affect other organs.

No one knows the exact cause of primary brain cancer. One possibility is that as the brain and spinal cord were forming, a problem with the cells occurred. Secondary brain tumors are the result of different cancers that have spread.

Treatments vary depending upon the type and location of the tumor. If it is possible to remove a tumor, surgery is usually performed, followed by radiation. Some patients receive chemotherapy as well.

The chance of surviving a brain tumor depends on its type, location, and treatment. But there is a very good chance that if the tumor can be removed and additional treatment is given, the cancer can be cured.

Other Cancers

Other cancers that teens are more likely to get—although they are generally rare—include testicular cancer and rhabdomyosarcomas.

Although testicular cancer is actually rare in teen guys, overall it is the *most common* cancer in males ages 15 to 35. Testicular cancer is almost always curable if it is caught and treated early. Teen guys should learn how to examine their testicles regularly to detect any abnormal lumps or bumps, which are usually the earliest sign of testicular cancer.

Rhabdomyosarcomas (pronounced: **rab**-doe-my-uh-sar-**koe**-mas), or soft tissue sarcomas, are less common cancers that mostly occur in infants, kids, and teens. With these cancers, cancer cells grow in the soft tissues of the skeletal muscles (the body's muscles that a person controls for movement). Though these cancers can occur anywhere in the body, rhabdomyosarcomas most frequently happen within the muscles in the trunk, arms, or legs. The types of treatment used and chances for recovery depend upon where the rhabdomyosarcoma is located and whether the cancer has spread to other areas of the body.

Chapter 3

Cancer Among Adolescents: Understanding The Statistics

Statistics are often used in news reports or in talking about someone's risk for getting cancer or whether a treatment will work. These statistics can be confusing or misleading if you do not understand how they are used. Statistics are collected and analyzed to help people better understand what is being observed. There are many examples of how statistics are used in our daily life—average temperature, median house price, etc. In addition, statistics are used to understand the probability or chance of something happening—of winning the lottery or being struck by lightning. Statistics help people make a "best guess" of any one situation but they cannot guarantee that something will or won't happen.

Statistics are often used in cancer to help guide decision-making about identifying people at risk for getting cancer and identifying the best test or treatment. But they can't be used to know, for certain, what will happen to any one person. Below is an understanding of some of the more commonly used statistics:

- **Mean (Average):** An average, or mean, is when all the numbers are added up and divided by the number of people (or whatever is being measured). For example, let's take the average age of a group of people.

About This Chapter: The information in this chapter is reprinted with permission from CancerSource. For additional information on childhood cancer and other cancers, visit the CancerSource website at www.cancersource.com. © 2003 CancerSource. All Rights Reserved.

In the group is a person who is 20 years old and another person who is 60 years old. The total of their ages is 80 and if you divide by two (the number of people), then the average age would be 40 and yet neither person is 40. Similarly, the average age at retirement or death can be calculated but it does not mean that any one person actually retires or dies at that age.

- **Median:** The median is the halfway point when counting a group of numbers. Half the numbers are below and half are above the median. For example, housing prices may range from $50,000 to $350,000. If

> ### ✎ Weird Words
>
> <u>Ependymal Tumors</u>: A type of brain tumor that usually begins in the central canal of the spinal cord. Ependymal tumors may also develop in the cells lining the ventricles of the brain, which produce and store the special fluid (cerebrospinal fluid) that protects the brain and spinal cord. Also called ependymomas.
>
> <u>Epithelial Carcinoma</u>: Cancer that begins in the cells that line an organ.
>
> <u>Hepatoblastoma</u>: A type of liver tumor that occurs in infants and children.
>
> <u>Retinoblastoma</u>: An eye cancer that most often occurs in children younger than five years. It occurs in hereditary and nonhereditary (sporadic) forms.
>
> Source: Excerpted from "Cancer.gov Dictionary," National Cancer Institute, December 2003. The full text of this dictionary is available online at http://www.cancer.gov/dictionary.

five houses are $50,000, $60,000, $85,000, $350,000 and $350,000 each, the median price is $85,000. The average or mean price is $179,000.

Every year, the American Cancer Society publishes *Facts & Figures*, a booklet that lists the number of people expected to get cancer during that year, how long someone may survive, and the number of people expected to die from cancer that year. This information is provided by type of cancer, state, gender, age, etc. Other cancer-related behaviors, such as the number of people smoking or getting Pap smears or mammograms, are also published. This information is calculated using formulas and statistical models based on previously collected data. These statistics do not take into account a person's individual risk factors such as family history, behaviors, or early detection practices. Below are some statistics covered in *Facts & Figures*:

- **Lifetime risk:** The lifetime risk is one person's chance of getting or dying from cancer over a lifetime. That risk changes based on the person's age. For example, the lifetime risk of a woman in the U.S. getting breast cancer is a one in eight chance if she lives to be 85. The risk will change over her lifetime and will be lower when she is younger and higher when she is older.

- **Relative risk:** The relative risk compares the risk of people getting a cancer with certain risk factors (family history or certain behaviors like smoking) to a similar group of people without those risk factors. It is usually referred to as X-times or X-fold relative risk when compared to the other group of people. For example, men who smoke have a 20 times increase in dying from lung cancer than non-smoking men.

- **Incidence rates:** The incidence rate is the number of people who will get a particular cancer for every 100,000 people. This allows comparisons across different groups of people (by state, age, or some other factor). This is different than the actual number of people getting cancer. For example, it was estimated that 488 men and 361 women per 100,000 people in Massachusetts would get cancer in 2001. This statistic compares to 449 for men and 340 for women in California. The actual number of people who were diagnosed with cancer in 2001 may be different.

♣ It's A Fact!!
Cancer Among Adolescents 15–19 Years Old: A Summary

The spectrum of malignancies that occur in adolescents is distinctive when compared to those that occur in young children and those that occur in older adults. The embryonal cancers that predominate among young children (e.g., neuroblastoma, Wilms' tumor, retinoblastoma, ependymoma, and hepatoblastoma) are very uncommon among 15–19 year olds. Similarly, the epithelial carcinomas of adults (e.g., lung, breast, colon) rarely occur in 15–19 year olds. While some types of acute leukemias and central nervous system (CNS) cancers are shared with both the older adult and the young childhood populations, the 15–19 year old group experiences high rates of a set of tumors (including germ cell tumors, Hodgkin's disease, and the bone cancers) that are relatively characteristic of the adolescent/young adult age group.

The annual incidence of cancer in adolescents increased from 183 per million for 1975–79 to 203.8 per million from 1990–95. The largest contributor to this increase was the germ cell, trophoblastic, and other gonadal tumor category (specifically testicular and ovarian germ cell tumors), with smaller contributions from non-Hodgkin's lymphoma (NHL), osteosarcoma, and acute lymphoblastic leukemia (ALL).

Rates of specific cancer types differed substantially by sex and by race. For sex, these differences were most remarkable for thyroid cancer (much more common in females) and for the bone tumors, ALL, and NHL (the latter three more common among males). Black 15–19 year olds had much lower incidence rates of Ewing's sarcoma, testicular germ cell tumors, and melanoma than did whites, and modestly lower incidence rates of ALL and thyroid cancer.

Five-year survival for 15–19 year olds increased from 69% to 77% from 1975–84 to 1985–94, with a 90% survival rate or better for several diagnoses (Hodgkin's disease, germ cell tumors, thyroid cancer, and melanoma). However, for some cancers, the survival rates remained less than 60% (including osteosarcoma, Ewing's sarcoma, ALL, and acute myelogenous leukemia [AML]).

Source: Excerpted and adapted from Smith MA, Gurney JG, and Ries LAG, "Cancer Among Adolescents 15–19 Years Old," in Ries LAG, Smith MA, Gurney JG, Linet M, Tamra T, Young JL, Bunin GR (eds). *Cancer Incidence and Survival among Children and Adolescents: United States SEER Program 1975-1995*, National Cancer Institute, SEER Program. NIH Pub. No. 99-4649. Bethesda, MD, 1999. Full text available online at http://seer.cancer.gov/publications/childhood/adolescents.pdf.

Cancer Among Adolescents: Understanding The Statistics

- **Relative survival rate:** The relative survival rate is the number of people surviving with cancer after adjusting for normal events occurring that affect life expectancy such as accidents, dying of other diseases, etc. The people included in this statistic reflect how many people with cancer are alive after a certain time (usually 5 years). They may still have cancer or be free of their cancer. An individual's prognosis may be different than this statistic based on many factors, such as general health, type and stage of the cancer, response to treatment, etc.

- **Mortality rates:** The mortality rate is the number of people who will die from a particular cancer for every 100,000 people. This allows comparisons across different groups of people (by state or some other factor). This is different than the actual number of people dying from cancer. For example, 215 men and 148 women per 100,000 people in Massachusetts and 183 men and 135 women per 100,000 in California were expected to die of cancer in 2001. The actual number of people who died in 2001 may be different.

People with cancer may want to know their prognosis. The prognosis is the likely outcome or course of a person's cancer—the chance of recovery or recurrence and of dying from their disease. Like other statistics, this information is a prediction of the chance of things occurring and is based on a variety of factors. These factors include type and stage of the cancer, type and response to treatment, and other personal factors such as general health. All of this information can help people make decisions about changing behaviors, taking tests or treatments, and overall outlook. But one should always remember that this information can never guarantee that something will or won't happen.

Related Sites

- "The median isn't the message": http://www.cancerguide.org/median_not_msg.html
- American Cancer Society, *Cancer Facts and Figures*: http://www.cancer.org/docroot/STT/stt_0
- Surveillance, Epidemiology, and End Results (SEER) Program of the National Cancer Institute: http://www.seer.cancer.gov

- National Center for Health Statistics (NCHS): http://www.cdc.gov/nchs
- Understanding Prognosis and Cancer Statistics: http://cis.nci.nih.gov/fact/8_2.htm

Chapter 4
Leukemia In Teens

Teens generally get one of two types of leukemia:
- Acute Lymphocytic Leukemia (ALL)
- Acute Myeloid or Myelogenous Leukemia (AML)

OK, So What Is Leukemia?

Leukemia is a form of cancer that starts in the bone marrow where all your blood is made. The bone marrow is a spongy material inside your bones where blood cells are produced and mature. Different types of blood cells are made in healthy bone marrow:

- Red blood cells carry oxygen and nutrients to all cells in your body.
- Platelets are cells that help your blood to clot and stop bleeding.
- White cells help fight infection. The white cells are responsible for recognizing foreign substances like bacteria and viruses. White blood cells can

---

About This Chapter: The information in this chapter is reprinted with permission from Teens Living with Cancer, a co-sponsored project of the Melissa's Living Legacy Foundation and The Children's Oncology Group. © 2003. All rights reserved. The Melissa's Living Legacy Foundation is a non-profit organization providing resources to help teens with cancer have meaningful, life-affirming experiences throughout all stages of their disease. The Children's Oncology Group is a National Cancer Institute-supported clinical trials cooperative group devoted exclusively to childhood and adolescent cancer research. For additional information, visit www.teenslivingwithcancer.org.

communicate with each other to help fight infection. Some types of white blood cells make antibodies to destroy these foreign substances, and other white cells ingest the foreign substance (a little like Pac-Man).

You have different types of white blood cells: lymphoid and myeloid. The type of white blood cell that goes crazy determines the type of leukemia you have.

> ### ✎ Weird Words
>
> <u>Acute Lymphoblastic Leukemia (ALL)</u>: A quickly progressing disease in which too many immature white blood cells called lymphoblasts are found in the blood and bone marrow. Also called acute lymphocytic leukemia.
>
> <u>Acute Myelogenous Leukemia (AML)</u>: A quickly progressing disease in which too many immature blood-forming cells are found in the blood and bone marrow. Also called acute myeloid leukemia or acute nonlymphocytic leukemia.
>
> Source: Excerpted from "Cancer.gov Dictionary," National Cancer Institute, December 2003. The full text of this dictionary is available online at http://www.cancer.gov/dictionary.

Those Darn Blast Cells

Although the exact cause is unknown, something happens that makes very young cells multiply but never grow or mature to become useful or functional. These abnormal cells are called leukemia blasts, or just blasts, and are one indicator of leukemia.

What's so bad about blasts in your bone marrow and blood? These abnormal cells are taking up space and pushing out the normal, healthy cells in your bone marrow. The blasts take up all the room in your bone marrow and you cannot make normal, healthy blood cells. This puts you at risk for infections (low white blood count), anemia (low red blood count), and bleeding (low platelet count).

Not Another Bone Marrow Biopsy

A bone marrow sample is essential for an accurate diagnosis. The biggest sources of bone marrow in your body are your hips, the long bones of your legs, your breastbone and all the vertebrae of your spine. This explains why your bone marrow test may have been done in your hipbone. This is a big bone that contains lots of bone marrow and is a relatively safe place to do the test.

It will be extremely important to keep checking your bone marrow after your treatment is underway. You need to be sure that your treatment is clearing the leukemia cells from your bone marrow.

Speaking Of Treatment

The primary treatment for leukemia includes chemotherapy and maybe radiation, in some cases. Bone marrow transplantation is also sometimes used. Your specific diagnosis will determine what happens next. Your treatment will be planned by a team of cancer specialists with experience and expertise in treating leukemia. Working together with you and your parents, they will recommend the best plan of action.

Checking Counts

Most of the time your blood counts will be checked to determine the status of your bone marrow. This will help your medical team know how your chemotherapy is working. Your counts will also give clues about what you might need to supplement your own body's supply of blood.

For example, if you are having headaches or feeling dizzy because your bone marrow can't make enough red blood cells, you will probably need a transfusion to help decrease your anemia. Transfusions of platelets can also be done if you are having problems with bleeding.

"But It's Only A Little Fever"

You may have been warned about high fevers. Why are fevers such a big deal? Good question. Fevers are one sign of infection. If you have good counts and plenty of healthy white blood cells to fight infections, then a fever is not a huge problem. But if your white blood count is low, this is a big deal.

Serious infections can settle in your blood stream or other parts of your body (sepsis). If you don't have a good supply of white blood cells and you have a fever over 38° C or 100.5° F, you will automatically be treated with antibiotics to help you fight off bacteria that can cause very serious, potentially life-threatening infections.

> ✔ **Quick Tip**
> Lymphocytic?
> How to pronounce it:
> Lim-fo-sih-tick.

Acute Lymphocytic Leukemia

With acute lymphocytic leukemia (ALL), you have an increased number of white blood cells called lymphocytes. This specific type of white blood cell, made in your lymph glands and bone marrow, has gotten out of control in your body.

Treatment For ALL

There are generally four phases of treatment for ALL according to the National Cancer Institute:

1. The first phase, called induction chemotherapy, is aimed at achieving remission. Remission is when bone marrow, examined under the microscope, has no visible leukemia cells (or blasts). The red blood cells, platelets, and white blood cells also appear normal.

2. The second phase, called central nervous system (CNS) prophylaxis, is preventive therapy (just in case). It uses intrathecal (within the spinal cord) and/or high-dose systemic (throughout your body) chemotherapy to kill any leukemia cells in your CNS. It is also to prevent the spread of cancer cells to your brain and spinal cord, even if no cancer has been detected there. Radiation therapy to the brain may also be given, in addition to chemotherapy, for this purpose.

3. Once you go into remission and there are no signs of leukemia, a third phase of treatment, called consolidation or intensification therapy, is given. Consolidation uses high-dose chemotherapy to attempt to kill any

remaining leukemia cells. Sometime CNS prophylaxis is given with this phase of treatment.

4. The fourth phase of treatment, called maintenance therapy, uses chemotherapy to maintain remission.

Being diagnosed with ALL is rough. There are lots of blood tests, many admissions to the hospital, feeling crummy, and plenty of disruptions to your usual daily routines. On the brighter side, you have the most common type of cancer in children. That's good because treatments are very effective for this form of leukemia.

Acute Myeloid (Myelogenous) Leukemia

With AML, you have an increased number of abnormal myeloid cells (these are also white blood cells and include neutrophils and monocytes). Immature neutrophils are called myelocytes. You may hear these names of various white cells during your treatment.

How Did I Get To Be So Special?

For some reason, AML is less common in kids than ALL (acute lymphocytic leukemia). Treatment for AML is more intense than for other kinds of leukemia. The abnormal cells in AML can become resistant to some kinds of chemotherapy that should destroy them but don't. This can make your cancer more difficult to treat but don't worry—there are many types of treatment available.

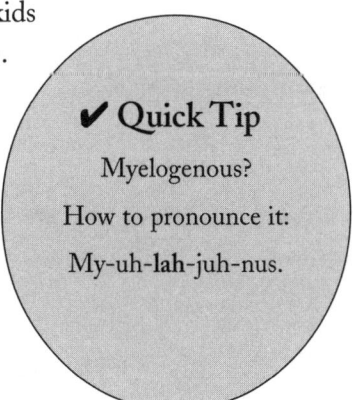

> ✔ **Quick Tip**
> Myelogenous?
> How to pronounce it:
> My-uh-lah-juh-nus.

Treatment For AML

There are different phases in the treatment of AML. The first phase, called induction chemotherapy, is aimed at achieving remission. Remission is when bone marrow, examined under the microscope, has no visible leukemia cells (or blasts). The red blood cells, platelets, and white blood cells also appear normal. What happens next depends on your individual circumstance.

Option A: Bone Marrow Transplant

If you have brothers or sisters, their blood may be compared to yours to see if you "match." That means they have the same proteins on their white blood cells and that their cells are genetically compatible.

If your brother or sister is a "match," you may have a bone marrow transplant after you've achieved remission. Prior to bone marrow transplantation, high doses of chemotherapy and/or radiation are given. The good news is that these high doses are effective at killing off any remaining cancer cells.

The doses are so high, however, they also destroy your ability to make new blood cells. After the high dose treatment, your donor's marrow is given to you through an infusion into one of your veins. It amazingly finds its way into the bone marrow spaces in your bones and starts making new blood cells.

If you do not have a sibling who can donate bone marrow, your medical team and you might decide to look for another bone marrow donor.

Option B: More Chemotherapy

If your medical team feels a bone marrow transplant is not an option, you may continue with more chemotherapy.

The Bottom Line

Be sure to discuss all the details of your AML treatment plan with your medical team. It is important that you understand everything that will be happening to your body so you can stay strong and make good decisions.

The road ahead of you may be a rocky one but you will manage it better if you are in the driver's seat. Remember—lots of kids with your same disease have made it!

I'm In Remission—Why More Chemo?

Many kids want to know why they have to keep getting chemotherapy even though they are in remission. This is another good question.

Remission is very important to achieve. It means that when the bone marrow is evaluated under the microscope, 95% of all the cells must be normal and there must be a good mixture of white blood cells, red cells, and platelets. No blasts allowed! Your treatment will continue even though you are in remission to make sure that every last blast is destroyed by the chemotherapy.

> ☞ **Remember!!**
> **Hang In There**
>
> Getting rid of leukemia is demanding and difficult work, filled with some difficult turns. You need to be just as tough and determined to keep the leukemia out of your bone marrow as those blasts are determined to stay in your body. Get help from your doctors and nurses so they can answer your questions and help you adapt to life with this disease. Count on your parents, family and friends for support.
>
> Try to meet other kids who are having treatment or who have already been through chemo. They can give you advice and encouragement.

Chapter 5

Lymphoma In Teens

Teenagers typically get one of two kinds of lymphoma: Hodgkin's disease and non-Hodgkin's lymphoma.

So, What Is Lymphoma?

Lymphoma is a cancer of the lymph system. Your lymph system includes lymph cells, lymph nodes, your thymus, spleen, tonsils and adenoids. This system has two important functions:

1. It helps your circulatory system carry nutrients *to* parts of your body and waste products *from* certain parts of your body.

2. It also helps your body recognize, trap, and destroy foreign cells, such as bacteria and virus.

Because of the importance of your lymph system, it is found throughout your body. Many times when you go to the doctor with a cold, the doctor

---

About This Chapter: The information in this chapter is reprinted with permission from Teens Living with Cancer, a co-sponsored project of the Melissa's Living Legacy Foundation and The Children's Oncology Group. © 2003. All rights reserved. The Melissa's Living Legacy Foundation is a non-profit organization providing resources to help teens with cancer have meaningful, life-affirming experiences throughout all stages of their disease. The Children's Oncology Group is a National Cancer Institute-supported clinical trials cooperative group devoted exclusively to childhood and adolescent cancer research. For additional information, visit www.teenslivingwithcancer.org.

feels for lymph nodes in your neck, but they're also found above your collarbone, in your chest and abdomen, under your arms, and in your groin.

Most teenagers with lymphoma have either Hodgkin's disease (cancer of the lymph tissue) or non-Hodgkin's lymphoma (cancer of the cells of the immune system that circulate throughout the body).

What's Next?

Your specific disease and its stage of development will determine your individual treatment plan but it will likely include some combination of the following treatments:

- Chemotherapy (using drugs to kill cancer cells and shrink tumors) is the primary treatment for lymphoma. Chemotherapy is called a systemic treatment because the drugs enter your bloodstream, travel through your body, and kill cancer cells throughout your body. Chemotherapy may also be put into your spinal fluid (intrathecal chemotherapy) to treat certain types of non-Hodgkin's lymphoma that spread to the brain.

- Low dose radiation therapy (using x-rays or other high-energy rays to kill cancer cells and shrink tumors) is also sometimes used.

- Bone marrow transplantation is sometimes used to treat lymphoma because lymphoma cells can become resistant to treatment with radiation therapy and/or chemotherapy.

> ### ❧ Weird Words
>
> <u>Hodgkin's Disease</u>: A malignant disease of the lymphatic system that is characterized by painless enlargement of lymph nodes, the spleen, or other lymphatic tissue. It is sometimes accompanied by symptoms such as fever, weight loss, fatigue, and night sweats.
>
> <u>Non-Hodgkin's Lymphoma</u>: A group of cancers of the lymphoid system, including acute lymphoblastic leukemia, B-cell lymphoma, Burkitt's lymphoma, diffuse cell lymphoma, follicular lymphoma, immunoblastic large cell lymphoma, lymphoblastic lymphoma, mantle cell lymphoma, mycosis fungoides, post-transplantation lymphoproliferative disorder, small non-cleaved cell lymphoma, and T-cell lymphoma.
>
> Source: Excerpted from "Cancer.gov Dictionary," National Cancer Institute, December 2003. The full text of this dictionary is available online at http://www.cancer.gov/dictionary.

High doses of chemotherapy are given before bone marrow transplantation. Because this can destroy your bone marrow, healthy marrow is taken from your bones before treatment or sometimes from a sibling donor.

If you are able to use your own cells, your stem cells are collected after a round of chemo, then frozen while you go through transplant conditioning—high dose chemotherapy and/or radiation. The stem cells or marrow that was taken out is then thawed and given back to you through a needle in a vein. This type of transplant is called an autologous transplant (getting back your own stem cells).

If the stem cells or marrow given to you is taken from another person, the transplant is called an allogeneic transplant.

Hodgkin's Disease

If you just found out you have Hodgkin's disease, you probably want to know more about it. Just knowing you have a type of cancer can be overwhelming and scary enough, but not knowing anything about it can sometimes make it worse. So, here goes.

How Do You Know It's Hodgkin's?

Your Hodgkin's disease was caused by an unknown trigger that causes an abnormal growth of cells in your lymph system. It can show up in enlarged lymph nodes in your neck, armpits, or chest and is usually not painful. A special cell, called a Reed-Sternberg cell, was identified during your diagnosis.

What Do Stages Mean?

You may have heard that your disease has stages based on the spread of the disease.

- Stage I: Limited to a single lymph node region.

- Stage II: Limited to one side of the diaphragm (the breathing muscle that separates the chest from the abdomen).

- Stage III: Involves lymph nodes on both sides of the diaphragm.

- Stage IV: Widespread disease found not only in the lymph tissue but also in the lungs, liver, bone marrow, skin or central nervous system.

Knowing the extent of your disease will help the doctors decide what treatment is best. If your disease involves just one part of your lymph system, you may be treated with radiation only. However, if your disease is more extensive, involving more than one part of your lymph system or spreading outside the lymph system, you might also get chemotherapy.

The Bottom Line

Many chemotherapy drugs are effective for treating Hodgkin's. This makes the outlook for a cure very good. Currently, greater than ninety percent of kids treated for Hodgkin's disease survive. This is very good news!

♣ **It's A Fact!!**

A few statistics and characteristics may help you put your disease in perspective. Hodgkin's disease accounts for 16% of all teen cancers. It usually occurs during the teen years and is more likely to affect guys than girls. We know that the virus causing "mono" (mononucleosis) has been associated with Hodgkin's disease. However, most kids who have "mono" will not develop Hodgkin's disease, so that relationship is unclear.

Non-Hodgkin's Lymphoma (NHL)

So, what is non-Hodgkin's lymphoma? What does that really mean for me? Finding out you have cancer is pretty scary but not knowing anything about the type of cancer you have is even more frightening. Here's some information to help you understand.

How many other kids get NHL? (not the National Hockey League!)

First, like many other kinds of teen cancers, there is no known cause for your disease. Some statistics and facts may help to put your disease in perspective. Non-Hodgkin's lymphoma (NHL) accounts for about 8% of all teen cancers each year in the United States. Guys are three times more likely to get this disease than girls.

How Do You Know It's Non-Hodgkin's?

Non-Hodgkin's lymphoma might start in any part of your lymph system: tonsils, thymus, bone, small intestine, spleen, or in lymph glands anywhere in your body. Your doctor will examine you carefully and check for swelling or lumps in your neck, underarms, groin, and abdomen.

A chest x-ray will usually be done to check for swelling in your chest. If the lymph nodes don't feel normal, or a lump is found in your chest or abdomen, your doctor may do a biopsy.

Three different types of non-Hodgkin's lymphoma occur in teens. The type of NHL is determined by the way the cells from your biopsy looked under a microscope. This is called the "histology" of your cancer. (Histology is the science of studying tissues.)

The types of NHL are: large cell lymphoma, small non-cleaved cell (Burkitt's or non-Burkitt's) lymphoma, and lymphoblastic lymphoma.

Non-Hodgkin's lymphoma sometimes looks like leukemia (ALL) because both involve malignant lymphocytes (white blood cells found in your lymph nodes), but most kids with NHL do not have bone marrow problems.

Stages Of Non-Hodgkin's

The type of lymphoma and the extent of your disease at diagnosis determine your treatment. You have probably heard your doctor describe the extent of your disease in stages:

- Stage I: Single tumor site in an isolated area, not including disease in the chest or abdomen.
- Stage II: Single tumor that may involve local lymph nodes; two or more lymph nodes or tumor areas on the same side of the diaphragm (breathing muscle that separates the chest from the abdomen); or a primary tumor in the intestinal tract.
- Stage III: Several tumors on opposite sides of the diaphragm; two or more lymph node areas above and/or below the diaphragm; chest tumors; large abdominal tumors; or all tumors near the brain or spine.

- Stage IV: Any of the above with a tumor involving the central nervous system or bone marrow.

Now What?

NHL progresses or spreads very rapidly, so your treatment will be aggressive. If you have localized disease, it may be able to be surgically removed.

You may also receive radiation to cure localized disease. If you had chest disease when you were diagnosed causing trouble breathing, you may have been given radiation at that time.

Chemotherapy is given to treat extensive disease or prevent your disease from spreading to other areas of your body through your bloodstream. Bone marrow transplantation may be an option.

Be sure to ask your medical team all the details of your treatment plan. You will be able to make better decisions about how to take care of yourself if you have all the information you need.

Over the past twenty years, the treatment for your disease has improved a great deal, and most teens like you will be cured of NHL.

> **☞ Remember!!**
> Chemotherapy (using drugs to kill cancer cells and shrink tumors), low dose radiation therapy (using x-rays or other high-energy rays to kill cancer cells and shrink tumors), and bone marrow transplantation are sometimes used to treat lymphoma. These treatments have improved over the past decades, and today the outlook for most teens with lymphoma is positive.

Chapter 6

Bone Cancer In Teens: Ewing's Sarcoma And Osteosarcoma

Ewing's Sarcoma

Ewing's sarcoma actually refers to a family of tumors found in bone and soft tissues. It is a cancer that can develop anywhere in your body, although it usually starts in one of your bones—most commonly one of the bones in your hip, upper arm or thigh.

- Generally (87% of the time), this tumor will grow in the middle of one of your long bones or in the bones of your spine, ribs, or pelvis.

- Occasionally, Ewing's can also develop outside of your bone. When this happens it is referred to as extra-osseous.

- Primitive neuroectodermal tumor (PNET)—also known as peripheral neuroepithelioma—is a related tumor in the Ewing's sarcoma family.

> About This Chapter: The information in this chapter is from two documents "Ewing's Sarcoma" and "Osteosarcoma," both reprinted with permission from Teens Living with Cancer, a co-sponsored project of the Melissa's Living Legacy Foundation and The Children's Oncology Group. © 2003. All rights reserved. The Melissa's Living Legacy Foundation is a non-profit organization providing resources to help teens with cancer have meaningful, life-affirming experiences throughout all stages of their disease. The Children's Oncology Group is a National Cancer Institute-supported clinical trials cooperative group devoted exclusively to childhood and adolescent cancer research. For additional information, visit www.teenslivingwithcancer.org.

- A PNET in your chest wall is referred to as an Askin's tumor.

(NOTE: Don't get hung up on all these medical names unless you're interested. If you just say you have a "Ewing's sarcoma" you'll be close enough.)

What's The First Step?

If you had some of the common symptoms of Ewing's—pain, stiffness, or tenderness in the bone—your doctor probably ordered x-rays and other tests plus a biopsy to see if there were any cancer cells. This is important to determine the level of your disease and decide the best treatment plan.

Levels Of Ewing's Sarcoma

> ### ✎ Weird Words
>
> Ewing's Sarcoma: A type of bone cancer that usually forms in the middle (shaft) of large bones. Also called Ewing's sarcoma/primitive neuroectodermal tumor (PNET).
>
> Osteosarcoma: A cancer of the bone that usually affects the large bones of the arm or leg. It occurs most commonly in young people and affects more males than females.
>
> Source: Excerpted from "Cancer .gov Dictionary," National Cancer Institute, December 2003. The full text of this dictionary is available online at http://www.cancer.gov/dictionary.

Both Ewing's sarcoma and PNETs are described as:

- Localized—in only one part of your body
- Metastatic—spread to other parts of your body

The most common place for this cancer to spread to is your lungs, although these tumors can also spread to your other bones or your bone marrow. This is one of the biggest problems with Ewing's sarcoma and other bone cancers. Most everyone with Ewing's or PNET has micrometastatic disease (disease spread) that can't always be seen on CT scans, bone scans, or bone marrow tests.

If your tumor is on your chest wall, you may have fluid around the lungs that also has cancerous cells.

So, Now What?

Your treatment plan will be determined by your medical team based on your specific diagnosis. Generally, it will look something like this:

- You will be treated with chemotherapy for both your primary tumor as well as any metastasis (even if it doesn't show up in your scans).
- If the tumor is in an area that allows it to be removed without a problem (for example, on your femur), then you will have surgery.
- After your tumor is removed, you may also be treated with radiation therapy.
- If your tumor is in an area where surgery would cause significant cosmetic or functional impairment (for example, on your head), then you will receive radiation therapy for local control.

Moving Right Along

Think of your medical team—your docs, nurses, specialists—as partners in your life for the next several months. Keep asking for all the information you need, so you know exactly what is going to happen. You will make better decisions about your care if you know what to expect.

Since your type of tumor was identified, there has been great progress in treatment. The road ahead may be tough but you know what they say, *"When the going gets tough, the tough get going."*

♣ **It's A Fact!!**

Ewing's sarcoma is named after Dr. James Ewing who described the tumor in the 1920's.

Ewing's sarcoma accounts for about 2% of all teen cancers. Approximately 200 children in the United States will be diagnosed each year with this disease. However, Ewing's sarcoma occurs most frequently in teenagers. Guys are at a slightly higher risk than girls and it is extremely rare in African Americans.

Osteosarcoma

Osteosarcoma is a cancer that begins in your bone forming cells. It is the most common type of tumor in the group of bone cancers called osteogenic sarcomas.

The First Signs And Steps

You might have first noticed something was wrong when you started having pain or swelling in or near one of your bones. The pain might have been worse at night or when you were exercising. These are usually the most common symptoms.

Your doctor probably ordered x-rays and blood tests and suggested that you see a specialist called an orthopedic oncologist. When osteosarcoma is suspected, a biopsy is often the next step to see if there are any cancer cells in the tissue.

About 90% of all osteosarcomas are located in the extremities (arms and legs) and most often in the bones around the knee.

Levels Of Osteosarcoma

Unlike some cancers, osteosarcoma does not really have a staging system but does have different levels:

- Localized—in only one part of your body
- Metastatic—spread to other parts of your body

The most common site of metastasis is your lung. It is believed that roughly 80% of people with osteosarcoma have micrometastatic (not evident) disease when they are diagnosed, even if it cannot be seen on x-rays and CT scans.

So, What Do We Do Now?

Your therapy will likely consist of chemotherapy and surgery.

- You will probably receive chemotherapy initially to shrink your tumor and kill any metastatic cells (cells that have spread to other parts of your body).

> ♣ **It's A Fact!!**
>
> About 5% of all teens with cancer are diagnosed with osteosarcoma. It is associated with rapid growth, so it is rarely seen in kids before puberty. Osteosarcoma affects more guys (usually between ages 15–19) than girls (usually between ages 10–14) and most kids are taller than average.

- Surgery is usually then performed using a limb salvage procedure, when possible. Limb salvage is a procedure in which your tumor, your bone, and some of the surrounding tissues are removed and then replaced with a bone graft or titanium rod.

  If your cancer has spread to other parts of your body and did not respond to your initial chemotherapy, these lesions might need to be surgically removed also.

  If your tumor has spread beyond the bone to the nerves and blood vessels, part or all of your limb may need to be amputated. Teens who have limbs amputated are usually fitted with a prosthesis (pros-**sthee**-sis), or artificial limb.

  Most kids adapt really well and are able to return to all their normal activities—even sports and dancing.

- After you recover from your surgery, you will have more chemotherapy to continue to treat any metastatic disease. This is referred to as adjuvant therapy.

> ☞ **Remember!!**
>
> First, many support resources are available to help you cope. You just need to find the one that works best for you. Counseling, physical therapy, teen support groups, your family and friends—all are available to help.
>
> Most importantly, most teens with osteosarcoma do recover. The overall survival rate for localized disease is 70–75%. Keep seeing yourself among this group! Visualize yourself leading the pack at the Boston Marathon! The road may seem hard at times, but with determination and persistence, you will make it.
>
> *"Slow and steady wins the race."*

Chapter 7

Germ Cell Tumors In Teens

Did you say "germ cells"? Yes, but not the kind of germs that cause infection.

What Is A Germ Cell?

Germ cells develop into the reproductive sex organs—testicles in guys and ovaries in girls. Germ cells can travel to other areas of the body, such as the chest, abdomen, tailbone, or brain.

Types Of Germ Cell Tumors

The major types of germ cell tumors that teens get are:

- Testicular—within the testes of older boys.

- Sacral—in the sacrum, a triangular-shaped section of fused bone located between the hip bones at the base of the spine and the tailbone.

About This Chapter: The information in this chapter is reprinted with permission from Teens Living with Cancer, a co-sponsored project of the Melissa's Living Legacy Foundation and The Children's Oncology Group. ©2003. All rights reserved. The Melissa's Living Legacy Foundation is a non-profit organization providing resources to help teens with cancer have meaningful, life-affirming experiences throughout all stages of their disease. The Children's Oncology Group is a National Cancer Institute-supported clinical trials cooperative group devoted exclusively to childhood and adolescent cancer research. For additional information, visit www.teenslivingwithcancer.org.

- Chest
- Ovarian—found in egg-making cells in a girl's ovaries.

Treatment For Germ Cell Tumors

There are two primary treatment options for germ cell tumors:

- surgery (cutting the tumor out)
- chemotherapy (using drugs to kill tumor cells)

If the tumor cannot be completely removed, chemotherapy may also be given.

> **Weird Word**
>
> Germ Cell Tumors: Tumors that begin in the cells that give rise to sperm or eggs. They can occur virtually anywhere in the body and can be either benign or malignant.
>
> Source: Excerpted from "Cancer.gov Dictionary," National Cancer Institute, December 2003. The full text of this dictionary is available online at http://www.cancer.gov/dictionary.

What's Next?

Treatment for germ cell tumors has improved drastically. Combination chemotherapy has improved so much that most patients (80%) can expect to be cured. While response to chemotherapy is quite good, some patients with germ cell tumors may have a recurrence or relapse.

Close follow-up for a long period of time is very important as relapses/recurrences have been known to happen as long as 10 years from diagnosis.

> **♣ It's A Fact!!**
>
> Germ cell tumors account for about 16% of teen cancers in the U.S. Adolescents and very young children are at increased risk for developing these tumors.

Chapter 8

Skin Cancer: Facts, Figures, And Questions

Facts And Statistics About Skin Cancer

The number of skin cancer cases has increased in the United States. Since 1981, the incidence of melanoma has increased an average of 7 percent per year to a rate of 14.3 per 100,000 in 1997. Melanoma is the most common cancer among people 25 to 29 years old.

The three major types of skin cancer are basal cell carcinoma, squamous cell carcinoma, and melanoma.

Basal cell and squamous cell carcinomas can cause substantial illness and, if untreated, can cause considerable damage and disfigurement. If detected and treated early, however, these carcinomas have a cure rate of more than 95%.

Malignant melanoma causes more than 75% of all deaths from skin cancer. This disease can spread to other organs, most commonly the lungs and liver. Malignant melanoma diagnosed at an early stage usually can be cured,

---

About This Chapter: "Facts and Statistics about Skin Cancer" is excerpted from "Choose Your Cover: Facts and Statistics About Skin Cancer," Centers for Disease Control and Prevention (CDC), last reviewed February 7, 2002, full text available at http://www.cdc.gov/chooseyourcover/skin.htm. "A Teen Asks About A Mole" is excerpted with permission from the TeenHealthFX website, www.teenhealthfx.com. Copyright © 2002 Atlantic Health System. All Rights Reserved.

but melanoma diagnosed at a late stage is more likely to spread and cause death.

Exposure to the sun's ultraviolet (UV) rays appears to be the most important environmental factor in developing skin cancer. This makes skin cancer a largely preventable disease when sun protective practices and behaviors are consistently applied and utilized. UV radiation is also a factor in the development of lip cancer, making sun protection even more important. UV rays from artificial sources of light, such as tanning beds and sun lamps are just as dangerous as those from the sun, and should also be avoided. Unfortunately, despite the fact that both tanning and burning can increase one's risk of skin cancer, most Americans do not protect themselves from UV rays.

Who Is At Risk?

Although anyone can get skin cancer, individuals with certain risk factors are particularly at risk. Some risk factors for skin cancer are:

- Lighter natural skin color
- Family history of skin cancer
- Personal history of skin cancer
- Constant exposure to the sun through work and play
- A history of sunburns early in life
- Skin that burns, freckles, gets red easily, or becomes painful in the sun
- Blue or green eyes
- Blond or red hair
- Certain types and a large number of moles

> ✔ **Quick Tip**
>
> Areas that are often missed when applying sunscreen include face, lips, ears, neck, feet, and hands.

Skin Cancer: Facts, Figures, And Questions

> **☞ Remember!!**
>
> The three major types of skin cancer are:
>
> - basal cell carcinoma
> - squamous cell carcinoma
> - melanoma

A Teen Asks About A Mole

Dear TeenHealthFX,

Is it possible to get more than one malignant melanoma (cancerous mole) at one time? I'm pretty sure I have one on my upper thigh, as it is brown with black spots, but I also have one below my breast. My mum won't take me to the doctor. I'm going out of my mind.

—Signed: Skin Cancer Questions

Dear Skin Cancer Questions,

TeenHealthFX understands how concerned you must be to discover moles and spots on your skin that you feel look abnormal. It is possible to have multiple cancerous or precancerous moles at the same time, so that is why getting suspicious marks on your body checked by a healthcare professional is important. With early detection the seriousness of many health concerns can be reduced.

The symptoms that you are describing can be caused by both normal and abnormal body changes; they may or may not be signs of something serious. Since we cannot offer a diagnosis, getting checked out is a good idea because a healthcare professional can not only examine you, but also will take a complete history and make a schedule for follow-up appointments.

To get your mother to assist you in obtaining medical care, start by showing her your letter to TeenHealthFX. Let her know that you are beginning to feel anxious about these symptoms, and would feel more at ease if a doctor examined you. If she still refuses to help you, talk to your school nurse, or you can visit a doctor on your own by using some of the resources for teens that may exist in your community.

Here are some skin cancer facts:

- Skin cancer IS preventable in most cases.

- Protection from the sun's harmful rays is an important part of prevention. Stay inside when the sun's rays are strongest—mid-morning to mid-afternoon. Wear a sunscreen with an SPF (Sun Protection Factor) of at least 15. Remember to apply sunscreen to your face, ears, neck, feet, and hands (areas that are often neglected).

- Do not use tanning beds, they also expose people to harmful rays.

- Check yourself for any moles or marks that are abnormal looking, or that change shape, size, or color. Look for marks that are not symmetrical, have irregular borders, and have uneven colors.

- Visit a healthcare provider (dermatologists are specially trained to treat skin, hair, and nail concerns) to discuss any moles or marks that seem suspicious.

—Signed: TeenHealthFX

✔ **Quick Tip**

For more information on this, check out "Reducing Cancer Risk" on the TeenHealthFX website (www.teenhealthfx.com) for some tips on cancer prevention or visit the American Cancer Society website (www.cancer.org).

Chapter 9

What You Should Know About Common Cancers In Older Family Members

Breast Cancer

Breast Cancer Is A Disease In Which Malignant (Cancer) Cells Form In The Tissues Of The Breast

The breast is made up of lobes and ducts. Each breast has 15 to 20 sections called lobes, which have many smaller sections called lobules. Lobules end in dozens of tiny bulbs that can produce milk. The lobes, lobules, and bulbs are linked by thin tubes called ducts.

Each breast also has blood vessels and lymph vessels. The lymph vessels carry an almost colorless fluid called lymph. Lymph vessels lead to organs called lymph nodes. Lymph nodes are small bean-shaped structures that are found throughout the body. They filter substances in lymph and help fight

> About This Chapter: Text for this chapter was excerpted and adapted from the following documents: PDQ® Cancer Information Summary. National Cancer Institute; Bethesda, MD. Breast Cancer (PDQ®): Treatment-Patient, updated 06/2003; Male Breast Cancer (PDQ®): Treatment-Patient, updated 07/2003; Colon Cancer (PDQ®): Treatment-Patient, updated 08/2003; Non-Small Cell Lung Cancer (PDQ®): Treatment-Patient, updated 06/2003; Small Cell Lung Cancer (PDQ®): Treatment-Patient, updated 09/2003; Prostate Cancer (PDQ®): Treatment-Patient, updated 07/2003. All documents available at http://cancer.gov, and accessed December 10, 2003.

infection and disease. Clusters of lymph nodes are found near the breast in the axilla (under the arm), above the collarbone, and in the chest.

The most common type of breast cancer is ductal carcinoma, which begins in the cells of the ducts. Cancer that begins in the lobes or lobules is called lobular carcinoma and is more often found in both breasts than are other types of breast cancer. Inflammatory breast cancer is an uncommon type of breast cancer in which the breast is warm, red, and swollen.

> ♣ **It's A Fact!!**
> **Age And Health History Can Affect The Risk Of Developing Breast Cancer**
>
> Anything that increases your chance of getting a disease is called a risk factor. Risk factors for breast cancer include:
>
> - Older age
> - Menstruating at an early age
> - Older age at first birth or never having given birth
> - A personal history of breast cancer or benign (noncancer) breast disease
> - A mother or sister with breast cancer
> - Treatment with radiation therapy to the breast/chest
> - Breast tissue that is dense on a mammogram
> - Hormone use (such as estrogen and progesterone)
> - Drinking alcoholic beverages
> - Caucasian race

Common Cancers In Older Family Members

Breast Cancer Is Sometimes Caused By Inherited Gene Mutations (Changes)

The genes in cells carry the hereditary information that is received from a person's parents. Hereditary breast cancer makes up approximately 5% to 10% of all breast cancer. Some altered genes related to breast cancer are more common in certain ethnic groups.

Women who have an altered gene related to breast cancer and who have had breast cancer in one breast have an increased risk of developing breast cancer in the other breast. These women also have an increased risk of developing ovarian cancer, and may have an increased risk of developing other cancers. Men who have an altered gene related to breast cancer also have an increased risk of developing this disease. (See "Male Breast Cancer," below.)

Tests have been developed that can detect altered genes. These genetic tests are sometimes done for members of families with a high risk of cancer.

Tests That Examine The Breasts Are Used To Detect (Find) And Diagnose Breast Cancer

A doctor should be seen if changes in the breast are noticed. The following tests and procedures may be used:

- **Mammogram:** An x-ray of the breast.
- **Biopsy:** The removal of cells or tissues so they can be viewed under a microscope to check for signs of cancer. If a lump in the breast is found, the doctor may need to cut out a small piece of the lump. A pathologist views the tissue under a microscope to look for cancer cells. Four types of biopsies are as follows:
    - **Excisional biopsy:** The removal of an entire lump or suspicious tissue.
    - **Incisional biopsy:** The removal of part of a lump or suspicious tissue.
    - **Core biopsy:** The removal of part of a lump or suspicious tissue using a wide needle.

- **Needle biopsy or fine-needle aspiration biopsy:** The removal of part of a lump, suspicious tissue, or fluid, using a thin needle.

- **Estrogen and progesterone receptor test:** A test to measure the amount of estrogen and progesterone (hormones) receptors in cancer tissue. If cancer is found in the breast, tissue from the tumor is examined in the laboratory to find out whether estrogen and progesterone could affect the way cancer grows. The test results show whether hormone therapy may stop the cancer from growing.

Certain Factors Affect Treatment Options And Prognosis (Chance Of Recovery)

The treatment options and prognosis (chance of recovery) depend on the stage of the cancer (whether it is in the breast only or has spread to other places in the body), the type of breast cancer, certain characteristics of the cancer cells, and whether the cancer is found in the other breast. A woman's age, menopausal status (whether a woman is still having menstrual periods), and general health can also affect treatment options and prognosis.

Male Breast Cancer

Male Breast Cancer Is A Disease In Which Malignant (Cancer) Cells Form In The Tissues Of The Breast

Breast cancer may occur in men. Men at any age may develop breast cancer, but it is usually detected (found) in men between 60 and 70 years of age. Male breast cancer makes up less than 1% of all cases of breast cancer.

The following types of breast cancer are found in men:

- **Infiltrating ductal carcinoma:** Cancer that has spread beyond the cells lining ducts in the breast. Most men with breast cancer have this type of cancer.

- **Ductal carcinoma in situ:** Abnormal cells that are found in the lining of a duct; also called intraductal carcinoma.

- **Inflammatory breast cancer:** A type of cancer in which the breast looks red and swollen and feels warm.

Common Cancers In Older Family Members

- **Paget's disease of the nipple:** A tumor that has grown from ducts beneath the nipple onto the surface of the nipple.

Lobular carcinoma in situ (abnormal cells found in one of the lobes or sections of the breast), which sometimes occurs in women, has not been seen in men.

Tests That Examine The Breasts Are Used To Detect (Find) And Diagnose Breast Cancer In Men

A doctor should be seen if changes in the breasts are noticed. Typically, men with breast cancer have lumps that can be felt. A biopsy can be done to check for cancer. The following are different types of biopsies:

- **Needle biopsy:** The removal of part of a lump, suspicious tissue, or fluid, using a thin needle. This procedure is also called a fine-needle aspiration biopsy.
- **Core biopsy:** The removal of part of a lump or suspicious tissue using a wide needle.
- **Excisional biopsy:** The removal of an entire lump or suspicious tissue.

> ♣ **It's A Fact!!**
>
> Risk factors for breast cancer in men may include the following:
>
> - Exposure to radiation
> - Having a disease related to high levels of estrogen in the body, such as cirrhosis (liver disease) or Klinefelter's syndrome (a genetic disorder)
> - Having several female relatives who have had breast cancer, especially relatives who have an alteration of the BRCA2 gene
> - Male breast cancer is sometimes caused by inherited gene mutations (changes).

After the tissue or fluid has been removed, a pathologist views it under a microscope to check for cancer cells.

Survival For Men With Breast Cancer Is Similar To Survival For Women With Breast Cancer

Survival for men with breast cancer is similar to that for women with breast cancer when their stage at diagnosis is the same. Breast cancer in men, however, is often diagnosed at a later stage. Cancer found at a later stage may be less likely to be cured.

Certain Factors Affect Prognosis (Chance Of Recovery) And Treatment Options

The prognosis (chance of recovery) and treatment options depend on the following:

- The stage of the cancer (whether it is in the breast only or has spread to other places in the body)
- The type of breast cancer
- Certain characteristics of the cancer cells
- Whether the cancer is found in the other breast
- The patient's age and general health

Colon Cancer

Colon Cancer Is A Disease In Which Malignant (Cancer) Cells Form In The Tissues Of The Colon

The colon is part of the body's digestive system. The digestive system removes and processes nutrients (vitamins, minerals, carbohydrates, fats, proteins, and water) from foods and helps pass waste material out of the body. The digestive system is made up of the esophagus, stomach, and the small and large intestines. The first six feet of the large intestine are called the large bowel or colon. The last six inches are the rectum and the anal canal. The anal canal ends at the anus (the opening of the large intestine to the outside of the body).

Common Cancers In Older Family Members

> ♣ **It's A Fact!!**
> ## Age And Health History Can Affect The Risk Of Developing Colon Cancer
>
> Risk factors include the following:
> - Age 50 or older
> - A family history of cancer of the colon or rectum
> - A personal history of cancer of the colon, rectum, ovary, endometrium, or breast.
> - A history of polyps (small noncancerous growths) in the colon
> - A history of ulcerative colitis (ulcers in the lining of the large intestine) or Crohn's disease
> - Certain hereditary conditions, such as familial adenomatous polyposis and hereditary nonpolyposis colon cancer (HNPCC; Lynch Syndrome)

Possible Signs Of Colon Cancer Include A Change In Bowel Habits Or Blood In The Stool

These and other symptoms may be caused by colon cancer or by other conditions. A doctor should be consulted if any of the following problems occur:

- A change in bowel habits
- Blood (either bright red or very dark) in the stool
- Diarrhea, constipation, or feeling that the bowel does not empty completely
- Stools that are narrower than usual
- General abdominal discomfort (frequent gas pains, bloating, fullness, or cramps)
- Weight loss with no known reason
- Constant tiredness
- Vomiting

McLean County Unit #5
204-Kingsley

♣ It's A Fact!!
Teens And Colon Cancer

Colon cancer (also called colorectal cancer) occurs very infrequently in people under the age of 50. In fact, the number of teens that have been diagnosed is so low that exact figures were unavailable.

The American Cancer Society recommends that screening for colon cancer starts after a person has entered adulthood, but if someone is experiencing symptoms, regardless of their age, a healthcare provider should examine them.

Symptoms To Discuss With A Healthcare Provider

- Bleeding from the rectum
- Abdominal pain
- Blood in the stool
- Change in bathroom habits

Risk Factors For Colon Cancer

- Aging (most cases occur in people over age 50)
- Personal history of polyps, colorectal cancer, or inflammatory bowel disease
- Family history of polyps or colorectal cancer
- Diets high in fat, calories, protein, meat, and alcohol and low in whole grains, fruits, and vegetables
- Smoking
- Sedentary (or inactive) lifestyle

Prevention Tips

- Eat a diet rich in fruits, vegetables, and whole grains
- Eat a diet low in fat
- Exercise regularly
- Don't smoke, or if you do smoke, quit

Source: Excerpted with permission from the TeenHealthFX website, www.teenhealthfx.com. Copyright © 2002 Atlantic Health System. All Rights Reserved.

Common Cancers In Older Family Members 57

Tests That Examine The Rectum, Rectal Tissue, And Blood Are Used To Detect (Find) And Diagnose Colon Cancer

The following tests and procedures may be used:

- **Fecal occult blood test:** A test to check stool (solid waste) for blood that can only be seen with a microscope. Small samples of stool are placed on special cards and returned to the doctor or laboratory for testing.

- **Digital rectal exam:** An exam of the rectum. The doctor or nurse inserts a lubricated, gloved finger into the rectum to feel for lumps or abnormal areas.

- **Barium enema:** A series of x-rays of the lower gastrointestinal tract. A liquid that contains barium (a silver-white metallic compound) is put into the rectum. The barium coats the lower gastrointestinal tract and x-rays are taken. This procedure is also called a lower GI series.

- **Sigmoidoscopy:** A procedure to look inside the rectum and sigmoid (lower) colon for polyps, abnormal areas, or cancer. A sigmoidoscope (a thin, lighted tube) is inserted through the rectum into the sigmoid colon. Polyps or tissue samples may be taken for biopsy.

- **Colonoscopy:** A procedure to look inside the rectum and colon for polyps, abnormal areas, or cancer. A colonoscope (a thin, lighted tube) is inserted through the rectum into the colon. Polyps or tissue samples may be taken for biopsy.

- **Biopsy:** The removal of cells or tissues so they can be viewed under a microscope to check for signs of cancer.

Certain Factors Affect Treatment Options And Prognosis (Chance of Recovery)

The treatment options and prognosis (chance of recovery) depend on the stage of the cancer (whether the cancer is in the inner lining of the colon only, involves the whole colon, or has spread to other places in the body) and the patient's general health.

Lung Cancer

The lungs are a pair of cone-shaped breathing organs that are found within the chest. The lungs bring oxygen into the body and take out carbon dioxide, which is a waste product of the body's cells. Each lung has sections called lobes. The left lung has 2 lobes. The right lung, which is slightly larger, has 3 lobes. A thin membrane called the pleura surrounds the lungs. Two tubes called bronchi lead from the trachea (windpipe) to the right and left lungs. The bronchi are sometimes also involved in lung cancer. Tiny air sacs called alveoli and small tubes called bronchioles make up the inside of the lungs.

There are two types of lung cancer: non-small cell lung cancer and small cell lung cancer.

Non-Small Cell Lung Cancer

There Are Five Types Of Non-Small Cell Lung Cancer

The five types of non-small cell lung cancer have different kinds of cancer cells. The cancer cells of each type grow and spread in different ways. The types of non-small cell lung cancer are named for the kinds of cells found in the cancer and how the cells look when viewed under a microscope:

- **Squamous cell carcinoma:** Cancer that begins in squamous cells, which are thin, flat cells that look like fish scales. This is also called epidermoid carcinoma.
- **Adenocarcinoma:** Cancer that begins in cells that have glandular (secretory) properties.
- **Large cell carcinoma:** Cancer in which the cells are large and look abnormal when viewed under a microscope.
- **Adenosquamous carcinoma:** Cancer that begins in cells that look flattened when viewed under a microscope. These cells also have glandular (secretory) properties.
- **Undifferentiated carcinoma:** Cancer cells that do not look like normal cells and multiply uncontrollably.

Common Cancers In Older Family Members

Certain Factors Affect Prognosis (Chance Of Recovery) And Treatment Options

The prognosis (chance of recovery) and treatment options depend on the following:

- The stage of the cancer (whether it is in the lung only or has spread to other places in the body)
- The tumor size
- The type of lung cancer
- Whether there are symptoms
- The patient's general health

For Most Patients With Non-Small Cell Lung Cancer, Current Treatments Do Not Cure The Cancer

If lung cancer is found, participation in one of the many clinical trials being done to improve treatment should be considered. Clinical trials are taking place in most parts of the country for patients with all stages of non-small cell lung cancer. Information about ongoing clinical trials is available from the National Cancer Institute's website (www.cancer.gov).

> ✔ **Quick Tip**
>
> To help reduce your risk of developing lung cancer, don't smoke.
>
> Cigarette smoking is the most common cause of lung cancer. Risk factors for small cell lung cancer include:
>
> - Smoking cigarettes, cigars, or pipes now or in the past
> - Being exposed to second hand smoke
> - Being exposed to asbestos or radon

Small Cell Lung Cancer

There Are Three Types Of Small Cell Lung Cancer

These three types include many different types of cells. The cancer cells of each type grow and spread in different ways. The types of small cell lung cancer are named for the kinds of cells found in the cancer and how the cells look when viewed under a microscope:

- Small cell carcinoma (oat cell cancer)
- Mixed small cell/large cell carcinoma
- Combined small cell carcinoma

Possible Signs Of Small Cell Lung Cancer Include Coughing, Chest Pain, And Shortness Of Breath

These and other symptoms may be caused by small cell lung cancer or by other conditions. A doctor should be consulted if any of the following problems occur:

- A cough that doesn't go away
- Shortness of breath
- Chest pain that doesn't go away
- Wheezing
- Coughing up blood
- Hoarseness
- Swelling of the face and neck
- Loss of appetite
- Unexplained weight loss
- Unusual tiredness

Tests And Procedures That Examine The Lungs Are Used To Detect (Find) And Diagnose Small Cell Lung Cancer

The following tests and procedures can help diagnose small cell lung cancer:

- **Chest x-ray:** An x-ray of the organs and bones inside the chest. An x-ray is a type of energy beam that can go through the body and onto film, making a picture of areas inside the body.
- **Physical exam and history:** An exam of the body to check general signs of health, including checking for signs of disease, such as lumps or anything else that seems unusual. A history of the patient's health habits and past illnesses and treatments will also be taken.
- **Sputum cytology:** A microscope is used to check for cancer cells in the sputum (mucus coughed up from the lungs).
- **Laboratory tests:** Medical procedures that test samples of tissue, blood, urine, or other substances in the body. These tests help to diagnose disease, plan and check treatment, or monitor the disease over time.

- **Bronchoscopy:** A procedure to look inside the trachea and large airways in the lung for abnormal areas. A bronchoscope (a thin, lighted tube) is inserted through the nose or mouth into the trachea and lungs. Tissue samples may be taken for biopsy.
- **Fine needle aspiration biopsy:** The removal of part of a lump, suspicious tissue, or fluid, using a thin needle. A pathologist views the tissue or fluid under a microscope to look for cancer cells. This procedure is also called a needle biopsy.
- **Thoracentesis:** Removal of fluid from the pleural cavity (the space between the lungs and chest wall) through a needle inserted between the ribs.

Certain Factors Affect Prognosis (Chance Of Recovery) And Choice Of Treatment

The prognosis (chance of recovery) and choice of treatment depend on the stage of the cancer (whether it is in the chest cavity only or has spread to other places in the body), the patient's gender and general health, and LDH (lactate dehydrogenase, a substance found in the blood that may indicate cancer when blood levels are higher than normal) level.

For Most Patients With Small Cell Lung Cancer, Current Treatments Do Not Cure The Cancer

If lung cancer is found, participation in one of the many clinical trials being done to improve treatment should be considered. Clinical trials are taking place in most parts of the country for patients with all stages of small cell lung cancer. Information about ongoing clinical trials is available from the National Cancer Institute's website (www.cancer.gov).

Prostate Cancer

Prostate Cancer Is A Disease In Which Malignant (Cancer) Cells Form In The Tissues Of The Prostate

The prostate is a gland in the male reproductive system located just below the bladder (the organ that collects and empties urine) and in front of the rectum (the lower part of the intestine). It is about the size of a walnut and surrounds part of the urethra (the tube that empties urine from the bladder). The prostate gland produces fluid that makes up part of the semen.

Prostate cancer is found mainly in older men. As men age, the prostate may get bigger and block the urethra or bladder. This may cause difficulty in urination or can interfere with sexual function. The condition is called benign prostatic hyperplasia (BPH), and although it is not cancer, surgery may be needed to correct it. The symptoms of benign prostatic hyperplasia or of other problems in the prostate may be similar to symptoms for prostate cancer.

Possible Signs Of Prostate Cancer Include A Weak Flow Of Urine Or Frequent Urination

These and other symptoms may be caused by prostate cancer or by other conditions. A doctor should be consulted if any of the following problems occur:

- Weak or interrupted flow of urine
- Frequent urination (especially at night)
- Difficulty urinating
- Pain or burning during urination
- Blood in the urine or semen
- Nagging pain in the back, hips, or pelvis
- Painful ejaculation

Tests That Examine The Prostate And Blood Are Used To Detect (Find) And Diagnose Prostate Cancer

The following tests and procedures may be used:

- **Digital rectal examination:** An exam of the rectum. The doctor or nurse inserts a lubricated, gloved finger into the rectum and feels the prostate through the rectal wall for lumps or abnormal areas.
- **Prostate-specific antigen (PSA) test:** A test that measures the level of PSA in the blood. PSA is a substance made by the prostate that may be found in an increased amount in the blood of men who have prostate

Common Cancers In Older Family Members

cancer. PSA levels may also be high in men who have an infection or inflammation of the prostate or benign prostatic hyperplasia (BPH; an enlarged, but noncancerous, prostate).

- **Transrectal ultrasound:** A procedure in which an endoscope (a thin, lighted tube) is inserted into the rectum to check the prostate. The endoscope is used to bounce high-energy sound waves (ultrasound) off internal tissues or organs and make echoes. The echoes form a picture of body tissues called a sonogram. Transrectal ultrasound may be used during a biopsy procedure.

- **Biopsy:** The removal of cells or tissues so they can be viewed under a microscope to check for signs of cancer. There are two types of biopsy procedures used to diagnose prostate cancer:

    - **Transrectal biopsy:** The removal of tissue from the prostate by inserting a thin needle through the rectum and into the prostate. This procedure is usually done using transrectal ultrasound to help guide the needle. A pathologist views the tissue under a microscope to look for cancer cells.

    - **Transperineal biopsy:** The removal of tissue from the prostate by inserting a thin needle through the skin between the scrotum and rectum and into the prostate. A pathologist views the tissue under a microscope to look for cancer cells.

A pathologist will examine the sample to check for cancer cells and determine the Gleason score. The Gleason score ranges from 2–10 and describes how likely it is that a tumor will spread. The lower the number, the less likely the tumor is to spread.

Certain Factors Affect Treatment Options And Prognosis (Chance of Recovery)

The treatment options and prognosis (chance of recovery) depend on the stage of the cancer (whether it affects part of the prostate, involves the whole prostate, or has spread to other places in the body), the Gleason score, the level of PSA, and the patient's age and general health.

Part 2
Risks, Rumors, And Controversies

Chapter 10
Tobacco And Cancer Risk

Health Effects of Smoking Among Young People

Among young people, the short-term health consequences of smoking include respiratory and nonrespiratory effects, addiction to nicotine, and the associated risk of other drug use. Long-term health consequences of youth smoking are reinforced by the fact that most young people who smoke regularly continue to smoke throughout adulthood.

- Cigarette smokers have a lower level of lung function than those persons who have never smoked.

- Smoking reduces the rate of lung growth.

About This Chapter: "Health Effects of Smoking Among Young People," reviewed November 2000, and "Cigarette Smoking-Related Mortality," reviewed April 2003 is taken from *Tobacco Information and Prevention Source (TIPS)*, National Center for Chronic Disease Prevention and Health Promotion. "Teen Opinions on Smoking" is from "TIPS 4 Youth: Facts You Should Know," Centers for Disease Control, April 8, 2003, available online at http://www.cdc.gov/tobacco/tips_4_youth/facts.htm; "Smokeless Tobacco and Cancer: Questions and Answers," National Cancer Institute (NCI), May 30, 2003, full text available online at http://www.cis.nci.nih.gov/fact/3_63.htm; "Environmental Tobacco Smoke," National Cancer Institute (NCI), February 14, 2000, available online at http://www.cis.nci.nih.gov/fact/3_9.htm; "Questions and Answers about Cigar Smoking and Cancer," National Cancer Institute (NCI), March 7, 2000, available online at http://www.cis.nci.nih.gov/fact/3_65.htm; and "The Truth about 'Light' Cigarettes: Questions and Answers," National Cancer Institute (NCI), January 3, 2003, available online at http://www.cis.nci.nih.gov/fact/3_74.htm.

- On average, someone who smokes a pack or more of cigarettes each day lives 7 years less than someone who never smoked.
- Smoking at an early age increases the risk of lung cancer. For most smoking-related cancers, the risk rises as the individual continues to smoke.

Cigarette Smoking-Related Mortality

Cigarette smoking is the single most preventable cause of premature death in the United States. Each year, more than 400,000 Americans die from cigarette smoking. In fact, one in every five deaths in the United States is smoking related. Every year, smoking kills more than 276,000 men and 142,000 women.

Deaths from lung cancer among women have increased significantly. If you think that breast cancer is the number one cancer killer among women, think again. Since the mid-1980s lung cancer deaths among women have exceeded breast cancer deaths.

Men who smoke increase their risk of death from lung cancer by more than 22 times and from bronchitis and emphysema by nearly 10 times. Women who smoke increase their risk of dying from lung cancer by nearly 12 times and the risk of dying from bronchitis and emphysema by more than 10 times. Smoking triples the risk of dying from heart disease among middle-aged men and women.

Annually, exposure to secondhand smoke (or environmental tobacco smoke) causes an estimated 3,000 deaths from lung cancer among American adults. Scientific studies also link secondhand smoke with heart disease.

> ✔ **Quick Tip**
>
> *How can you quit smoking for your health—and for the ones you love?*
>
> For more information about smoking and advice on quitting, contact:
>
> Organization: Centers for Disease Control and Prevention
> Telephone: 1-800-CDC-1311 (1-800-232-1311)
> Website: http://www.cdc.gov/tobacco
>
> Organization: National Cancer Institute
> Telephone: Smoking Quitline 1-877-44U-QUIT (1-877-448-7848)
> Website: http://www.smokefree.gov

The Truth About "Light" Cigarettes: Questions And Answers

Many smokers choose "low-tar," "mild," or "light" cigarettes because they think that light cigarettes may be less harmful to their health than "regular" or "full-flavor" cigarettes.

After all, the smoke from light cigarettes feels smoother and lighter on the throat and chest—so lights must be healthier than regulars, right? Wrong.

The truth is that light cigarettes do **not** reduce the health risks of smoking. The only way to reduce your risk, and the risk to others around you, is to stop smoking completely.

What about the lower tar and nicotine numbers on light cigarette packs and in ads for lights?

These numbers come from smoking machines that "smoke" every brand of cigarettes exactly the same way.

These numbers do not really tell how much tar and nicotine a particular smoker may get because people do not smoke cigarettes the same way the machines do. And no two people smoke the same way.

How do light cigarettes trick the smoking machines?

Tobacco companies designed light cigarettes with tiny pinholes on the filters. These "filter vents" dilute cigarette smoke with air when light cigarettes are "puffed" on by smoking machines, causing the machines to measure artificially low tar and nicotine levels.

Many smokers do not know that their cigarette filters have vent holes. The filter vents are uncovered when cigarettes are smoked on smoking machines. However, without realizing it and because they cannot avoid it, many smokers block the tiny vent holes with their fingers or lips—which basically turns the light cigarette into a regular cigarette.

Because people, unlike machines, crave nicotine, they may inhale more deeply; take larger, more rapid, or more frequent puffs; or smoke a few extra cigarettes each day to get enough nicotine to satisfy their craving. This is called "compensating," and it means that smokers end up inhaling more tar, nicotine, and other harmful chemicals than the machine-based numbers suggest.

Cigarette makers can also make the paper wrapped around the tobacco of light cigarettes burn faster so that the smoking machines get in fewer puffs before the cigarettes burn down. The result is that the machine measures less tar and nicotine in the smoke of the cigarette.

What is the scientific evidence about the health effects of light cigarettes?

The Federal Government's National Cancer Institute (NCI) concluded that light cigarettes provide no benefit to smokers' health. (National Cancer Institute. *Risks Associated with Smoking Cigarettes with Low Machine-Measured Yields of Tar and Nicotine*. Smoking and Tobacco Control Monograph 13. Bethesda, MD: NCI, 2001.)

According to the NCI report, people who switch to light cigarettes from regular cigarettes are likely to inhale the same amount of hazardous chemicals, and they remain at high risk for developing smoking-related cancers and other diseases.

> ♣ It's A Fact!!
> - The lower tar and nicotine numbers on light cigarette packs and in ads are misleading.
> - Light cigarettes trick the smoking machines so that they record artificially low tar and nicotine levels.
> - Light cigarettes provide no benefit to smokers' health.
> - Resources are available for people who want to quit smoking.

There is also no evidence that switching to light or ultra-light cigarettes actually helps smokers quit.

What do tobacco companies say about the health effects of light cigarettes?

The tobacco industry's own documents show that companies were well aware that smokers of light cigarettes compensate by taking bigger puffs.

Industry documents also show that the companies were aware early on of the difference between machine-measured yields of tar and nicotine and what the smoker actually inhales.

The NCI report concluded that strategies used by the tobacco industry to advertise and promote light cigarettes were intended to reassure smokers and to prevent them from quitting, and to lead consumers to perceive filtered and light cigarettes as safer alternatives to regular cigarettes.

Questions And Answers About Cigar Smoking And Cancer

What are the health risks associated with cigar smoking?

Scientific evidence has shown that cancers of the oral cavity (lip, tongue, mouth, and throat), larynx, lung, and esophagus are associated with cigar smoking. Furthermore, evidence strongly suggests a link between cigar smoking and cancer of the pancreas. In addition, daily cigar smokers, particularly those who inhale, are at increased risk for developing heart and lung disease.

Like cigarette smoking, the risks from cigar smoking increase with increased exposure. For example, compared with someone who has never smoked, smoking only one to two cigars per day doubles the risk for oral and esophageal cancers. Smoking three to four cigars daily can increase the risk of oral cancers to more than eight times the risk for a nonsmoker, while the chance of esophageal cancer is increased to four times the risk for someone who has never smoked. Both cigar and cigarette smokers have similar levels of risk for oral, throat, and esophageal cancers.

The health risks associated with occasional cigar smoking (less than daily) are not known. About three-quarters of cigar smokers are occasional smokers.

What is the effect of inhalation on disease risk?

One of the major differences between cigar and cigarette smoking is the degree of inhalation. Almost all cigarette smokers report inhaling while the majority of cigar smokers do not because cigar smoke is generally more irritating. However, cigar smokers who have a history of cigarette smoking are more likely to inhale cigar smoke. Cigar smokers experience higher rates of lung cancer, coronary heart disease, and chronic obstructive lung disease than nonsmokers, but not as high as the rates for cigarette smokers. These lower rates for cigar smokers are probably related to reduced inhalation.

How are cigars and cigarettes different?

Cigars and cigarettes differ in both size and the type of tobacco used. Cigarettes are generally more uniform in size and contain less than 1 gram of tobacco each. Cigars, on the other hand, can vary in size and shape and can measure more than 7 inches in length. Large cigars typically contain between 5 and 17 grams of tobacco. It is not unusual for some premium cigars to contain the tobacco equivalent of an entire pack of cigarettes. U.S. cigarettes are made from different blends of tobaccos, whereas most cigars are composed primarily of a single type of tobacco (air-cured or dried burley tobacco). Large cigars can take between 1 and 2 hours to smoke, whereas most cigarettes on the U.S. market take less than 10 minutes to smoke.

♣ It's A Fact!!

- Health risks associated with both cigars and cigarettes are strongly linked to the degree of smoke exposure.
- All cigar and cigarette smokers, whether or not they inhale, directly expose the lips, mouth, tongue, throat, and larynx to smoke and its carcinogens.

How are the health risks associated with cigar smoking different from those associated with smoking cigarettes?

Health risks associated with both cigars and cigarettes are strongly linked to the degree of smoke exposure. Since smoke from cigars and cigarettes are composed of many of the same toxic and carcinogenic (cancer causing) compounds, the differences in health risks appear to be related to differences in daily use and level of inhalation.

Tobacco And Cancer Risk

Most cigarette smokers smoke every day and inhale. In contrast, as many as three-quarters of cigar smokers smoke only occasionally, and the majority do not inhale.

All cigar and cigarette smokers, whether or not they inhale, directly expose the lips, mouth, tongue, throat, and larynx to smoke and its carcinogens. Holding an unlit cigar between the lips also exposes these areas to carcinogens. In addition, when saliva containing smoke constituents is swallowed, the esophagus is exposed to carcinogens. These exposures probably account for the fact that oral and esophageal cancer risks are similar among cigar smokers and cigarette smokers.

Cancer of the larynx occurs at lower rates among cigar smokers who do not inhale than among cigarette smokers. Lung cancer risk among daily cigar smokers who do not inhale is double that of nonsmokers, but significantly less than the risk for cigarette smokers. However, the lung cancer risk from moderately inhaling smoke from five cigars a day is comparable to the risk from smoking up to one pack of cigarettes a day.

What are the hazards for nonsmokers exposed to cigar smoke?

Environmental tobacco smoke (ETS), also known as secondhand or passive smoke, is the smoke released from a lit cigar or cigarette. The ETS from cigars and cigarettes contains many of the same toxins and irritants (such as carbon monoxide, nicotine, hydrogen cyanide, and ammonia), as well as a number of known carcinogens (such as benzene, nitrosamines, vinyl chloride, arsenic, and hydrocarbons). Because cigars contain greater amounts of tobacco than cigarettes, they produce greater amounts of ETS.

There are, however, some differences between cigar and cigarette smoke due to the different ways cigars and cigarettes are made. Cigars go through a long aging and fermentation process. During the fermentation process, high concentrations of carcinogenic compounds are produced. These compounds are released when a cigar is smoked. Also, cigar wrappers are less porous than cigarette wrappers. The nonporous cigar wrapper makes the burning of cigar tobacco less complete than cigarette tobacco. As a result, compared with cigarette smoke, the concentrations of toxins and irritants are higher in cigar smoke.

In addition, the larger size of most cigars (more tobacco) and longer smoking time produces higher exposures to nonsmokers of many toxic compounds (including carbon monoxide, hydrocarbons, ammonia, cadmium, and other substances) than a cigarette. For example, measurements of the carbon monoxide (CO) concentration at a cigar party and a cigar banquet in a restaurant showed indoor CO levels comparable to those measured on a crowded California freeway. Such exposures could place nonsmoking workers attending such events at significantly increased risk for cancer as well as heart and lung diseases.

Are cigars addictive?

Nicotine is the agent in tobacco that is capable of causing addiction or dependence. Cigarettes have an average total nicotine content of about 8.4 milligrams, while many popular brands of cigars will contain between 100 and 200 milligrams, or as many as 444 milligrams of nicotine.

> **Remember!!**
> Addiction studies of cigarettes and spit tobacco show that addiction to nicotine begins almost exclusively during adolescence and young adulthood when young people start using these tobacco products.

As with cigarette smoking, when cigar smokers inhale, nicotine is absorbed rapidly. However, because of the composition of cigar smoke and the tendency of cigar smokers not to inhale, the nicotine is absorbed predominantly through the lining of the mouth rather than in the lung. It is important to note that nicotine absorbed through the lining of the mouth is capable of forming a powerful addiction, as demonstrated by the large number of people addicted to smokeless tobacco. Both inhaled and noninhaled nicotine can be addictive. The infrequent use by the average cigar smoker, low number of cigars smoked per day, and lower rates of inhalation compared with cigarette smokers have led some to suggest that cigar smokers may be less likely to be dependent than cigarette smokers.

Addiction studies of cigarettes and spit tobacco show that addiction to nicotine occurs almost exclusively during adolescence and young adulthood when young people begin using these tobacco products. Also, several studies raise the concern that use of cigars may predispose individuals to the use of cigarettes. A recent survey showed that the relapse rate of former cigarette smokers who smoked cigars was twice as great as the relapse rate of former cigarette smokers who did not smoke cigars. The study also observed that cigar smokers were more than twice as likely to take up cigarette smoking for the first time than people who never smoked cigars.

What are the benefits of quitting?

There are many health benefits to quitting cigar smoking. The likelihood of developing cancer decreases. Also, when someone quits, an improvement in health is seen almost immediately. For example, blood pressure, pulse rate, and breathing patterns start returning to normal soon after quitting. People who quit will also see an improvement in their overall quality of life. People who decide to quit have many options available to them. Some people choose to quit all at once. Other options gaining popularity in this country are nicotine replacement products, such as patches, gum, and nasal sprays. If considering quitting, ask your doctor to recommend a plan that could best suit you and your lifestyle.

What are the current trends in cigar smoking?

Although cigar smoking occurs primarily among males between the ages of 35 and 64 who have higher educational backgrounds and incomes, recent studies suggest new trends. Most new cigar users today are teenagers and young adult males (ages 18 to 24) who smoke occasionally (less than daily).

♣ It's A Fact!!

- Most new cigar users today are teenagers and young adult males (ages 18 to 24) who smoke occasionally (less than daily).
- Cigar use has increased nearly five times among women and appears to be increasing among adolescent females as well.
- A number of studies have reported high rates of use among not only teens but preteens.

Smokeless Tobacco And Cancer

What is smokeless tobacco?

There are two types of smokeless tobacco—snuff and chewing tobacco. Snuff, a finely ground or shredded tobacco, is packaged as dry, moist, or in sachets (tea bag-like pouches). Typically, the user places a pinch or dip between the cheek and gum. Chewing tobacco is available in loose leaf, plug (plug-firm and plug-moist), or twist forms, with the user putting a wad of tobacco inside the cheek. Smokeless tobacco is sometimes called "spit" or "spitting" tobacco because people spit out the tobacco juices and saliva that build up in the mouth.

What harmful chemicals are found in smokeless tobacco?

Chewing tobacco and snuff contain 28 carcinogens (cancer-causing agents). The most harmful carcinogens in smokeless tobacco are the tobacco-specific nitrosamines (TSNAs). They are formed during the growing, curing, fermenting, and aging of tobacco. TSNAs have been detected in some smokeless tobacco products at levels many times higher than levels of other types of nitrosamines that are allowed in foods, such as bacon and beer.

Other cancer-causing substances in smokeless tobacco include N-nitrosamino acids, volatile N-nitrosamines, benzo(a)pyrene, volatile aldehydes, formaldehyde, acetaldehyde, crotonaldehyde, hydrazine, arsenic, nickel, cadmium, benzopyrene, and polonium-210.

All tobacco, including smokeless tobacco, contains nicotine, which is addictive. The amount of nicotine absorbed from smokeless tobacco is three to four times the amount delivered by a cigarette. Nicotine is absorbed more slowly from smokeless tobacco than from cigarettes, but more nicotine per dose is absorbed from smokeless tobacco than from cigarettes. Also, the nicotine stays in the bloodstream for a longer time.

What cancers are caused by or associated with smokeless tobacco use?

- Smokeless tobacco users increase their risk for cancer of the oral cavity. Oral cancer can include cancer of the lip, tongue, cheeks, gums, and the floor and roof of the mouth.

Tobacco And Cancer Risk

- People who use oral snuff for a long time have a much greater risk for cancer of the cheek and gum than people who do not use smokeless tobacco.
- The possible increased risk for other types of cancer from smokeless tobacco is being studied.

What are some of the other ways smokeless tobacco can harm users' health?

Some of the other effects of smokeless tobacco use include addiction to nicotine, oral leukoplakia (white mouth lesions that can become cancerous), gum disease, and gum recession (when the gum pulls away from the teeth). Possible increased risks for heart disease, diabetes, and reproductive problems are being studied.

Is smokeless tobacco a good substitute for cigarettes?

In 1986, the Surgeon General concluded that the use of smokeless tobacco "is not a safe substitute for smoking cigarettes. It can cause cancer and a number of noncancerous conditions and can lead to nicotine addiction and dependence." Since 1991, NCI has officially recommended that the public avoid and discontinue the use of all tobacco products, including smokeless tobacco. NCI also recognizes that nitrosamines, found in tobacco products, are not safe at any level. The accumulated scientific evidence does not support changing this position.

What about using smokeless tobacco to quit cigarettes?

Because all tobacco use causes disease and addiction, NCI recommends that tobacco use be avoided and discontinued. Several non-tobacco methods have been shown to be effective for quitting cigarettes. These methods include pharmacotherapies such as nicotine replacement therapy and bupropion SR, individual and group counseling, and telephone quitlines.

Who uses smokeless tobacco?

In the United States, the 2000 National Household Survey on Drug Abuse, which was conducted by the Substance Abuse and Mental Health Services Administration, reported the following statistics:

- An estimated 7.6 million Americans age 12 and older (3.4 percent) had used smokeless tobacco in the past month.

- Smokeless tobacco use was most common among young adults ages 18 to 25.

- Men were 10 times more likely than women to report using smokeless tobacco (6.5 percent of men age 12 and older compared with 0.5 percent of women).

People in many other countries and regions, including India, parts of Africa, and some Central Asian countries, have a long history of using smokeless tobacco products.

Where can people find help to quit using smokeless tobacco?

Several national organizations provide information about the health risks of smokeless tobacco and how to quit.

National Institute of Dental and Craniofacial Research's National Oral Health Information Clearinghouse offers educational booklets that discuss spit tobacco use in a colorful and graphic format. These booklets are designed specifically for young men who have decided to quit or are thinking about it. Website: http://www.nohic.nidcr.nih.gov.

Centers for Disease Control and Prevention's Office on Smoking and Health distributes a brochure for teens who are trying to quit cigarettes or smokeless tobacco. The Office also maintains a database of smoking and health-related materials. Website: http://www.cdc.gov/tobacco/how2quit.htm.

❧ Weird Words

Snuff: A finely ground or shredded tobacco that is either sniffed through the nose or placed between the cheek and gum.

Chewing Tobacco: Tobacco which is available in loose leaf, plug (plug-firm and plug-moist), or twist forms, which the user puts inside the cheek.

Carcinogens: Cancer-causing agents.

Oral Leukoplakia: White mouth lesions that can become cancerous.

National Spit Tobacco Education Program (NSTEP) has a mission to prevent people, especially young people, from starting to use tobacco, and to help users to quit. NSTEP offers information and materials on spit tobacco use, prevention, and cessation. Website: http://nstep.org.

American Cancer Society publishes a series of pamphlets with helpful tips and techniques for smokeless tobacco users who want to quit. Website: http://www.cancer.org.

American Academy of Family Physicians has a fact sheet with information on how to quit using smokeless tobacco. The fact sheet is available at http://familydoctor.org/handouts/177.html.

A number of other organizations provide information about where to find help to stop using smokeless tobacco. State and local health agencies often have information about community tobacco cessation programs. The local or county government section in the phone book (blue pages) has phone numbers for health agencies. Information to help smokers who want to quit is also available through community hospitals, the yellow pages (under "drug abuse and addiction"), public libraries, health maintenance organizations, health fairs, and community helplines.

What other resources are available?

A person's dentist or doctor can be a good source of information about the health risks of smokeless tobacco and about quitting. Friends, family members, teachers, and coaches can help a person quit smokeless tobacco use by giving them support and encouragement.

Teen Opinions On Smoking

Way more young people don't smoke than do. And most consider it a foul, unattractive habit. In fact, smoking is about the least popular thing you can do if you want to hang out with other teenagers. Table 10.1 shows what teens across the U.S. said in response to statements about tobacco.

Environmental Tobacco Smoke

Environmental tobacco smoke (ETS), also called "secondhand smoke," is the combination of two forms of smoke from burning tobacco products:

- Sidestream smoke, or smoke that is emitted between the puffs of a burning cigarette, pipe, or cigar; and

- Mainstream smoke, or the smoke that is exhaled by the smoker.

When a cigarette is smoked, about half of the smoke generated is sidestream smoke, which contains essentially the same compounds as those identified in the mainstream smoke inhaled by the smoker. Some of the chemicals in ETS include substances that irritate the lining of the lung and other tissues, carcinogens (cancer-causing compounds), mutagens (substances that promote genetic changes in the cell), and developmental

Table 10.1. Teen Opinions On Smoking

All numbers are percentages	AGREE	DISAGREE	NO OPINION or DON'T KNOW
Seeing someone smoke turns me off	67	22	10
I'd rather date people who don't smoke	86	8	6
It's safe to smoke for only a year or two	7	92	1
Smoking can help you when you're bored	7	92	1
Smoking helps reduce stress	21	78	3
Smoking helps keep your weight down	18	80	2
Chewing tobacco and snuff cause cancer	95	2	3
I strongly dislike being around smokers	65	22	13

Tobacco And Cancer Risk

toxicants (substances that interfere with normal cell development). Tobacco smoke is known to contain at least 60 carcinogens, including formaldehyde and benzo[a]pyrene, and six developmental toxicants, including nicotine and carbon monoxide.

Secondhand Smoke Facts

Secondhand smoke is the name for the sickening, poisonous smoke given off by a burning cigarette, cigar, or pipe. Smokers may claim to have a right to smoke, but nonsmokers have a more important right to breathe safe air. So the next time one of your friends lights up in front of you, fire off these facts about secondhand smoke.

- Secondhand smoke can produce six times the pollution of a busy highway when in a crowded restaurant.
- Secondhand smoke causes 30 times as many lung cancer deaths as all regulated pollutants combined.
- Secondhand smoke makes clothes and hair stink.
- Secondhand smoke causes wheezing, coughing, colds, earaches, and asthma attacks.
- Secondhand smoke fills the air with many of the same poisons found in the air around toxic waste dumps.
- Secondhand smoke wrecks the smell and taste of food.
- Secondhand smoke causes reddening, itching, and watering of the eyes.
- Secondhand smoke kills about 3,000 nonsmokers each year from lung cancer.
- Secondhand smoke causes up to 300,000 lung infections (such as pneumonia and bronchitis) in infants and young children each year.

Health Effects Associated With ETS Exposure

In 1986, two landmark reports were published on the association between ETS exposure and the adverse health effects in nonsmokers: one by the U.S. Surgeon General and the other by the Expert Committee on

Passive Smoking, National Academy of Sciences' National Research Council (NAS/NRC). Both of these reports concluded that:

- ETS can cause lung cancer in healthy adult nonsmokers;

- Children of parents who smoke have more respiratory symptoms and acute lower respiratory tract infections, as well as evidence of reduced lung function, than do children of nonsmoking parents; and

- Separating smokers and nonsmokers within the same air space may reduce but does not eliminate a nonsmoker's exposure to ETS.

In 1992, the U.S. Environmental Protection Agency (EPA) confirmed the above findings in its study on the respiratory health effects of ETS. In addition, the EPA classified ETS as a Group A carcinogen—a category reserved only for the most dangerous cancer-causing agents in humans. The EPA report, a compilation of 30 epidemiological studies that focused on the health risks of nonsmokers with smoking spouses, concluded that there is a strong association between ETS exposure and lung cancer. Scientists estimate that ETS is responsible for approximately 3,000 lung cancer deaths per year among nonsmokers in the United States. Recent studies and the EPA's report point to a 20-percent increased risk of lung cancer in nonsmokers due to ETS.

In response to evidence that ETS causes diseases beyond lung cancer and respiratory problems in children, the California Environmental Protection Agency (Cal/EPA) conducted a comprehensive assessment of the range of health effects connected with ETS exposure. In 1999, the National Cancer Institute (NCI) published the Cal/EPA's results as part of its Smoking and Tobacco Control monograph series in *Health Effects of Exposure to Environmental Tobacco Smoke*. Table 10.2 outlines the health effects that were found to have a significant association with ETS exposure.

Other health effects that were found to be possibly associated with ETS were as follows:

- Spontaneous abortion (miscarriage);

- Adverse impact on cognition and behavior during child development;

Tobacco And Cancer Risk

- Exacerbation of cystic fibrosis (a disease marked by overproduction of mucus in the lungs);

- Decreased lung function; and

- Cervical cancer.

However, further research is needed to confirm the link between the above health risks and ETS.

Carcinogenic Effects Of ETS

More than 3,000 chemicals are present in tobacco smoke, including at least 60 known carcinogens such as nitrosamines and polycyclic aromatic hydrocarbons. Some of these compounds become carcinogenic only after they are activated by specific enzymes (proteins that control chemical reactions) found in many tissues in the body. These activated compounds can then become part of deoxyribonucleic acid (DNA) molecules and possibly interfere with the normal growth of cells. Tobacco also contains nicotine, a chemical that causes physical addiction to smoking and makes it difficult for people to stop smoking.

Although much of the research into the carcinogenicity of ETS has focused on lung cancer, ETS has also been linked with other cancers, including those in the nasal sinus cavity, cervix, breast, and bladder. The role of ETS in the development of nasal sinus cancer has been investigated in three recent studies; all three showed a significant positive association between ETS exposure and the development of nasal sinus cancer in nonsmoking adults. Several studies that focused on ETS as a risk factor for cervical cancer have shown a possible association between ETS and cancer of the cervix, although no specific conclusions could be made. Similarly, studies of the relationship between ETS exposure and breast cancer suggested an association between the two, but the evidence was weak. Although active smoking has been identified as a cause of bladder cancer, the results of studies focusing on ETS and

> ♣ **It's A Fact!!**
>
> Nonsmokers who are exposed to ETS absorb nicotine and other compounds just as smokers do. As the exposure to ETS increases, the levels of these harmful substances in the body increase as well. Although the smoke to which a nonsmoker is exposed is less concentrated than that inhaled by smokers, research has demonstrated significant health risks associated with ETS.

bladder cancer have not been conclusive. More research is needed into the impact of ETS on nonsmokers' risk for cancers of the cervix, breast, and bladder.

Public Policies Restricting Smoking

Studies dating from the early 1970s have consistently shown that children and infants exposed to ETS in the home have significantly elevated rates of respiratory symptoms and respiratory tract infections. These findings prompted recommendations that ETS be eliminated from the environment of small children.

In adults, ETS can worsen existing pulmonary symptoms for people with asthma and chronic bronchitis, as well as for people with allergic conditions. Even individuals who are not allergic can suffer eye irritation, sore throat, nausea, and hoarseness. Contact lens wearers can find tobacco smoke very irritating.

Following the release of the 1986 reports by the Surgeon General and the NAS, many new laws, regulations, and ordinances were enacted that severely restrict or ban public smoking:

Table 10.2 Health Effects Associated With ETS Exposure

Developmental Effects	• Low birth weight or small for gestational age • Sudden Infant Death Syndrome (SIDS)
Respiratory Effects	• Acute lower respiratory tract infections in children • Asthma induction and exacerbation in children • Chronic respiratory symptoms in children • Eye and nasal irritation in adults • Middle ear infections in children
Carcinogenic Effects	• Lung Cancer • Nasal Sinus Cancer
Cardiovascular Effects	• Heart disease mortality • Acute and chronic coronary heart disease morbidity

Tobacco And Cancer Risk

> ### ✎ Weird Words
>
> <u>Developmental Toxicants</u>: Substances that interfere with normal cell development.
>
> <u>Enzymes</u>: Proteins that control chemical reactions.
>
> <u>Mutagens</u>: Substances that promote genetic changes in cells.
>
> <u>Secondhand Smoke</u>: The combination of two forms of smoke from burning tobacco products—sidestream smoke (smoke that is emitted between the puffs of a burning cigarette, pipe, or cigar) and mainstream smoke (the smoke that is exhaled by the smoker). Also called environmental tobacco smoke (ETS).

- On the Federal level, the General Services Administration issued regulations restricting smoking to designated areas only in Federal office buildings. Many agencies within the Public Health Service, which includes the National Institutes of Health, have banned smoking completely.

- By law, smoking on all airline flights of 6 hours or less within the United States is banned; however, in practice, all U.S. airlines have banned smoking on all domestic flights. All interstate bus travel is smoke free.

- ETS meets the criteria of the Occupational Safety and Health Administration (OSHA) for classification as a potential occupational carcinogen. (OSHA is the Federal agency responsible for health and safety regulations in the workplace.)

- The National Institute for Occupational Safety and Health (NIOSH) is another Federal agency that is concerned with ETS exposure in the workplace. NIOSH conducts ETS-related research, evaluates work sites for possible health hazards, and makes safety recommendations. NIOSH recommends that ETS be regarded as a potential occupational carcinogen, in conformance with the OSHA carcinogen policy, and that exposures to ETS be reduced to the lowest possible levels.

- Currently, nearly every state has some form of legislation to protect nonsmokers; some states require private employers to enact policies that protect employees who do not smoke.

Additional Resources About The Effects Of ETS

A 1999 NCI monograph *Health Effects of Exposure to Environmental Tobacco Smoke* can be viewed and downloaded or ordered from the National Cancer Institute's Cancer Information Service (www.cancer.gov). Additional information on the health effects of tobacco is available from the CDC's Tobacco Information and Prevention Source at http://www.cdc.gov/tobacco on the Internet. This program collects and distributes reports and news about tobacco, lists services available for people trying to quit using tobacco products, and produces publications about tobacco and the dangers of its use.

☞ Remember!!

What is the bottom line for smokers who want to protect their health?

There is no such thing as a safe cigarette. The only proven way to reduce your risk of smoking-related disease is to quit smoking completely.

Here's good news: Smokers who quit before age 50 cut their risk of dying in half over the next 15 years compared with people who keep smoking.

Quitting also decreases your risk of lung cancer, heart attacks, stroke, and chronic lung disease.

Chapter 11

Sun Exposure And Cancer Risk

Health Effects Of Overexposure To The Sun

This chapter provides a quick overview of the major health problems linked to overexposure to UV radiation. Understanding these risks and taking a few sensible precautions will help you to enjoy the sun while lowering your chances of sun-related health problems later in life.

Skin Cancer

The incidence of skin cancer in the United States has reached epidemic proportions. One in five Americans will develop skin cancer in their lifetime, and one American dies every hour from this devastating disease. Medical research is helping us understand the causes and effects of skin cancer, and many health and education groups are working to reduce the incidence of this disease.

Melanoma

Melanoma, the most serious form of skin cancer, is also one of the fastest growing types of cancer in the United States. Many dermatologists believe

---

About This Chapter: Text in this chapter was adapted and excerpted from "Health Effects of Overexposure to the Sun," US Environmental Protection Agency (EPA), 2003, available online at http://www.epa.gov/sunwise/uvandhealth.html; and "Sunscreen: The Burning Facts," EPA, EPA430-F-01-015, May 2001, available online at http://www.epa.gov/sunwise/doc/sunscreen.pdf. Reviewed and revised by David A. Cooke, M.D., on January 24, 2004

there may be a link between childhood sunburns and melanoma later in life. Melanoma cases in this country have more than doubled in the past two decades, and the rise is expected to continue.

Nonmelanoma Skin Cancers

Nonmelanoma skin cancers are less deadly than melanomas. Nevertheless, left untreated, they can spread, causing disfigurement and more serious health problems. More than 1.2 million Americans were predicted to develop nonmelanoma skin cancer in 2000 while more than 1,900 were estimated to die from the disease. There are two primary types of nonmelanoma skin cancers. These two cancers have a cure rate as high as 95 percent if detected and treated early. The key is to watch for signs and seek medical treatment.

Basal Cell Carcinomas are the most common type of skin cancer tumors. They usually appear as small, fleshy bumps or nodules on the head and neck, but can occur on other skin areas. Basal cell carcinoma grows slowly, and rarely spreads to other parts of the body. It can, however, penetrate to the bone and cause considerable damage.

✎ Weird Words

Basal Cell Carcinoma: A type of skin cancer that arises from the basal cells, small round cells found in the lower part or (base) of the epidermis, the outer layer of the skin.

Melanoma: A form of skin cancer that rises in melanocytes, the cells that produce pigment. Melanoma usually begins in a mole.

Squamous Cell Carcinoma: Cancer that begins in squamous cells, which are thin, flat cells resembling fish scales. Squamous cells are found in the tissue that forms the surface of the skin, the lining of the hollow organs of the body, and the passages of the respiratory and digestive tracts. Also called epidermoid carcinoma.

Source: Excerpted from "Cancer.gov Dictionary," National Cancer Institute, December 2003. The full text of this dictionary is available online at http://www.cancer.gov/dictionary.

Squamous Cell Carcinomas are tumors that may appear as nodules or as red, scaly patches. This cancer can develop into large masses, and unlike basal cell carcinoma, it can spread to other parts of the body.

Other Skin Damage

Other UV-related skin disorders include actinic keratoses and premature aging of the skin. Actinic keratoses are skin growths that occur on body areas exposed to the sun. The face, hands, forearms, and the "V" of the neck are especially susceptible to this type of lesion. Although pre-malignant, actinic keratoses are a risk factor for squamous cell carcinoma. Look for raised, reddish, rough-textured growths and seek prompt medical attention if you discover them. Chronic exposure to the sun also causes premature aging, which over time can make the skin become thick, wrinkled, and leathery. Since it occurs gradually, often manifesting itself many years after the majority of a person's sun exposure, premature aging is often regarded as an unavoidable, normal part of growing older. With proper protection from UV radiation, however, most premature aging of the skin can be avoided.

Cataracts And Other Eye Damage

Cataracts are a form of eye damage in which a loss of transparency in the lens of the eye clouds vision. If left untreated, cataracts can lead to blindness. Research has shown that UV radiation increases the likelihood of certain cataracts. Although curable with modern eye surgery, cataracts diminish the eyesight of millions of Americans and cost billions of dollars in medical care each year. Other kinds of eye damage include pterygium (i.e., tissue growth that can block vision), skin cancer around the eyes, and degeneration of the macula (i.e., the part of the retina where visual perception is most acute). All of these problems can be lessened with proper eye protection from UV radiation.

Immune Suppression

Scientists have found that overexposure to UV radiation may suppress proper functioning of the body's immune system and the skin's natural defenses. All people, regardless of skin color, might be vulnerable to effects including impaired response to immunizations, increased sensitivity to sunlight, and reactions to certain medications.

Sunscreen: The Burning Facts

Although the sun is necessary for life, too much sun exposure can lead to adverse health effects, including skin cancer. More than 1 million people in the United States are diagnosed with skin cancer each year, making it the most common form of cancer in the country, but it is largely preventable through a broad sun protection program. Ninety percent of skin cancers are linked to sun exposure.

By themselves, sunscreens might not be effective in protecting you from the most dangerous forms of skin cancer. However, sunscreen use is an important part of your sun protection program. Used properly, certain sunscreens help protect human skin from some of the sun's damaging ultraviolet (UV) radiation. But according to recent surveys, most people are confused about the proper use and effectiveness of sunscreens. The purpose of this section is to educate you about sunscreens and other important sun protection measures so that you can protect yourself from the sun's damaging rays.

How Does UV Radiation Affect My Skin? What Are The Risks?

UV rays can have a number of harmful effects on the skin. The two types of UV radiation that can affect the skin, UVA and UVB, have both been linked to skin cancer and a weakening of the immune system. They also

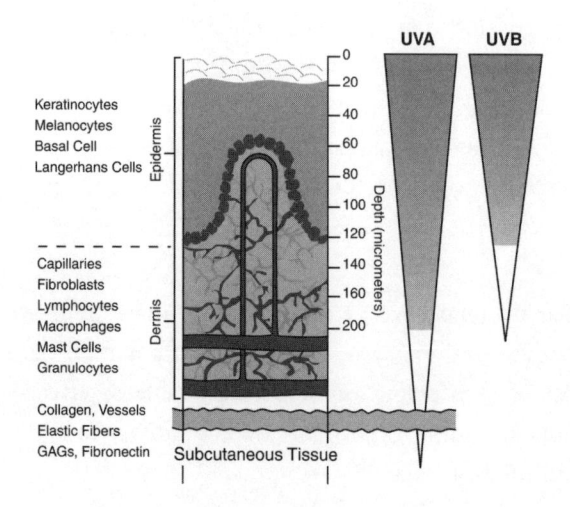

Figure 11.1 Penetration of UV Into the Skin

Sun Exposure And Cancer Risk

contribute to both premature aging of the skin and cataracts (a condition that impairs eyesight), and cause skin color changes.

UVA Rays

UVA rays, which are not absorbed by the ozone layer, penetrate deep into the skin and heavily contribute to premature aging. Up to 90 percent of the visible skin changes commonly attributed to aging are caused by sun exposure.

UVB Rays

These powerful rays, which are partially absorbed by the ozone layer, mostly impact the surface of the skin and are the primary cause of sunburn. Because of the thinning of the ozone layer, the effects of UVB radiation will pose an increased threat until the layer is restored in approximately 50 years.

Are Some People Predisposed To Adverse Health Effects Resulting From Sun Exposure?

Everybody, regardless of race or ethnicity, is subject to the potential adverse effects of overexposure to the sun. Some people might be more vulnerable to certain conditions, however.

Skin Type

Skin type affects the degree to which some people burn and the time it takes them to burn. The Food and Drug Administration (FDA) classifies skin type on a scale from 1 to 6. Individuals with lower number skin types (1 and 2) have fair skin and tend to burn rapidly and more severely. Individuals with higher number skin types (5 and 6), though capable of burning, have darker skin and do not burn as easily.

The same individuals who are most likely to burn are also most vulnerable to skin cancer. Studies have shown that individuals with large numbers of freckles and moles also have a higher risk of developing skin cancer. Although individuals with higher-number skin types are less likely to develop skin cancer, they should still take action to protect their skin and eyes from overexposure to the sun. Some dark-skinned individuals can and do get skin cancer.

Additional Factors

Certain diseases, such as lupus, can also make a person more sensitive to sun exposure. People who take medications that suppress the immune system, such as people with organ transplants or certain autoimmune diseases, are unusually prone to skin cancer, and their risk can be several hundred times that of other people. Some medications, such as antibiotics and antihistamines and even certain herbal remedies, can cause extra sensitivity to the sun's rays. Discuss these issues with your physician.

How Do Sunscreens Work? What Is the Sun Protection Factor (SPF)?

Sunscreens protect your skin by absorbing and/or reflecting UVA and UVB rays. The Food and Drug Administration (FDA) requires that all sunscreens contain a Sun Protection Factor (SPF) label. The SPF reveals the relative amount of sunburn protection that a sunscreen can provide an average user (tested on skin types 1, 2, and 3) when correctly used.

♣ **It's A Fact!!**

Not everyone burns or tans in the same manner. Whether individuals burn or tan depends on a number of factors, including their skin type, the time of year, and the amount of sun exposure they have received recently. The skin's susceptibility to burning can be classified as follows:

Skin Type	Tanning and Sunburning History
1	Always burns, never tans, sensitive to sun exposure
2	Burns easily, tans minimally
3	Burns moderately, tans gradually to light brown
4	Burns minimally, always tans well to moderately brown
5	Rarely burns, tans profusely to dark
6	Never burns, deeply pigmented, least sensitive

Though everyone is at risk for damage as a result of excessive sun exposure, people with skin types 1 and 2 are at the highest risk.

Source: Text adapted and excerpted from "Choose Your Cover: Questions and Answers," Centers for Disease Control and Prevention (CDC), November 2001, available online at http://www.cdc.gov/chooseyourcover/qanda.htm.

Sunscreens with an SPF of at least 15 are recommended. You should be aware that an SPF of 30 is not twice as protective as an SPF of 15; rather, when properly used, an SPF of 15 protects the skin from 93 percent of UVB radiation, and an SPF 30 sunscreen provides 97 percent protection (see Figure 11.2).

Although the SPF ratings found on sunscreen packages apply mainly to UVB rays, many sunscreen manufacturers include ingredients that protect the skin from some UVA rays as well. These "broad-spectrum" sunscreens are highly recommended.

What Are The Active Ingredients In Sunscreen?

Chemical (Organic) Ingredients

Broad-spectrum sunscreens often contain a number of chemical ingredients that absorb UVA and UVB radiation. Many sunscreens contain UVA-absorbing avobenzone or a benzophenone (such as dioxybenzone, oxybenzone, or sulisobenzone), in addition to UVB-absorbing chemical ingredients (some of which also contribute to UVA protection). In rare cases, chemical ingredients cause skin reactions, including acne, burning, blisters, dryness, itching, rash, redness, stinging, swelling, and tightening of the skin. Consult a physician if these symptoms occur. These reactions are most commonly associated with para-aminobenzoic acid (PABA)-based sunscreens and those containing benzophenones. Some sunscreens also contain alcohol, fragrances, or preservatives, and should be avoided if you have skin allergies.

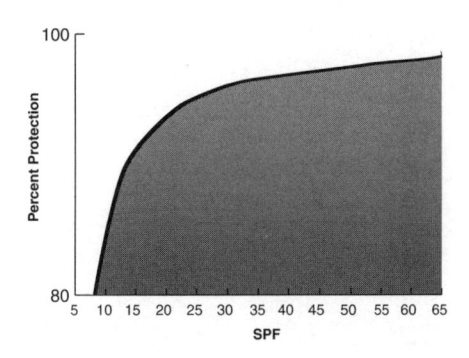

Figure 11.2 SPF versus UVB Protection

✔ **Quick Tip**

Action Steps For Sun Protection

Protecting yourself from overexposure to UV radiation is simple if you take the precautions listed below.

- **Limit time in the midday sun as much as possible.** The sun's UV rays are strongest between 10 a.m. and 4 p.m. To the extent you can, limit exposure to the sun during these hours.

- **Watch for the UV Index.** The UV Index provides important information to help you plan your outdoor activities in ways that prevent overexposure to the sun's rays. Developed by the National Weather Service (NWS) and EPA, the UV Index is issued daily in selected cities across the United States.

- **Wear sunglasses that block 99 to 100 percent of UV radiation.** Sunglasses that provide 99 to 100 percent UVA and UVB protection will greatly reduce sun exposure that can lead to cataracts and other eye damage. Check the label when buying sunglasses.

- **Wear a hat.** A hat with a wide brim offers good sun protection for your eyes, ears, face, and the back of your neck, areas particularly prone to overexposure to the sun.

- **Seek shade.** Staying under cover is one of the best ways to protect yourself from the sun.

- **Protect other areas of your body with clothing during prolonged periods in the sun.** Tightly-woven, loose-fitting, and full-length clothes are best for protection of exposed skin.

- **Always use a sunscreen when outside.** A sunscreen with a sun protection factor (SPF) of at least 15 blocks most harmful UV radiation. Apply sunscreen liberally and reapply every 2 hours when working, playing, or exercising outdoors. Even waterproof sunscreen can come off when you towel off sweat or water. Consult your physician about sunscreen use on children under 6 months of age. Also use lip balm of SPF 15.

- **Avoid sunlamps and tanning salons.** The light source from sunbeds and sunlamps damages the skin and unprotected eyes. It's a good idea to avoid artificial sources of UV light.

Source: Text adapted and excerpted from "The Sun, UV, and You: A Guide to Sunwise Behavior," EPA, June 1999, available online at http://www.epa.gov/sunwise/doc/SUNUVU.PDF.

Sun Exposure And Cancer Risk

Physical (Inorganic) Ingredients

The physical compounds titanium dioxide and zinc oxide reflect, scatter, and absorb both UVA and UVB rays. These ingredients, produced through chemical processes, do not typically cause allergic reactions. Using new technology, the particle sizes of zinc oxide and titanium dioxide have been reduced, making them more transparent.

Summary

All of the previously mentioned chemical and physical ingredients have been approved by the FDA. Figure 11.3 lists these ingredients and includes information regarding the type and amount of ray protection that they provide and their class.

FDA Monograph Sunscreen Ingredients	Amount of Ray Protection UVA	UVB	Chemical (C) or Physical (P)
Aminobenzoic acid (PABA)	○	●	C
Avobenzone	●	◐	C
Cinoxate	◐	●	C
Dioxybenzone	◑	●	C
Homosalate	○	●	C
Menthyl anthranilate	◑	●	C
Octocrylene	◐	●	C
Octyl methoxycinnamate	◐	●	C
Octyl salicylate	○	●	C
Oxybenzone	◑	●	C
Padimate O	○	●	C
Phenylbenzimidazole	○	●	C
Sulisobenzone	◑	●	C
Titanium dioxide	◑	●	P
Trolamine salicylate	○	●	C
Zinc Oxide	●	●	P

Protection Level: ● = extensive ◑ = considerable ◐ = limited ○ = minimal

Figure 11.3 Sunscreen Ingredients

Can I Get A Tan Without The Sun?

Sunless tanners and bronzers are applied to the skin like a cream and can provide a temporary, artificial tan. The only color additive currently approved by FDA for this purpose is dihydroxyacetone (DHA). Application can be difficult, and areas of the skin can react differently, resulting in an uneven appearance.

Bronzers stain the skin temporarily, and they can generally be removed with soap and water. They may streak after application and can stain clothes. Sunless tanners and bronzers might not contain active sunscreen ingredients. Read their labels to find out if they provide any sun protection.

Is A Suntan Healthy?

There is no such thing as a healthy suntan. Any change in your natural skin color is a sign of skin damage. Every time your skin color changes after sun exposure, your risk of developing sun-related ailments increases.

Will Sun Protection Deprive Me Of Vitamin D?

Sun exposure is not required to get a sufficient amount of vitamin D. Most people get an adequate amount of vitamin D in their diets. If you are concerned about not getting enough vitamin D, consider taking a multivitamin or drinking vitamin D-fortified milk daily. [Editor's Note: There is conflicting scientific evidence about the effect of sunscreen use on vitamin D production. Because of this uncertainty, taking a multivitamin containing vitamin D is reasonable precaution if you use sunscreen regularly.]

Are Tanning Lotions Safe?

The FDA considers it an important public health issue that users of suntanning products be told when the products do not contain a sunscreen and thus, do not protect against sunburn or other harmful effects to the skin. The FDA requires that all such products carry the following label:

"Warning This product does not contain a sunscreen and does not protect against sunburn. Repeated exposure of unprotected skin while tanning may increase the risk of skin aging, skin cancer, and other harmful effects to

Sun Exposure And Cancer Risk

> ### ♣ It's A Fact!!
>
> The UV Index describes the next day's likely levels of the intensity of UV rays. The index predicts UV levels on a 0 to 10+ scale:
>
> | Index Number Level | Intensity |
> |---|---|
> | 0 to 2 | Minimal |
> | 3 to 4 | Low |
> | 5 to 6 | Moderate |
> | 7 to 9 | High |
> | 10+ | Very High |
>
> While always taking precautions against overexposure, take special care to adopt the safeguards recommended above when the UV Index predicts exposure levels of moderate or higher.
>
> Some medications cause serious sun sensitivity, as do some diseases such as lupus erythematosus. The UV Index is not intended for use by seriously sunsensitive individuals. Consult your doctor about additional precautions you might need to take.
>
> Source: Text adapted and excerpted from "The Sun, UV, and You: A Guide to Sunwise Behavior," EPA, June 1999, available online at http://www.epa.gov/sunwise/doc/SUNUVU.PDF.

the skin even if you do not burn." (Title 21 of the Code of Federal Regulations, Section 740.19)

How Does The Outside Environment Influence Exposure?

The intensity of the sun's UV rays reaching the Earth's surface varies and should be considered when you plan outdoor activities. The National Weather Service issues the UV Index, a daily forecast of UV intensity.

You can obtain your local UV Index forecast daily from local weather stations or newspapers. The U.S. Environmental Protection Agency's website provides daily local UV forecasts for your ZIP code. The address is http://www.epa.gov/sunwise/uvindex.html. The higher the UV Index forecast, the stronger the sun will be and the greater the need to follow all the sun protection action steps.

In general, UV strength is greatest from 10 a.m. to 4 p.m. during sunny summer days. Up to 80 percent of UV rays pass through clouds, however, meaning that sunburn is possible on cloudy days as well. UV exposure is greater at low latitudes (nearer to the equator) and/or high altitudes. Snow, water, and sand also increase sun exposure by reflecting incoming UV rays, making it especially important for skiers, boaters, and beachcombers to wear clothing and hats and apply sunscreen.

How Do I Apply Sunscreen?

Use a broad-spectrum sunscreen with an SPF rating of 15 or higher. Apply sunscreen 20 minutes before going out into the sun (or as directed by the manufacturer) to give it time to absorb into your skin. Apply it well and regularly about one ounce every two hours (or as directed by the manufacturer) and more often if you are swimming or perspiring. A small tube containing between three and five ounces of sunscreen might only be enough for one person during a day at the beach.

Do not forget about lips, ears, feet, hands, bald spots and the back of the neck. In addition, apply sunscreen to areas under bathing suit straps, necklaces, bracelets, and sunglasses. Keep sunscreen until the expiration date or for no more than three years, because the sunscreen ingredients might become less effective over time.

According to the FDA, "water resistant" sunscreens must maintain their SPFs after 40 minutes of water immersion, while "very water resistant" sunscreens must maintain their SPF after 80 minutes of water immersion. Either type of water-resistant sunscreen must be reapplied regularly, as heavy perspiration, water, and towel drying remove the sunscreen's protective layer.

Is Sunscreen Fail-Safe?

Using sunscreen does not mean it is safe to spend more time in the sun, especially when the UV Index is high. Although a sunscreen with an SPF of 30 offers protection from sunburn, it does not block all of the sun's damaging rays. In fact, there is no evidence that sunscreens protect you from malignant melanoma, the deadliest form of skin cancer. There is only limited evidence that sunscreens protect you from several other types of skin cancer. To fully protect yourself, remember to seek shade, avoid peak hours of sun exposure, and wear protective clothing in addition to applying sunscreen.

Chapter 12

Cervical Cancer Risks Linked To Unprotected Sex

Human Papillomaviruses

Human papillomaviruses (HPVs) are a group of more than 100 types of viruses. They are called papillomaviruses because certain types may cause warts, or papillomas, which are benign (noncancerous) tumors. The HPVs that cause the common warts which grow on hands and feet are different from those that cause growths in the mouth and genital area. Some types of HPVs are associated with certain types of cancer.

Of the more than 100 types of HPVs, over 30 types can be passed from one person to another through sexual contact. HPV infection is one of the most common sexually transmitted diseases (STDs). Some types of HPVs may cause warts to appear on or around the genitals or anus. Genital warts (technically known as condylomata acuminatum) are most commonly associated with two HPV types, numbers 6 and 11. Warts may appear within several weeks after sexual contact with a person who has HPV, or they may take months or years to appear; or they may never appear. HPVs may also

---

About This Chapter: Text in this chapter is excerpted from "Human Papillomaviruses and Cancer," Cancer Facts Fact Sheet, National Cancer Institute (NCI), reviewed January 8, 2001, editorial changes made October 15, 2002, available online at http://cis.nci.nih.gov/fact/3_20.htm.

cause flat, abnormal growths in the genital area and on the cervix (the lower part of the uterus that extends into the vagina). HPV infections often do not cause any symptoms.

HPVs And Cancer Risk

HPVs are now recognized as the major cause of cervical cancer. Studies also suggest that HPVs may play a role in cancers of the anus, vulva, vagina, and penis, and some cancers of the oropharynx (the middle part of the throat that includes the soft palate, the base of the tongue, and the tonsils).

❧ Weird Words

Cervical Intraepithelial Neoplasia (CIN): A general term for the growth of abnormal cells on the surface of the cervix. Numbers from 1 to 3 may be used to describe how much of the cervix contains abnormal cells.

Colposcopy: Examination of the vagina and cervix using a lighted magnifying instrument called a colposcope.

Cryosurgery: Treatment performed with an instrument that freezes and destroys abnormal tissues.

Dysplasia: Cells that look abnormal under a microscope but are not cancer.

Human Papillomavirus (HPV): A virus that causes abnormal tissue growth (warts) and is often associated with some types of cancer.

Squamous Intraepithelial Lesion (SIL): A general term for the abnormal growth of squamous cells on the surface of the cervix. The changes in the cells are described a low grade or high grade, depending on how much of the cervix is affected and how abnormal the cells appear.

Source: Excerpted from "Cancer.gov Dictionary," National Cancer Institute, December 2003. The full text of this dictionary is available online at http://www.cancer.gov/dictionary.

Some types of HPVs are referred to as "low-risk" viruses because they rarely develop into cancer; these include HPV-6 and HPV-11. HPV viruses that can lead to the development of cancer are referred to as "high-risk." Both high-risk and low-risk types of HPVs can cause the growth of abnormal cells, but generally only the high-risk types of HPVs may lead to cancer. Sexually transmitted, high-risk HPVs have been linked with cancer in both men and women; they include HPV types 16, 18, 31, 33, 35, 39, 45, 51, 52, 56, 58, 59, 68, and 69. These high-risk types of HPVs cause growths that are usually flat and nearly invisible, as compared with the warts caused by HPV-6 and HPV-11. It is important to note, however, that the majority of HPV infections go away on their own and do not cause any abnormal growths.

> ♣ **It's A Fact!!**
> Of the more than 100 types of HPVs, over 30 types can be passed from one person to another through sexual contact.

Precancerous Cervical Conditions

Abnormal cervical cells can be detected when a Pap test is done during a gynecologic exam. Various terms have been used to describe the abnormal cells that may be seen in Pap tests. In the Bethesda system (the major system used to report the results of Pap tests in the United States), precancerous conditions are divided into low-grade and high-grade squamous intraepithelial lesions (SILs). Squamous cells are thin, flat cells that cover internal and external surfaces of the body, including the tissue that forms the surface of the skin, the lining of the hollow organs of the body, and the passages of the genital, respiratory, and digestive tracts. Other terms sometimes used to describe these abnormal cells are cervical intraepithelial neoplasia (CIN) and dysplasia. Low-grade SILs (mild dysplasias) are a common condition, especially in young women. The majority of low-grade SILs return to normal over months to a few years. Sometimes, low-grade SILs can progress to high-grade SILs. High-grade SILs are not cancer, but they may eventually lead to cancer and should be treated by a doctor.

Risk Factors For HPV And Cervical Cancer

Behaviors such as beginning sexual intercourse at an early age (especially age 16 or younger) and having many sexual partners increase the chance that a woman will develop an HPV infection in the cervix. Most HPV infections go away on their own without causing any type of abnormality. It is important to note that infection with high-risk HPV types may increase the chance that mild abnormalities will progress to more severe abnormalities or cervical cancer. Still, of the women who do develop abnormal cell changes with high-risk types of HPV, only a small percentage will develop cervical cancer if the abnormal cells are not removed. Studies suggest that whether a woman develops cervical cancer depends on a variety of factors acting together with high-risk HPVs. The factors that may increase the risk of cancer in women with HPV infection include smoking, having many children, and human immunodeficiency virus (HIV) infection.

Screening And Follow-Up For Precancerous Cervical Conditions

Screening for cervical cancer consists of regular Pap tests for women who are sexually active or who have reached 18 years of age. If high-grade abnormal cell changes are found on a Pap test, colposcopy and biopsy of any abnormal areas are recommended. (Colposcopy is a procedure in which a lighted magnifying instrument called a colposcope is used to examine the vagina and

♣ **It's A Fact!!**
Behaviors such as beginning sexual intercourse at an early age (especially age 16 or younger) and having many sexual partners increase the chance that a woman will develop an HPV infection in the cervix.

Cervical Cancer Risks Linked To Unprotected Sex

> **♣ It's A Fact!!**
>
> The factors that may increase the risk of cancer in women with HPV infection include:
>
> - smoking
> - having many children
> - human immunodeficiency virus (HIV) infection

cervix. Biopsy is the removal of a small piece of tissue for diagnosis.) If low-grade changes are found, repeat Pap tests or colposcopy may be recommended.

Treatment Of HPV Infection

Although there is currently no medical cure to eliminate a papillomavirus infection, the SILs and warts these viruses cause can be treated. Methods used to treat SILs include cryosurgery (freezing that destroys tissue), laser treatment (surgery using a high-intensity light), LEEP (loop electrosurgical excision procedure, the removal of tissue using a hot wire loop), as well as conventional surgery. Similar treatments may be used for external genital warts. In addition, three powerful chemicals (podophyllin, bichloroacetic acid, and trichloroacetic acid) will destroy external genital warts when applied directly to them. Podofilox (podophyllotoxin) can be applied topically either as a liquid or a gel to external genital warts. Imiquimod cream has also been approved to treat external warts. Also, fluorouracil cream (sometimes called 5-FU) may be used to treat the warts. Some doctors use interferon alpha to treat warts that have recurred after being removed by traditional means. Imiquimod and interferon alpha work by stimulating the immune (defense) system to fight the virus.

Current Research

The ASCUS/LSIL Triage Study (ALTS), a major study organized and funded by the National Cancer Institute (NCI), is currently evaluating different management approaches for women with mildly abnormal Pap test results. (ASCUS and LSIL are acronyms for the two mild abnormalities detected by Pap tests. ASCUS stands for atypical squamous cells of undetermined significance and LSIL for low-grade squamous intraepithelial lesions.) Preliminary findings from the ALTS study suggest that testing cervical samples for HPV is an excellent option to help direct follow-up for women with an

ASCUS Pap test result. Repeat Pap tests or direct referral to colposcopy remain options for the follow-up of ASCUS results. The final study results, which are expected to be published in about 3 years, will help women and their doctors decide what course of action to take when mild abnormalities show up on Pap tests.

Researchers at NCI and elsewhere are studying how HPVs cause precancerous changes in normal cells and how these changes can be prevented. They are using HPVs grown in the laboratory to find ways to prevent the infection and its associated disease and to create vaccines against the viruses. Vaccines for certain papillomaviruses, such as HPV-16 and HPV-18, are being studied in clinical trials (research studies with people) for cervical cancer; similar trials for other types of cancer are planned. Information about clinical trials is available from the Cancer Information Service (CIS) or on the clinical trials page of the NCI's website (1-800-4-CANCER or www.cancer.gov/clinicaltrials).

Laboratory research has indicated that HPVs produce proteins known as E5, E6, and E7. These proteins interfere with the cell functions that normally prevent excessive growth. For example, HPV E6 interferes with the human protein p53. p53 is present in all people and acts to keep tumors from growing. This research is being used to develop ways to interrupt the process by which HPV infection can lead to growth of abnormal cells and, eventually, cancer.

☞ **Remember!!**
HPVs are now recognized as the major cause of cervical cancer.

Chapter 13

Cancer Risks Associated With Heterocyclic Amines In Cooked Meats

Research has shown that cooking certain meats at high temperatures creates chemicals that are not present in uncooked meats. A few of these chemicals may increase cancer risk. For example, heterocyclic amines (HCAs) are the carcinogenic chemicals formed from the cooking of muscle meats such as beef, pork, fowl, and fish. HCAs form when amino acids (the building blocks of proteins) and creatine (a chemical found in muscles) react at high cooking temperatures. Researchers have identified 17 different HCAs resulting from the cooking of muscle meats that may pose human cancer risk.

Research conducted by the National Cancer Institute (NCI) as well as by Japanese and European scientists indicates that heterocyclic amines are created within muscle meats during most types of high temperature cooking.

Studies have further evaluated the relationship associated with methods of cooking meat and the development of specific types of cancer. One study conducted by researchers from NCI's Division of Cancer Epidemiology and Genetics found a link between individuals with stomach cancer and the consumption of cooked meats. The researchers assessed the diets and cooking

---

About This Chapter: Text in this chapter is from "Heterocyclic Amines in Cooked Meats," National Cancer Institute (NCI), July 22, 1996, available online at http://cis.nci.nih.gov/fact/3_25.htm. Reviewed by David A. Cooke, M.D. on January 24, 2004.

habits of 176 people diagnosed with stomach cancer and 503 people without cancer. The researchers found that those who ate their beef medium-well or well-done had more than three times the risk of stomach cancer than those who ate their beef rare or medium-rare. They also found that people who ate beef four or more times a week had more than twice the risk of stomach cancer than those consuming beef less frequently. Additional studies have shown that an increased risk of developing colorectal, pancreatic, and breast cancer is associated with high intakes of well-done, fried, or barbecued meats.

Four factors influence HCA formation: type of food, cooking method, temperature, and time. HCAs are found in cooked muscle meats; other sources of protein (milk, eggs, tofu, and organ meats such as liver) have very little or no HCA content naturally or when cooked. Temperature is the most important factor in the formation of HCAs. Frying, broiling, and barbecuing produce the largest amounts of HCAs because the meats are cooked at very high temperatures. One study conducted by researchers showed a threefold increase in the content of HCAs when the cooking temperature was increased from 200° to 250° C (392° to 482° F). Oven roasting and baking are done at lower temperatures, so lower levels of HCAs are likely to form, however, gravy made from meat drippings does contain substantial amounts of HCAs. Stewing, boiling, or poaching are done at or below 100° C (212° F); cooking at this low temperature creates negligible amounts of the chemicals. Foods cooked a long time ("well-done" instead of "medium") by other methods will also form slightly more of the chemicals.

Meats that are partially cooked in the microwave oven before cooking by other methods also have lower levels of HCAs. Studies have shown that microwaving meat prior to cooking helps to decrease mutagens by removing the precursors. Meats that were microwaved

> **Weird Words**

Amino Acids: The building blocks of proteins.

Creatine: A chemical found in muscles.

Heterocyclic Amines (HCAs): The carcinogenic chemicals formed from the cooking of muscle meats such as beef, pork, fowl, and fish.

for 2 minutes prior to cooking had a 90-percent decrease in HCA content. In addition, if the liquid that forms during microwaving is poured off before further cooking, the final quantity of HCAs is reduced.

One study has evaluated the content of HCAs in fast food restaurants. After evaluating five kinds of meat products from various fast food restaurant chains, the study concluded that there were low levels of HCAs found in fast food meat products due to factors such as cooking temperature and time. The study suggested that greater exposure to HCAs stems from home cooking and cooking in non-fast-food restaurants where food may be cooked to order and where a larger amount of meat is consumed.

> ♣ **It's A Fact!!**
> Four factors influence HCA formation:
> - type of food cooked
> - cooking method
> - temperature
> - time

Studies are being conducted to assess the amount of HCAs in the average American diet, but at present the maximum daily intake of HCAs in food has not been established. At the moment, no Federal agency monitors the HCA content of cooked meats (how much a person could be eating), there is no good measure of how much HCAs would have to be eaten to increase cancer risk, and there are no guidelines concerning consumption of foods with HCAs. Further research is needed before such recommendations can be made.

However, concerned individuals can reduce their exposure to HCAs by varying methods of cooking meats; microwaving meats more often, especially before frying, broiling, or barbecuing; and refraining from making gravy from meat drippings.

References

Adamson RH, Thorgeirsson UP. Carcinogens in foods: heterocyclic amines and cancer and heart diseases. *Adv Exp Med Biol* 1995; 369:211–20.

Adamson RH, Thorgeirsson UP, Snyderwine EG, et al. *Jpn J Cancer Res* 1990; 81:10–14.

Bjeldanes LF, Morris MM, Felton JS, et al. *Food Chem Toxicol* 1982; 20:357–63.

Bjeldanes LF, Morris MM, Timourian H, et al. *J Agric Food Chem* 1983; 31:18–21.

Bogen KT. Cancer potencies of heterocyclic amines found in cooked foods. *Food Chemical Toxicology* 1994; 32(6):505–15.

Dolara P, Commoner B, Vithayathil A, et al. *Mutation Res* 1979; 60:231–37.

Esumi H, Ohgaki H, Kohzen, E et al. *Jpn J Cancer Res* 1989; 80:1176–78.

Felton JS, Fultz E, Dolbeare FA, et al. Effect of microwave pretreatment on heterocyclic aromatic amine mutagens/carcinogens in fried beef patties. *Food Chemical Toxology* 1994; 32(10):897–903.

Felton JS, Knize MG. In: Hayatsu H, editor. Mutagens in food: detection and prevention. Florida, CRC Press, 1991.

Felton JS, Knize MG, Shen NH, et al. *Environ Health Perspect* 1986; 67:17–24.

Felton JS, Knize MG, Wood C, et al. *Carcinogenesis* 1984; 5:95–102.

Knize MG, Sinha R, Rothman N, et al. Heterocyclic amine content in fast-food meat products. *Food Chemical Toxology* 1995; 33:545–51.

Layton DW, Bogen KT, Knize MG, et al. Cancer risk of heterocyclic amines in cooked foods: an analysis and implications for research. *Carcinogenesis* 1995; 16(1):39–52.

Murray S, Gooderham NJ, Boobis AR, et al. *Carcinogenesis* 1989; 10(4):763–65.

Muscat JE, Wynder EL. The consumption of well-done meat and the risk of colorectal cancer. *American Journal of Public Health* 1994; 84:856–8.

Nader CJ, Spencer LK, Weller RA. *Cancer Letter* 1981; 13:147–151.

Pariza MW, Ashoor SH, Chu FS et al. *Cancer Letter* 1979; 7:63–69.

Sinha R, Rothman N, Brown ED, et al. High concentrations of the carcinogen 2-amino-1-methyl-6-phenylimidazo[4,5-b]pyridine (PhIP) occur in chicken but are dependent on cooking method. *Cancer Research* 1995; 55(20):4516–9.

Snyderwine EG. Some perspectives on the nutritional aspects of breast cancer research. Food-derived heterocyclic amines as etiologic agents in human mammary cancer. *Cancer* 1994; 74:1070–7.

Stavric B. Biological significance of trace levels of mutagenic heterocyclic aromatic amines in human diet: a critical review. *Food Chemical Toxology* 1994; 32(10):977–94.

Wakabayashi K, Ushiyama H, Takahashi M, et al. Exposure to heterocyclic amines. *Environmental Health Perspective* 1993; 99:129–34.

Chapter 14

Studying A Possible Link Between Obesity And Cancer Risk

Scientists have identified a number of factors that increase a person's chance of developing cancer. For example, they have found that cancer is related to the use of tobacco; what people eat and drink; exposure to ultraviolet radiation from the sun; and exposure to cancer-causing agents (carcinogens) in the environment and the workplace.

One factor under investigation is obesity. Obesity is different from overweight. People who are *overweight* have excess body weight, which can come from fat, muscle, bone, and/or water retention. People who are *obese* have an abnormally high, unhealthy proportion of body fat.

More than 50 percent of American adults are overweight to some extent, and almost 25 percent are obese. The number of people who are obese has increased steadily over the past 30 years. From 1960 to 1994, the prevalence of obesity among adults increased from 13.4 percent to 22.3 percent. From 1991 to 1998, obesity increased in every state of the United States, in both sexes, among smokers and nonsmokers, and across race/ethnicity, age, and educational levels. Because of this dramatic rise, even a small increase in cancer risk due to obesity is cause for concern.

> About This Chapter: Text in this chapter is excerpted from "Obesity and Cancer," Cancer Facts Fact Sheet, National Cancer Institute (NCI), reviewed September 24, 2001, available online at http://cis.nci.nih.gov/fact/3_70.htm.

Researchers have found a consistent relationship between obesity and a number of diseases, including diabetes, heart disease, high blood pressure, and stroke. Although study results related to cancer have been conflicting, with some showing an increased risk and others not showing such an association, obesity does appear to be linked to some types of cancer. Obesity appears to increase the risk of cancers of the breast, colon, prostate, endometrium (lining of the uterus), cervix, ovary, kidney, and gallbladder. Studies have also found an increased risk for cancers of the liver, pancreas, rectum, and esophagus. Although there are many theories about how obesity increases cancer risk, the exact mechanisms are not known. They may be different for different types of cancer. Also, because obesity develops through a complex interaction of heredity and lifestyle factors, researchers may not be able to tell whether the obesity or something else led to the development of cancer.

Measurement Of Overweight And Obesity

Definitions and measurements of overweight and obesity have varied over time, from study to study, and from one part of the world to

> ### ❧ Weird Words
>
> Body Mass Index (BMI): The body weight in kilograms divided by the height in meters squared (wt/ht^2) used as a practical marker to assess obesity; often referred to as the Quetelet Index. An indicator of optimal weight for health and different from lean mass or percent body fat calculations because it only considers height and weight.
>
> Obesity: The condition of having an abnormally high proportion of body fat. Most overweight persons are obese. Defined as a body mass index (BMI) of greater than or equal to 30. Subjects are generally classified as obese when body fat content exceeds 30 percent in women and 25 percent in men.
>
> Overweight: An excess of body weight but not necessarily body fat; a body mass index of 25 to 29.9 kg/m^2.
>
> Source: "Clinical Guidelines on the Identification, Evaluation, and Treatment of Overweight and Obesity in Adults: Glossary of Terms," pp. 167-177, http://www.nhlbi.nih.gov/guidelines/obesity/ob_gdlns.pdf, 1998.

another. The variety of ways of determining overweight and obesity affected the results of earlier studies and made it difficult to compare data across studies. Most researchers currently use a formula based on weight and height, known as Body Mass Index (BMI), to study obesity as a risk factor for cancer. A BMI calculator is available at http://www.nhlbisupport.com/bmi on the Internet.

Two components of the National Institutes of Health—the National Heart, Lung, and Blood Institute (NHLBI) and the National Institute of Diabetes and Digestive and Kidney Diseases (NIDDK)—convened a panel of experts to provide guidelines for the measurement of overweight and obesity. The report, which was released in June 1998, provided standard definitions for overweight and obesity that are consistent with the recommendations of many other countries and the World Health Organization. The panel identified overweight as a BMI of 25 to 30, and obesity as a BMI of 30 or more. Health risks increase gradually with increasing BMI. BMI is useful in tracking trends in the population because it provides a more accurate measure of overweight and obesity than weight alone. By itself, however, this measurement cannot give direct or specific information about a person's health.

> ♣ **It's A Fact!!**
>
> - Obesity appears to increase the risk of cancers of the breast, colon, prostate, endometrium (lining of the uterus), cervix, ovary, kidney, and gallbladder.
> - Studies have also found an increased risk for cancers of the liver, pancreas, rectum, and esophagus.

Research Findings

A study published in the January 2001 issue of *Cancer Causes and Control* evaluated the relationship between obesity and cancer risk. More than 28,000 Swedish patients who were diagnosed as obese were followed for up to 29 years. The researchers compared the incidence of cancer in these patients with the incidence in the general Swedish population. They found 33 percent more cases of cancer among the obese people than in the general population (25 percent more among men and 37 percent more among women). The obese patients had an increased risk for Hodgkin's disease (among men) and cancers of the endometrium, kidney, gallbladder, colon, pancreas, bladder, cervix, ovary, and brain. An association between obesity and liver cancer was also found, but that may be explained by the presence of diabetes and alcoholism in these patients. The researchers also found some associations between obesity and cancer that were not found by previous researchers, including non-Hodgkin's lymphoma (among women) and cancers of the small intestine and larynx. They recommended further study of the association between obesity and these types of cancer.

In another study, published in the November 2, 2000, issue of *The New England Journal of Medicine*, researchers examined the health records of 363,992 Swedish men who had at least one physical exam between 1971 and 1992, and were followed until their death or the end of 1995. Compared with men in the lowest range for BMI, men in the middle range had a 30- to 60-percent greater risk of renal cell cancer (the most common type of kidney cancer), and men in the highest range had nearly double the risk. There was also a direct association between higher blood pressure and a higher risk of renal cell cancer. A reduction in blood pressure appeared to lower the risk of renal cell cancer.

Obesity may also play a role in a type of esophageal cancer called adenocarcinoma. A study sponsored by the National Cancer Institute concluded that excess abdominal fat may lead to reflux disease (a condition in which liquid from the stomach backs up into the esophagus) by increasing pressure on the stomach. Reflux disease can cause inflammation of tissues at the

---

🕮 Weird Word

Adenocarcinoma: Cancer that begins in cells that line certain internal organs and that have glandular (secretory) properties.

Source: Excerpted from "Cancer.gov Dictionary," National Cancer Institute, December 2003. The full text of this dictionary is available online at http://www.cancer.gov/dictionary.

bottom of the esophagus and can lead to a precancerous condition called Barrett's esophagus, which may develop into cancer of the esophagus. The researchers noted that, although obesity may contribute to reflux disease, it is unclear exactly how obesity increases the risk of esophageal cancer. The research team is also studying dietary factors, but analyses have not been completed.

Research Needs

More research is needed to better understand the effect of obesity on the development of cancer. In particular, studies are needed to evaluate the combined effects of diet, body weight, and physical activity. For some types of cancer, such as colon and breast, it is not clear whether the increased cancer risk is due to extra weight, inadequate consumption of fruits and vegetables, or a high-fat, high-calorie diet. Lack of physical activity also contributes to obesity and appears to be associated with increased risk of cancers of the breast and colon. Physical inactivity may also be associated with other types of cancer, such as prostate cancer.

However, because physical activity level is difficult to measure, its impact on cancer may be underestimated due to misclassification. In the future, researchers may measure physical fitness, rather than level of physical activity. Physical fitness appears to predict heart disease better than measures of physical activity; the same may be true for cancer. The complex relationship between physical activity and obesity makes it important that researchers include both factors in future epidemiological investigations.

IARC Recommendations

In February 2001, a panel of experts met at the International Agency for Research on Cancer (IARC) in Lyon, France, and concluded that overweight and a sedentary lifestyle are associated with several diseases, including cancer. The panel recommended that prevention of obesity begin early in life, based on healthy eating habits and regular physical activity. The panel advised people who are overweight or obese to avoid gaining additional weight, and to lose weight through dietary changes and exercise. The IARC, which is part of the World Health Organization, coordinates and conducts research on the causes of cancer and develops scientific strategies for cancer control.

Resources

The following U.S. Government agencies have information about controlling weight and preventing overweight and obesity:

National Institute of Diabetes and Digestive and Kidney Diseases (NIDDK)
Weight-control Information Network (WIN)
One Win Way
Bethesda, MD 20892-3665
Telephone: 202-828-1025
Toll free: 1-877-946-4627
Fax: 202-828-1028
E-mail: win@info.niddk.nih.gov
Website: http://www.niddk.nih.gov/health/nutrit/win.htm

WIN is a national public information service of the NIDDK. WIN assembles and distributes information and publications about weight control, obesity, and nutritional disorders.

National Heart, Lung, and Blood Institute (NHLBI)
Obesity Education Initiative
Post Office Box 30105
Bethesda, MD 20824-0105
Telephone: 301-592-8573
Fax: 301-592-8563
Website: http://www.nhlbi.nih.gov

The NHLBI's Obesity Education Initiative seeks to reduce the risk of heart disease and overall morbidity and mortality from heart disease by reducing the prevalence of overweight and physical inactivity. The NHLBI website has information for health professionals as well as patients and the general public.

References

Blot WJ, McLaughlin JK. The changing epidemiology of esophageal cancer. *Seminars in Oncology.* 1999; 26(5 Suppl 15):2–8.

Chow W, Devesa SS, Warren JL; Fraumeni JF. Rising incidence of renal cell cancer in the United States. *Journal of the American Medical Association.* 1999; 281(17):1628–1631.

Chow W, Gridley G, Fraumeni JF, Jarvholm B. Obesity, hypertension, and the risk of kidney cancer in men. *The New England Journal of Medicine.* 2000; 343(18):1305–1311.

Devesa SS, Blot WJ, Fraumeni JF. Changing patterns in the incidence of esophageal and gastric carcinoma in the United States. *Cancer.* 1998; 83(10):2049–2053.

Giacosa A, Franceschi S, La Vecchia C, Favero A, Andreatta R. Energy intake, overweight, physical exercise, and colorectal cancer risk. *European Journal of Cancer Prevention.* 1999; 8 Suppl 1:S53–S60.

Hill HA, Austin H. Nutrition and endometrial cancer. *Cancer Causes and Control.* 1996; 7(1):19–32.

Khaodhiar L, McCowen KC, Blackburn GL. Obesity and its comorbid conditions. *Clinical Cornerstone.* 1999; 2(3):17–31.

McCann J. Obesity, cancer links prompt new recommendations. *Journal of the National Cancer Institute.* 2001; 93(12):901–902.

McLaughlin JK, Lipworth L. Epidemiologic aspects of renal cell cancer. *Seminars in Oncology.* 2000; 27(2):115–123.

McTiernan A, Ulrich C, Slate S, Potter J. Physical activity and cancer etiology: associations and mechanisms. *Cancer Causes and Control.* 1998; 9(5):487–509.

National Institute of Diabetes and Digestive and Kidney Diseases. Overweight, obesity, and health risk. National Task Force on the Prevention and Treatment of Obesity. *Archives of Internal Medicine.* 2000:160(7):898–904.

Rao GN. Influence of diet on tumors of hormonal tissues. *Progress in Clinical and Biological Research.* 394:41–56.

Shepard RJ, Shek PN. Associations between physical activity and susceptibility to cancer: possible mechanisms. *Sports Medicine.* 1998; 26(5):293–315.

Shike M. Body weight and colon cancer. *The American Journal of Clinical Nutrition.* 1996 63(3 Suppl):442S–444S.

Silverman DT, Swanson CA, Gridley G, et al. Dietary and nutritional factors and pancreatic cancer: a case-control study based on direct interviews. *Journal of the National Cancer Institute.* 1998; 90(22):1710–1719.

Steinmetz KA, Potter JD. Vegetables, fruit, and cancer prevention: a review. *Journal of the American Dietetic Association.* 1996; 96(10):1027–1039.

Tominaga S. Major avoidable risk factors of cancer. *Cancer Letters.* 1999:143 Suppl 1:S19–S23.

Wideroff L, Gridley G, Mellemkjaer L, et al. Cancer incidence in a population-based cohort of patients hospitalized with diabetes mellitus in Denmark. *Journal of the National Cancer Institute.* 1997; 89(18):1360–1365.

Wolk A, Gridley G, Svensson M, et al. A prospective study of obesity and cancer risk (Sweden). *Cancer Causes and Control.* 2001; 12(1):13–21.

Chapter 15

Oral Contraceptives: Risks Are Difficult To Evaluate

Introduction

Oral contraceptives (OCs) first became available to American women in the early 1960s. The convenience, effectiveness, and reversibility of action of birth control pills (popularly known as "the pill") have made them the most popular form of birth control in the United States. However, concerns have been raised about the role that hormones might play in a number of cancers, and how hormone-based OCs contribute to their development.

This chapter addresses only what is known about OC use and the risk of developing cancer. It does not deal with the role of menopausal hormone use or the most serious side effect of OC use—the increased risk of cardiovascular disease for certain groups of women.

Oral Contraceptives

Currently, two types of OCs are available in the United States. The most commonly prescribed OC contains two man-made versions of natural female hormones (estrogen and progesterone) that are similar to the hormones

---

About This Chapter: Text in this chapter is excerpted from "Oral Contraceptives and Cancer Risk," Cancer Facts Fact Sheet, National Cancer Institute (NCI), reviewed November 3, 2003, available online at http://cis.nci.nih.gov/fact/3_13.htm.

the ovaries normally produce. Estrogen stimulates the growth and development of the uterus at puberty, causes the endometrium (the inner lining of the uterus) to thicken during the first half of the menstrual cycle, and influences breast tissue throughout life, but particularly from puberty to menopause.

Progesterone, which is produced during the last half of the menstrual cycle, prepares the endometrium to receive the egg. If the egg is fertilized, progesterone secretion continues, preventing release of additional eggs from the ovaries. For this reason, progesterone is called the "pregnancy-supporting" hormone, and scientists believe that it has valuable contraceptive effects. The man-made progesterone used in OCs is called progestogen or progestin.

The second type of OC available in the United States is called the minipill. It contains only a progestogen. The minipill is less effective in preventing pregnancy than the combination pill, so it is prescribed less often.

Because medical research suggests that cancers of the female reproductive organs depend on naturally occurring sex hormones for their development and growth, scientists have been investigating a possible link between OC use and cancer risk. Researchers have focused a great deal of attention on OC users over the past 40 years. This scrutiny has produced a wealth of

♣ It's A Fact!!

- There is evidence of an increased risk of breast cancer for women under age 35 who are recent users of oral contraceptives (OCs).

- Studies have consistently shown that using OCs reduces the risk of ovarian cancer.

- There is evidence that long-term use of OCs may increase the risk of cancer of the cervix.

- There is some evidence that OCs may increase the risk of certain cancerous liver tumors.

data on OC use and the development of certain cancers, although results of these studies have not always been consistent.

Breast Cancer

A woman's risk of developing breast cancer depends on several factors, some of which are related to her natural hormones. Hormonal factors that increase the risk of breast cancer include conditions that may allow high levels of hormones to persist for long periods of time, such as early age at first menstruation (before age 12), late age at menopause (after age 55), having children after age 30, and not having children at all.

Because many of the risk factors for breast cancer are related to natural hormones, and because OCs work by manipulating these hormones, there has been some concern about the possible effects of medicines such as OCs on breast cancer risk, especially if women take them for many years. Sufficient time has elapsed since the introduction of OCs to allow investigators to study large numbers of women who took birth control pills for many years. Even so, the results of some of these studies have not been consistent.

In an NCI-sponsored study published in 2003, researchers examined risk factors for breast cancer among women ages 20 to 34 compared with women ages 35 to 54. Researchers analyzed data from 2,202 women who were diagnosed with breast cancer between 1990 and 1992, and 2,209 women who did not have breast cancer. The results indicated that the risk of breast cancer was significantly increased for women ages 20 to 34 who had used OCs for at least 6 months. The risk associated with OC use was strongest for women who had used OCs within 5 years of breast cancer diagnosis. Although also elevated, the risk was weaker for women over age 35 and those who used OCs for longer periods of time.

A 1996 analysis of worldwide epidemiologic data conducted by the Collaborative Group on Hormonal Factors in Breast Cancer found that women who were current or recent users of birth control pills had a slightly elevated risk of developing breast cancer. However, 10 years or more after they stopped using OCs, their risk of developing breast cancer returned to the same level as if they had never used birth control pills. In addition, breast cancers diagnosed in women after 10 or more years of not using OCs were less advanced than breast cancers diagnosed in women who had never used OCs. To conduct this analysis, the researchers examined the results of 54 studies. The analysis involved 53,297 women with breast cancer and 100,239 women without breast cancer. More than 200 researchers participated in this combined analysis of their original studies, which represented about 90 percent of the epidemiological studies throughout the world that had investigated the possible relationship between OCs and breast cancer.

The return of risk to normal levels after 10 years or more of not taking OCs was consistent regardless of family history of breast cancer, reproductive history, geographic area of residence, ethnic background, differences in study design, dose and type of hormone, and duration of use. The change in risk also generally held true for age at first use; however, for reasons that were not fully understood, there was a continued elevated risk among women who had started to use OCs before age 20.

The findings of the Women's Contraceptive and Reproductive Experience (Women's CARE) study were in contrast to those described above. The Women's CARE study examined the use of OCs as a risk factor for breast cancer in women ages 35 to 64. Researchers interviewed 4,575 women who were diagnosed with breast cancer between 1994 and 1998, and 4,682 women who did not have breast cancer. Investigators collected detailed information about the participants' use of OCs, reproductive history, health,

✎ Weird Words

Estrogen: Hormone which stimulates the growth and development of the uterus at puberty, causes the endometrium (the inner lining of the uterus) to thicken during the first half of the menstrual cycle, and influences breast tissue throughout life, but particularly from puberty to menopause.

Human Papillomavirus (HPV): A virus that causes abnormal tissue growth (warts) and is often associated with some types of cancer.

Progesterone: Hormone which is produced during the last half of the menstrual cycle and prepares the endometrium to receive the egg.

Progestogen or Progestin: The man-made progesterone used in oral contraceptives.

and family history. The results, which were published in 2002, indicated that current or former use of OCs among women ages 35 to 64 did not significantly increase the risk of breast cancer. The findings were similar for white and black women. Factors such as longer periods of use, higher doses of estrogen, initiation of OC use before age 20, and OC use by women with a family history of breast cancer were not associated with an increased risk of the disease.

Ovarian And Endometrial Cancers

Studies have consistently shown that using OCs reduces the risk of ovarian cancer. In a 1992 analysis of 20 studies of OC use and ovarian cancer, researchers from Harvard Medical School found that the risk of ovarian cancer decreased with increasing duration of OC use. Results showed a 10 to 12 percent decrease in risk after 1 year of use, and approximately a 50 percent decrease after 5 years of use. This association between OC use and decreased risk of ovarian cancer has also been observed among women who have certain genetic changes in the BRCA1 or BRCA2 gene that increase their risk of ovarian cancer.

The results of the Cancer and Steroid Hormone Study (CASH), which was conducted by the Centers for Disease Control and Prevention and published in 1987, indicated that the longer a woman had used OCs, the lower her risk of ovarian cancer. The decrease in risk persisted long after OC use stopped. The risk-reducing effect of OCs appeared in both older and younger women, and in women with and without children. Several hypotheses have been offered to explain how oral contraceptives might protect against ovarian cancer, such as a reduction in the number of ovulations a woman has during her lifetime, but the exact mechanism is still not known.

Researchers have also found that OC users have a reduced risk of endometrial cancer. Findings from the CASH study and other reports show that combination OC use can protect against the development of endometrial cancer. The level of risk reduction is greater in women who have used OCs for a longer time, and the protection apparently persists after women have stopped taking OCs.

The reduction in risk of ovarian and endometrial cancers from OC use does not apply to the sequential type of pill, in which each monthly cycle contains 16 estrogen pills followed by 5 estrogen-plus-progesterone pills. (Sequential OCs were taken off the market in 1976, so few women have been exposed to them.) Researchers believe OCs reduce ovarian and endometrial cancer risk only when the estrogen content of birth control pills is balanced by progestogen in the same pill.

Cancer Of The Cervix

There is evidence that long-term use of OCs (10 or more years) may be associated with an increased risk of cancer of the cervix (the narrow, lower portion of the uterus). A 2003 analysis by the International Agency for Research on Cancer found an increased risk of cervical cancer with longer use of OCs. Researchers analyzed data from 28 studies that included 12,531 women with cervical cancer. The data suggested that the risk of cervical cancer may decrease after OC use stops. However, more research is needed to determine the extent to which women remain at risk for cervical cancer after they stop using OCs.

Human Papillomavirus (HPV)

Of the more than 100 types of human papillomavirus (HPV), over 30 types can be passed from one person to another through sexual contact. HPVs are some of the most common sexually transmitted infections. Approximately 15 HPVs are known to cause cervical cancer. Compared to non-OC users,

✔ **Quick Tip**

Women who are concerned about their risk for cancer are encouraged to talk with their health care provider. More information is also available from the Cancer Information Service (1-800-4-CANCER or http://cis.nci.nih.gov).

women who use OCs may be less likely to use barrier methods of contraception (such as condoms). Because condoms are partially effective in preventing HPV infection, OC users who do not use condoms may be at increased risk of becoming infected with HPV. Therefore, the increased risk of cervical cancer that some studies found to be caused by prolonged OC use may actually be the result of HPV infection.

Researchers are studying whether other factors such as multiple births and the use of OCs work together with sexually transmitted agents (such as HPVs) in the development of cervical cancer. Findings from an analysis of 10 studies suggested that long-term use of OCs may increase the risk of cervical cancer by up to 4 times in women who are infected with HPV.

However, in another long-term study published in 2002, researchers concluded that OC use did not increase the risk of cervical cancer in a well-screened population. The researchers followed a group of HPV-diagnosed women for 10 years. The participants were asked questions about OC use (but not the duration of use), smoking, and number of children. The results showed that HPV-diagnosed women who used OCs did not have a higher risk of cervical cancer than women who did not use OCs.

More research is needed into the exact nature of the association between OC use and risk of cervical cancer. One reason the association is unclear is that the major risk factor for cervical cancer (history of genital HPV infection) is related to sexual behavior. Because sexual behavior may be different between women who use OCs and those who have never used them, it is difficult for researchers to determine the exact role that OCs may play in the development of cervical cancer.

Liver Tumors

There is some evidence that OCs may increase the risk of certain malignant (cancerous) liver tumors. However, the risk is difficult to evaluate because of different patterns of OC use and because these tumors are rare in American women (the incidence is approximately 2 cases per 100,000 women). A benign (noncancerous) tumor of the liver called hepatic adenoma has also been found to occur, although rarely, among OC users. These tumors do not spread, but they may rupture and cause internal bleeding.

Reducing Risks Through Screening

Studies have found that breast cancer screening with mammograms reduces the number of deaths from breast cancer for women ages 40 to 69. Women who are at increased risk for breast cancer should seek medical advice about when to begin having mammograms and how often to be screened. A high-quality mammogram, with a clinical breast exam (an exam done by a professional health care provider), is the most effective way to detect breast cancer early.

Abnormal changes in the cervix can often be detected by a Pap test and treated before cancer develops. Women who have begun to have sexual intercourse or are age 21 should check with their doctor about having a Pap test.

Chapter 16

Cancer Risk Controversies About Cell Phones And Other Electronics

Cellular Telephone Use And Cancer

Recently, there has been concern that the use of hand-held cellular telephones may be linked with an increased risk of cancer. In response to this concern, and the rapidly rising number of cellular telephone users worldwide, studies have been conducted to determine whether there is an association between cellular telephone use and an increased risk of certain types of cancer. Although the majority of these studies have not supported any such association, scientists caution that more research needs to be done before conclusions can be drawn about the risk of cancer from cellular telephones.

Concerns About Cellular Telephone Use And Human Health

The number of people using cellular telephones has risen dramatically during the past decade, and is expected to continue increasing. According to the Cellular Telecommunications Industry Association (CTIA), there are

---

About This Chapter: Text in this chapter is excerpted from "Cellular Telephone Use and Cancer," Cancer Facts Fact Sheet, National Cancer Institute (NCI), reviewed January 4, 2002, available online at http://cis.nci.nih.gov/fact/3_72.htm; and "Magnetic Field Exposure and Cancer Studies at the NCI," Cancer Facts Fact Sheet, NCI, May 19, 1999, available online at http://cis.nci.nih.gov/fact/3_46.htm. Reviewed by David A. Cooke M.D. on January 24, 2004.

currently over 110 million wireless telephone users in the United States. This number is increasing at a rate of about 46,000 new subscribers per day. Experts estimate that by 2005 there will be over 1.26 billion wireless telephone users worldwide.

The concern about an increased risk of cancer with cellular telephone use is related to the radiation that the device produces. Like televisions, alarm systems, computers, and all other electrical devices, cellular telephones emit electromagnetic radiation. In the United States, cellular telephones operate in a frequency ranging from about 800 to 2100 megahertz (MHZ). In that range, the radiation produced is in the form of non-ionizing radiofrequency (RF) radiation. AM/FM radios, VHF/UHF televisions, and cordless telephones operate at lower radio frequencies than cellular phones; microwave ovens, radar, and satellite-stations operate at higher radio frequencies. RF radiation is different from ionizing radiation, which can present a health risk at certain doses. Ionizing radiation is produced by devices such as x-ray machines. It is not yet known whether the non-ionizing radiation emitted by cellular telephones poses a cancer risk. Because so many people use cellular telephones, it is important to learn whether RF radiation affects human health, and to provide reassurance if it does not.

> ♣ **It's A Fact!!**
>
> According to the Cellular Telecommunications Industry Association (CTIA), there are currently over 110 million wireless telephone users in the United States. This number is increasing at a rate of about 46,000 new subscribers per day.

A cellular telephone user's level of exposure to RF radiation depends on several factors. These factors include the amount of cellular telephone traffic, the quality of the transmission, how far the antenna is extended, and the size of the handset. A cellular telephone's main source of RF energy is its antenna. Therefore, the closer the antenna is to the head, the greater a person's expected exposure to RF radiation. The amount of RF radiation absorbed decreases rapidly with increasing distance between the antenna and the user.

Cancer Risk Controversies

The antenna of hand-held cellular telephones is in the handset, which is typically held against the side of the head while the phone is in use. The antenna of a car cellular telephone is mounted on the outside of the car, some distance from the user. Transportable cellular telephones or "bag phones" have an antenna in a portable unit separate from the handset. Most of the studies conducted on cellular telephone use and cancer risk have focused on hand-held models, since they deliver the most RF radiation to the user.

The intensity of RF radiation emitted by cellular telephones also depends on the power level of the signal sent to and from the nearest base station. A given geographical region is divided into zones or cells, each of which is equipped with a base station. When a call is placed from a cellular telephone, a signal is sent from the antenna of the phone to the nearest base station antenna. The base station routes the call through a switching center, where the call can be transferred to another cellular telephone, another base station, or to the local land-line telephone system. The farther a cellular telephone is from the base station antenna, the higher the power level needed to maintain the connection. This distance, in part, determines the amount of RF radiation exposure to the user.

RF radiation can be harmful at high levels because it produces heat. Some people have speculated that the heat produced by RF radiation from hand-held cellular telephones may be associated with brain tumors, because the antenna is held close to the user's head. However, the heat generated by a cellular telephone is small in comparison with the large amount of heat generated by RF radiation in a microwave oven. It is generally agreed that the amount of heat produced by a cellular telephone is too small to cause cancer.

Conclusions

Overall, most of the studies cited do not support a link between cellular telephone use and an increased risk of cancer. However, all of the studies have limitations, and it would be premature to conclude that the use of hand-held cellular telephones is not associated with cancer. One limitation is the relatively short amount of time that cellular telephones have been widely available. Cancers that take a long time to develop would not have been detected by these studies.

♣ It's A Fact!!
Why is radiation bad for a person?

Radiation is energy that travels in the form of waves or particles. When we hear the word "radiation," we generally think of nuclear power plants, nuclear weapons, or radiation treatments for cancer. Microwaves, radar, electrical power lines, cellular phones, and sunshine are also radiation sources.

Inhalation, ingestion, and direct exposure are the methods that radiation can affect the body. Exposure by the inhalation pathway occurs when people breathe radioactive materials into the lungs. Radioactive particles can lodge in the lungs and remain for a long time. A transfer of energy occurs, which can damage the surrounding tissues. This damage can eventually lead to cancer or other diseases.

Exposure by ingestion occurs when someone swallows radioactive materials. Large amounts of energy can be released, causing damage to tissues. All of the organs in the digestive system may become affected.

The third method for transmission of radiation is direct or external exposure from radioactive material. The concern about exposure to different kinds of radiation varies. Gamma rays, which are exceptionally harmful can be slowed by dense material (shielding), such as lead, and can be stopped if the material is thick enough.

Radiation is dangerous because of the way it damages the tissues, can cause cancer, and other serious symptoms and illness. The government has set standards and made regulations to attempt to reduce the amount of exposure that people have.

For more information about this topic, contact your local health department or check out the Environmental Protection Agency website (www.epa.gov) for specific information.

Source: Excerpted with permission from the TeenHealthFX website, www.teenhealthfx.com. Copyright © 2002 Atlantic Health System. All Rights Reserved.

Cancer Risk Controversies

> ### ◈ Weird Words
>
> <u>Electric and Magnetic Fields (EMF)</u>: An area containing electromagnetic energy (electromagnetic radiation). Electromagnetic radiation consists of waves of electrical and magnetic energy moving together through space. Also called electromagnetic energy.
>
> <u>Ionizing Radiation</u>: Very high energy electromagnetic radiation that strips electrons away from their normal locations in atoms and molecules.
>
> <u>Non-Ionizing Radiofrequency (RF) Radiation</u>: Levels of electromagnetic radiation that are too low to strip electrons away from their normal locations in atoms and molecules.
>
> Source: "Glossary," U.S. Food and Drug Administration (FDA), updated April 3, 2002, available online at http://www.fda.gov/cellphones/wireless-glossary.html.

Researchers suggest that future studies need to address the effects of long-term, heavy use of cellular telephones, and the differences between analogue and digital technologies. Analogue and digital telephones operate at different frequencies and power levels. Although many of the cellular telephones tested in prior studies used analogue technology, most cellular telephones today are based on digital technology.

Additional studies of cellular telephone use and cancer risk are under way in the United States and internationally to address these remaining issues. For example, the U.S. Food and Drug Administration (FDA), a Federal Government agency that monitors the safety of wireless phones, and the Cellular Telecommunications Industry Association (CTIA) are working jointly to evaluate the health effects of cellular telephone use. They will plan studies to determine the possible health effects of repeated or long-term exposure to cellular telephones, and select topics for future research.

What Consumers Can Do If They Are Concerned About The Health Effects Of Cellular Telephones

The FDA has suggested some steps that cellular telephone users can take if they are concerned about potential health risks, but do not want to give up their mobile phones:

- Reserve the use of cellular telephones for shorter conversations, or for when a conventional phone is not available;

- Switch to a type of mobile phone with a headset to place more distance between the antenna and the phone user;

- For use in the car, switch to a mobile phone with the antenna mounted outside the vehicle.

The Federal Communications Commission (FCC) is a Federal Government agency that regulates interstate and international communications by radio, television, wire, satellite, and cable. The FCC provides consumers with

> ✔ **Quick Tip**
>
> The National Institute of Environmental Health Sciences (NIEHS), the nation's principal agency for environmental health research and information, recommends that anyone concerned about the possible health effects of magnetic fields may do the following to reduce exposure:
>
> - Increase the space between a person and devices that may emit magnetic fields.
>
> - Avoid standing too close to computers, microwave ovens, or televisions.
>
> - Reduce the time of exposure to possible magnetic fields by turning off devices such as electric blankets when not in use.
>
> - Avoid keeping such devices as electric alarm clocks too close to the bed.
>
> - Discourage children from playing near high power lines or transformers.
>
> - Avoid activities near magnetic field sources.
>
> For more information on this subject, please refer to the National Institute of Environmental Health Sciences' website at http://www.niehs.nih.gov/emfrapid/home.htm on the Internet.

information on human exposure to RF radiation from wireless phones and other devices. The Commission's website, which is located at http://www.fcc.gov/oet/rfsafety on the Internet, allows consumers to find information about the specific absorption rate (SAR) of cellular telephones produced and marketed within the last 1 to 2 years. The SAR corresponds to the relative amount of RF energy absorbed into the head of a cellular telephone user. Consumers can access this information using the phone's FCC ID number, which is usually located on the case of the phone. Instructions for obtaining information about the SAR are available on the FCC's website.

Magnetic Field Exposure And Cancer

Electric and magnetic fields (EMF) arise from the motion of electric charges. They are characterized as non-ionizing radiation when they lack sufficient energy to remove electrons from atoms. In contrast, the energy in ionizing radiation, such as x-rays and gamma rays, can break atomic bonds and cause chromosomal changes. EMFs are emitted from devices that produce, transmit, or use electric power. These include power lines; transmitters; and common household items, such as electric clocks, shavers, computers, televisions, electric blankets, heated waterbeds, and microwave ovens. The intensity of the field drops off as distance from the source increases.

For the past few years, public concern has been growing over the possible health effects of EMFs produced by power transmission and distribution lines located near residential areas, as well as from electrical devices used in the home. Over the past 15 years, there have been numerous studies of children and adults evaluating residential exposures to electric and magnetic fields in relation to the risk of cancer. Recently, research has focused on magnetic fields. The findings have been inconsistent.

To evaluate the possible effects of magnetic fields on human health, scientists rely on epidemiological studies. However, these studies are often difficult to conduct due to the need to enroll a large number of subjects to detect potential small increases in risk; the difficulty in estimating exposure after it has occurred; the necessity for minimizing selection bias; the need to obtain high participation rates; the effort to minimize the number of surrogate, or next-of-kin respondents; and the necessity for considering potential confounding variables.

Chapter 17

Are There Any Cancer Risks Associated With Artificial Sweeteners And Fluoridated Water?

Artificial Sweeteners

Questions about artificial sweeteners and cancer arose when early studies showed that cyclamate, one of several types of artificial sweeteners, caused bladder cancer in laboratory animals. However, results from research studies do not provide clear evidence of an association between artificial sweeteners and human cancer.

Cyclamate

Because the findings in animals suggested that cyclamate might increase the risk of bladder cancer in humans, the U.S. Food and Drug Administration (FDA) banned the use of cyclamate in 1969. More recent animal studies have failed to demonstrate that cyclamate is a carcinogen (a substance known to cause cancer) or a co-carcinogen (a substance that enhances the

---

About This Chapter: Text in this chapter is from "Artificial Sweeteners," National Cancer Institute (NCI), September 3, 2003, available online at http://cis.nci.nih.gov/fact/pdfdraft/3_risk/fs3_19.pdf; and "Fluoridated Water," National Cancer Institute (NCI), October 10, 2000, available online at http://cis.nci.nih.gov/fact/pdfdraft/3_risk/fs3_15.pdf.

effect of a cancer-causing substance). However, other issues must be resolved before cyclamate can be approved for commercial use as a food additive in the United States.

Saccharin

Animal studies have linked saccharin, another artificial sweetener, with the development of bladder cancer. For this reason, Congress required that all food containing saccharin bear the following warning label: "Use of this product may be hazardous to your health. This product contains saccharin, which has been determined to cause cancer in laboratory animals." Congress also mandated that further studies of saccharin be performed.

The National Cancer Institute (NCI) and FDA have looked at the possible role of saccharin in causing bladder cancer in humans. People in the study (which included a large number of elderly people) who used this artificial sweetener had no greater risk of bladder cancer than people in the population as a whole. However, researchers looked at the data for those people who were heavy saccharin users (six or more servings of sugar substitute or two or more 8-ounce servings of diet drink daily) and found some evidence of an increased risk of bladder cancer, particularly for those who heavily ingested the sweetener as a table top sweetener or through diet sodas. The results of the NCI-FDA study, together with findings of additional research with laboratory animals, suggest that consumption of saccharin is not a major risk factor for bladder cancer in humans. For these reasons, Congress removed the warning label in December of 2000.

Aspartame

Aspartame, an artificial sweetener distributed under several trade names (for example, NutraSweet® or Equal®), was approved in 1981 by the FDA after tests showed that it did not cause cancer in laboratory animals, although not all of the laboratory experiments agreed. Interest in aspartame was renewed by a 1996 report suggesting that an increase in the number of people with

♣ **It's A Fact!!**
Common artificial sweeteners include: cyclamate, saccharin, aspartame, and stevia.

brain tumors between 1975 and 1992 might be associated with the introduction and use of this sweetener in the United States. However, an analysis of then-current NCI statistics showed that the overall incidence of brain and central nervous system cancers began to rise in 1973, 8 years prior to the approval of aspartame, and continued to rise until 1985. Moreover, increases in overall brain cancer incidence occurred primarily in people 70 and older, a group that was not exposed to the highest doses of aspartame since its 1981 introduction. These and other data do not point to a clear link, based on animal or human studies, between the use of aspartame and the development of brain tumors. The FDA still considers aspartame safe.

> **✎ Weird Words**
>
> Carcinogen: A substance that is known to cause cancer.
>
> Co-carcinogen: A substance that enhances the effect of a cancer-causing substance.
>
> Dental caries: Cavities.

Stevia

In recent years, a sweetening product called stevia (stevioside or steviol) has received much public attention. It is 250 to 300 times sweeter than sugar. To date, the FDA has not approved it for use as a sweetener in the United States, but stevia may be sold as a dietary supplement. Researchers have found that the main chemical in stevia can be converted in the laboratory to a compound that causes changes in genes. More study is needed to learn whether the same changes, which might lead to cancer, could occur in people.

Fluoridated Water

Virtually all water contains fluoride. In the 1940s, scientists discovered that the higher the level of natural fluoride in the community water supply, the fewer the dental caries (cavities) among the residents. Currently, more than half of all Americans live in areas where fluoride is added to the water supply to bring it up to the level considered best for dental health.

The possible relationship between fluoridated water and cancer has been debated at length. However, a February 1991 Public Health Service (PHS) report on the results of a year-long survey showed no evidence of an association between fluoride and cancer in humans. The survey, which involved a review of more than 50 human epidemiological studies produced over the past 40 years, led the investigators to conclude that optimal fluoridation of drinking water "does not pose a detectable cancer risk to humans as evidenced by extensive human epidemiological data reported to date."

In one of the studies reviewed for the PHS report, scientists at the National Cancer Institute evaluated the relationship between the fluoridation of drinking water and the number of deaths due to cancer in the United States during a 36-year period, and the relationship between water fluoridation and number of new cases of cancer during a 15-year period. After examining more than 2.2 million cancer death records and 125,000 cancer case records in counties using fluoridated water, the researchers concluded that there was no indication of increased cancer risk associated with fluoridated drinking water.

In 1993, the Subcommittee on Health Effects of Ingested Fluoride of the National Research Council conducted an extensive literature review concerning

☞ Remember!!

- Artificial sweeteners are regulated by the U.S. Food and Drug Administration (FDA).
- There is no evidence that the regulated artificial sweeteners on the market in the United States are related to cancer risk in humans.
- As new sweetening products come on the market, the FDA continues to investigate any possible short- or long-term health risks that these products might create.

Artificial Sweeteners And Fluoridated Water

the association between fluoridated drinking water and increased cancer risk. The review included more than 50 human epidemiological studies and six animal studies. The Subcommittee concluded that none of the data demonstrated an association between fluoridated drinking water and cancer.

A report by the Centers for Disease Control and Prevention supported these findings. The report concluded that studies to date have produced "no credible evidence" of an association between fluoridated drinking water and an increased risk for cancer.

The Environmental Protection Agency (EPA) website has more information about drinking water and health. It includes information about drinking water quality and standards. The website is located at http://www.epa.gov/safewater/dwhealth.html on the Internet.

References

Bucher JR, Hejtmancik MR, Toft JD 2d, Persing RL, Eustis SL, Haseman JK. Results and conclusions of the National Toxicology Program's rodent carcinogenicity studies with sodium fluoride. *International Journal of Cancer* 1991;48(5):733–737.

Centers for Disease Control and Prevention. Public Health Service report on fluoride benefits and risks. *Journal of the American Medical Association* 1991;266(8):1061–1062, 1066–1067.

Centers for Disease Control and Prevention. Achievements in public health, 1900–1999: fluoridation of drinking water to prevent dental caries. *Morbidity and Mortality Weekly Report* 1999;48(41):933–940.

National Research Council, Subcommittee on Health Effects of Ingested Fluoride. Carcinogenicity of Fluoride. In: *Health Effects of Ingested Fluoride*. Washington, D.C.: National Academy Press, 1993.

National Toxicology Program. NTP technical report on the toxicology and carcinogenesis studies of sodium fluoride (CAS No. 7681–49–4) in F344/N rats and B6C3F1 mice (drinking water studies). In: *Toxicology and carcinogenesis studies of sodium fluoride*. Research Triangle Park, NC: U.S. Department of Health and Human Services, 1990.

United States Department of Health and Human Services, Committee to Coordinate Environmental Health and Related Programs, Ad Hoc Subcommittee on Fluoride. Review of fluoride benefits and risks: report of the Ad Hoc Subcommittee on Fluoride of the Committee to Coordinate Environmental Health and Related Programs. Washington, D.C.: Public Health Service, Department of Health and Human Services, 1991.

Chapter 18

Cancer Myths And Rumors

Ten Breast Cancer Myths Debunked

Could that sexy underwire bra cause breast cancer? What about that frozen yogurt you just ordered? Or hormone therapy? And how would you know if you had the disease until it was too late anyway? Don't new studies show that examining your breasts and getting mammograms are useless?

Amid all the rumors and controversies surrounding breast cancer these days—what causes it, how to diagnose and treat it—it's hard to know what to think. Or do. One thing we can tell you is that being able to separate fact from fiction could make the difference between life and death.

About This Chapter: Text in this chapter was taken from "10 Biggest Breast Cancer Myths," by Marisa Weiss, MD and Barbara Loecher, reprinted with permission of *Prevention* Magazine. Copyright 2003 Rodale, Inc. All rights reserved. Text under "Antiperspirants/Deodorants and Breast Cancer," was excerpted and adapted from Fact Sheet 3.66, National Cancer Institute (NCI), February 4, 2003; full text available online at http://www.cis.nci.nih.gov/fact/3_66.htm. Text under "Tampons," was excerpted and adapted from U.S. Food and Drug Administration (FDA), July 23, 1999, available at http://www.fda.gov/cdrh/consumer/tamponsabs.html. Text under "Plastics and the Microwave," is by Michelle Meadows, *FDA Consumer*, November/December 2002, available at http://www.fda.gov/fdac/features/2002/602_plastic.html. Text under "Reregistration of the Insect Repellent DEET," is from the U.S. Environmental Protection Agency (EPA), April 28, 1998; available at http://www.epa.gov/pesticides/factsheets/chemicals/deet.htm.

Myth 1: Having a risk factor for breast cancer means you'll develop the disease. No risk factor either alone or in combination with others means you'll definitely get breast cancer. There are various factors that may increase your risk of developing the disease. Some of these appear to increase your risk only slightly. They include smoking, drinking (more than five alcoholic drinks per week year after year), getting your first menstrual period before age 12, continuing to have periods after age 50, and not having your first full-term pregnancy until after age 30. If you have a number of these, the increase in risk can start to be more meaningful.

♣ It's A Fact!!

Missed Diagnoses:
What Young Women Need To Know

Randi Rosenberg's gynecologist was sure she didn't have breast cancer. She was so sure that, despite the lump she'd found in Rosenberg's breast, she advised against a mammogram.

"My OB/GYN said, 'Young women usually have lumpy breasts; I wouldn't worry about it,'" recalls Rosenberg, then 31. So Rosenberg didn't worry about it. Not until 6 months later, that is, when she saw a general practitioner for a routine physical. After feeling the lump, he ordered an immediate mammogram—even escorting Rosenberg down the hall to the radiologist.

The mammogram showed nothing amiss. But the astute doctor, aware that mammography is more likely to miss abnormalities in young women's breasts because their breast tissue is denser than older women's, ordered a follow-up sonogram. It found cancer, but almost a full year had passed since the lump was originally discovered.

Every year, 11,000 American women who, like Rosenberg, are 40 or younger are diagnosed with breast cancer. And about 1,300 die of it. Breast cancer appears to be more aggressive in younger than older women. It's the leading cause of cancer death in women under 40.

That said, even an inherited genetic abnormality in your family doesn't necessarily mean you're going to get breast cancer. Abnormalities in the so-called breast cancer genes BRCA1 and BRCA2 are very strong risk indicators. But 20 to 60% of women with these inherited abnormalities will not develop breast cancer.

Myth 2: If there is no breast cancer in your family, then you're not at risk for the disease. Every woman is at risk for breast cancer. So are some men! For any individual woman, an inherited abnormality is the strongest risk

---

"I was lucky; many young women who go a full year without a diagnosis don't find their aggressive cancers still confined to their breast," says the now 37-year-old Rosenberg, who heads her own marketing and consulting firm in New York City and volunteers as president of the Young Survival Coalition (YSC), an international nonprofit organization for young women with breast cancer.

The YSC website includes information on breast cancer among young women, advice on getting top-notch care, and bulletin boards aimed at creating a sense of community for young women with the disease. Members talk about the prevalence of breast cancer among young women to school groups and young professionals. They attend major medical meetings, among other things, to raise awareness among doctors that young women do, in fact, get breast cancer.

The group is also collaborating with research teams on studies focusing on young women. One, with researchers at the University of Connecticut, is an epidemiological study to identify risk factors for early-onset breast cancer.

For more information, or to join, call toll-free (877) YSC-1011 (972-1011), or visit Young Survival Coalition.

Source: "Missed Diagnoses: What Young Women Need to Know," by Barbara Loecher, reprinted with permission of *Prevention* Magazine. Copyright 2003 Rodale, Inc. All rights reserved.

factor, but only about 10% of all cases of breast cancer are due to inherited abnormalities. About 85% of women who develop the disease don't have a family history. That's why it's important for all women to get screened regularly.

Myth 3: Breast cancer is passed only from your mother, not your father. We now know that breast cancer genes can be inherited from your dad's side of the family. So ask relatives about cases on both sides and in both men and women. About 1,500 cases of male breast cancer are diagnosed in the U.S. each year. In fact, male breast cancer is most closely associated with a BRCA2 abnormality. So if there's a man in the family who's had breast cancer, be sure to tell your doctor.

Myth 4: No matter what your risk factors are, you really don't have to worry about breast cancer until you're through menopause. The odds of getting the disease do increase as you age. But breast cancer can occur at any age.

That's why all women need to be vigilant. Though experts recommend yearly mammograms starting at age 40, your doctor may suggest that you start even earlier if you have a family history of breast cancer at a young age.

Mammography isn't the ideal screening test for women younger than 40 because it can't "see through" their dense breast tissue. So your doctor may also recommend ultrasound or magnetic resonance imaging (MRI). You may be able to enroll in a study of MRI for breast cancer detection for women at increased risk. To find a clinical trial, go to the searchable database at http://ClinicalTrials.gov.

Myth 5: Wearing a bra or using antiperspirants and deodorants increases your risk of breast cancer. These are two Internet rumors that never seem to quit. It's not true that wearing a bra, especially underwire bras, traps toxins by limiting lymph and bloodflow in your breasts, increasing risk. There's also no proof for the claims that antiperspirants and deodorants cause cancer by keeping the body from sweating out the cancer-causing substances that build up in the breasts, or because they contain harmful chemicals that are absorbed through the skin.

Myth 6: If you have small breasts, you're much less likely to get breast cancer. Size doesn't matter. Any woman with breasts can get it.

Myth 7: New research shows that using hormone therapy (HT)—even for a short period of time—causes breast cancer. Many women were understandably concerned when a major study found that HT combining estrogen and progestin increased risks of invasive breast cancer slightly. A more recent study also showed that combination therapy boosts breast cancer risk somewhat, however, it was able to offer some reassurance: This risk appeared to return to normal six months after women stopped using the therapy. This seems to be the case for women who've been on HT for just months and those who've used it for more than five years.

One more thing: It's important to note that no studies have found a boost in breast cancer risk for women using estrogen-only therapy. This type of therapy is prescribed solely for women who have had hysterectomies, because estrogen taken alone can cause cancer in the lining of the uterus (endometrial cancer).

Myth 8: Eating high-fat foods and dairy products boosts your risk. A number of studies have found that women who live in countries where diets tend to be lower in fat have a lower risk of breast cancer. But the majority of studies focusing on women in the U.S. haven't found a solid link between dietary fat consumption and breast cancer risk. Why are these findings contradictory? It may be that women in other countries are at lower risk for other reasons: They exercise more, eat less, weigh less, smoke less, or have a different genetic profile or environmental interaction that makes them less susceptible. One thing we do know: Postmenopausal obesity is a risk factor that does put you at risk for breast and other cancers, so it pays to maintain a healthy weight.

As for dairy products, the study results are mixed. But Harvard's Nurses' Health Study, a large-scale study of 120,000 women, recently found that premenopausal women who ate a lot of dairy products, especially low-fat and fat-free ones, ran a lower risk of breast cancer. The study found no link between dairy product consumption and breast cancer risk in women who are past menopause.

Myth 9: Mammograms can prevent breast cancer. A recent Harris survey of more than 500 women found that about 30% thought mammograms could prevent breast cancer. The truth: While mammograms can detect breast cancer, they can't prevent it.

Myth 10: Newer studies actually show mammograms are worthless. Two studies, including a recent review study done by Danish scientists, did suggest

---

♣ It's A Fact!!
Abortion-Cancer Link Is Rejected

A report stemming from a workshop sponsored by the National Cancer Institute (NCI) in Bethesda, MD, concludes that abortions don't increase a woman's risk of developing breast cancer. This controversial issue was reviewed in late February 2003 during a meeting of clinicians, epidemiologists, and basic scientists who study how early reproductive events influence breast cancer risk. There's a large body of evidence, for example, that young women have a reduced breast cancer risk if they've had a baby.

The workshop was organized after members of Congress last summer inquired into the validity of an NCI fact sheet stating that abortions don't increase a woman's breast cancer risk. Several studies have suggested such a connection, but subsequent larger studies have not *(SN: 1/11/97, p. 20)*. NCI responded to the inquiry by withdrawing its fact sheet and convening the meeting.

Workshop participants reviewed published research and, in a closed-door session, listened to presentations on unpublished data from additional studies. "There is strong evidence that there is no association between induced abortions and breast cancer risk," says Daniel Medina of Baylor College of Medicine in Houston, who summarized the workshop's conclusions.

The investigators also agreed that there's compelling evidence that full-term pregnancies do have a protective effect in young women and called for more research in that area. The workshop findings have been presented to NCI, which will consider re-releasing the fact sheet.

Source: Republished with permission of SCI Service Inc. from *Science News*, Volume 163, Number 11. Copyright © 2003 SCI Service Inc.; permission via Copyright Clearance Center.

that getting a regular mammogram didn't lower a woman's risk of dying of breast cancer. But several other new studies, including one done by the U.S. Preventive Services Task Force, totally disagree. You can maximize the benefit of mammography screening by seeking out the best facilities and staff in your area. Look for the radiology center that handles the most breast cancer cases in the region. Go to a radiologist who specializes in reading mammograms, and ask, "How many mammograms do you read each year?" More tends to be better. A study published in the *Journal of the National Cancer Institute* found that radiologists who read more than 300 mammograms a month were more accurate.

Antiperspirants/Deodorants And Breast Cancer

Articles in the press and on the Internet have warned that underarm antiperspirants or deodorants cause breast cancer. The reports have suggested that these products contain harmful substances, which can be absorbed through the skin or enter the body through nicks caused by shaving.

Scientists at the National Cancer Institute (NCI) are not aware of any research to support a link between the use of underarm antiperspirants or deodorants and the subsequent development of breast cancer. The U.S. Food and Drug Administration, which regulates food, cosmetics, medicines, and medical devices, also does not have any evidence or research data to support the theory that ingredients in underarm antiperspirants or deodorants cause cancer.

The results of a study looking for a relationship between breast cancer and underarm antiperspirants/deodorants were reported in the *Journal of the National Cancer Institute* in October 2002. The findings did not show any increased risk for breast cancer in women who reported using an underarm antiperspirant or deodorant. The results also showed no increased breast cancer risk for women who reported using a blade (nonelectric) razor and an underarm antiperspirant or deodorant, or for women who reported using an underarm antiperspirant or deodorant within 1 hour of shaving with a blade razor. These conclusions were based on interviews with 813 women with breast cancer and 793 women with no history of breast cancer.

People who are concerned about their cancer risk are encouraged to talk with their doctor.

Tampons

The Food and Drug Administration (FDA) regulates the safety and effectiveness of medical devices, including tampons. Recently it has come to the agency's attention that allegations about tampons are being spread over the Internet. It is alleged that tampons are contaminated by asbestos and dioxin during manufacture, and that rayon fibers cause toxic shock syndrome (TSS). The available scientific evidence does not support these rumors. The following information will help answer concerns.

Asbestos Concerns

Unfounded rumors on the Internet have suggested that U.S. tampon manufacturers add asbestos to their products to promote excessive menstrual bleeding

---

♣ It's A Fact!!

Does A Shampoo Additive (Sodium Lauryl Sulfate) Cause Cancer?

Source: Reprinted with permission from Go Ask Alice!—Columbia University's Health Q&A Internet Service, www.goaskalice.columbia.edu. Copyright © 2002 by The Trustees of Columbia University.

Hi Alice!

I was wondering about the chemical Sodium Laureth Sulfate. I have received several forwarded e-mails about this causing cancer by a lawyer looking into the matter. This chemical was said to be in many shampoos to create a nice lather, but it's actually a garage cleaner and is a cheap substance for the manufacturer, and in the past, only 1 in 2000 would get cancer from this, and now it's about 1 in 10. I was just curious if it really causes cancer, or is it just a prank? And if it really does cause cancer, what kind of cancer is it? Thank you. I would appreciate an honest answer.

Dear Reader,

Wash those e-mails right out of your hair; they are hoaxes being perpetrated on innocent cyber-surfers in various forms and attributed to several different "experts," all spouting claims that commonly used health or beauty items

Cancer Myths And Rumors

in order to sell more tampons. FDA has no evidence of asbestos in tampons or any reports regarding increased menstrual bleeding following tampon use.

Before any tampon is marketed in the U.S., FDA reviews its design and materials. Asbestos is not an ingredient in any U.S. brand of tampon, nor is it associated with the fibers used in making tampons. Moreover, tampon manufacturing sites are subject to inspection by FDA to assure that good manufacturing practices are being followed. Therefore, these inspections would likely identify any procedures that would expose tampon products to asbestos. If any tampon product was contaminated with asbestos, it would be as a result of tampering, which is a crime. Thus far, FDA has received no reports of tampering. Anyone having knowledge of tampon tampering is urged to notify FDA or a law enforcement officer.

---

are actually cancerous. Other products that have been the target of Internet smear campaigns include tampons and antiperspirants.

According to the American Cancer Society, neither Sodium Lauryl Sulfate, nor its more potent cousin Sodium Laureth Sulfate, causes cancer. Both of these additives are cleansers (a.k.a. detergents) that remove oil and dirt from hair and skin. Sodium Laureth Sulfate is also used as an ingredient in household cleaners, so it could be in detergents that you use to clean your garage, your bathroom, or your car. This does not necessarily mean that it is toxic—only that it does a pretty good job of removing grime and grease from everyday surfaces. The concentrations of these two additives that are used in cosmetic cleaners are much lower than the concentrations used in household cleaners (because, hopefully, your face has less ground-in grime than your garage floor).

Sodium Laureth Sulfate has been shown to cause skin or eye irritation in some people, so the more mild Sodium Lauryl Sulfate is typically used in baby shampoos and other products advertised as being "more gentle" on skin and/or eyes. As with any product, if you experience discomfort or irritation when using a cleanser containing either detergent ingredient, you need to find an alternative that's free of these substances. But if your favorite, most trusted shampoo contains these cleansers, there is no reason to start having bad hair days in the name of health.

Alice

Dioxin And Rayon Concerns

There are also allegations that some tampons contain toxic amounts of the chemical dioxin. The term "dioxin" or "dioxins" actually refers to a number of related chemical compounds. State-of-the art testing of tampons and tampon materials that can detect even trace amounts of dioxin has shown that dioxin levels are at or below the detectable limit. No risk to health would be expected from these trace amounts.

Tampons currently sold in the U.S. are made of cotton, rayon, or blends of rayon and cotton. Rayon is made from cellulose fibers derived from wood pulp. In this process the wood pulp is bleached. At one time, bleaching the wood pulp was a potential source of trace amounts of dioxin in tampons, but that bleaching method is no longer used. Rayon raw material used in U.S. tampons is now produced using elemental chlorine-free or totally chlorine free bleaching processes. These methods for purifying wood pulp are described below:

Elemental chlorine-free bleaching refers to methods **that do not use elemental chlorine gas** to purify the wood pulp. These methods include the use of chlorine dioxide as the bleaching agent as well as totally chlorine-free processes. Some elemental chlorine-free bleaching processes can theoretically generate dioxins at extremely low levels, and dioxins are occasionally detected in trace amounts in mill effluents and pulp. In practice, however, this method is considered to be dioxin free.

Totally chlorine-free bleaching refers to use of bleaching agents that contain no chlorine. These methods are also dioxin-free. Totally chlorine-free methods include, for example, use of hydrogen peroxide as the bleaching agent.

The Environmental Protection Agency (EPA) has worked with wood pulp producers to promote use of dioxin-free methods because dioxin is an environmental pollutant. Because of decades of pollution, dioxin can be found in the air, water and ground. Therefore, while the methods used for manufacturing tampons today are considered to be dioxin-free processes, traces of dioxin may still be present in the cotton or wood pulp raw materials used to make tampons. Thus, there may be trace amounts of dioxin present from environmental sources in cotton, rayon, or rayon/cotton tampons.

When questions about dioxin arose a number of years ago, FDA asked tampon manufacturers to provide information about their pulp purification processes and the potential for dioxin contamination. Manufacturers of rayon tampons are also asked to routinely monitor dioxin levels in the raw material used or the finished tampons. Manufacturers have provided FDA with test results of studies conducted at independent laboratories, using the most sensitive test methods available. Dioxin monitoring is a highly technical assay performed at only a few independent expert laboratories in the U.S. The detectable limit of this assay is currently approximately 0.1 to 1 parts per trillion of dioxin.

Using these tests, dioxin levels in the rayon raw materials for tampons are reported to be at or below the detectable limit of the state-of-the-art dioxin assay, that is, approximately 0.1 to 1 parts per trillion. FDA's risk assessment indicates that this exposure is many times less than normally present in the body from other environmental sources, so small that any risk of adverse health effects is considered negligible. A part per trillion is about the same as one teaspoon in a lake fifteen feet deep and a mile square.

Toxic Shock Syndrome (TSS)

There are also allegations that rayon in tampons causes TSS, and dryness or ulcerations of vaginal tissues.

TSS is a rare but potentially fatal disease caused by a bacterial toxin. (Different bacterial toxins may cause TSS, depending on the situation, but most often *streptococci* and *staphylococci* are responsible.) Although scientists have recognized an association between TSS and tampon use, the exact connection remains unclear. Tampons made with rayon do not appear to have a higher risk of TSS than cotton tampons of similar absorbency.

Vaginal dryness and ulcerations may occur when women use tampons more absorbent than needed for the amount of their menstrual flow. Ulcerations have also been reported in women using tampons between menstrual periods to try to control excessive vaginal discharge or abnormal bleeding. Women may avoid problems by choosing a tampon with the minimum absorbency needed to control menstrual flow and using tampons only during active menstruation.

To help women compare absorbency from brand to brand, FDA requires that manufacturers measure absorbency using a standard method and describe absorbency on the package using standardized terms. Thus, the terms "junior," "regular," "super," and "super plus," always describe a specific range of tampon absorbency regardless of the brand.

Plastics And The Microwave

Stories about the dangers of chemicals leaching from plastic into microwaved food have circulated on the Internet for years. As a result, the Food and Drug Administration continues to receive inquiries from concerned consumers.

Consumers can be confident as they heat holiday meals or leftovers in the microwave that the FDA carefully reviews the substances used to make plastics designed for food use. These include microwave-safe plastic coverings that keep food from splattering and microwave-safe containers that hold frozen dinners. Even microwavable popcorn bags, which look like paper, actually contain a metallized plastic film that allows them to reach high temperatures so the corn can fully pop.

Under the food additive provisions of the Federal Food, Drug, and Cosmetic Act, new substances used to make plastics for food use are classified as "food contact substances." They must be found safe for their intended use before they can be marketed.

"It's true that substances used to make plastics can leach into food," says Edward Machuga, Ph.D., a consumer safety officer in the FDA's Center for Food Safety and Applied Nutrition. "But as part of the approval process, the FDA considers the amount of a substance expected to migrate into food and the toxicological concerns about the particular chemical." The agency has assessed migration levels of substances added to regulated plastics and has found the levels to be well within the margin of safety based on information available to the agency. The FDA will revisit its safety evaluation if new scientific information raises concerns.

One chemical called diethylhexyl adipate (DEHA) has received a lot of media attention. DEHA is a plasticizer, a substance added to some plastics to make them flexible. DEHA exposure may occur when eating certain foods wrapped in plastics, especially fatty foods such as meat and cheese. But the levels are very low. The levels of the plasticizer that might be consumed as a result of plastic film use are well below the levels showing no toxic effect in animal studies.

Other claims have asserted that plastics contain dioxins, a group of contaminants labeled as a "likely human carcinogen" by the Environmental Protection Agency. "The FDA has seen no evidence that plastic containers or films contain dioxins and knows of no reason why they would," Machuga says.

Machuga says that consumers should be sure to use any plastics for their intended purpose and in accordance with directions. If you don't find instructions for microwave use, you should use a different plate or container that you know is microwave-safe. Such containers are made to withstand high temperatures. For example, carry-out containers from restaurants and margarine tubs should not be used in the microwave. Also, discard containers that hold prepared microwavable meals after you use them because they are meant for one-time use.

Microwave-safe plastic wrap should be placed loosely over food so that steam can escape, and should not directly touch your food. "Some plastic wraps have labels indicating that there should be a one-inch or greater space between the plastic and the food during microwave heating," Machuga says.

Always read directions, but generally, microwave-safe plastic wraps, wax paper, cooking bags, parchment paper, and white microwave-safe paper towels are safe to use. Covering food helps protect against contamination, keeps moisture in, and allows food to cook evenly. Never use plastic storage bags, grocery bags, newspapers, or aluminum foil in the microwave.

Does The Insect Repellent DEET Cause Cancer?

What Is DEET?

DEET (chemical name, N,N-diethyl-meta-toluamide) is the active ingredient in many insect repellent products. It is used to repel biting pests such as mosquitoes and ticks, including ticks that may carry Lyme disease. Every year, approximately one-third of the U.S. population is expected to use DEET. Products containing DEET currently are available to the public in a variety of liquids, lotions, sprays, and impregnated materials (e.g., wrist bands). Formulations registered for direct application to human skin contain from 4 to 100% DEET. Except for a few veterinary uses, DEET is registered for use by consumers, and it is not used on food.

> ♣ **It's A Fact!!**
>
> ## Does DEET Cause Cancer?
>
> - Animals: Rats and mice did not develop cancer when fed high daily doses of DEET over their lifetime.
>
> - Humans: No direct relationship between DEET use and carcinogenicity in humans has been established.
>
> - U.S. EPA has classified DEET as a group D carcinogen (not classifiable as to human carcinogenicity). The U.S. EPA needs further animal testing data to completely evaluate DEET.
>
> - Cancer: The U.S. EPA has strict guidelines that require testing of pesticides for their potential to cause cancer. These studies involve feeding laboratory animals large daily doses of the pesticide over most of the lifetime of the animal. Based on these tests, and any other available information, EPA gives the pesticide a rating for its potential to cause cancer in humans. For example, if a pesticide does not cause cancer in animal tests, then the EPA considers it unlikely the pesticide will cause cancer in humans. Testing for cancer has not been done on human subjects.
>
> Source: Excerpted with permission from "DEET: General Fact Sheet," produced by the National Pesticide Information Center (NPIC), March 2000. © National Pesticide Information Center. For the most recent version of this fact sheet including references, or additional information about pesticides, visit http://npic.orst.edu, or call 800-858-7378. NPIC is a cooperative effort of Oregon State University and the U.S. Environmental Protection Agency.

Cancer Myths And Rumors

DEET is designed for direct application to human skin to repel insects, rather than kill them. After it was developed by the U.S. Army in 1946, DEET was registered for use by the general public in 1957. Approximately 230 products containing DEET are currently registered with EPA by about 70 different companies.

What Decision Did EPA Make Concerning The Use Of DEET?

EPA issued a Reregistration Eligibility Decision (RED) for the chemical DEET. After completing a comprehensive re-assessment of DEET, EPA concluded that, as long as consumers follow label directions and take proper precautions, insect repellents containing DEET do not present a health concern. Human exposure is expected to be brief, and long-term exposure is not expected. Based on extensive toxicity testing, the Agency believes that the normal use of DEET does not present a health concern to the general population.

Most of the changes to DEET registrations required by EPA concern label directions and claims. The Agency also is encouraging companies to provide a company telephone number or toll-free number on all product labels for consumers to call for additional product information and to report incidents. The Agency has determined that registrants may distribute and sell DEET products bearing old labels for 26 months from the date of issuance of the RED, and stores may continue to sell these products for 50 months from the date of issuance.

What Benefits Do DEET Products Offer?

DEET's most significant benefit is its ability to repel potentially disease-carrying insects and ticks. The Centers for Disease Control (CDC) receives nearly 10,000 reports of Lyme disease (transmitted by deer ticks) and 1,000 reports of encephalitis (transmitted by mosquitoes) annually. Both of these diseases can cause serious health problems or even death in the case of encephalitis. Where these diseases are endemic, the CDC recommends use of insect repellents when out-of-doors. Studies submitted to EPA indicate that DEET repels ticks for about three to eight hours, depending on the percentage of DEET in the product.

For More Information about DEET

For medical information, please call the National Pesticide Information Center (NPIC) at 1-800-858-7378 (6:30 a.m. to 4:30 p.m., Pacific Time, 7 days/week, except holidays). For a copy of the RED, call EPA at (703) 305-5805, or for more information at (703) 305-5017.

✔ **Quick Tip**

How To Use DEET Products Safely

Consumers can reduce their own risks when using DEET by reading and following products labels. Statements on all DEET product labels will be revised to include the following directions:

- Read and follow all directions and precautions on this product label.
- Do not apply over cuts, wounds, or irritated skin.
- Do not apply to hands or near eyes and mouth of young children.
- Do not allow young children to apply this product.
- Use just enough repellent to cover exposed skin and/or clothing.
- Do not use under clothing.
- Avoid over-application of this product.
- After returning indoors, wash treated skin with soap and water.
- Wash treated clothing before wearing it again.
- Use of this product may cause skin reactions in rare cases. The following additional statements will appear on the labels of all aerosol and pump spray formulation labels:
- Do not spray in enclosed areas.
- To apply to face, spray on hands first and then rub on face. Do not spray directly onto face.

Part 3
Cancer Detection, Diagnosis, And Treatment

Chapter 19

Screening Tests For Various Cancers

What Is Screening?

Screening is looking for cancer before a person has any symptoms. This can help find cancer at an early stage. When abnormal tissue or cancer is found early, it may be easier to treat. By the time symptoms appear, cancer may have begun to spread.

Scientists are trying to better understand which people are more likely to get certain types of cancer. They also study the things we do and the things around us to see if they cause cancer. This information helps doctors recommend who should be screened for cancer, which screening tests should be used, and how often the tests should be done.

It is important to remember that your doctor does not necessarily think you have cancer if he or she suggests a screening test. Screening tests are given when you have no cancer symptoms.

About This Chapter: Text in this chapter was excerpted and adapted from the following documents: PDQ® Cancer Information Summary. National Cancer Institute; Bethesda, MD. Breast Cancer (PDQ®): Screening-Patient, updated 9/2003; Colorectal Cancer (PDQ®): Screening-Patient, updated 6/2003; Lung Cancer (PDQ®): Screening-Patient, updated 11/2003; Oral Cancer (PDQ®): Screening-Patient, updated 6/2003; Prostate Cancer (PDQ®): Screening-Patient, updated 6/2003; Skin Cancer (PDQ®): Screening-Patient, updated 6/2003. All documents available at http://cancer.gov. Accessed December 10, 2003.

If a screening test result is abnormal, you may need to have more tests done to find out if you have cancer. These are called diagnostic tests.

Different Tests Are Used To Screen For Cancer

Some screening tests are used because they have been shown to be helpful both in finding cancers early and decreasing the chance of dying from these cancers. Other tests are used because they have been shown to find cancer in some people; it is not yet known if use of these tests will decrease the risk of dying from cancer.

Scientists study screening tests to find those with the fewest risks and most benefits. Cancer screening trials also are meant to show whether early detection (finding cancer before it causes symptoms) decreases a person's chance of dying from the disease. For some types of cancer, finding and treating the disease at an early stage may result in a better chance of recovery.

Clinical trials that study cancer screening methods are taking place in many parts of the country. Information about ongoing clinical trials is available from the NCI Cancer.gov website.

Breast Cancer Screening

Three Tests Are Commonly Used To Screen For Breast Cancer

Breast Self-Exam (BSE): Breast self-exam is an exam to check your own breasts for lumps or anything else that seems unusual.

Clinical Breast Exam (CBE): A clinical breast exam is an exam of the breast by a doctor or other health professional. The doctor will carefully feel the breasts and under the arms for lumps or anything else that seems unusual.

> ♣ **It's A Fact!!**
>
> Three tests are commonly used to screen for breast cancer:
>
> - Breast self-exam (BSE)
> - Clinical breast exam (CBE)
> - Mammogram

Screening Tests For Various Cancers

Mammogram: A mammogram is an x-ray of the breast. This test may find tumors that are too small to feel. The ability of this test to find breast cancer may depend on the size of the tumor, the density of the breast tissue, and the skill of the radiologist.

If a lump or other abnormality is found using one of these three tests, ultrasound may be used to learn more. It is not used by itself as a screening test for breast cancer. Ultrasound is a procedure in which high-energy sound waves (ultrasound) are bounced off internal tissues or organs and make echoes. The echoes form a picture of body tissues called a sonogram.

Other Screening Tests Are Being Studied In Clinical Trials

Magnetic Resonance Imaging (MRI)

MRI is a procedure that uses a magnet, radio waves, and a computer to make a series of detailed pictures of areas inside the body. This procedure is also called nuclear magnetic resonance imaging (NMRI).

MRI tests are used to make decisions about breast masses that have been found by a clinical breast exam or a breast self-exam. MRIs also help show the difference between cancer and scar tissue. MRI does not use any x-rays. Scientists are studying MRI to find out how helpful it is in screening for breast cancer.

Screening clinical trials are taking place in many parts of the country. Information about ongoing clinical trials is available from the NCI Cancer.gov website.

Colorectal Cancer Screening

Cancer of the colon or rectum is often called colorectal cancer. The colon and the rectum are part of the large intestine, which is part of the digestive system.

Screening Tests For Colorectal Cancer

Fecal Occult Blood Test: Special cards are coated with a stool sample and returned to the physician or lab. This test examines a patient's solid waste (stool) for occult (hidden) blood. Studies show that a fecal occult blood test performed every one or two years in people between the ages of 50–80 years decreases the number of deaths due to colorectal cancer.

Sigmoidoscopy: Sigmoidoscopy is an examination in which a doctor uses a thin, flexible tube with a light to look inside the rectum and colon for polyps, tumors, or abnormal areas. Studies suggest that fewer people may die

---

♣ It's A Fact!!
No Scope: CT Scan Works As Well As Colonoscopy

For anyone seeking to avoid the unpleasantness and discomfort of a colonoscopy, here's good news: A computed tomography (CT) scan that provides a "virtual colonoscopy" of the large intestine is just as adept at detecting signs of cancer as is a viewing device moved through the colon, a new study finds.

A team led by researchers at the National Naval Medical Center in Bethesda, MD, used a CT scanner to generate three-dimensional images of the colon, an emerging technique that seems to be more accurate than typical two-dimensional CT scanning. The 3-D images consistently revealed polyps growing inside the colon. Such growths aren't necessarily cancerous, but some can develop into tumors.

The scientists performed CT scans on 1,233 people, average age 58, who were free of signs of cancer. Next, without knowing the CT results, other doctors conducted a colonoscopy on each volunteer. In this procedure, a physician inserts a flexible, camera-tipped tube into a sedated patient's colon via the rectum and withdraws it gradually while watching a video screen for polyps.

In this generally healthy group of volunteers, only two cancerous polyps showed up. CT scanning spotted both, but colonoscopy found only one. Of 38 worrisome polyps at least one centimeter in diameter, 45 turned up in the CT scans and 42 were detected by the colonoscopy. Between them, the tests turned up 554 polyps deemed to have malignant potential.

"The results were quite comparable," says study coauthor Pauline A. Mysliwiec, a gastroenterologist now at the University of California, Davis, Medical Center in Sacramento. The report appears in the Dec. 4 *New England Journal of Medicine*.

Patients spent an average of 14 minutes in the CT scanning room, where they received a sometimes-uncomfortable infusion of air into the colon. A

Screening Tests For Various Cancers

of colorectal cancer if they have regular screening by sigmoidoscopy after the age of 50 years.

Digital Rectal Examination: A digital rectal examination is performed during an office visit or prior to sigmoidoscopy or colonoscopy. For this examination, the doctor or nurse inserts a lubricated gloved finger into the

---

colonoscopy took 32 minutes during which patients were sedated to a dreamlike state.

Colon cancer kills nearly 60,000 people annually in the United States, even though it is largely preventable through polyp detection and removal. The Centers for Disease Control and Prevention in Atlanta reported earlier this year that fewer than half of US residents over age 50 have had a colonoscopy or a sigmoidoscopy, a similar but less-thorough exam.

A physician who detects polyps during a colonoscopy routinely removes them using equipment built into the scope. A CT scan revealing a large polyp triggers a colonoscopy for the growth's removal.

However, colonoscopy has drawbacks as a screening tool. It risks perforating the colon, and the sedated patient requires up to an hour of recovery time and a ride home, say Martina M. Morrin and J. Thomas LaMont of Harvard Medical School in Boston in an article accompanying the new study. If the new findings are replicated and doctors can agree on how big a CT-detected polyp needs to be to warrant immediate removal, then "virtual colonoscopy is ready for prime time," Morrin and LaMont say.

The price tag for such a CT scan is "still being worked out," says John H. Bond, a gastroenterologist at the University of Minnesota and the Veterans Affairs Medical Center in Minneapolis. Once medical authorities agree that a CT scan is as good as colonoscopy, he predicts that Medicare and insurance companies will pay for CT—probably within the next two years.

"A lot of people are going to opt for this procedure," Bond says.

Source: Republished with permission of SCI Service, Inc. From *Science News*, Volume 164, Number 23. Copyright © 2003 SCI Service, Inc.; permission via Copyright Clearance Center.

rectum and feels for lumps or abnormal areas. The evidence available does not suggest that digital rectal examination is effective in decreasing mortality from colorectal cancer.

Barium Enema: Barium enema is a procedure in which a liquid containing barium is put into the rectum and colon by way of the anus. Barium is a silver-white metallic compound that helps to show the image of the lower gastrointestinal tract on an x-ray. Barium enema may be effective in detecting large polyps.

Colonoscopy: Colonoscopy is an examination of the inside of the colon and rectum using a thin, lighted tube (called a colonoscope) inserted into the rectum. If the doctor sees polyps or other abnormal tissue during the procedure, they can be removed and further examined under a microscope. Studies suggest that colonoscopy is a more effective screening method than barium enema.

Lung Cancer Screening

Two Tests Have Commonly Been Used To Screen For Lung Cancer

It has not yet been shown that screening for lung cancer with either of the following tests decreases the chance of dying from lung cancer.

Chest x-ray: A chest x-ray is an x-ray of the organs and bones inside the chest. An x-ray is a type of energy beam that can go through the body and onto film, making a picture of areas inside the body.

Sputum cytology: Sputum cytology is a procedure in which a sample of sputum (mucus that is brought up from the lungs by coughing) is viewed under a microscope to check for cancer cells.

Other Tests Are Being Studied In Clinical Trials

Spiral CT Scan

Spiral CT scan is a procedure that makes a series of very detailed pictures of areas inside the body using an x-ray machine that scans the body in a spiral path. The pictures are made by a computer linked to the x-ray machine. This procedure is also called a helical CT scan.

Screening clinical trials are taking place in many parts of the country. Information about NCI's lung screening trial can be found at the National Lung Screening Trial (NLST) website. Information about other clinical trials is available from the NCI Cancer.gov website.

Oral Cancer Screening

The oral cavity is made up of the following parts of the mouth: the lips, the lining of the lips and cheeks, the teeth, the floor of the mouth under the tongue, the front two-thirds of the tongue, the bony top of the mouth, the gums, and the small area behind the wisdom teeth. Oral cancer can affect any or all of these areas.

Screening Tests For Oral Cancer

Screening for oral cancer may be done during a physical examination by the dentist or doctor. The areas of the mouth that are inspected for early detection are: the floor of the mouth, the front and sides of the tongue, and the soft palate. However, it is not known if screening decreases the risk of dying from oral cancer.

Prostate Cancer Screening

The prostate is a gland in males that is involved in the production of semen. It is located between the bladder and the rectum. The normal prostate gland is the size of a walnut and surrounds the urethra, the tube that carries urine from the bladder.

♣ It's A Fact!!

The three screening tests for prostate cancer are: digital rectal examination (DRE); prostate-specific antigen (PSA) test; and transrectal ultrasonography.

Screening Tests For Prostate Cancer

Digital Rectal Examination: A digital rectal examination (DRE) is performed by a doctor during a regular office visit. For this examination, the doctor inserts a gloved finger into the rectum and feels the prostate gland through the rectal wall to check for bumps or abnormal areas. Although this test has been used for many years, whether DRE is effective in decreasing the number of deaths from prostate cancer has not been determined.

Transrectal Ultrasonography: During this examination, high-frequency sound waves are sent out by a probe about the size of the index finger, which is inserted into the rectum. The waves bounce off the prostate gland and produce echoes that a computer uses to create a picture called a sonogram. Doctors examine the sonogram for echoes that might represent abnormal areas. Whether ultrasonography is effective in decreasing mortality from prostate cancer has not been determined.

Prostate-Specific Antigen (PSA): For this test, a blood sample is drawn and the amount of prostate-specific antigen (PSA) present is determined in a laboratory. PSA is a marker that, if present in higher than average amounts, may indicate prostate cancer cells. However, PSA levels may also be higher in men who have noncancerous prostate conditions. Scientists are studying ways to improve the reliability of the PSA test.

Because unnecessary treatment due to false screening results could be harmful, research is being done to determine the most reliable method for prostate cancer screening. For example, scientists at the National Cancer Institute are studying the value of early detection by DRE and PSA on reducing the number of deaths caused by prostate cancer.

Skin Cancer Screening

The skin is the body's outermost covering and offers protection from heat and light, injury, and infection. It also helps regulate body temperature and stores water, fat, and vitamin D. The skin is made up of two main layers: the outer epidermis and the inner dermis.

There are three main types of skin cancer: basal cell carcinoma and squamous cell carcinoma (which are referred to as nonmelanoma skin cancer) and melanoma. Melanoma is the rarest and most serious form of the disease. The epidermis is made up of squamous cells, basal cells, and melanocytes. Melanocytes are the cells from which melanoma begins to develop.

> ♣ **It's A Fact!!**
> There are three main types of skin cancer:
> - basal cell carcinoma
> - squamous cell carcinoma
> - melanoma

Screening For Skin Cancer

Routine examination of the skin increases the chance of finding skin cancer early. Most melanomas that appear in the skin can be seen by the naked eye. If an area on the skin looks abnormal, a biopsy is usually done. The doctor may remove all or part of the growth. To check for cancer cells, the tissue is looked at under a microscope by a pathologist. Because melanoma can be hard to diagnose, you should consider having your biopsy sample looked at by a second pathologist.

Usually, there is a lengthy period when the tumor expands beneath the top layer of skin but does not invade the deeper skin layers. This period allows for early detection and full recovery if the tumor is discovered before spreading deeper.

Cancer Screening Limitations And Risks

Screening Tests Have Risks

Decisions about screening tests can be difficult. Not all screening tests are helpful and most have risks. Before having any screening test, you may want to discuss the test with your doctor. It is important to know the risks of the test and whether it has been proven to reduce the risk of dying from cancer.

The Risks Of Breast Cancer Screening

Finding Cancer May Not Improve Health Or Help A Woman Live Longer

Screening may not help you if you have fast-growing breast cancer or if it has already spread to other places in your body. Also, some breast cancers never cause symptoms or become life-threatening, but cancer may be found on a screening mammogram and treated. It is not known if treatment of these cancers would help you live longer than if no treatment were given, and treatments for cancer may have serious side effects.

False-Negative Test Results Can Occur

Screening test results may appear to be normal even though breast cancer is present. A woman who receives a false-negative test result (one that shows there is no cancer when there really is) may delay seeking medical care even if she has symptoms.

One in five cancers may be missed by mammography. False-negatives occur more often in younger women than in older women because the breast tissue of younger women is more dense. The size of the tumor, the rate of tumor growth, the level of hormones, such as estrogen and progesterone, in the woman's body, and the skill of the radiologist can also affect the chance of a false-negative result.

False-Positive Test Results Can Occur

Screening test results may appear to be abnormal even though no cancer is present. A false-positive test result (one that shows there is cancer when there really isn't) can cause anxiety and is usually followed by more tests (such as biopsy), which also have risks.

Most abnormal test results turn out not to be cancer. False-positives are more common in younger women, women who have had previous breast biopsies, women with a family history of breast cancer, and women who take hormones, such as estrogen and progesterone. The skill of the doctor also can affect the chance of a false-positive result.

Mammograms Expose The Breast To Radiation

Being exposed to radiation is a risk factor for breast cancer. The risk of developing breast cancer from screening mammograms is greater with higher doses of radiation and in younger women. For women older than 40 years of age, the benefits of an annual screening mammogram may be greater than the risks from radiation exposure.

No matter how old you are, if you have risk factors for breast cancer you should ask for medical advice about when to begin having mammograms and how often to be screened.

The Risks Of Lung Cancer Screening

Finding Lung Cancer May Not Improve Health Or Help You Live Longer

Screening may not improve your health or help you live longer if you have advanced lung cancer or if it has already spread to other places in your body.

Some cancers never cause symptoms or become life-threatening, but if found by a screening test, the cancer may be treated. It is not known if treatment of these cancers would help you live longer than if no treatment were given, and treatments for cancer may have serious side effects.

False-Negative Test Results Can Occur

Screening test results may appear to be normal even though lung cancer is present. A person who receives a false-negative test result (one that shows there is no cancer when there really is) may delay seeking medical care even if there are symptoms.

False-Positive Test Results Can Occur

Screening test results may appear to be abnormal even though no cancer is present. A false-positive test result (one that shows there is cancer when there really isn't) can cause anxiety and is usually followed by more tests (such as biopsy), which also have risks. A biopsy to diagnose lung cancer can cause part of the lung to collapse. Sometimes surgery is needed to reinflate the lung.

Chest X-Rays Expose The Chest To Radiation

Radiation exposure from chest x-rays may increase the risk of developing certain cancers, such as breast cancer.

Your doctor can advise you about your risk for lung cancer and your need for screening tests.

Chapter 20

How To Perform A Breast Self-Examination

Four-Step Breast Self-Exam

Step 1. Stand up and place one hand behind your head. Hold the fingers of the other hand flat. Gently touch every part of the breast below the raised arm. Feel for lumps, bumps, or thickening. Now do the other breast.

Step 2. Stand in front of a mirror. Place your hands on your hips. Inspect each breast for changes in size, shape, and form. Do it again with your arms raised above your head. (See Figure 20.1)

Step 3. Lie back with a pillow or folded towel under your right shoulder. Place your right hand behind your head. Examine every part of your breast with the fingers of the left hand held flat. Gently press in small circles. Start at the top outermost edge and spiral in to the nipple. Feel for lumps, bumps, or thickening. Now do the other breast. Be sure to follow a consistent pattern. You may want to use one of the patterns shown in Figure 20.2.

> About This Chapter: Text in this chapter begins with "Four-Step Breast Self-Exam," excerpted from "The Gynecological Visit and Exam: Your Key to Good Health" and reprinted with permission from Planned Parenthood® Federation of American, Inc. ©2002 PPFA. All rights reserved. For additional information, visit www.plannedparenthood.org. "Do It Yourself: Monthly Breast Self-Exam," a second method of breast exam, is from a document by Holden Comprehensive Care Center staff, last revised June 2002. Copyright protected material used with permission of the author and the University of Iowa's Virtual Children's Hospital, www.vh.org/VCH. Available online at http://www.vh.org/adult/patient/cancercenter/doityourself/index.html.

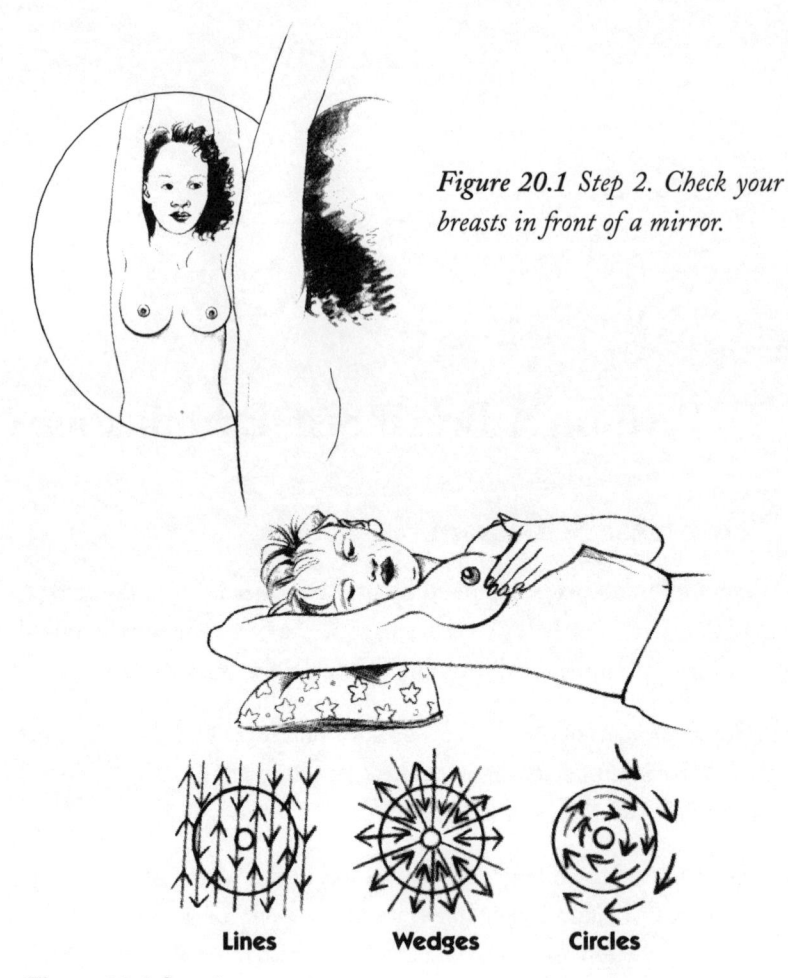

Figure 20.1 Step 2. Check your breasts in front of a mirror.

Figure 20.2 Step 3, with examination patterns.

Figure 20.3 Step 4. Don't forget under your arm.

How To Perform A Breast Self-Examination

Do not miss any part of the breast.

Step 4. Rest your arm on a firm surface like the top of a bookshelf. Examine the underarm. Feel for lumps, bumps, or thickening in the same way. Now do the other underarm.

In time, you will become familiar with the usual feel and changes of your breasts. The more familiar you become, the more easily you will recognize any abnormalities that may develop. Ask your clinician for further guidance.

Do It Yourself: Monthly Breast Self-Exam

This simple 3-step procedure could save your life by finding breast cancer early when it is most curable.

In The Shower

Examine your breasts during bath or shower; hands glide easier over wet skin. Fingers flat, move gently over every part of each breast. Use right hand to examine left breast, left hand for right breast. Check for any lump, hard knot, or thickening.

Before A Mirror

Inspect your breasts with arms at your sides. Next raise your arms high overhead. Look for any changes in contour of each breast, a swelling, dimpling of skin or changes in the nipple.

Then rest palms on hips and press down firmly to flex your chest muscles. Left and right breast will not exactly match—few women's breasts do. Regular inspection shows what is normal for you and will give you confidence in your examination.

Lying Down

To examine your right breast, put a pillow or folded towel under your right shoulder. Place right hand behind your head—this distributes breast tissue more evenly on the chest.

With left hand, fingers flat, press gently in small circular motions around an imaginary clock face. Begin at outermost top of your right breast for 12 o'clock, then move to 1 o'clock, and so on around the circle back to 12. A ridge of firm tissue in the lower curve of each breast is normal. Then move in an inch, toward the nipple, keep circling to examine every part of your breast, including nipple. This requires at least three more circles. Now slowly repeat procedure on your left breast with a pillow under your left shoulder and left hand behind head. Notice how your breast structure feels.

Finally, squeeze the nipple of each breast gently between thumb and index

---

♣ **It's A Fact!!**

Paget's Disease Of The Breast: Questions And Answers

What Is Paget's Disease Of The Breast?

Paget's disease of the breast is an uncommon type of cancer that occurs in one to four percent of all people with breast cancer. It is sometimes called mammary Paget's disease. Paget's disease of the breast can develop in men, but it is very rare. This type of cancer was named after Sir James Paget, a scientist who noted an association between changes in the appearance of the nipple and underlying breast cancer.

Scientists do not know exactly how Paget's disease of the breast occurs, but two major theories have been suggested. In one theory, cancer cells called Paget cells break off from a tumor (an abnormal mass of tissue) in the breast and move through the milk ducts in the breast to the surface of the nipple. In the other theory, the skin cells of the nipple spontaneously become cancerous Paget cells.

What Are The Symptoms Of Paget's Disease Of The Breast?

Symptoms of Paget's disease of the breast include itching, burning, redness, and scaling of the skin on the nipple and areola. The areola is the circular area of darker-colored skin that surrounds the nipple. There may be a bloody discharge from the nipple, and the nipple may appear flattened against the breast. In up to 30 percent of cases, however, there are no visible skin changes. Almost

finger. Any discharge, clear or bloody should be reported to your doctor immediately.

This self-exam is not a substitute for periodic examinations by a qualified physician.

The best time to do breast self-examination is right after your period, when the breasts are not tender or swollen. If you don't have regular periods, do it on the same day each month.

---

half of all patients with Paget's disease of the breast also have a lump in the breast that can be felt at the time of diagnosis. It is important to see a health care provider about any of these symptoms, or if the symptoms do not completely disappear after treatment. They may be caused by Paget's disease of the breast, other types of breast cancer, or a less serious skin condition.

How Is Paget's Disease Of The Breast Diagnosed?

If the health care provider suspects Paget's disease, a sample of any nipple discharge may be examined under a microscope for Paget cells, or a biopsy of the nipple will be done. In a biopsy, the doctor removes a small sample of nipple tissue. A pathologist examines the tissue under a microscope to see if Paget cells are present.

Most people with Paget's disease of the breast also have an underlying breast cancer. That is why the health care provider usually orders a mammogram (x-ray of the breast). However, women with symptoms of Paget's disease who do not have a lump that can be felt often have normal mammograms. These women may need to have other breast imaging techniques, such as ultrasound or MRI (magnetic resonance imaging). In an ultrasound, high-frequency sound waves that humans cannot hear are bounced off tissues and internal organs. Their echoes produce a picture called a sonogram. In an MRI, a magnet linked to a computer creates detailed pictures of areas inside the breast.

Source: Text excerpted and adapted from "Paget's Disease of the Breast: Questions and Answers," National Cancer Institute (NCI), March 18, 2002. Full text available online at http://www.cis.nci.nih.gov/fact/6_39.htm.

Chapter 21

Testicular Cancer And The Importance Of Self-Examination

At age 25, Lance Armstrong was one of the world's best cyclists. He proved it by winning the World Championships, the Tour DuPont, and multiple Tour de France stages. Lance Armstrong seemed invincible and he had a bright future. Entering the peak of his career, Lance felt "bulletproof." But he wasn't. Suffering with a severe pain in his groin, Armstrong went to see a doctor who diagnosed the problem: the cycling champion had testicular cancer and it had spread to his lungs and stomach.

Scott Hamilton rose to the top with technical wizardry, athleticism, enthusiasm and a natural flair to entertain. He used it to become a world and Olympic champion. But that zeal for life was severely tested when, at the age of 29 during the Stars on Ice tour, a doctor confirmed that the source of the lingering ache in Hamilton's stomach was testicular cancer.

An All-American football player at Wake Forest, Brian Piccolo was a tougher-than-nails, gutsy running back who faced opponents that towered over him. After graduation he signed as a free agent with the Chicago Bears and became close friends with all-Pro running back Gayle Sayers. Brian Piccolo

About This Chapter: This information is reprinted with permission from www.TeenGrowth.com. © 2003. All rights reserved.

seemed so durable and sturdy that he was the player called on to get the first down. At the age of 26, Brian Piccolo was diagnosed with testicular cancer and his story was later told in the movie "Brian's Song."

Who Gets Testicular Cancer?

Cancer of the testicles—the egg-shaped male sex glands located in a pouch of skin called the scrotum—usually occurs in men between the ages of 15 and 35, although it can strike any male at any time. In the year 2000, an estimated 7,600 cases of testicular cancer were diagnosed in the United States, and a little less than 400 of men with this cancer died. Disturbingly, the incidence of testicular cancer around the world has basically doubled in the past 30–40 years. For unknown reasons, the disease is about four times more common in white men than in black men. Children born with an undescended testicle have an increased risk of getting testicular cancer regardless of whether surgery is done to correct the problem. (Parents should see that their infant boys are

♣ It's A Fact!!

- Testicular cancer can be one of two general types: seminoma or nonseminoma.

- This disease occurs most often in men between the ages of 15 and 39. It accounts for only one percent of all cancers in men.

- Risk factors include having an undescended testicle, a previous testicular cancer, or having a brother or father who has had testicular cancer.

- Symptoms include a lump, swelling, or enlargement in the testicle; an ache in the lower abdomen, back, or groin; and pain or discomfort in a testicle or in the scrotum.

- Diagnosis generally involves blood tests, ultrasound, and biopsy.

- Treatment can often cure testicular cancer, but regular follow-up exams are extremely important.

Source: Text excerpted and adapted from "Testicular Cancer: Questions and Answers," National Cancer Institute (NCI), August 14, 2003. Full text available online at http://www.cis.nci.nih.gov/fact/6_34.htm.

checked at birth for undescended testicles.) Other risk factors include a family history of testicular cancer, having an identical twin with testicular cancer, and a past injury to the scrotum.

What Are The Symptoms Of Testicular Cancer?

The earliest symptoms of testicular cancer are pain, swelling, or hardness in the testis. Testicular cancer can also cause a number of other symptoms. Listed below are warning signs that men should watch for:

- A lump in either testicle; the lump typically is pea-sized, but sometimes it might be as big as a marble or even an egg.
- Any enlargement of a testicle.
- A significant shrinking of a testicle.
- A feeling of heaviness in the scrotum.
- A sudden collection of fluid in the scrotum.
- Pain or discomfort in a testicle or in the scrotum.
- Enlargement or tenderness of the breasts.

> **Weird Words**
>
> Epididymis: A soft, tube like structure behind the testicle that collects and carries sperm.
>
> Testicles: The egg-shaped male sex glands located in a pouch of skin called the scrotum.

How To Examine Your Testicles

Most testicular cancers are found by men themselves, by accident or when doing a testicular self-examination. It is common knowledge that a monthly breast self-exam for women is an effective part of early breast cancer detection. For men, starting at age 15, monthly self-exams of the testicles are also an effective way of detecting testicular cancer at an early—and very curable—stage.

The self-exam for testicular cancer is best performed after a warm bath or shower (heat relaxes the scrotum, making it easier to spot anything abnormal).

The National Cancer Institute recommends following these steps every month:

1. Stand in front of a mirror. Check for any swelling on the scrotal skin.

2. Examine each testicle with both hands. Place the index and middle fingers under the testicle with the thumbs placed on top. Roll the testicle gently between the thumbs and fingers. You shouldn't feel any pain when doing the exam. Don't be alarmed if one testicle seems slightly larger than the other; that's normal. The testicles are smooth, oval-shaped, and rather firm.

3. Find the epididymis, the soft, tube like structure behind the testicle that collects and carries sperm. Once you are familiar with this structure, you won't mistake it for a suspicious lump. Cancerous lumps usually are found

> ### ☞ Remember!!
>
> Men with testicular cancer should discuss their concerns about sexual function and fertility with the doctor. If a man is to have treatment that might lead to infertility, he may want to ask the doctor about sperm banking (freezing sperm before treatment for use in the future). This procedure can allow some men to produce children after loss of fertility.
>
> Source: Text excerpted and adapted from "Testicular Cancer: Questions and Answers," National Cancer Institute (NCI), August 14, 2003. Full text available online at http://www.cis.nci.nih.gov/fact/6_34.htm.

Testicular Cancer Self-Examination

on the sides of the testicle but can also show up on the front. Lumps on the epididymis are not cancerous.

4. If you find a lump, see your doctor right away. The abnormality may not be cancer, but if it is, it will spread if not stopped by treatment. Waiting and hoping will not fix anything.

Men who examine themselves regularly (once a month) become familiar with the way their testicles normally feel. Any changes in the way they feel from month-to-month should be checked by a doctor.

Testicular cancer is treated by surgery, radiation therapy, and medication. In most cases, surgery is done to remove the testicle. Sometimes it also is necessary to remove lymph nodes in the abdomen if the cancer has spread. Anti-cancer drugs are recommended when there are signs that the cancer has spread, or if the doctor suspects that undetected cancer cells remain in the body after surgery or irradiation.

Only 15 years ago testicular cancer was considered a difficult and dangerous type of tumor. It cost Brian Piccolo his life at the age of 27. Advances in treatment, along with improved diagnosis, now mean that most men found to have testicular cancer will survive the disease. Today, the overall cure rate for testicular cancer, when detected early, is above 90 percent! Cyclist Lance Armstrong and figure skater Scott Hamilton appear to be two of the lucky ones.

Men in their late teens to early 30's often consider themselves invincible. The last thing they are thinking about is that there is something out there that can stop them. But testicular cancer can. Fortunately this deadly but treatable disease can be detected early by regular self-examination.

Chapter 22

How Cancer Is Diagnosed

Throughout your diagnosis and treatment, you will have tons of different tests. Some will be more routine than others, and you'll get used to them. Others will just be annoying because you don't want to be bothered. Unfortunately, some may be uncomfortable or painful. Here are the most common tests you will have.

X-Rays

The subspecialty of medicine called Radiology was developed from the discovery of the x-ray by Wilhelm Conrad Roentgen in 1895. X-rays are a form of electromagnetic radiation that have high energy and short wavelength and are able to pass through various substances including body tissue.

When x-rays are passed through parts of your body, an image is created. Denser tissue, such as bones, blocks more of the rays than less dense tissues, such as the lung. The results are recorded using special photographic film.

> About This Chapter: The information in this chapter is reprinted with permission from Teens Living with Cancer, a co-sponsored project of the Melissa's Living Legacy Foundation and The Children's Oncology Group. ©2003. All rights reserved. The Melissa's Living Legacy Foundation is a non-profit organization providing resources to help teens with cancer have meaningful, life-affirming experiences throughout all stages of their disease. The Children's Oncology Group is a National Cancer Institute-supported clinical trials cooperative group devoted exclusively to childhood and adolescent cancer research. For additional information, visit www.teenslivingwithcancer.org.

When you have an x-ray you have to remove all metal objects. The part of your body to be scanned is placed between the x-ray machine (that produces the rays) and a special screen used to obtain the image. You have to stay as still as possible for a few seconds. It is completely painless and there are no side effects.

The radiologist will look at the images and prepare a report with the results.

MRI—Magnetic Resonance Imaging

Magnetic resonance imaging (MRI) is a non-invasive procedure using magnetism and radio waves to provide detailed images of your body and its soft tissue structures. MRIs help diagnose your disease, monitor the progress of your treatment or help understand other medical situations that arise.

In most cases, there is no special preparation for an MRI scan. You can eat and drink normally on the day of the scan although it is best to avoid large amounts of coffee or other things that might make you restless.

Depending on what part of your body is being scanned, you might have to wear a gown, but usually you can wear regular clothes (without heavy metal attachments). Because of the strong magnetism, it is very important not to bring any metal into the scan room. You will be asked to remove your watch, keys, coins, earrings, and anything else metallic.

For the actual procedure, you lie on your back on a movable scanning table that moves into the MRI scanner. Depending on what type of scan is necessary, the table moves you into the machine head or feet first. Once the body part to be scanned is in the exact center of the magnetic field, the scan begins.

Most kids have no trouble during the procedure but some feel claustrophobic. To make you more comfortable, the inside of the scanner is well lit, and has a fan that gently blows fresh air. Even though the technician is in another room during the procedure, he or she can see you at all times and you can see through a mirror positioned at eye level inside the machine. You can also talk to the technician through an intercom system. If you want, you can usually bring someone with you in the room (check with the technician first).

How Cancer Is Diagnosed

Most MRI scans take between 30 and 90 minutes. Your only job is to remain completely still because even slight movement can spoil the images. During the scan you will hear a variety of sounds such as humming and hammering. It may sound like the technician is hitting the side of the scanner with a large hammer. These sounds are normal. You may be given earplugs or stereo headphones to muffle the noise (in most MRI centers you can even bring your own cassette or CD). But don't be surprised if the music is drowned out by the noise.

Other than maybe being a little uncomfortable (and loud), an MRI is completely painless and you should have no side effects to worry about.

CAT (Or CT) Scan

CAT stands for computerized axial tomography (sometimes referred to as CT scans). CAT scans combine x-rays and computers to produce very detailed cross sectional images of your body.

Depending on what part of your body is to be scanned, you may be given something called "contrast" to make things show up better on the scan. The contrast is given through an IV. If you are having an abdominal scan, you may have to drink it. It tastes really terrible but it's important. Just make sure it's cold and that you have a good "chaser" nearby—soda or juice.

The good thing about CTs is that they are quick but you need to lie very still to get a good scan. After the scan is done, it can be computer reconstructed to show three-dimensional images of the part of your body that was scanned.

Because the machine produces x-rays, the technician is in a separate room near the computer but can talk with you through an intercom. You will probably be alone in the room, unless you request that someone be with you. That person will need to wear a lead vest as protection against the x-rays.

Nuclear Scan: Bone, Gallium

Nuclear scans provide images of your internal organs and bones not possible with conventional x-rays. Instead of being bombarded with x-rays, a low level radioactive compound is injected, swallowed, or inhaled into your body. The amount of radiation received from the radioisotope is very low—about the same as from a dental x-ray. So don't worry—you won't glow.

After your body has had time to absorb the radioactive material, a special imaging camera, that looks like an x-ray machine, is passed over the part of your body to be examined.

Bone scans and gallium scans are the most common nuclear scans for kids with cancer. They are usually used together with other tests to make a definite diagnosis.

Bone Scans

Bone scans can show abnormalities long before they show up in x-rays, which is why your doctor probably ordered one. The radioactive compound is given through an IV and is absorbed by your bones as it travels through your body. You have to drink a lot of water or juice right after the isotope is injected to clear your body of radioactive material not absorbed by your bones.

The bone scan may take about an hour and you have to lie very still while the camera moves back and forth. You might be asked to change positions several times to get different images. Because no x-rays are emitted, you can have someone stay in the treatment room with you.

The radioactive material or tracer concentrates in areas where there is a lot of activity, so to speak—like normal growing bone or in bone tumors or bone infections. These areas will show up as "hot spots" on the scan.

Gallium Scan

A gallium scan is a whole body nuclear scan that helps detect tumors and inflammations. Gallium citrate is the radioactive compound that is injected through an IV. It accumulates in areas where there is rapid cell growth, such as tumors and sites of infection, helping your doctors make an accurate diagnosis and providing appropriate follow-up.

There is nothing special you have to do to prepare for the scan. The imaging is done 24–48 hours after the radioisotope is injected and takes 30–60 minutes, during which you have to lie still.

How Cancer Is Diagnosed

Ultrasound

Ultrasound scans are images of your internal organs created by using sound waves. High frequency waves are directed at your body and then reflected (echoed) back to a scanner that creates an image of the area scanned.

A special gel is spread on the skin over the area to be examined. This helps to define the area as clearly as possible by enhancing the transmission and reception of the sound waves. The ultrasound scanner or transducer looks like a small paint roller that the technician moves over the area to be scanned. It is completely painless but the gel can sometimes feel a bit cold.

There is nothing special that you have to do to prepare for an ultrasound and there are no side effects.

Echocardiogram (Echo)

An echocardiogram is an ultrasound test specifically for your heart. If your treatment plan includes anthracyclines, which are potentially damaging to your heart, you will probably have this test done periodically.

Echocardiograms, like other ultrasounds, use reflected sound waves to create an image of your heart. A special gel is applied over the area to be examined and a scanner is then moved over the area. It is completely painless but the gel can sometimes feel a bit cold.

Electrocardiogram (ECG Or EKG)

Your heart generates electrical impulses causing it to beat or contract. The electrocardiogram (ECG or EKG) records your heart's rhythms and electrical impulses through 10 electrodes that are placed on your chest, arms and legs. The test takes only 5–10 minutes to complete and is completely painless. It is usually done right in your hospital room or treatment room.

If you are taking certain chemotherapy drugs called anthracyclines, you will probably have an EKG prior to treatment and then again, periodically throughout your treatment. Because anthracyclines can cause damage to your heart muscle, your doctor will closely monitor your heart's function and adjust your treatment plan if necessary.

Audiogram

This test evaluates your hearing. If your treatment plan includes the drug cisplatinum, you will likely have a number of audiograms. A possible side effect of cisplatinum is hearing loss so you will probably have a baseline test done prior to starting the drug, and then periodically throughout your treatment.

If you notice any change in your hearing, be sure to tell your medical team.

Pulmonary Function Test

A pulmonary function test measures how well your lungs function, specifically how much air your lungs can hold, and how effectively they work. It also looks at the forcefulness of your breathing.

You may have a pulmonary function test because some chemotherapy drugs affect lung functioning.

Lumbar Puncture Or Spinal Tap

A lumbar puncture or spinal tap may be used to diagnose as well as treat your cancer. The term lumbar refers to your lower back between the pelvis and the ribs. You might have several spinal taps throughout your treatment.

During a spinal tap, a very small needle is inserted between two bones (vertebrae) of your spine. Using this needle, a small amount of spinal fluid is withdrawn to check for cancer in your central nervous system. A chemotherapy drug may also be injected through this needle to treat your cancer (referred to as intrathecal chemotherapy).

Spinal taps take only about 20 minutes. Usually, you are asked to lie on your side and "curl up into a ball," knees bent and pulled up as far as possible with your chin touching your chest. In this position, the bones or vertebrae in your spine separate, letting the needle pass between the vertebrae and into the spinal canal.

A local anesthetic is used to numb the skin before the needle is inserted. Even with the local anesthetic, you might still feel some discomfort. Try to use relaxation techniques like deep breathing and visual imagery to stay calm.

How Cancer Is Diagnosed

When the test is done, a piece of sterile tape is applied to your skin where the needle was inserted. Your medical team will tell you exactly what to do after the procedure, but you will usually be told to lie flat on your back for at least an hour to prevent a headache (caused by the temporary imbalance of your spinal fluid). Even with this precaution, you may still have a headache for several days that is worse when you sit or stand up. Sometimes drinking caffeine—cola or coffee—will help the headache subside.

Bone Marrow Aspirate And Biopsy

You will likely have many bone marrow biopsies throughout your treatment. This test is extremely important for accurately diagnosing some types of cancer as well as tracking the progress of your therapy. This procedure is usually performed by one of your doctors or nurse practitioners.

The bone marrow is a soft tissue inside some of your larger bones. The bone marrow produces red and white blood cells and platelets. By examining a small amount of your bone marrow, usually taken from your hip bone in an area called the ileac crest, your doctors can make important decisions about your care.

Guidelines about sedation or anesthesia differ from one hospital to another. You may receive medication to sedate you (put you to sleep). Some common drugs used are fentanyl and propofol, and they may be administered by an anesthesiologist. Ask your medical team about this.

The procedure will probably be done in a treatment room where you lie face down on an examining table. A small blanket or towel may be placed under your hips to raise them. If you receive sedation medicine, you will begin to feel sleepy very soon and will not feel any of the procedure. Some kids really like the feeling from propofol—very dreamy and relaxing. If you want, you can bring a walk-man or CD player to help you stay calm.

After you are asleep (if you are sedated), the biopsy area is cleansed and a local anesthetic is injected to numb the skin. If you are not sedated, you will feel the prick of the needle and the local anesthetic will sting at first.

A biopsy needle is then inserted through your hip bone into your bone marrow. A small amount of bone marrow is pulled up into a syringe for testing. If you are not asleep, you may feel some pressure and pain as the needle is pushed into your bone.

Once the bone marrow is extracted, a new needle will be placed in the same hole to get a small specimen of bone for further testing. The needle is pressed forward and rotated in both directions. This forces a tiny sample of bone into the needle. If a good sample is not gotten, the doctor or nurse doing the procedure may need to try again. The needle is then removed and a pressure bandage is applied (to stop bleeding).

A bone marrow technician will examine the bone marrow and prepare a report for your doctor. This usually takes a few days.

✎ Weird Words

Biopsy: The removal of cells or tissues for examination under a microscope. When only a sample of tissue is removed, the procedure is called an incisional biopsy or core biopsy. When an entire lump or suspicious area is removed, the procedure is called an excisional biopsy. When a sample of tissue or fluid is removed with a needle, the procedure is called a needle biopsy or fine-needle aspiration.

Computed Tomography (CT) Scan: A series of detailed pictures of areas inside the body taken from different angles; the pictures are created by a computer linked to an x-ray machine. Also called computerized axial tomography (CAT) scan.

Lymph Node: A rounded mass of lymphatic tissue that is surrounded by a capsule of connective tissue. Lymph nodes filter lymph (lymphatic fluid), and they store lymphocytes (white blood cells). They are located along lymphatic vessels. Also called a lymph gland.

Magnetic Resonance Imaging (MRI): A procedure in which a magnet linked to a computer is used to create detailed pictures of areas inside the body. Also called nuclear magnetic resonance imaging.

Nuclear Magnetic Resonance Imaging (NMRI): A procedure in which radio waves and a powerful magnet linked to a computer are used to create detailed pictures of areas inside the body. These pictures can show the difference be-

How Cancer Is Diagnosed

Your back may be sore for a few days. Tylenol may help relieve the soreness. If you have multiple bone marrow biopsies throughout your treatment, your doctor or nurse will try to alternate sides to reduce scar tissue build up. After a while, you will begin to feel like a pin cushion but unfortunately it's necessary.

Blood Tests

Blood tests will become part of your life with cancer, so it's important that you understand what they're for. Various types of blood tests help diagnose your cancer. Sometimes, they are the first indicators of disease. Blood tests are also used to track the progression of your disease as well as help make decisions about your treatment.

---

tween normal and diseased tissue. NMRI makes better images of organs and soft tissue than other scanning techniques, such as CT or X-ray. NMRI is especially useful for imaging the brain, spine, the soft tissue of joints, and the inside of bones. Also called magnetic resonance imaging (MRI).

Tumor Marker: A substance sometimes found in the blood, other body fluids, or tissues. A high level of tumor marker may mean that a certain type of cancer is in the body. Examples of tumor markers include CA 125 (ovarian cancer), CA 15-3 (breast cancer), CEA (ovarian, lung, breast, pancreas, and gastrointestinal tract cancers), and PSA (prostate cancer). Also called biomarker.

Ultrasonography: A procedure in which high-energy sound waves (ultrasound) are bounced off internal tissues or organs and make echoes. The echoes form a picture of body tissues called a sonogram. Also called ultrasound.

X-Ray: A type of high-energy radiation. In low doses, x-rays are used to diagnose diseases by making pictures of the inside of the body. In high doses, x-rays are used to treat cancer.

Source: Terms excerpted from "Cancer.gov Dictionary," December 2003, and from "When Cancer Recurs: Meeting the Challenge," April 1997, both produced by the National Cancer Institute, December 2003. The full text of this dictionary is available online at http://www.cancer.gov/dictionary.

Your doctor will often order a complete blood count (CBC). Your blood "counts" will be closely tracked throughout treatment.

Three primary types of blood cells are formed in your bone marrow: red cells, white cells, and platelets. Plasma is the liquid part of your blood in which the other cells travel. Certain kinds of cancer will affect the normal production of these cells. Some of the treatments you will receive, especially chemotherapy, will also affect your body's ability to produce blood cells. Here are some of the most important "counts" you will track:

Table 22.1 Blood Count Summary Chart

Type of Blood Cell	Normal Range	Possible Signs of Low Counts	What to do when counts are low
Red: carries oxygen	Hematocrit: 35–45% Hemoglobin: 12–14g/µl	• Pale skin • Tired, no energy • Shortness of breath	• Have red blood transfusions • Get extra rest • Eat well
White: fights infections	4.8–10.8 mill/µl	• Fever • Cough • Infections • Redness around sores	• Report fever over 100.5° F and 38.0° C • Start antibiotics • Wash hands often and well • Avoid crowded public places • Don't get any body piercings or tattoos • Take extra precaution if sexually active. Abstinence is best until your counts recover.
Platelets: stops bleeding	150–400 thousands/µl	• Bruising • Bleeding • Petechiae (small red spots)	• Have platelet transfusions • Avoid rough activity, like contact sports. • Don't get any body piercings or tattoos • Take extra precaution if sexually active. Abstinence is best until your counts recover.

How Cancer Is Diagnosed

Red Blood Cells (RBC)

Your red cells are primarily responsible for carrying oxygen throughout your body.

Hemoglobin (Hgb)

Red cells contain hemoglobin, the molecule that carries oxygen and carbon dioxide in your blood throughout your body. If your hemoglobin is low, you will be anemic with symptoms like pale skin, shortness of breath, and fatigue. You may have low hemoglobin at diagnosis as well as during treatment because of your bone marrow's inability to produce new red cells.

Hematocrit (Hct)

Hematocrit refers to the volume of red blood cells in your system. (This is also called packed cell volume—PCV.) Your hematocrit count is the ratio of red cells to plasma (the liquid part of your blood). It is expressed as a percentage. As an example, if your hematocrit is 30 it means that 30% of the blood that was drawn is red cells; the remaining 70% is plasma.

When you are on chemotherapy, your marrow's ability to make new red cells is decreased, so your hematocrit will go down. Because there is less oxygen in your body, you will feel tired and have little energy. If your hematocrit drops below about 18 percent, you will probably need a red blood transfusion. Your medical team will tell you the best thing to do.

White Blood Cells

Your white blood cells are responsible for fighting infection. Because cancer treatment affects your body's ability to produce white cells, your risk of infection becomes very high.

White Blood Cell Differential (Diff)

The differential (or diff) refers to the distribution of different kinds of white cells in your blood. Each type of white cell will be listed as a percentage of the total. Neutrophils are the most important infection-fighting white cells. On your lab reports, the "differential" or "diff" will show the percentage of each type of white cell, all together equaling 100%. As an example:

- Segmented neutrophils (or segs) 49%
- Band neutrophils (or bands) 10%
- Basophils 1%
- Eosinophils 1%
- Lymphocytes 29%
- Monocytes 10%

Absolute Neutrophil Count (ANC)

This count is a measure of your body's ability to fight infection. It is the percent of neutrophils (segs + bands) multiplied by the total white blood count (WBC). The magic number is an ANC of 1,000 or more. When your ANC is less than 1,000, you are at very high risk for infection.

IMPORTANT: If you have a fever higher than 100.5° F or 38.5° C and your ANC is less than 1,000, you will usually be admitted to the hospital to begin antibiotic treatment. Because the fever may be caused by a bacterial infection, extreme caution must be taken. Even if you feel perfectly fine, this precaution is necessary. Spending a few days in the hospital—just in case—is much better than taking a chance with a potentially life-taking infection.

Here's an easy way to calculate your ANC using example blood count results:

- WBC = 1,000
- Segs = 49%
- Bands = 10%
- Add the segs and bands: 49 + 10 = 59
- Multiply by total WBC: 59 x 1,000 = 59,000
- Divide by 100: 59,000 / 100 = 590 ANC

Platelets

Platelets are the cells in your blood necessary to stop bleeding. Because chemotherapy affects your bone marrow's ability to produce platelets, you will probably need platelet transfusions during your treatment.

How Cancer Is Diagnosed

Signs of low platelet count include:

- Bruising with no apparent cause
- Any unusual bleeding (nosebleeds, bleeding gums, vaginal or anal bleeding, prolonged bleeding from a cut)
- Petechiae (small red or purple spots on the skin)

Table 22.1 helps to summarize the important things to know about blood counts. Some labs use different measures to report results. Just be sure you are comparing apples to apples.

Blood Cultures

If your ANC (absolute neutrophil count) is less than 1,000 and you develop a fever of more than 100.5° F or 38.0° C, the risk of serious bacterial infection is high. You will probably be hospitalized and started on IV antibiotics. In order to know exactly what antibiotics best kill the bacteria, blood cultures might be drawn.

What this means is blood is drawn from your central line, and sent to the lab to see what type of bacteria grows in the culture medium (a substance that germs grow in). The most effective antibiotic to treat the specific bacteria can then be administered.

Vital Signs

Get used to this. Your "vital signs" will be taken often (which can be annoying in the middle of the night). These include:

Temperature

Taking your temperature is important to detect possible infection. Most hospitals will record temps in Centigrade degrees. Your temperature can be taken in a number of ways:

- Oral: In your mouth.
- Auxiliary: In your armpit.
- Rectal: In your buttocks.
- Aural: In your ear.

If you don't already have one, you should have a reliable thermometer at home. Remember that a fever over 100.5° F or 38.0° C requires a call to your doctor if you are neutropenic.

Blood Pressure

Your blood pressure is a measure of the force of your blood against the walls of your arteries. Blood pressure is recorded as two numbers—the systolic pressure (as the heart beats) over the diastolic pressure (as the heart relaxes between beats).

The measurement is written one above the other, with the systolic number on top and the diastolic number on the bottom. Normal blood pressure is about 120/80. Many things affect your blood pressure including being nervous, scared, or stressed out. High or low blood pressure can be an indicator of a serious medical problem, so it is watched closely.

Your blood pressure might be taken manually with a blood pressure cuff and a stethoscope or electronically with a digital readout.

Respiration

Your respiration rate is simply the rate at which you are breathing. If you notice the person taking your vital signs is staring at you funny while taking your temperature, he or she is probably watching you breathe. They count how many times you breathe in and out over a period of time.

Pulse

Usually while taking your temperature or blood pressure, the person taking your vital signs feels your wrist to check your pulse. The pulse represents the beating of your heart, specifically the ejection of blood from the left ventricle to the general circulation of the body.

Chapter 23

Who's Who In The Health Care System

Medical Doctors

Primary Oncologists

A doctor specializing in cancer who is in charge of and responsible for your care, sometimes working in a team with other oncologists. This physician stays in communication with your primary care pediatrician or physician.

Attending Physician

One of a team of doctors responsible for your care. In your hospital, a team of oncologists may work together to care for you on rotating schedules. You may have a primary oncologist but still be seen by other attending physicians while you are in the hospital or clinic. Don't worry—in most hospitals all the doctors work as a team and constantly share information about how you are doing and what you need.

About This Chapter: The information in this chapter is reprinted with permission from Teens Living with Cancer, a co-sponsored project of the Melissa's Living Legacy Foundation and The Children's Oncology Group. ©2003. All rights reserved. The Melissa's Living Legacy Foundation is a non-profit organization providing resources to help teens with cancer have meaningful, life-affirming experiences throughout all stages of their disease. The Children's Oncology Group is a National Cancer Institute-supported clinical trials cooperative group devoted exclusively to childhood and adolescent cancer research. For additional information, visit www.teenslivingwithcancer.org.

Radiation Oncologist

A doctor who specializes in using radiation to treat cancer. This physician often puts together your radiation treatment plan and may be responsible for your scans and x-rays.

Surgeon

A doctor who performs operations. You may have different types of surgeons involved in your care for different reasons. For example, a general surgeon may insert your central catheter; an orthopedic surgeon may be involved if you have bone cancer; a neurosurgeon may remove your brain tumor, etc.

Oncology Fellow

A doctor who has finished residency training and doing additional training to become a specialist in oncology. A fellow is a fully certified physician who works closely with the attending physicians to make decisions regarding your treatment. The fellow sometimes has more time than your primary doctor to really talk about things that concern you.

Resident

A doctor who has graduated from medical school and is getting more clinical training in the hospital before

---

☞ Remember!!

Typical members of your health care team may include:

- medical doctors
- nurses
- inter-disciplinary team members

Doctors who may take care of you include:

- oncologist
- surgeon
- oncology fellow
- resident
- anesthesiologist
- psychiatrist
- radiologist

Members of the nursing staff include:

- nurse practitioner
- advanced practice nurse
- nursing aide
- patient care technician

There are many other health care workers who are members of your medical team, including:

- social worker
- child life specialist
- psychologist
- nutritionist
- registered dietitian
- clergy
- phlebotomist

Who's Who In The Health Care System

becoming fully certified. Residents rotate through several specialty areas, including oncology, and work with your other doctors. The residents you see in the hospital will change when their rotations end. This is sometimes annoying because you are always seeing new faces during rounds who may not know your medical history. Try to be patient—we all have to learn somewhere.

Anesthesiologist

A doctor who specializes in giving medicines or other agents that prevent or relieve pain, especially during surgery. An anesthesiologist will always be part of your team when you have surgery. For some procedures like bone marrow biopsies, an anesthesiologist may administer some type of anesthesia and monitor your body functions.

Psychiatrist

A medical doctor that specializes in providing psychotherapy or general psychological help. Because they are medical doctors, psychiatrists can also prescribe medication, such as antidepressants or medication to help you sleep.

Radiologist

A physician with advanced training in diagnosing diseases by interpreting x-rays and other types of imaging studies, for example, CT scans and MRIs.

Nurses

Nurse Practitioner Or Advanced Practice Nurse

A registered nurse with additional education and clinical training in oncology. Nurse practitioners work with your doctors and do many things including: performing physical examinations and procedures, diagnosing patient problems, ordering lab tests and medications, and teaching you about issues related to your care. In some hospitals, you may spend much more time with your nurse practitioner than your doctor. Nurse practitioners usually wear white lab coats like the doctors, not scrubs like the other nurses.

Staff Nurse

A registered nurse who provides the care you require both while you are in the hospital and as an outpatient in the clinic. The nurse may draw your blood, administer chemotherapy and/or medications, teach you about your cancer and treatment, and help arrange follow-up.

Nursing Aides, Patient Care Technicians

The aides in your hospital may have one of several different titles, but they probably all do essentially the same jobs. They often check vitals: blood pressure, temperature, pulse, etc.—and usually have the dubious honor of checking the levels of bodily wastes that you leave behind for closer examination. They might also do things like change your linens, bring in your food trays, and take care of minor problems.

Inter-Disciplinary Team Members

Social Worker

A trained professional who helps you and your family adjust to your illness, access hospital and community resources, and deal with problems. Sometimes you may not feel like talking with the social worker about things that are on your mind. They always want to know, "How are you feeling?" It's OK if you don't want to talk. If you do, they're available.

Child Life Specialist

A child development expert who offers age-appropriate activities to help meet your social and emotional needs. In some hospitals, child life specialists supervise activity rooms, coordinate activities, and help you deal with difficult procedures and treatments.

Clinical Psychologist

A therapist skilled in administering tests to determine at what level you are functioning intellectually and emotionally. Psychologists can help if you are feeling depressed or sad or having problems dealing with your disease. Psychologists are not medical doctors but have a doctoral degree in psychology and counseling. They are referred to as "doctor."

Who's Who In The Health Care System

Nutritionists

Registered dietitians are knowledgeable about the nutritional needs of oncology patients. They are nutrition experts who evaluate eating patterns and problems and recommend nutritional options. When you are going through various treatments (chemotherapy, radiation, surgery, etc.) you may not feel like eating. The nutritionist can help you keep your strength up which is very important during treatment.

Chaplains

Members of the clergy (ministers, priests, rabbis, etc.) who are available to help you with your spiritual issues, concerns or needs.

Physical, Occupational, Speech, And Respiratory Therapists

Individuals with advanced training in their specialty area who may help you with specific problems related to your cancer or its treatment. There are several different kinds of therapists: physical therapists, occupational therapists, speech therapists, and respiratory therapists.

Phlebotomists

Individuals who draw your blood when you do not have a central venous catheter like a Broviac or medi-port.

Chapter 24

Hospitalization And Surgery For Cancer Treatment

What About Hospitalization?

Being in the hospital is often scary for any child, especially at first. It is a whole new world to learn about—new people and strange machines, procedures, and routines. Adding a touch of home by having pictures of family members and friends, drawings, and other personal things in your room can help make the hospital a less scary place. These homey touches can help start a conversation between the hospital staff and yourself.

One of the scariest things for many children is being separated from their parents and siblings. Many hospitals and treatment centers help your family and you spend as much time together as possible by allowing you to have

---

About This Chapter: "What About Hospitalization?" is excerpted and adapted from *Young People With Cancer: A Handbook for Parents*, January 2001, pages 53–54. Full text is available online at http://www.cancer.gov/cancerinfo/youngpeople. "Surgery" is reprinted with permission from Teens Living with Cancer, a co-sponsored project of the Melissa's Living Legacy Foundation and The Children's Oncology Group. © 2003. All rights reserved. The Melissa's Living Legacy Foundation is a non-profit organization providing resources to help teens with cancer have meaningful, life-affirming experiences throughout all stages of their disease. The Children's Oncology Group is a National Cancer Institute-supported clinical trials cooperative group devoted exclusively to childhood and adolescent cancer research. For additional information, visit www.teenslivingwithcancer.org.

visitors anytime and having beds for parents in the child's room or bedrooms nearby. If the hospital does not have beds for your parents, you might ask if they can sleep in a chair near your bed.

Most hospitals have playrooms or activity rooms for children who are patients. These rooms often have toys, games, arts and crafts supplies, and tape players, giving children a chance to play and talk with each other in much the same way that they do with their friends at home or in school. The playroom setting allows children to relax and become more comfortable in the hospital. Playroom staff, trained in working with children who have serious illnesses, can talk to parents and other members of the treatment team about the fears or concerns a child may share through play.

If you cannot get out of bed to go to the playroom or activity room, child-life workers—trained staff who help coordinate play, schoolwork, and other activities for patients—may make bedside visits.

✎ Weird Word

Central Venous Access Catheter: A tube surgically placed into a blood vessel for the purpose of giving intravenous fluid and drugs. It also can be used to obtain blood samples. This device avoids the need for separate needle insertions for each infusion or blood test. Examples of these devices include Hickman catheters, which require clamps to make sure the valve is closed, and Groshong catheters, which have a valve that opens as fluid is withdrawn or infused and remains closed when not in use.

Source: Excerpted from "Cancer.gov Dictionary," National Cancer Institute, December 2003. The full text of this dictionary is available online at http://www.cancer.gov/dictionary.

Hospitalization And Surgery For Cancer Treatment

For older children who are trying to separate themselves from their parents and be more on their own, being in the hospital may thwart their drive for independence. At a time when young people are normally doing more on their own, cancer makes them rely on adults more. As a result, adolescents may make it known, loudly and often, that they are unhappy. They may refuse treatment, break hospital rules, miss outpatient appointments, and rebel in other ways.

Children of any age will often cooperate more if given treatment choices that do not cause problems with their care. Your parents can help you become more independent by allowing you to share the responsibility for your care. Some hospitals also make a special effort to help children cope with illness and being in the hospital, such as allowing teenagers to dress in street clothes whenever possible and to have friends visit. Some hospitals have equipment that allows you to interact with your classmates in the classroom.

Surgery

Surgery is a primary treatment method for many types of solid tumors, especially when the cancer has not spread (metastasized) to other parts of your body. This involves surgical removal of all or part of your tumor.

Surgery is rarely used as the only treatment method. It is often preceded by radiation or chemotherapy, with the intent of shrinking your tumor; or followed by radiation or chemotherapy, to destroy any remaining cancer cells and reduce the risk of reoccurrence. The type of surgery you may have will depend on your type of cancer, the location of your tumor, its size and other factors.

Surgery also plays an important role in the diagnosis of your cancer. Often, cancer can only be correctly identified when cells are viewed under a microscope or tested in a laboratory. This is done through a procedure called a biopsy that takes a small sample of tissue to examine. It may be done under general anesthesia or, as in the case of a bone marrow biopsy, with little or no medication. Additionally, central lines (Broviacs, Medi-ports, etc.) are surgically implanted, either under local or general anesthesia.

Surgical methods have improved over the years reducing the potential impact to your healthy tissue as well as minimizing the potential side effects and reducing risks. Talk with your medical team about treatment options, including various surgical methods.

Chapter 25

Chemotherapy, Radiation Therapy, And Immunotherapy

Chemotherapy

First of all, what is chemo?

Chemotherapy (often referred to as "chemo") is the most common treatment for cancer. To some extent, it is used in almost all treatment plans. Chemotherapy basically means using drugs to treat disease. When you think of it this way, taking aspirin for a headache is a form of chemotherapy. Of course, chemotherapy for cancer is much more powerful. But then, cancer is much more serious than a headache.

About This Chapter: This chapter includes "Your Treatment Plan: Chemotherapy," and "Your Treatment Plan: Radiation," reprinted with permission from Teens Living with Cancer, a co-sponsored project of the Melissa's Living Legacy Foundation and The Children's Oncology Group. © 2003. All rights reserved. The Melissa's Living Legacy Foundation is a non-profit organization providing resources to help teens with cancer have meaningful, life-affirming experiences throughout all stages of their disease. The Children's Oncology Group is a National Cancer Institute-supported clinical trials cooperative group devoted exclusively to childhood and adolescent cancer research. For additional information, visit www.teenslivingwithcancer.org. "Immunotherapy," is excerpted and adapted from *Young People With Cancer: A Handbook for Parents*, National Cancer Institute (NCI), January 2001, pages 46–48.

How does it work?

Chemotherapy works by seeking out and destroying rapidly growing and dividing cells (that's why your hair falls out). Because cancer cells grow and divide in a disorderly and rapid manner, they are very susceptible to chemo drugs. Unfortunately, unlike surgery and radiation that target specific areas, chemotherapy affects healthy cells as well, causing many unpleasant side effects (more on that later).

🕮 Weird Words

<u>Adjuvant Therapy</u>: Treatment given after the primary treatment to increase the chances of a cure. Adjuvant therapy may include chemotherapy, radiation therapy, or hormone therapy.

<u>Chemotherapy</u>: Treatment with anticancer drugs.

<u>Induction Chemotherapy</u>: Treatment designed to be used as a first step toward shrinking the cancer and in evaluating response to drugs and other agents. Induction therapy is followed by additional therapy to eliminate whatever cancer remains.

<u>Radiation Therapy</u>: The use of high-energy radiation from x-rays, gamma rays, neutrons, and other sources to kill cancer cells and shrink tumors. Radiation may come from a machine outside the body (external-beam radiation therapy), or from materials called radioisotopes. Radioisotopes produce radiation and can be placed in or near the tumor or in the area near cancer cells. This type of radiation treatment is called internal radiation therapy, implant radiation, interstitial radiation, or brachytherapy. Systemic radiation therapy uses a radioactive substance, such as a radiolabeled monoclonal antibody, that circulates throughout the body. Also called radiotherapy, irradiation, and x-ray therapy.

Source: Excerpted from "Cancer.gov Dictionary," National Cancer Institute, December 2003. The full text of this dictionary is available online at http://www.cancer.gov/dictionary.

Chemotherapy, Radiation Therapy, And Immunotherapy

How is chemo given?

Chemotherapy, like other drugs, can be administered in a variety of ways. The most common is intravenously, usually through a central line (Broviac or medi-port) that has been surgically implanted before the start of treatment. Some chemo drugs are given orally, either in pill or liquid form. Others are given by an injection. Still others are administered to the central nervous system through a lumbar puncture (spinal tap). This is referred to as intrathecal.

There are dozens of drugs currently being used to treat cancer. Your chemotherapy treatment will probably consist of more than one drug used in combination with others. This is called combination chemotherapy and is generally more effective in killing cancer cells. It also reduces the chance that you will develop a tolerance to one particular drug.

But aren't the side effects terrible?

Yes...and no.

Most teens are concerned about the possible side effects of chemotherapy. You—and most kids—just want to get on with your life and would really rather not be bothered with all of this. You have things to do.

Unfortunately, you may have to put those things on hold for a while until the chemo has a chance to do its thing. Everyone reacts differently to the chemo drugs. This is a function of what kinds of drugs you get, what the dosages are, your general physical condition, and sometimes your mental and emotional stamina.

The most common side effects of chemotherapy include:

- Nausea/vomiting
- Hair loss
- Fatigue (low red blood)
- Increased chance of infection (low white blood)
- Mouth sores
- Diarrhea/constipation
- Increased chance of bleeding (low platelets)

Often, you will experience a cumulative effect from your chemo—it might not hit you right away but will sort of build up over time. Be sure to talk with your medical team about which side effects you can expect and how best to deal with them. There are many medications that can prevent some side effects before they happen.

What can I do about this?

To help overcome any anxiety about your chemo treatment, ask your medical team for a copy of your treatment plan.

This should include:

- A list of the drugs to be used and dosages
- The schedule of treatment
- Description, timing, and likelihood of side effects
- Plans to minimize and deal with side effects

Be sure to ask as many questions as you need to about what to expect throughout your chemotherapy treatment. Understanding your treatment is the key to controlling your emotions and sense of well-being. Talking with other teens might also be helpful. Just remember—every person reacts differently, and one kid's terrible experience might not be yours.

Radiation

What is radiation therapy anyway?

Radiation therapy is the use of high-energy rays or particles to kill cancer cells. Don't worry, the levels you will be exposed to will be safe and will not make you glow in the dark.

Radiation therapy may be used alone or in combination with chemotherapy and surgery to help cure your cancer. The most common teen cancers treated with radiation are brain tumors, leukemia, lymphoma, neuroblastoma, and certain sarcomas. Radiation is also part of the treatment plan for bone marrow transplants.

Chemotherapy, Radiation Therapy, And Immunotherapy

How does radiation work?

Cancer is the overgrowth of abnormal cells. One way to stop the cancer from growing is to interfere with the cell's ability to multiply. Radiation, used at high doses, causes cellular changes that stop the cell's ability to multiply, and it eventually kills the cancer cell.

The most common form of radiation therapy for teens is external beam irradiation. If radiation is given to the entire body, it is called total body irradiation or TBI (this is the procedure prior to bone marrow transplants).

Getting Started

Your radiation therapy must be planned very carefully because both cancer cells and normal cells are damaged by the radiation. The goal is to wipe out the cancer while doing as little damage as possible to your healthy cells.

First, a radiation oncologist reviews all of your records and examines you. Then treatment recommendations are discussed with you and your parents and a plan is developed that includes one or two sessions called simulations (basically getting everything set up).

During the simulation, you lie on a flat x-ray table in what is called the treatment position. To help you keep the same position during each treatment, an immobilization device (like a mask or a mold) may be used. These are not necessary for everyone and are never used for TBI.

A CT scan or x-rays are done so the radiation oncologist can design the exact area to be radiated. Several small marks, or tattoos, are marked on your skin to help identify the area to be treated. These marks are permanent, so you don't have to worry about them washing off. They are very small and over time will hardly be noticeable.

Special shielding "blocks" are designed to shape the radiation beam and help shield normal tissues. Special computer plans are developed that give the best radiation dose to the selected treatment field.

In a second set-up simulation, the shielding blocks are placed in the machine and an x-ray is taken. The radiation oncologist compares this x-ray with the simulation x-ray to ensure accuracy.

The Actual Treatment

Everything is now ready. During treatment, you lie on a table in the treatment position, and the radiation machine (called a linear accelerator) moves itself over and around you to aim the radiation beam directly at your tattoos.

The treatments are very short, usually lasting less than 30 minutes each. Most of this time is spent getting the treatment fields accurately positioned. You will not feel anything during the treatment but must lie very still.

No one is allowed to stay in the room with you during the actual irradiation. You are observed on monitors and can speak to the therapists if necessary. You can also bring a tape or CD to listen to if you want. Radiation is usually given once or twice a day for a number of weeks, but your medical team will tell you your exact schedule.

What about side effects?

Side effects are related to the treatment dose and the area that is being treated. Most side effects of radiation—although sometimes unpleasant—are not serious and can often be controlled.

The most common side effects are:

- Nausea/vomiting
- Diarrhea/constipation
- Fatigue or weakness
- Skin redness or irritation
- Loss of appetite (mouth sores; food may taste weird)
- Hair loss (if you had radiation to your head)

Radiation often has a cumulative effect—you might not notice many side effects right away but over time they build up. Be sure to talk with your medical team about which side effects you can expect and how best to deal with them.

What can I do about this?

To help overcome any worry about your radiation treatment, make sure you know the plan—your treatment schedule, possible side effects and how

Chemotherapy, Radiation Therapy, And Immunotherapy

to deal with them. It's important that you understand the role radiation therapy plays in your overall treatment plan.

Understanding your treatment is one way to stay in control of your mental and emotional well-being. Talking with other teens might also be helpful. Just remember—every person is different. One teen's experience might be very different from yours.

Immunotherapy

The immune system—the body's system for defending itself—knows when substances that should not be there, such as bacteria and viruses, are in the body and then attacks them. The system also knows when cells have changed, such as when cells become cancerous, and then attacks them. Immunotherapy, also known as biological therapy, was developed to take advantage of the body's own ability to fight disease.

In immunotherapy, substances called biological response modifiers (BRMs) are given to cancer patients. BRMs are substances that are normally made by the body to fight cancer and other diseases. Scientists can make large amounts of BRMs to use in cancer treatment. These BRMs destroy cancer cells and change the way the body reacts to a tumor. They may also help the body replace noncancerous cells destroyed by chemotherapy.

Several types of BRMs are used to treat cancer. Four are discussed here: cytokines, interleukins, colony-stimulating factors, and monoclonal antibodies.

- Cytokines are proteins formed in small amounts by all human cells to help control the working of cells. Interferon, one type of cytokine, helps the immune system slow the rate of growth and division of cancer cells, causing them to become sluggish and die. In children who have cancer, these agents have been tested against leukemia, osteosarcoma, brain tumors, and neuroblastoma.

- Interleukins, another type of cytokine, are made by lymphocytes. Interleukin-2, one of the most studied interleukins, causes certain kinds of white blood cells to grow and destroy tumors.

- Colony-stimulating factors are proteins that cause bone marrow cells to develop platelets, red blood cells, and white blood cells.

- Monoclonal antibodies recognize specific antigens, substances that the body senses do not belong or regards as "outsiders," on the surface of cancer cells. These antibodies can be directed against a certain cell type. They can be used to attack and damage or destroy cancer cells. They may also be used to deliver anticancer drugs or radiation directly to specific cancer cells. This technique is still being developed and is used only in clinical trials.

Weird Words

Antigens: Substances that the body senses do not belong or regards as "outsiders."

Biological Response Modifiers (BRMs): Substances that are normally made by the body to fight cancer and other diseases. Four types of BRMs used to treat cancer are: cytokines, interleukins, colony-stimulating factors, and monoclonal antibodies.

Side Effects Of Immunotherapy

Depending on the exact type of treatment, immunotherapy often causes flu-like symptoms such as chills, fever, muscle aches, weakness, loss of appetite, nausea, vomiting, diarrhea, and, at times, a rash. Sometimes the patient will bleed or bruise easily. Depending on how serious these problems are, hospitalization may be needed during treatment. These side effects usually go away after treatment ends. Ask your doctor about coping with the side effects.

Chapter 26

Bone Marrow Transplants: Treatment, Side Effects, And Possible Complications

Simply said, bone marrow transplantation (BMT) is the transfusion of bone marrow from one individual to another or, in some cases, to the same person. That's the easy part. It's what happens before and after the actual infusion that gets tricky.

Why Is Bone Marrow Transplant Necessary?

You may be facing a bone marrow transplant for one of two reasons:

1. Your medical team believes this treatment is the best way to prevent a relapse in certain cancers that are more likely to come back again.

2. Your cancer has not responded well to previous therapy and you have either relapsed or never gained remission.

About This Chapter: The information in this chapter is reprinted with permission from Teens Living with Cancer, a co-sponsored project of the Melissa's Living Legacy Foundation and The Children's Oncology Group. ©2003. All rights reserved. The Melissa's Living Legacy Foundation is a non-profit organization providing resources to help teens with cancer have meaningful, life-affirming experiences throughout all stages of their disease. The Children's Oncology Group is a National Cancer Institute-supported clinical trials cooperative group devoted exclusively to childhood and adolescent cancer research. For additional information, visit www.teenslivingwithcancer.org.

The types of teen cancers most often treated with BMT are:

- Leukemia (ALL, AML)
- Lymphoma (Hodgkin's, non-Hodgkin's)
- Sarcomas (rhabdo or Ewing's)
- Neuroblastoma
- Myelodysplasia (rare in teens)
- Medulloblastoma

A Little Bit About Your Bone Marrow

Bone marrow is the spongy material found in the cavities of your bones, where all your blood cells are produced (the process, in case you are interested, is called hematopoiesis).

Each type of blood cell—red (carries oxygen), white (fights infection), and platelet (helps stop bleeding)—develops from a stem cell made in your marrow. These cells divide and produce all the different cells

> ### ✎ Weird Words
>
> Bone Marrow Transplantation: A procedure to replace bone marrow destroyed by treatment with high doses of anticancer drugs or radiation. Transplantation may be autologous (an individual's own marrow saved before treatment), allogeneic (marrow donated by someone else), or syngeneic (marrow donated by an identical twin).
>
> Peripheral Stem Cell Transplantation: A method of replacing blood-forming cells destroyed by cancer treatment. Immature blood cells (stem cells) in the circulating blood that are similar to those in the bone marrow are given after treatment to help the bone marrow recover and continue producing healthy blood cells. Transplantation may be autologous (an individual's own blood cells saved earlier), allogeneic (blood cells donated by someone else), or syngeneic (blood cells donated by an identical twin). Also called peripheral stem cell support.
>
> Source: Excerpted from "Cancer.gov Dictionary," National Cancer Institute, December 2003. The full text of this dictionary is available online at http://www.cancer.gov/dictionary.

Bone Marrow Transplants

that mature and become fully functional in your body. As old cells wear out and die, stem cells divide and produce new ones.

Most stem cells are found in the bone marrow, but some stem cells called peripheral blood stem cells (PBSCs) can be found in the bloodstream. Umbilical cord blood from newborn babies also contains stem cells.

But When You Have Cancer...

Chemotherapy and radiation are often used to treat cancer. As you know, both of these therapies not only destroy cancer cells but normal ones as well. Doses have to be carefully monitored to reduce the risk of damaging your bone marrow beyond repair yet still kill the cancer.

When you have a bone marrow transplant, very high doses of chemotherapy and radiation are administered which essentially destroy your own marrow, but also, you hope, all the cancer. The new marrow which is transfused from a donor, or in some cases, yourself, "rescues" the old marrow which has been destroyed by the intensive treatment. If all goes well, new cells will be normal, and the cancer will be cured.

Types Of BMTs

There are different types of transplants depending on how and from whom the new marrow is donated:

1. **Syngeneic transplant:** The person donating the bone marrow or stem cells is an identical twin.

2. **Allogeneic transplant:** The person giving the bone marrow or stem cells is a genetically matched family member (usually a brother or sister). If you don't have a sibling to be a donor, you may have a type of allogeneic transplant called a matched unrelated transplant or MUD. The donor is unrelated to you but has matching marrow.

3. **Autologous transplant:** Depending on your specific situation, you may be your own donor. If you have a type of cancer that does not affect your marrow or if you are in remission after another form of treatment, your own marrow can be harvested and frozen for future use.

4. **Peripheral blood stem cell transplant:** With this type of transplant, the donor's cells are collected from his or her circulating blood instead of from bone marrow. Essentially, it's the same as a bone marrow transplant except that the stem cells were collected in a different way.

5. **Umbilical Cord Blood Transplant:** This is usually unrelated, and may be available if an adequate match is not found from the bone marrow registry. Frozen stem cells from a newborn's umbilical cord are available from a cord blood registry.

So, What Exactly Will Happen?

The time line will look something like this:

1. A decision will be made between you and your medical team to proceed with bone marrow transplant. This may either be a first step or a next step if earlier treatments were unsuccessful.

2. The search for a suitable donor will begin. If you have an identical twin, he or she may be the first choice. If not, other siblings will be tested to see if their marrow is genetically matched to yours. This is called HLA (human leukocyte antigen) typing, done through blood tests to make sure their marrow is compatible with you.

3. If you have no siblings or none that match, your medical team may recommend looking for an unrelated donor in a national registry of people who have volunteered to be donors. The transplant coordinator in your hospital will help you with this.

4. Once a donor has been identified, a plan will be created that will include several steps for both you and your donor.

    - The donor will go through a series of tests to be absolutely certain that a good match has been found. The potential donor also is carefully screened to be sure that he or she is totally committed to going forward. Once your treatment starts, it is critical that the donor continue with the process.

Bone Marrow Transplants

- You will begin what's called conditioning treatment. This sometimes includes total body radiation (TBI) for a number of sessions over a few days plus high dose chemotherapy. This conditioning treatment is designed to kill all cancer cells in your body, but it also destroys your marrow in the process.

- At this point, you are very susceptible to life-threatening infection and must take strict precautions. Visitors must be sure to wash their hands very well before coming into your room. You must not be exposed to anyone who is sick, even with a little cold. You might be instructed to wear a sterile mask when around other people. These precautions must be followed until your new marrow is working.

- Everything will be timed perfectly, so that your donor's marrow is harvested (or removed) the day before you receive it. The donor goes to a hospital in whatever city he or she lives for the harvest. In a procedure much like a bone marrow biopsy but longer, marrow is taken from your donor. The donor is usually able to go home that same day. If your donor lives in another city, the marrow will be flown to your hospital where you will be waiting.

- After all the planning and preparation, some teens find the actual transplant to be a bit anticlimactic. Unlike other organ transplants, there is no surgery for you on the day of the procedure. The new marrow is simply given to you intravenously through your central line (Broviac or Hickman). It looks much like a blood transfusion (of which you have had many, by now). But the stem cells you are getting have a very special function. They miraculously find their way directly into your bone marrow where they will hopefully begin producing new blood cells.

- It usually takes a couple of weeks for your new marrow to engraft—or begin making new blood after a bone marrow transplant. With a peripheral stem cell transplant, engraftment usually begins a little earlier. Once the new marrow engrafts, your counts will continue to climb. If there are no complications, you should be able to go home in 4–6 weeks.

Possible Complications

There are several things that your medical team will be closely monitoring following your transplant:

- Failure to engraft: Sometimes (very rarely) the new marrow will not "take" or engraft. Your medical team will guide you to making the best decision about what to do in this case.

- Infections: This poses one of your greatest dangers. If you develop a high fever (100.5° F or 38° C), you will likely be treated with antibiotics.

- Graft-versus-host disease (GVH or GVHD): When your new marrow "takes", you develop the immune system of your donor. In some cases, your new immune system sees the rest of you as foreign—it doesn't recognize you—and begins to attack. In other words, the new marrow (graft) is fighting you (host). This is called graft-versus-host disease. The most common symptoms are skin rash, diarrhea, and jaundice. If you develop any of these symptoms, there is medication to treat them. Uncontrolled GVH can be very serious and potentially life threatening.

> **Remember!!**
> Bone marrow transplant is a very rough ordeal. If you stay focused on the goal of getting better and take one step at a time, you'll get through this.

What Happens After My BMT?

After you are discharged from the hospital, you will be closely monitored for signs of graft-versus-host disease as well as possible infections. You may need to take many medications while your immune system is still recovering and also have injections of a growth factor called G-CSF (growth colony stimulating factor) to boost your white blood cells. Make sure the EMLA (eutectic mixture of local anesthetics) cream is handy—the G-CSF stings if it goes in too fast.

Periodic bone marrow biopsies will also be done to ensure that you are disease free.

Chapter 27

Supportive Care During Cancer Treatment: Blood Transfusions, Antibiotics, And Supplemental Nutrition

In addition to your main therapies (chemo, radiation, surgery, bone marrow transplantation), you will have some treatments that are generally referred to as supportive care. They include blood transfusions, antibiotics, and supplemental nutrition.

Blood Transfusions

Throughout your treatment, you are likely to need blood transfusions for two primary reasons:

1. Your cancer is affecting your bone marrow's ability to produce blood normally (leukemia, as an example).

About This Chapter: The information in this chapter is reprinted with permission from Teens Living with Cancer, a co-sponsored project of the Melissa's Living Legacy Foundation and The Children's Oncology Group. ©2003. All rights reserved. The Melissa's Living Legacy Foundation is a non-profit organization providing resources to help teens with cancer have meaningful, life-affirming experiences throughout all stages of their disease. The Children's Oncology Group is a National Cancer Institute-supported clinical trials cooperative group devoted exclusively to childhood and adolescent cancer research. For additional information, visit www.teenslivingwithcancer.org. Text under "Marijuana Use In Supportive Care For Cancer Patients" is excerpted the National Cancer Institute (NCI) Fact Sheet No. 8.4, December 12, 2000, available online at http://www.cis.nci.nih.gov/fact/8_4.htm.

2. Your treatment—chemo and/or radiation—is destroying your healthy blood cells as well as the cancer cells.

In either case, you may need additional blood products to keep you going if your blood counts are too low.

Let's Talk About Donated Blood

If you need a transfusion, the blood you receive will usually come from a local blood bank (like the Red Cross) where people donate their blood for others, like you, who need this life-saving treatment.

Very strict guidelines about blood donation, preparation, and storage have drastically reduced the risks with receiving donated blood. Donors are carefully screened before they donate and then their blood is tested to ensure that it does not contain any diseases. You may worry about getting AIDS or other diseases from a blood transfusion. That's understandable, but put your mind to rest—the risk is almost non-existent.

What's A Transfusion Like?

Typically you will need either red blood cells or platelets. Only on very rare occasions—if you have a serious infection and are not responding to antibiotics—will you receive white blood cells.

Before you receive a transfusion, a sample of your blood is tested to be sure that the blood you receive is compatible with yours. You will probably receive some medications before the transfusion (like Tylenol® and Benadryl®) to prevent any possible reactions.

If you have a central line, the blood will be transfused right through it. If not, you will need to have an IV started. Plan on bringing a good book or a pillow if you need red blood because it takes a while—2–4 hours for one unit of red cells. Platelets are much quicker—only about 20–30 minutes per bag.

Bags of red cells are usually connected to an IV pump to keep a steady flow during the transfusion. Platelet bags are usually just hung and allowed to drip by gravity. Because platelets are very delicate cells with a much shorter life than red cells, it is best to transfuse them as quickly as possible. Nurses

Supportive Care During Cancer Treatment

have been known to hang bags of platelets from the ceiling to get them in as fast as possible.

Are There Any Side Effects?

When you receive a red blood or platelet transfusion, the white cells are filtered from the donated blood. However, even after being filtered, a few white cells might remain. If you have a reaction to the transfusion, these white cells are probably responsible.

Transfusion reactions can include:

- Fever and chills
- Rash
- Hot flushes

Be sure to let someone on your medical team know if you start to feel any of these side effects.

Antibiotic Therapy

Get used to this equation: Neutropenia + Fever = Antibiotics

When your counts are low during treatment, fevers are taken very seriously. If your temperature is higher than 100.5° F or 38° C, you must call your doctor. It will seem like a pain sometimes, especially if you have something else planned, but your life could depend on it. Really! Don't take any chances. When your white count is low, infections can quickly get out of control and your body has no means to defend itself.

When you spike a fever while neutropenic, you will be put on antibiotics which are given either IV or orally. You may need to be admitted to the hospital for a few days, as a precaution, until blood cultures are negative.

You may also have to take routine antibiotics to prevent possible infection, particularly *Pneumocystis* pneumonia (PCP). This lung infection is very serious if it develops. The antibiotic you'll probably take is called Bactrim® or Septra®.

Nutrition

While you are going through treatment, there may be times when you either don't feel like eating or are just not able. During chemotherapy, as an example, you may develop mouth sores that make eating really tough. Chemo also does pretty nasty things to the inside of your gut and you may not have a normal appetite.

Lots of things—treatment, infections, fevers, the general "blahs"—sometimes make eating difficult. But it is important that you stay nourished so you can keep fighting this disease. Your body needs nutrition to heal just like a car needs gas to run.

When your eating patterns are disrupted, you may be put on some form of extra nutrition. These might include:

Hyperalimentation: Hyper-Al or TPN (Total Parenteral Nutrition)

A method of intravenous nutrition consisting of carbohydrates, protein, minerals, and fats to provide basic nutrition when you aren't able to eat by mouth. This usually looks like a bag of yellow and/or milky fluid and goes in through your central line.

Feeding Tubes

Naso-gastric (NG) or feeding tubes are also used to provide nutrition when you aren't able to eat by mouth. A very small plastic tube is inserted by a nurse from your nose to your stomach so liquid nutrition can be given. This isn't as horrible as it sounds at first, and it is a very safe way to keep you strong when you can't get enough calories or protein in your regular diet.

Nutritional Supplements

There are many different kinds of supplements out there—start taste-testing a few to find one you like. (Adding these to your diet may prevent

> **✔ Quick Tip**
> Supplemental nutrition can be provided in several ways:
> - hyperalimentation
> - naso-gastric (NG) or feeding tubes
> - nutritional supplements

you from needing TPN or NG tubes.) Some examples are: Ensure/PediaSure, Mighty Shakes, Enlive juice boxes, Carnation Instant Breakfast, Scandi Shakes. If you feel adventurous—try your own unique recipe by adding ice cream, fruit, etc. to these in a blender.

Marijuana Use In Supportive Care For Cancer Patients: A Medical Controversy

Cancer, and cancer therapies and their side effects, may cause a variety of problems for cancer patients. Chemotherapy-induced nausea and vomiting, and anorexia and cachexia are conditions that affect many individuals with cancer.

Nausea And Vomiting

Some anticancer drugs cause nausea and vomiting because they affect parts of the brain that control vomiting and/or irritate the stomach lining. The severity of these symptoms depends on several factors, including the chemotherapeutic agent(s) used, the dose, the schedule, and the patient's reaction to the drug(s). The management of nausea and vomiting caused by chemotherapy is an important part of care for cancer patients whenever it occurs. Although patients usually receive antiemetics, drugs that help control nausea and vomiting, there is no single best approach to reducing these symptoms in all patients. Doctors must tailor antiemetic therapy to meet each individual's needs, taking into account the type of anticancer drugs being administered; the patient's general condition, age, and related factors; and, of course, the extent to which the antiemetic is helpful.

There has been much interest in the use of marijuana to treat a number of medical problems, including chemotherapy-induced nausea and vomiting in cancer patients. Two forms of marijuana have been used: compounds related to the active chemical constituent of marijuana taken by mouth and marijuana cigarettes. Dronabinol (Marinol®), a synthetic form of the active marijuana constituent delta-9-tetrahydrocannabinol (THC), is available by prescription for use as an antiemetic. In 1985, the U.S. Food and Drug Administration approved its use for the treatment of nausea and vomiting associated with cancer chemotherapy in patients who had not responded to the standard antiemetic drugs.

National Cancer Institute (NCI) scientists feel that other antiemetic drugs or combinations of antiemetic drugs have been shown to be more effective than synthetic THC as "first-line therapy" for nausea and vomiting caused by anticancer drugs. Examples include drugs called serotonin antagonists, including ondansetron (Zofran®) and granisetron (Kytril®), used alone or combined with dexamethasone (a steroid hormone); metoclopramide (Reglan®) combined with diphenhydramine and dexamethasone; high doses of methylprednisolone (a steroid hormone) combined with droperidol (Inapsine®); and prochlorperazine (Compazine®). Continued research with other agents and combinations of these agents is under way to determine their usefulness in controlling chemotherapy-induced nausea and vomiting. However, NCI scientists believe that synthetic THC may be appropriate for some cancer patients who have chemotherapy-induced nausea and vomiting that cannot be controlled by other antiemetic agents. The expected side effects of this compound must be weighed against the possible benefits. Dronabinol often causes a "high" (loss of control or sensation of unreality), which is associated with its effectiveness; however, this sensation may be unpleasant for some individuals.

> **Weird Words**
>
> Anorexia: The loss of appetite or desire to eat.
>
> Cachexia: A wasting condition in which the patient has weakness and a marked and progressive loss of body weight, fat, and muscle.
>
> Antiemetic: Drug that helps control nausea and vomiting.

Marijuana cigarettes have been used to treat chemotherapy-induced nausea and vomiting, and research has shown that THC is more quickly absorbed from marijuana smoke than from an oral preparation. However, any antiemetic effects of smoking marijuana may not be consistent because of varying potency, depending on the source of the marijuana contained in the cigarette.

Anorexia And Cachexia

Anorexia, the loss of appetite or desire to eat, is the most common symptom in cancer patients. It may occur early in the disease process or later, in

Supportive Care During Cancer Treatment

cases where the cancer progresses. Cachexia is a wasting condition in which the patient has weakness and a marked and progressive loss of body weight, fat, and muscle. Anorexia and cachexia frequently occur together, but cachexia may occur in patients who are eating an adequate diet but have malabsorption of nutrients. Maintenance of body weight and adequate nutritional status can help patients feel and look better, and maintain or improve their performance status. It may also help them better tolerate cancer therapy.

There are a variety of options for supportive nutritional care of cancer patients, including changes in diet and consumption of foods, enteral or parenteral feeding (delivery of nutrients by tube), and the use of drugs. An NCI-supported study to evaluate the effects of THC and megestrol acetate (a synthetic female hormone) used alone and in combination for treatment-related and cancer-related anorexia and cachexia completed patient accrual earlier this year. Researchers will compare the appetite, weight, and rate of weight change among patients treated with THC to patients treated with megestrol acetate or with both therapies. Researchers will also evaluate the effects of the drugs alone or in combination on nausea and vomiting, assess for toxic effects of the drugs, and evaluate differences in quality of life among those patients who were treated with THC.

The Institute of Medicine (IOM), part of the National Academy of Sciences, has published a report assessing the scientific knowledge of health effects and possible medical uses of marijuana. The IOM project was funded by the White House Office of National Drug Control Policy. The IOM released its report on March 17, 1999.

♣ It's A Fact!!

Copies of the report, *Marijuana and Medicine: Assessing the Science Base*, are available from National Academy Press, Lockbox 285, 2101 Constitution Avenue, NW., Washington, DC 20055; (202) 334-3313 or 1-888-624-8373. The full text of the IOM report is also available online at http://pompeii.nap.edu/books/0309071550/html/index.html.

Chapter 28

Complementary And Alternative Treatments In Cancer Care

There are a multitude of alternative treatments available to help the person with cancer. They can be used in conjunction with, or separate from, surgery, chemotherapy, and radiation therapy. Alternative treatment of cancer is a complicated arena and a trained health practitioner should be consulted.

Although the effectiveness of complementary therapies such as acupuncture in alleviating cancer pain has not been clinically proven, many cancer patients find it safe and beneficial. Bodywork therapies such as massage and reflexology ease muscle tension and may alleviate the side effects such as

> About This Chapter: Beginning text in this chapter was taken from *GALE ENCYCLOPEDIA OF MEDICINE, 1ST EDITION*, by Lata Cherath, 2, Gale Group, © 1999, Gale Group. Reprinted by permission of The Gale Group. Text also excerpted and adapted from the following documents: PDQ® Cancer Information Summary. National Cancer Institute; Bethesda, MD. 714-X (PDQ ®): Treatment-Patient, updated 7/2003; Cancell/Entelev (PDQ ®): Treatment-Patient, updated 7/2003; Cartilage (Bovine and Shark) (PDQ ®): Treatment-Patient, updated 7/2003; Coenzyme Q_{10} (PDQ ®): Treatment-Patient, updated 7/2003; Essiac/Flor-Essence (PDQ ®): Treatment-Patient, updated 7/2003; Hydrazine Sulfate (PDQ ®): Treatment-Patient, updated 8/2003; Laetrile/Amygdalin (PDQ ®): Treatment-Patient, updated 7/2003; Mistletoe Extracts (PDQ ®): Treatment-Patient, updated 11/2003; Newcastle Disease Virus (PDQ ®): Treatment-Patient, updated 7/2003; Selected Vegetables/Sun's Soup (PDQ ®): Treatment-Patient, updated 7/2003. All NCI documents available at: http://cancer.gov. Accessed December 10, 2003.

nausea and vomiting. Homeopathy and herbal remedies used in Chinese traditional herbal medicine have also been shown to alleviate some of the side effects of radiation and chemotherapy and are being recommended by many doctors.

Certain foods including many vegetables, fruits and grains are believed to offer protection against various cancers. However, isolation of the individual constituent of vegetables and fruits that are anti-cancer agents has proven difficult. In laboratory studies, vitamins such as A, C and E, as well as compounds such as isothiocyanates and dithiolthiones found in broccoli, cauliflower, and cabbage, and beta-carotene found in carrots have been shown to protect against cancer. Studies have shown that eating a diet rich in fiber as found in fruits and vegetables reduces the risk of colon cancer. Exercise and a low fat diet help control weight and reduce the risk of endometrial, breast, and colon cancer.

Certain drugs, which are currently being used for treatment, could also be suitable for prevention. For example, the drug tamoxifen (Nolvadex®), that has been very effective against breast cancer, is currently being tested by the National Cancer Institute, for its ability to prevent cancer. Similarly, retinoids derived from vitamin A are being tested for their ability to slow the progression or prevent head and neck cancers. Certain studies have suggested that cancer incidence is lower in areas where soil and foods are rich in the mineral selenium. More trials are needed to explain these intriguing connections.

714-X

- The main ingredient of 714-X is naturally derived camphor that is chemically modified by the addition of an extra nitrogen atom.

- It is claimed that 714-X protects and stabilizes the immune system and restores its ability to fight cancer.

- No study of 714-X has been published in a peer-reviewed, scientific journal to show it is safe or effective in treating cancer.

- 714-X is not approved for use in the United States.

Complementary And Alternative Treatments

Cancell/Entelev

- Cancell/Entelev has been promoted by its manufactures as an effective therapy for cancer and a number of other diseases.

- Cancell/Entelev is a mixture of common chemicals, none of which is known to be effective in treating any type of cancer.

- No animal study or human study of Cancell/Entelev has been published in a peer-reviewed, scientific journal to show that it is safe or effective in treating cancer.

- Cancell/Entelev is not approved for use in the United States.

♣ **It's A Fact!!**

Cancell/Entelev is also known by the following names: Sheridan's Formula, Jims Juice, Crocinic Acid, JS-114, JS-101, 126-F, and Cantron.

Cartilage (Bovine And Shark)

- Bovine (cow) cartilage and shark cartilage have been studied as treatments for cancer and other medical conditions for more than 30 years.

- Numerous cartilage products are sold commercially in the United States as dietary supplements.

- Three principal mechanisms of action have been proposed to explain the antitumor potential of cartilage: 1) it kills cancer cells directly; 2) it stimulates the immune system; and 3) it blocks the formation of new blood vessels (angiogenesis), which tumors need for unrestricted growth.

- At least 3 different inhibitors of angiogenesis have been identified in bovine cartilage, and 2 angiogenesis inhibitors have been purified from shark cartilage.

- Few human studies of cartilage as a treatment for cancer have been reported to date, and the results are inconclusive.

- Additional clinical trials of cartilage as a treatment for cancer are now being conducted.

Coenzyme Q_{10}

- Although several naturally occurring forms of coenzyme Q have been identified, Q_{10} is the predominant form found in humans and most mammals, and it is the form most studied for therapeutic potential.

- Coenzyme Q_{10} is made naturally by the human body.

- Coenzyme Q_{10} helps cells to produce energy, and it acts as an antioxidant.

- Coenzyme Q_{10} has shown an ability to stimulate the immune system and to protect the heart from damage caused by certain chemotherapy drugs.

♣ **It's A Fact!!**
Coenzyme Q_{10} is also known as: Co Q_{10}, Q_{10}, vitamin Q_{10}, ubiquinone, and ubidecarenone.

✎ Weird Words

<u>Angiogenesis Inhibitor</u>: A substance that may prevent the formation of blood vessels. In anticancer therapy, an angiogenesis inhibitor prevents the growth of blood vessels from surrounding tissue to a solid tumor.

<u>Antioxidant</u>: A substance that prevents damage caused by free radicals. Free radicals are highly reactive chemicals that often contain oxygen. They are produced when molecules are split to give products that have unpaired electrons. This process is called oxidation.

<u>Coenzyme Q_{10}</u>: A benzoquinone compound synthesized naturally by the human body. The "Q" and the "10" in the name refer to the quinone chemical group and the 10 isoprenyl chemical subunits, respectively, that are part of this compound's structure. The term "coenzyme" denotes it as an organic (contains carbon atoms), nonprotein molecule necessary for the proper functioning of its protein partner (an enzyme or an enzyme complex).

Source: Excerpted from "Cancer .gov Dictionary," National Cancer Institute, December 2003. The full text of this dictionary is available online at http://www.cancer.gov/dictionary.

Complementary And Alternative Treatments

> ### ✥ Weird Words
>
> <u>Essiac</u>: Herbal tea mixture that is reported to contain four herbs: burdock *root (Arctium lappa)*, Indian rhubarb root (*Rheum palmatum*, sometimes known as Turkish rhubarb), sheep sorrel (*Rumex acetosella*), and the inner bark of slippery elm (*Ulmus fulva* or *Ulmus rubra*).[1]
>
> <u>Flor-Essence</u>: Herbal tea mixture that is reported to contain the same four herbs as Essiac, plus four "potentiating" herbs: watercress (*Nasturtium officinale*), blessed thistle (*Cnicus benedictus*), red clover (*Trifolium pratense*), and kelp (*Laminaria digitata*).[2]
>
> **References**
>
> 1. Essiac. Kirkland, Canada: Altramed Health Products, 2002. Available online at: http://www.essiac-resperin.com. Last accessed April 2, 2003.
>
> 2. Flora Manufacturing & Distributing Ltd.: Flora Flor-Essence®. Available online at: http://www.florahealth.com/Flora/Home/canada/Products/R8070.asp. Last accessed April 3, 2003.

- Low blood levels of coenzyme Q_{40} have been detected in patients with some types of cancer.

- No report of a randomized clinical trial of coenzyme Q_{40} as a treatment for cancer has been published in a peer-reviewed, scientific journal.

- Coenzyme Q_{40} is marketed in the United States as a dietary supplement.

Essiac/Flor-Essence

- Essiac and Flor-Essence are herbal tea mixtures originally developed in Canada. These products are marketed as dietary supplements.

- Proponents have claimed that Essiac and Flor-Essence can help detoxify the body, strengthen the immune system, help relieve pain, improve quality of life, and reduce tumor size.

- Molecules with antioxidant, anti-inflammatory, anticancer, or immunostimulatory activity have been identified in the individual herbs in these formulas.

- No data are available from animal or human studies to suggest that Essiac or Flor-Essence can be effective in the treatment of patients with cancer.

> ☞ **Remember!!**
>
> There are hundreds of kinds of cancer, and specific "standards of care" for each of them are used in modern (scientific) medical treatment. Breast cancer may be treated with surgery, radiation, chemotherapy or a combination of these methods. Alternative therapies to standard medical practice, now often called "complementary" or "integrated" therapies, may include allopathic and homeopathic approaches, eastern (Asian) medicine, herbs, vitamins, nutritional supplements, dietary changes, massage, meditation and other treatments. Some alternative therapies may be helpful in combination with traditional medical treatment, particularly for relief of symptoms, and they are often integrated into the overall treatment plan. But by definition, alternative therapies remain scientifically unproven for treatment or cure, and in some cases can be dangerous. It's important that patients with cancer discuss alternative therapies with their physician, since some approaches, like herbal medications, might interfere or interact with the medical treatments being used.
>
> Cancer in an older relative can be very frightening. If you are worried about a family member, it's important that you discuss your concerns with a trusted adult.
>
> Source: This information is reprinted with permission from www.TeenGrowth.com. © 2003. All rights reserved.

Hydrazine Sulfate

- Hydrazine sulfate is a chemical that has been studied as a treatment for cancer and as a treatment for the body wasting (i.e., cachexia) associated with this disease.

- It has been claimed that hydrazine sulfate limits the ability of tumors to obtain glucose, which is a type of sugar used by cells to create energy.

- Hydrazine sulfate has been shown to increase the incidence of lung, liver, and breast tumors in laboratory animals, suggesting it may cause cancer.

- There is only limited evidence from animal studies that hydrazine sulfate has anticancer activity.

Complementary And Alternative Treatments

- Hydrazine sulfate has shown no anticancer activity in randomized clinical trials, and data concerning its effectiveness in treating cancer-related cachexia are inconclusive.
- Hydrazine sulfate has been marketed in the United States as a dietary supplement or a nutraceutical by some companies; however, its use as an anticancer drug outside of clinical trials has not been approved by the Food and Drug Administration (FDA).

Laetrile/Amygdalin

- Laetrile is another name for the chemical amygdalin, which is found in the pits of many fruits and in numerous plants.
- Cyanide is thought to be the main anticancer component of laetrile.
- Laetrile was first used as a cancer treatment in Russia in 1845 and, in the United States, in the 1920s.
- Laetrile has shown little anticancer activity in animal studies and no anticancer activity in human clinical trials.
- Laetrile is not approved for use in the United States.

> **Weird Word**
>
> Laetrile: An acronym (laevorotatory and mandelonitrile) used to describe a purified form of the chemical amygdalin, a cyanogenic glucoside (a plant compound that contains sugar and produces cyanide) found in the pits of many fruits and raw nuts and in other plants, such as lima beans, clover, and sorghum.

Mistletoe Extracts

- Mistletoe is a semiparasitic plant that has been used for centuries to treat numerous human ailments.
- Extracts of mistletoe have been shown to kill cancer cells in the laboratory and to stimulate the immune system.
- Mistletoe is used mainly in Europe, where a variety of different extracts are manufactured and marketed as injectable prescription drugs.

These extracts are not available commercially in the United States.

- Although mistletoe plants and berries are considered poisonous to humans, few serious side effects have been associated with mistletoe extract use.

- The use of mistletoe as a treatment for cancer has been investigated in more than 30 clinical studies. Reports of improved survival and/or quality of life have been common, but nearly all of the studies had major weaknesses that raise doubts about the reliability of the findings.

- At present, the use of mistletoe cannot be recommended outside the context of well-designed clinical trials. Such trials will be valuable to determine more clearly whether mistletoe can be useful in the treatment of specific subsets of cancer patients.

> ♣ **It's A Fact!!**
>
> Mistletoe is used mainly in Europe, where commercially available extracts are marketed under a variety of brand names, including:
>
> - Iscador
> - Eurixor
> - Helixor
> - Isorel
> - Iscucin
> - Plenosol
> - ABNOBAviscum
>
> Some extracts are marketed under more than one name. For example, Iscador, Isorel, and Plenosol are also sold as Iscar, Vysorel, and Lektinol, respectively. All of these products are prepared from *Viscum album Loranthacea* (*Viscum album L.* or European mistletoe). They are not available commercially in the United States.

Newcastle Disease Virus

- NDV is usually thought to be an avian (i.e., bird) virus, but it also infects humans. Although NDV causes a potentially fatal, noncancerous disease (Newcastle disease) in birds, it causes only minor illness in humans.

- NDV appears to replicate (i.e., reproduce) substantially better in human cancer cells than it does in most normal human cells.

- Individual strains of NDV are classified as lytic or nonlytic. Viruses of both strain types can kill cancer cells, but lytic strains have the potential to do this more quickly because they damage the plasma membrane of infected cells. Nonlytic strains appear to kill by interfering with cell metabolism.

- Lytic strains of NDV have been studied in humans for their ability to kill cancer cells directly, but viruses of both strain types have been used to make vaccines in an attempt to stimulate the immune system to fight cancer.

- NDV-based anticancer therapy has been reported to be of benefit in more than a dozen clinical studies, but the results of these studies must be considered inconclusive because the study designs were weak and the study reports were generally incomplete.

> ### ✎ Weird Words
>
> Lytic: Strain of NDV which kills cancer cells by damaging the plasma membrane of infected cells.
>
> Newcastle Disease Virus (NDV): A paramyxovirus that causes Newcastle disease in a wide variety of birds (most notably, in chickens). This often fatal disease is characterized by inflammation of respiratory tract and of either the brain or the gastrointestinal tract. NDV can also infect humans, but, in humans, it is generally not very virulent, causing only mild flu-like symptoms or conjunctivitis and/or laryngitis.
>
> Nonlytic: Strain of NDV which appears to kill cancer cells by interfering with cell metabolism.

Selected Vegetables/Sun's Soup

- "Selected Vegetables" and "Sun's Soup" are names given to several different mixtures of vegetables and herbs that have been studied as treatments for cancer. These mixtures were developed by a single individual.

- At present, two formulations of Selected Vegetables/Sun's Soup are marketed in the United States as dietary supplements.

- The vegetables and herbs in Selected Vegetables/Sun's Soup are thought to have anticancer and/or immune system–stimulating properties.

- It has been reported that treatment with Selected Vegetables/Sun's Soup lengthened the survival of patients with advanced non-small cell lung cancer or other types of malignant tumors. However, different formulations of Selected Vegetables/Sun's Soup were used in the studies reported to date, making the comparison of results across studies difficult, and design weaknesses in the studies raise doubts about the reliability of the findings.

- Additional clinical studies of Selected Vegetables/Sun's Soup are being conducted or contemplated.

♣ It's A Fact!!

"Selected Vegetables" and "Sun's Soup" are names given to several different mixtures of vegetables and herbs that have been studied as treatments for cancer and other medical conditions.

The original formulation contained *Lentinus edodes* (shiitake mushroom), mung bean, *Hedyotis diffusa* (also known by the Chinese herbal name Bai Hua She She Cao), *Scutellaria barbata* (barbat skullcap; also known by the Chinese herbal name Ban Zhi Lian).

A second formulation, specifically named "Selected Vegetables" (or "SV"), is a freeze-dried vegetable and herb product, is marketed in the United States as a dietary supplement under the names "Freeze-dried SV" or "DSV."

A third formulation, called "Frozen SV" or "FSV," like SV/DSV, is marketed in the United States as a dietary supplement.

SV/DSV and FSV are reported to contain soybean, shiitake mushroom, mung bean, red date, scallion, garlic, leek, lentil, Hawthorn fruit, onion, ginseng, Angelica root, licorice, dandelion root, senega root, ginger, olive, sesame seed, and parsley.

Chapter 29

What Is Standard Therapy Versus A Clinical Trial?

Your doctor may recommend a standard therapy or a clinical trial. Standard therapy is the best treatment available outside of clinical trials for a specific type and stage of cancer.

A cancer clinical trial is a research study. In a clinical trial, a new treatment is used with a group of patients to find out:

- if it is safe
- if it destroys the cancer
- if it has side effects and how severe they might be
- if it is better than standard therapy

These new treatments are first tested in the laboratory and on animals. If a treatment shows promise of being better than the standard therapy, it is tested with patients in a clinical trial.

Most clinical trials are carried out in steps called phases. Each phase answers different questions about the treatment. Patients may be eligible for

---

About This Chapter: This chapter contains excerpts adapted from "What Is a Standard Therapy Versus a Clinical Trial?" *Young People With Cancer: A Handbook for Parents*, January 2001, pages 12–14. Full text is available online at http://www.cancer.gov/cancerinfo/youngpeople.

studies in different phases, depending on their general condition and the type and stage of their cancer.

- **Phase I studies** test new treatments in humans to determine if the treatment can be given safely and if it has harmful side effects. Researchers look for the best dose and the best way to deliver the treatment. Because less is known about the possible risks and benefits in Phase I, these studies usually include only a limited number of patients who would not be helped by other treatments.

- **Phase II studies** focus on learning whether the new treatment actually has an anticancer effect. As in Phase I, only a small number of people take part because of the risks and unknowns involved.

- **Phase III studies** compare the results of people receiving the new treatment with results of people receiving standard therapy. In most cases, studies move into Phase III testing only after a treatment shows promise in Phases I and II. Phase III studies may include hundreds of people around the country.

- **Phase IV studies** evaluate the side effects of the new treatment—once it has been approved and is being marketed—that were not apparent in the Phase III trial. Thousands of people are involved in a Phase IV trial.

> ✔ **Quick Tip**
>
> You may ask your doctor to obtain information from PDQ®, or you may call the NCI-supported Cancer Information Service (CIS) at 1-800-4-CANCER (1-800-422-6237) or TTY at 1-800-332-8615 to ask for a PDQ® search. Read more about PDQ® on the NCI CancerNet website at http://www.cancer.gov/search/clinicaltrials/usersguides. To find out about NCI trials taking place on the main campus of the National Institutes of Health in Bethesda, Maryland, you may also call the NCI's Pediatric Oncology Branch at 1-877-624-4878. To search for open clinical trials in your area, visit www.clinicaltrials.gov.

What Is Standard Therapy Versus A Clinical Trial?

Clinical trials have played an important role in producing new and better treatments. About two-thirds of children with cancer are treated in clinical trials.

You, your parents, and your doctor can learn about clinical trials from PDQ®—NCI's cancer information database. PDQ® contains:

- descriptions of current clinical trials, including information about the purpose of the study, who is eligible for the study, details of the treatment program, and the names and addresses of doctors and places conducting the study.
- the latest treatment information for most types of cancer (also available by fax at 1-800-624-2511 or 301-402-5874).

Chapter 30

Uses And Side Effects Of Cancer Drugs

Drugs, drugs, and more drugs! Your head will spin trying to remember all the drugs you will be taking. Not to mention trying to pronounce their names. This chapter will list the most common, how they are given, and the most common side effects.

Chemotherapy Drugs

If your treatment plan includes chemotherapy, you'll get to know some of these drugs, often given in various combinations.

Asparaginase (a-SPARE-a-gin-ase)—Given by injection. Most common side effects:

- Changes in blood clotting
- Fever and chills
- Allergic reaction
- Lethargy, sleepiness and confusion

About This Chapter: The information in this chapter is reprinted from "All Drugged Up: Understanding Your Medications" with permission from Teens Living with Cancer, a co-sponsored project of the Melissa's Living Legacy Foundation and The Children's Oncology Group. ©2003. All rights reserved. The Melissa's Living Legacy Foundation is a non-profit organization providing resources to help teens with cancer have meaningful, life-affirming experiences throughout all stages of their disease. The Children's Oncology Group is a National Cancer Institute-supported clinical trials cooperative group devoted exclusively to childhood and adolescent cancer research. For additional information, visit www.teenslivingwithcancer.org.

Bleomycin (blee-oh-MY-sin) (Blenoxane)—Given through IV or injection. Most common side effects:

- Fever and chills
- Skin and nail changes
- Loss of appetite
- Nausea and vomiting
- Changes to the lungs

Busulfan (byoo-SUL-fan) (Myleran)—Given through IV or taken by mouth. Most common side effects:

- Bone marrow depression (lowering counts)
- Nausea, vomiting, and diarrhea
- Hair loss
- Mouth sores
- Seizures
- Skin changes

Carboplatin (KAR-bo-plat-in) (Paraplatin)—Given through IV. Most common side effects:

- Bone marrow depression (lowering counts)
- Nausea and vomiting
- Poor appetite
- May affect your kidneys
- Will lower your pH ct.
- Hearing loss

Carmustine (kar-MUS-teen) (BCNU)—Given through IV. Most common side effects:

- Nausea and vomiting
- Changes to the skin
- Bone marrow depression (lowering counts)

Cisplatin (siss-PLAT-in) (Platinol)—Given through IV. Most common side effects:

- Nausea and vomiting (may get worse after a few days)
- Your kidneys may be affected
- Changes to your skin
- Hearing loss
- May cause numbness or tingling in hands or feet

IMPORTANT: Drink lots of fluid while on this drug. Keep anti-nausea meds nearby.

Uses And Side Effects Of Cancer Drugs

Cyclophosphamide (sye-kloe-FOSS-fa-mide) (Cytoxan)—Given through IV or taken by mouth. Most common side effects:

- Bone marrow depression (lowering counts)
- Hair loss
- Bladder irritation
- Nausea and vomiting
- Poor appetite

> ♣ **It's A Fact!!**
>
> Drugs used in cancer treatment fall into several categories:
> - Chemotherapy
> - Anti-nausea (anti-emetic)
> - Pain Meds
> - Anti-depressants
> - Steroids

Cytarabine (sye-TARE-a-been) (ARA-C; Cytosar)—Given by injection, IV or intrathecal (injected into fluid around spinal cord). Most common side effects:

- Bone marrow depression (lowering counts)
- Nausea/vomiting/diarrhea
- Eye irritation
- Mouth sores
- Rash
- A flu-like effect

Dacarbazine (da-KAR-ba-zeen) (DTIC-Dome)—Given through IV. Most common side effects:

- Nausea and vomiting, poor appetite
- Flu-like effect
- Bone marrow depression (lowering counts)
- Hair loss

Daunorubicin (daw-noe-ROO-bi-sun) (Daunomycin)—Given through IV. Most common side effects:

- Nausea and vomiting
- Hair loss
- Mouth sores
- Bone marrow depression (lowering counts)
- Discolored urine

IMPORTANT: This kind of chemo (anthracycline) may affect your heart muscle. Check with your doctor before exercising or weightlifting.

Doxorubicin (dox-oh-ROO-bi-sin) (Adriamycin)—Given through IV. Most common side effects:

- Hair loss
- Nausea, vomiting, and diarrhea
- Bone marrow depression (lowering counts)
- Mouth sores
- Discolored urine
- Skin and nail changes
- Sensitivity to the sun

IMPORTANT: This kind of chemo (anthracycline) may affect your heart muscle. Check with your doctor before exercising and weightlifting.

Etoposide (e-TOE-poe-side) (VP-16)—Given through IV or taken by mouth. Most common side effects:

- Bone marrow depression (lowering counts)
- Nausea and vomiting, and diarrhea
- Hair loss
- Temporary taste alterations
- Mouth sores
- Skin changes

5-Fluorouracil (floor-oh-YOOR-a-sill) (5-FU)—Given through IV or taken by mouth. Most common side effects:

- Mouth sores
- Diarrhea
- Eye sensitivity
- Skin changes
- Bone marrow depression (lowering counts)
- Nausea and vomiting
- Hair loss
- Sensitivity of the skin to sunlight
- Rashes

Fludarabine (flu-DAHR-a-been) (Fludara)—Given through IV or taken by mouth. Most common side effects:

- Bone marrow depression

Hydroxyurea (hye-DROX-ee-yoo-REE-ah) (Hydrea)—Taken by mouth. Most common side effects:

- Bone marrow depression (lowering counts)
- Skin changes

Uses And Side Effects Of Cancer Drugs

Idarubicin (eye-dah-ROO-bah-sin) (Idamycin)—Given through IV or taken by mouth. Most common side effects:

- Bone marrow depression (lowering counts)
- Nausea and vomiting
- Mouth sores and ulcers
- Hair loss

IMPORTANT: This kind of chemo (anthracycline) may affect your heart muscle. Check with your doctor before exercising or weightlifting.

Ifosfamide (eye-FOSS-fah-mide) (Ifex)—Given through IV. Most common side effects:

- Bone marrow depression (lowering counts)
- Nausea and vomiting
- Hair loss
- Irritation of the bladder
- Changes to nails

Lomustine (loe-MUS-teen) (CCNU; CeeNU)—Taken by mouth. Most common side effects:

- Nausea and vomiting
- Mouth sores
- Bone marrow depression (lowering counts)

Mechlorethamine (me-klor-ETH-a-meen) (Nitrogen Mustard)—Given through IV. Most common side effects:

- Nausea and vomiting
- Hair loss
- Rash

Melphalan (MEL-fa-lan) (Alkeran)—Given through IV or taken by mouth. Most common side effects:

- Bone marrow depression (lowering counts)
- Nausea and vomiting
- Mouth sores
- Diarrhea
- Hair loss
- Skin changes

Mercaptopurine (mer-kap-toe-PYOOR-een) (Purinethol)—Taken by mouth. Most common side effects:

- Bone marrow depression (lowering counts)
- Mouth sores
- Skin changes

Methotrexate (meth-o-TREX-ate)—Given by mouth, injection, IV or intrathecal (injected into fluid around spinal cord). Most common side effects:

- Bone marrow depression (lowering counts)
- Mouth sores
- Diarrhea, nausea, vomiting
- Skin changes, rash, hair loss

Mitoxantrone (my-toe-ZAN-trone) (Novantrone®)—Given through IV. Most common side effects:

- Bone marrow depression (lowering counts)
- Discolored urine
- Nausea and vomiting
- Mouth sores
- Hair loss
- Whites of eyes may have a slight blue tint

This is a blue colored medicine.

IMPORTANT: This kind of chemo (anthracycline) may affect your heart muscle. Check with your doctor before exercising or weightlifting.

Paclitaxel (PACK-lih-tax-el) (Taxol®)—Given through IV. Most common side effects:

- Bone marrow depression (lowering counts)
- Mouth sores
- Diarrhea, nausea, vomiting
- Hair loss
- Skin changes
- Aching or pain in joints and muscles (usually after 2–3 days. Gets better within 5–7 days)
- Numbness or tingling in hands or feet
- Allergic reaction

Procarbazine (pro-KAR-ba-zeen) (Matulane)—Given through IV or taken by mouth. Most common side effects:

- Bone marrow depression (lowering counts)
- Nausea and vomiting
- Alcohol should be avoided while taking this drug
- Delayed low pH. ct.

Uses And Side Effects Of Cancer Drugs

Teniposide (ten-IP-oh-side) (Vumon)—Given through IV. Most common side effects:

- Nausea, vomiting, or diarrhea
- Fever, chills
- Allergic reaction

6-Thioguanine (six-thigh-oh-GWAN-neen) (6-TG)—Taken by mouth. Most common side effects:

- Bone marrow depression (lowering counts)
- Skin changes
- Raised levels of uric acid in the blood
- Mouth sores

Vinblastine (vin-BLAS-teen) (Velban)—Given through IV. Most common side effects:

- Bone marrow depression (lowering counts)
- Nausea, vomiting, and diarrhea
- Hair loss
- Mouth sores
- Constipation
- Numbness or tingling in hands or feet

Vincristine (vin-KRIS-teen) (Oncovin; VCR)—Given through IV. Most common side effects:

- Abdominal cramps and constipation
- Jaw pain
- Numbness or tingling in hands or feet

Anthracyclines

Anthracyclines are a group of chemotherapy drugs used to treat a variety of childhood cancers. There is both good and bad news associated with anthracyclines. The good news: significantly increased survival rates. The bad news: possible heart problems that may not show up for 10–15 years.

Anthracyclines include daunorubicin, doxorubicin, idarubicin, and mitoxantrone.

If anthracyclines are part of your treatment plan, it is important that you know it so you can take the necessary precautions.

So, What's The Problem?

An article written by Nancy Keene and Dr. Kevin Oeffinger, M.D. (*Late Effects to the Heart, 2000 Candlelighters Childhood Cancer Foundation Newsletter*) sums up how your heart functions.

The heart is a large muscle that is divided into four chambers and is designed to pump the blood around the body. The upper chambers or rooms are called atria and the lower chambers are called ventricles. The blood returning from the body enters the right atrium, is squeezed into the right ventricle, and then is pumped into the blood vessels in the lungs.

It is here that the oxygen we breathe is transferred into many small blood vessels in the lungs. The blood, now rich with oxygen, returns to the left atrium and then is squeezed into the left ventricle, the largest and most powerful of the chambers. The left ventricle contracts to circulate the blood to the entire body.

OK, You Might Be Asking, "So What's The Big Deal With Anthracyclines?"

We know that these drugs can effect the functioning of your heart's left ventricle. This is a problem when your heart needs to work harder, like during exercise or strenuous activity. The weakened left ventricle—responsible for pumping oxygen-rich blood back into your body—may not be capable of this heavy duty pumping action.

What Do I Have To Do?

If you are going to be taking anthracyclines, you will probably have some baseline tests (EKG and ECHO cardiogram) done before you start taking the drug. These tests will be repeated throughout your treatment and then annually or as often as your doctor suggests.

You also have to restrict activities that put a heavy strain on your heart. Two sports in particular should be avoided: football and weight lifting. You can still participate in many other sports and are encouraged to do so. You can still dance, swim, and play tennis, basketball, soccer, and baseball.

Uses And Side Effects Of Cancer Drugs

Just remember that the effects of anthracyclines are long lasting and need life-long attention. As you get older, you should always take these precautions to stay on the safe side.

Anti-Nausea Drugs

Anti-nausea (or anti-emetic) drugs will become your best friends during your chemotherapy treatment. Your medical team is the best source of information about which drugs will work best for you.

Most teens going through chemotherapy will take one or the other of the following two drugs for nausea: Ondansetron (Zofran) or Granisetron (Kytril). These are both given through IV or by mouth.

Depending on your response to the chemo, you may also take some of the following drugs to prevent or treat nausea. You will come to learn which ones work best for you:

- Diphenhydramine (Benadryl)*
- Promethazine (Phenergan)*
- Metoclopramide (Reglan)
- Prochlorperazine (Compazine)
- Dexamethasone (Decadron)
- Dronabinol (Marinol)*
- Lorazepam (Ativan)*
- Inapsine (Droperidol)*

Most common side effects:

- Dry mouth
- Drowsiness and light-headedness (those marked with *)

Pain Medications

You may be given various types of pain medications (often referred to as "narcotics"). Your medical team is the best source of information about which pain medications will best control your pain, if you have any.

One goal is to be as pain free as possible when you are in treatment. You have enough other things to worry about without trying to deal with unnecessary pain. You may feel that you have to be totally brave and completely stoic. You don't.

You might be hesitant to take pain meds because you—or your parents—are afraid you will become addicted to them. When given in a controlled manner for short periods of time, addiction to these drugs is not a worry. If you are on a certain drug for a longer period of time, your body may become tolerant to it and you may need to gradually taper off.

Don't be afraid to ask for pain meds if you need them.

Commonly used pain medications:

- Morphine (Morphine)
- Hydromorphone (Dilaudid)
- Oxycodone (Percocet)
- Codeine (Codeine)
- Methadone (Dolophine)
- Meperidine (Demerol)
- Fentanyl (Fentanyl)

These are usually given by injection, liquid, pill or IV. Sometimes they are given as a rectal suppository.

Common side effects:

- Sedation
- Light-headedness
- Dizziness
- Constipation
- Sometimes nausea or vomiting

Local Anesthetic To Prevent Pain

EMLA is an anesthetic cream that numbs your skin. It's great if you need to have a needle stick for an IV, access your medi-port, or have an injection. It can also be used for procedures like spinal taps and bone marrow aspirations.

All you have to do is apply it to your skin about 1–2 hours before the procedure, cover it with an airtight dressing, and it will numb the area. You don't feel a thing (if you wait long enough). EMLA (eutectic mixture of local anesthetics) is only sold with a prescription.

Anti-Depressants

The use of anti-depressants by teens with cancer is not uncommon. Depression or feelings of sadness, disruption in your eating or sleeping patterns, or having trouble coping with all that is going on can occur anytime during or after your treatment.

Uses And Side Effects Of Cancer Drugs

Depression is caused by a lack of a chemical in your brain called serotonin. Anti-depressant medication helps increase your serotonin levels. You need to take these drugs for a few weeks before you feel any change.

Commonly used anti-depressants:

- Sertraline (Zoloft)
- Paroxetine (Paxil)
- Fluoxetine (Prozac)
- Citalopram (Celexa)

Most common side effects:

- Drowsiness or agitation
- Dry mouth
- Nausea
- Constipation
- Headache

Steroids

This type of medication is often used in the treatment of several different kinds of cancers and other diseases. **Don't confuse this kind of steroid with the illegal, anabolic type that have been used to bulk muscles.**

Your body normally produces a natural form of steroid called cortisol. You will make less cortisol while you're taking steroid medication. This is why you always taper off this medication—so you own body starts making the normal amounts of cortisol again. Commonly used steroids:

- Methylprednisolone (Solumedrol): Taken through IV
- Cortisone: Taken by injection into the muscle
- Prednisone: Taken by mouth
- Hydrocortisone: Taken through IV, by mouth, or in a cream for the skin

Common side effects:

- Increased appetite
- Weight gain
- Mood swings
- Fullness in cheeks
- High blood pressure
- Stomach upset or ulcers
- Osteoporosis (weakens bones)

Chapter 31

Managing Side Effects Of Cancer Treatments

Weird Body Issues

Are you losing hair, growing hair in strange places—feeling fat or looking scrawny? These and many other strange things may happen to your body while undergoing chemo and/or radiation. There aren't always easy ways to solve some of these problems, but let's talk about them and learn from other teens what helps.

Plumbing Problems

Constipation, vomiting, diarrhea, hemorrhoids, mouth sores… (OK, skip this section if you're eating right now.)

Some drug is probably causing one or more of these problems. The good news is there's probably another drug to help it go away.

About This Chapter: The information in this chapter is reprinted from "Weird Body Issues" with permission from Teens Living with Cancer, a co-sponsored project of the Melissa's Living Legacy Foundation and The Children's Oncology Group. ©2003. All rights reserved. The Melissa's Living Legacy Foundation is a non-profit organization providing resources to help teens with cancer have meaningful, life-affirming experiences throughout all stages of their disease. The Children's Oncology Group is a National Cancer Institute-supported clinical trials cooperative group devoted exclusively to childhood and adolescent cancer research. For additional information, visit www.teenslivingwithcancer.org.

Don't be afraid to tell someone your plumbing is messed up. Don't feel bad asking—even if it's 3 A.M. There are lots of options, so if one thing isn't working, then ask to try something different. Advocate for yourself.

Nausea And Vomiting

What comes first—the chicken or the egg? Can you have one without the other? Same riddle with nausea and vomiting. One often leads to the other, which sometimes starts the whole cycle again.

Nausea and vomiting may be a problem throughout your treatment. Others, depending on their treatment and their own reactions, may have little or no problem. But if you are one of those who experience nausea and vomiting as a side effect of your treatment, here a few things to know:

The Warning Signs

Nausea is that queasy, yucky feeling in your stomach that tells your brain—*"Get to the bathroom and quick!"* You might begin to feel a little dizzy or warm. Your throat might start to feel funny, your knees a little wobbly. The room may begin to spin. Keep a bucket handy if you think you can't get to the bathroom.

> **✎ Weird Word**
>
> Antiemetics: Drugs that prevent or reduce nausea and vomiting.
>
> Source: Excerpted from "Cancer.gov Dictionary," National Cancer Institute, December 2003. The full text of this dictionary is available online at http://www.cancer.gov/dictionary.

Sometimes you may only feel nauseous and not actually vomit. Some kids say they feel better when they do vomit. On the other hand, vomiting may make you feel more nauseous. And so it goes....

What Causes Nausea And Vomiting

Nausea and vomiting are two common side effects of various cancer treatments.

Chemotherapy: Chemotherapy affects the parts of your stomach and your brain that detect toxic or poisonous substances. (How comforting is that?) This causes you to feel sick. Your body tries to rid itself of these toxins. (It's so smart.) Because chemo is given through your veins, it cannot be expelled out of your body like food and stays in your body to treat the cancer. Unfortunately, everything else that is in your stomach is purged—sometimes very unpleasantly.

Radiation: Radiation can also cause nausea and vomiting, especially if it is given near your gastrointestinal tract (small intestines and stomach) or to you brain. The nausea/vomiting cycle works the same as above.

Other things to blame: Certain other drugs used to treat the side effects of cancer may cause nausea and vomiting. Some pain meds, like Demerol, as an example, might make you feel sick. Constipation and diarrhea can also make some teens feel nauseous. Having nausea and diarrhea at the same time is unpleasant.

General anxiety and emotions, as well as other triggers like certain odors (especially hospital food) can make you sick to your stomach. Anesthesia before a surgical procedure also may make you sick. Unfortunately, you don't know what is going to make you vomit until it happens. All you can do, sometimes, is try to not let it happen again.

Do's And Don'ts

- *Anti-Nausea Drugs*

    - Be sure you take an anti-nausea drug *before* chemo or radiation.

    - At the first sign of nausea, tell your nurse you need drugs. Don't be too proud to ask. That's what they're for. Sometimes you can prevent nausea before it hits.

    - Keep a trusty bucket nearby for emergencies.

    - Keep a record of what makes you sick as well as what drugs worked well to prevent nausea.

- *Foods*
  - Don't eat just before treatment. Try to eat a few hours before and then eat frequent, light meals throughout the day. Good nutrition is important to keep your strength.
  - Avoid greasy, fried foods, dairy products, and acidic things like orange juice and Italian salad dressing. They are hard to digest.
  - Try to stay away from food smells. One of two things will happen: they will either make you sick or make you hungry for things you can't eat. Neither is a good thing. (*Tip: foods that are cold or at room temperature have fewer odors than warm foods.*)
  - Try eating hard candy (Altoids work great) or chewing gum to cover up any bad tastes of chemotherapy.
  - Be gentle on your stomach after vomiting. Start with ice chips or "de-fizzed" soda (stir it vigorously to release the carbonation).
  - Have someone (mothers are good for this) taste test all your hospital food. Don't even let it in the door if it looks, tastes, or smells suspect.

- *Rest And Relaxation*
  - Whenever possible, get lots of fresh air. Open a window or go outside, if you can.
  - Get good at distraction therapy—do something, anything, to keep your mind off vomiting. For some teens, playing video games before a treatment session helps ward off anticipatory nausea (getting sick just thinking about it).
  - Have friends visit when you're getting chemo; play games or watch TV together.
  - Visualize yourself not vomiting—the old "mind over matter" strategy. Sometimes it works.

- Breathe! Breathing deeply and focusing your attention may help relax you. The more relaxed you are, the better your chances of not losing your dinner.
- Try to sleep during and after your treatment. Some anti-nausea meds will make you sleepy anyway. You need all the energy you can get.

Side Effects Of The Side Effect

If your nausea and vomiting get really bad, you might not be able to eat or drink adequately. Preventing dehydration and keeping your electrolytes in balance is important. Your medical team might recommend extra fluids to be given intravenously (IV). You might also be given supplemental nutrition to give you an extra boost.

Diarrhea And Constipation

Nobody wants to talk about this topic. It's embarrassing. But when you have cancer, everything is fair game. All privacy goes out the window, so let's just get it on the table (so to speak).

This subject is difficult to put into words. Lots of expressions are used to describe this bodily function. Your docs and nurses will use "bowel movement" (BM for short) and "stool" (not the kind you sit on). Don't be surprised if they simply ask, *"Have you pooped today?"* You probably have your own favorite term.

Diarrhea

Diarrhea is a common, and uncomfortable, side effect of cancer treatment. You know you have diarrhea when, with no warning, you get a severe stomach cramp or stomach ache and then—heaven help anyone in your way.

What Causes Diarrhea?

The most likely cause is chemotherapy. But certain medicines like antibiotics, as well as some infections, can also be responsible.

During chemotherapy, the fast growing cells that make up your intestine wall are attacked, along with the cancer cells. This makes the lining of your intestine thinner and unable to work properly. This makes your bowel movement softer and more watery than usual.

Here's the trouble with having bad diarrhea. You spend a lot of time in the bathroom—not a pleasant place for many reasons, not the least of which is the putrid odors produced by your body. This alone is enough to make you nauseous. If you notice a significant decline of visitors, this may be why. Keep the air freshener handy.

More importantly, the cramps may be really painful. Just remember, that this too will pass. If your diarrhea continues for a while, your docs might prescribe extra IV fluids to prevent dehydration and keep necessary nutrients in balance.

Is There Any Thing I Can Do?

Yes. Here's a list of ideas:

- DRINK! Clear liquids are best: water, broth, sports drinks (Gatorade), un-fizzy ginger ale. If drinking makes you nauseous sip slowly and make sure your drinks are at room temperature. Very hot or cold drinks tend to make the diarrhea worse.

- Eat small amounts. Eat frequently, rather than three large meals. It's easier on your digestive system.

- Eat low-fiber, high potassium foods: white bread, rice, or noodles, mashed potatoes, bananas, oranges (unless you have mouth sores), creamed cereals, chicken, turkey, or fish (with no skin). Avoid high-fiber foods that make cramping worse: whole grain breads and cereals, raw veggies, nuts, popcorn, or beans.

- Stay away from fried, greasy, highly spiced foods. Also stay away from caffeine (coffee, tea, soft drinks), alcohol, and sweets. They irritate your digestive system.

- Avoid milk and milk products. This includes ice cream, especially if you notice it making your diarrhea worse.

- Ask your medical team about medicines. Don't use over the counter medications without first checking with your doctor.

- Keep lots of toilet paper and reading material in the bathroom.

One Last Thing

Personal hygiene is really important if you have bouts of diarrhea. It is easy to get a very sore buttocks with all the activity going on in that area. If your white counts are low, the last thing you want is an infection. Just one more embarrassing thing that will need to be examined. Ask your nurse about specially designed wipes or creams that can help the process.

Constipation

Constipation, of course, is the opposite problem of diarrhea. What a crazy game this cancer makes us play. Either you can't stop going to the bathroom or you can't go at all. Seems like there should be an easier way.

This, too, is an embarrassing topic to talk about but it is very important. If you have a problem with constipation, find someone with whom you can talk. Nurses have seen it all and are comfortable talking about stool problems.

What Causes Constipation?

Constipation is a very uncomfortable side effect for some teens with cancer. Some chemotherapy drugs and other medications can cause your intestines to slow down. When things don't move along your digestive tract the way they're supposed to, your normal bowel patterns change.

A change in your diet as well as your normal routine also can cause you to be constipated.

Problems Caused By Constipation

You may have painful stomachaches caused by the inactivity in your intestines. As a result, your bowel movements get hard and difficult to pass out of your body.

Pushing hard to eliminate stool could cause a bleeding tear in the skin around your anus. If your platelets are low, the bleeding could be heavy. If your white counts are low, you could develop an infection from the break in your skin.

If you are constipated and nothing is moving through your intestines, you may feel nauseous and vomit. As in life, one thing often leads to another.

What Should I Do?

- First, if you notice any signs of constipation—or you haven't had a bowel movement in a few days or you notice blood on the toilet paper—tell someone. Your medical team may prescribe medication (laxatives or stool softeners) to help move things along.
- Be sure to drink plenty of fluids. Warm or hot drinks sometimes work best.
- Eat a well-balanced diet with plenty of fruits, vegetables, and high-fiber foods: whole grain breads and cereals, popcorn, nuts. (Check with your medical team for any food restrictions)
- Avoid cheese, chocolate, and eggs. These can cause constipation.
- Get out of bed (if you are able) and exercise. Just walking around the nurse's station or down the hall will help keep your intestines active. It will also make you feel better overall.

Mouth Sores

You probably know by now that chemotherapy targets rapidly dividing cancer cells. Unfortunately, some normal cells also divide rapidly and are affected. Specifically in this section, we'll talk about the effects of chemo on the rapidly dividing cells in your mouth and throat.

What Causes Mouth Problems?

First, chemotherapy can cause sores in your mouth and throat. You may hear these sores referred to as *mucositis*, *stomatitis*, or *mouth ulcers*. Secondly, mouth sores may become infected by the many germs that live in your mouth, especially if your white blood count is low. You may also experience a sense of dryness in your mouth, making it difficult to swallow.

Mouth problems can make it very painful to eat and drink. For many teens, mouth pain can be the most painful side effect of cancer treatment.

What Can You Do?

You might be able to prevent mouth sores from developing with good oral hygiene. Here are some tips:

Managing Side Effects Of Cancer Treatments

- Visit the dentist **before** you start chemo. When your counts go down, it will be difficult to have dental care. Use a soft bristled toothbrush and fluoride toothpaste.

- Brushing your teeth often—but gently—will not only keep your teeth and mouth clean, it will get rid of some of the nasty tastes of certain chemo drugs. Rinse your toothbrush well and store it in a dry place to prevent germs from growing.

- Ask your medical team to suggest a mild or medicated mouthwash. "Swish" often.

These are the things to look for—despite all these precautions, you might still develop some problems.

- Sores or raw areas
- White spots or patches
- Pain in your mouth or throat
- Unusual bleeding, usually around your gums

If you notice any of these symptoms, here are some ideas to help you cope:

- If you weren't using one already, you may need to start using an antibacterial mouthwash. Ask your medical team to recommend one of several different kinds. *But beware—none of them tastes great.* **Use it anyway.** The bad taste doesn't even come close to the pain of bad mouth sores.

- Most hospitals will have soft, foam brushes for your use. You can still keep your mouth clean without dealing with rough bristles.

- Ask your medical team for medication to treat the problem. There may be something you can put directly on the sores to ease the pain. As with all available meds, *don't be afraid to ask.* That's what they're for.

- Eating may become difficult if your mouth is really sore. Try eating soft foods like ice cream, milkshakes, mashed potatoes, macaroni and cheese, etc. Avoid acidic, spicy, or rough foods. *Don't try to eat a hard shell taco supreme.*

- If eating becomes really tough, you may need some extra IV nutrition known as TPN (Total Parenteral Nutrition). This will keep you healthy until your counts come back up and your mouth heals.

Temperature Control

Hot—cold. Cold—hot. *Get the heating pad. No, get the ice packs!* Would you make up your mind, for crying out loud? There will be times during your treatment when your body's thermostat will be completely wacky. In this section, you'll read about fevers and why you **absolutely can't** ignore them. You'll also read about a weird reaction called shaking chills or rigors.

Fever

First rule: If you have a fever, call your doctor. Here's why:

Fevers And Infection

Infections are a big deal when you have cancer. Chemotherapy wreaks havoc on your healthy cells as well as the cancer cells. In particular, your white blood count is very low after chemo (neutropenia).

You are very susceptible to infection without the protection of your white cells. If you do get an infection, your ability to fight it is diminished. You're hit with a double whammy—easy to get an infection and hard to fight it.

Fevers are the most common sign of infection. **If you have a fever over 100.5° F or 38° C, you must call your doctor immediately.** You will probably be started on antibiotics and may need to stay in the hospital until your fever comes down. Don't be surprised if your doctor is very strict about this. At times, this will be a pain—especially if you don't feel sick—but it is very important. Infections can get out of control very quickly—**don't put yourself in danger.**

What Causes A Fever?

Ever wonder what causes a fever when you have an infection? In a nutshell, here's what happens.

When foreign substances (like germs) enter your system, something called cytokines are released which re-set your body's thermostat. It's like adjusting

Managing Side Effects Of Cancer Treatments 263

the thermostat in a room when you want it warmer. Your body knows it needs more heat to fight the intruding germ—your immune system works better at a higher temperature.

Your body's first response is to tighten up or constrict your blood vessels. This reduces the amount of heat lost through your skin and raises your temperature a little.

The surface air feels cooler as your body temperature begins to rise. Even if you put on more clothes (adding warmth), you may begin to shiver. This causes your muscles to contract, producing more heat. Before you know it, you have a fever.

Once again, a double whammy—you shiver because you're cold but the shivers cause a fever which makes you feel sick. Like we said, first you're cold, then you're hot, then you need to get cool again.

Actually, a fever is your body's way of protecting itself. Fevers are good things—in a way. A natural defense mechanism.

When the infection goes away (with antibiotics), your body no longer needs as much heat. You may hear the expression, "Your fever is breaking." You begin to sweat, so you have to take off all the extra covers and clothes in order to cool off. Hot—cold.

Treating The Fever

- Your doctor may recommend you take acetaminophen (Tylenol). This will not cure the infection but it will take care of some of the uncomfortable symptoms: fever, body aches, etc. Don't take Tylenol or any other drugs without your medical team's knowledge. Drugs can mask a fever and keep you from getting treatment for the infection that caused the fever in the first place.

- ***Don't take aspirin or ibuprofen*** (Motrin, Advil). These may promote bleeding, which is not good if your platelets are low.

- If you are chilly or shaking, stay warm. Cover up with blankets. You could also try a heating pad.

- If you get too hot, cover yourself with a light sheet. Have someone (your trusted caregiver) place cool washcloths on your forehead.

- Drink plenty of fluids. Your body uses lots of fluids during a fever, so keep drinking.

To Help Prevent Infections

- Avoid other people who are sick—even with a cold. Don't take any chances.

- Wash your hands often, especially after going to the bathroom, before eating, or if you've been in a public place where there might be germs on door handles, railings, etc.

- Tell others to wash their hands carefully before coming in contact with you.

- Be careful not to get any cuts or scrapes. Bacteria can enter an open wound very easily. If you do get cut, wash it well with soap and water and cover the area with a bandage. Use lotions and moisturizers to prevent drying, chapping, and cracking.

- Have good oral hygiene: brush your teeth often, replace your toothbrush at least every three months or after a mouth infection, visit the dentist when your counts are normal.

- Be careful what you eat. Make sure your food has been prepared properly.

- Make sure you use sterile procedures when changing your central line dressing and when flushing your lines. This is a common source of infection.

- Avoid large, indoor crowds when your counts are low. As an example, if you go to a movie, see an afternoon matinee when the crowds are smaller. Large rock concerts where people are piled on top of each other—not a good idea for lots of reasons.

Shaking Chills

Shaking chills are just what they sound like—literally shaking because you are very cold.

Managing Side Effects Of Cancer Treatments

What Causes Shaking Chills Or Rigors?

The shaking chills are sometimes referred to as rigors. They are kind of like shivering when you have an infection and fever, but much more intense. Teens usually get shaking chills from very bad infections, some drugs, and sometimes during blood transfusions.

If you read the section on fever, you will learn what causes your body to have a fever. Essentially, when your body senses a foreign substance—germs, drugs, someone else's blood—it responds by increasing your body temperature, so it can fight off the perceived intruder.

When your body temperature rises, the surface air feels cold and you begin to shiver. Sometimes the shivers are very intense and become shaking chills or rigors.

One common anti-fungal medicine that often causes rigors is amphotericin. If this happens to you, your medical team may be able to switch you to a different type of amphotericin called liposomal amphotericin.

You may also have the shaking chills when getting a blood transfusion. Even though the white blood cells (which often cause a reaction) have been filtered out of donated blood, a few remaining cells may cause you to have this reaction.

Many teens describe this as one of the most frightening side effects of treatment. If you have this reaction, you will start feeling very cold. Soon, despite all efforts to get warm, you may begin shaking uncontrollably. The first time it happens you may think you are having some kind of seizure. This can be very scary.

After a while, the chills and shaking will subside and you will feel very warm. Off come the blankets and heating pads and out come the cool washcloths. Read more about this in the fever section.

What Should I Do?

- The first thing you need to do is let someone know what is happening. Your nurse will assure you that it will soon pass and is not serious.

- Next, try to relax. The experience will be less jarring if you're not all tensed up. Try to breathe deeply and focus on it passing—it will, trust us.

- Then, you need to get warm. Have someone pile on the blankets, especially around your arms and legs. Heating pads also work well. Some teens say it helps if another person holds them very close to absorb some of the shaking.

- When the chills stop, you may be really, really hot. Remove the heating pads and ask someone to put cool washcloths on your forehead and neck.

- If you have the shaking chills, record all the details in your journal or notebook: *when did it happen, what were you taking, how long did it last, what helped you feel better.* Keeping good notes like this will help your medical team find ways to prevent it from happening again.

- There are often medications that can be given before transfusions and certain drugs to help prevent the shaking chills or rigors.

Chapter 32

Long-Term Side Effects Of Childhood Cancer Therapy

Years ago, doctors didn't know how to treat kids with cancer, and a lot of kids died. Now, doctors know more about treating kids with cancer, so more are surviving. But, doctors are finding out that when kids who have treatment (like surgery, chemotherapy or radiation therapy) for cancer get older, some of them can have new problems from the cancer or the treatments. These problems are called late effects. Kids who survive cancer have to watch out for late effects for the rest of their lives. Doctors are trying to figure out why people have late effects so, in the future, cancer survivors won't have to worry about them.

Having cancer does not mean that you will definitely have late effects when you get older. Late effects can depend on:

- the type of cancer you had
- how old you were when you were diagnosed and treated
- the type of treatment you received

About This Chapter: The information in this chapter is reprinted from "Late Effects of Childhood Cancer" with permission from CancerSource. For additional information on childhood cancer and other cancers, visit the CancerSource website at www.cancersource.com. © 2003 CancerSource. All Rights Reserved.

♣ It's A Fact!!
Early Cancer Therapy And Heart Problems

Numerous studies have indicated that children who receive certain chemotherapy drugs and chest-radiation treatments for cancer face a heightened risk of heart disease later in life. In a new study, researchers report that cardiovascular symptoms show up as early as 10 years after treatment.

Steven Lipshultz of the University of Rochester in New York and his colleagues documented the risk by examining 176 young-adult cancer survivors and 64 of their siblings who never had cancer. The former patients had been treated for leukemia, lymphoma, or another cancer an average of 15 years before the study.

Compared with their siblings, the cancer survivors had more signs of atherosclerosis, the accumulation of fatty plaques in arteries that underpins heart disease. The former patients also had significantly greater weakening of the heart muscle, a higher pulse rate, and higher blood concentrations of a compound called homocysteine that's linked with heart disease. They also were less physically active.

These differences were present even though most people in both groups were outwardly healthy and less than 21 years old—an age when doctors would expect to see few signs of heart disease, Lipshultz says. The indicators suggest the cancer survivors had heart damage and were working harder to maintain circulation, Lipshultz says.

The treatments received by the cancer patients included radiation to the chest and chemotherapy with drugs called anthracyclines. Previous research indicated that such treatments cause chronic inflammation that can damage heart cells, notes Melissa Hudson of St. Jude Children's Research Hospital in Memphis, Tenn.

Hudson says doctors today are better shielding children's hearts from radiation and giving them lower doses of anthracyclines than when the children in Lipshultz' study received treatment.

Source: Republished with permission of SCI Service, Inc. from *Science News*, Volume 163, Number 25. Copyright © 2003 SCI Service, Inc.; permission via Copyright Clearance Center.

Long-Term Side Effects Of Childhood Cancer Therapy

Common Late Effects

There are some common late effects for kids who survive cancer. Some kids may have just one late-term effect, while others may have many. Some kids don't have any late effects. As a cancer survivor, you should see a doctor every year for a check-up. This way, your doctor can watch you to make sure you don't develop any late effects. Talk to your doctor about the type of cancer and the treatments you had. You can ask your doctor about your risks of getting late effects.

Heart Problems

Certain types of chemotherapy and radiation can cause heart problems in childhood cancer survivors. If your doctor says that you may be at risk for heart problems, you will have to have your heart checked regularly. Your doctor may also tell you that you cannot lift weights.

Second Cancers

It's scary to think about, but some people get another cancer after their first cancer is cured. Developing a second cancer is rare, but it can happen. You could get a second cancer from the treatment you received to cure your first cancer. Also, cancer runs in some families. And, if you do things that would increase your risk of getting cancer, such as smoking, you could also develop a second cancer.

Hormone Problems

The body makes hormones to control certain functions. For example, the ovaries produce the hormone estrogen. Estrogen, along with other hormones, controls a woman's menstrual cycle. Certain types of cancer and cancer treatments can affect hormones, sometimes causing late effects. Here are some examples.

- **Growth problems.** Certain types of surgery and radiation can affect growth hormones. During treatment, you may stop growing or you may grow slowly. Many kids grow after treatment ends, but some don't, or they grow slowly.

- **Puberty problems.** Certain hormones control puberty. Some cancer treatments can cause puberty to start early or to begin late. Puberty is when your sexual organs begin to work. This means that you can have children. Girls usually start puberty at age 13. This is when they get their period, their breasts grow, and hair grows under their arms and on their vagina. Boys usually start puberty at age 14. This is when their testicles and penises grow, and hair grows under their arms, on their face, and on their testicles.

- **Sexual organ problems.** Cancer treatments can also damage the male and the female reproductive hormones and organs. In males, the testes produce the hormone testosterone. In females, the ovaries produce the hormone estrogen. Problems with your testes or ovaries can depend on how old you were when you began your cancer treatment. You may have problems having sex or having children. For girls, this may mean experiencing hot flashes, lack of interest in sex, or not having a regular period or any at all.

Fertility Problems

Some types of radiation and chemotherapy can cause fertility problems. Many childhood cancer survivors can have children, but some cannot. Others have trouble getting pregnant. But, some people who are told that they cannot have children still can. If you have sex, practice safer sex.

Not being able to have children is very upsetting for many people. Your doctor may suggest that you talk to a counselor about how you feel. If you cannot have children, later in life you may decide that you'd like to try other ways of having children, such as adopting. Or, you may decide to see a doctor called a fertility specialist. He or she can tell you about other ways to have children.

You may also worry that if you have children they will not be healthy. Most childhood cancer survivors have healthy children. However, some cancers run in families. You can get genetic testing to find out if you have a type of cancer that runs in families.

Learning Disabilities

Some childhood cancer survivors have trouble learning. If you have trouble learning, it may be because of the type of cancer you had or the treatments

Long-Term Side Effects Of Childhood Cancer Therapy

you received. For example, brain tumors and many treatments for brain tumors can cause learning and memory problems.

If you are having problems learning in school, tell your parents or teacher. You may need to have some tests to check your brain and how it's working. You may feel frustrated that you cannot keep up with the other kids. Or, you may feel dumb. You're not dumb. You can still go to school and go on to college. You just may need some extra help in school or you may need to learn in a different way than you previously learned. You may need to do things differently than other students.

Other Late Effects

The examples above are common late effects. Other late effects that you could develop later in life include problems with your bones, teeth, muscles, hearing, sight, breathing, stomach, kidneys, bladder, blood, and bone marrow.

Emotional Problems

Some childhood cancer survivors have emotional problems after they've survived cancer. Some kids worry that cancer will come back. Or, they get scared thinking about going to their doctor's appointment for their yearly checkup. These kinds of worries are natural. But, if you worry too much, you may become depressed. Or, if you can't stop thinking about your cancer, you may have post-traumatic stress disorder. You can get help for these problems and get better.

Depression

Depression is a serious illness. If you are depressed, you may:

- focus on the bad things
- not enjoy life
- feel that life is not worth living
- feel that you are a burden
- feel that you don't deserve any help
- not have energy
- stay away from friends and family

If you are depressed, it may feel hard to get help. But you need help. Talk to your doctor, parent, teacher, or friend if you feel depressed. You may need counseling or medicine called an anti-depressant.

Post-Traumatic Stress Disorder

Some childhood cancer survivors develop post-traumatic stress disorder. This means that someone has seen a death or came close to death or a serious injury and is having a hard time adjusting. People used to think that only soldiers coming home from war had it. Sometimes people in abusive relationships, survivors of car accidents, and survivors of serious illnesses, such as cancer, have post-traumatic stress disorder. If you have this condition, it can feel like you are still fighting cancer every day. It can feel like you are reliving your illness and treatment. Or, if you had a friend from treatment die and you feel guilty for being alive, you may also have it. If you have post-traumatic stress disorder, you may:

- have dreams or flashbacks about your cancer or treatment
- feel very scared, angry, or upset if you are reminded of your illness or treatment
- not remember things
- avoid your loved ones and friends
- have trouble sleeping
- have trouble concentrating

If you think that you have post-traumatic stress disorder, it's important to talk about how you feel. You may need to go to counseling and take medicine. You may also need to learn new ways to cope with your feelings and how to relax.

It's important to talk to your doctor about late effects. He or she can tell you which problems you could be at risk for. Remember though, you may not develop any late effects. See your doctor every year for a check up. That way, if you do get a late-term effect, your doctor may be able to catch it early and treat it. And, remember that if you feel worried or depressed, you should talk to someone. Living with cancer was very hard. Sometimes surviving it can be hard too. There is help.

Part 4

Coping Strategies For Adolescents With Cancer

Chapter 33

School And Cancer: Advice On Staying Current, Getting In The Swing, And Finding Help If You Need It

School—

"I can't ever go back there. How can I go to school looking like this? It would be just too weird to go in a wheelchair."

On the other hand:

"I really miss my friends. It will be great to feel "normal" again. I can't believe I actually miss school."

If you've been out of school during treatment, you might be nervous about going back. Who wouldn't be after all you've been through? These thoughts from kids like you might help.

> About This Chapter: The information in this chapter is reprinted from "Dealing with Others: Back To School" with permission from Teens Living with Cancer, a co-sponsored project of the Melissa's Living Legacy Foundation and The Children's Oncology Group. © 2003. All rights reserved. The Melissa's Living Legacy Foundation is a non-profit organization providing resources to help teens with cancer have meaningful, life-affirming experiences throughout all stages of their disease. The Children's Oncology Group is a National Cancer Institute-supported clinical trials cooperative group devoted exclusively to childhood and adolescent cancer research. For additional information, visit www.teenslivingwithcancer.org.

People Change

First, understand that "normal" will never be normal again. Don't expect things to be the same because they won't. They can't. You're different and you'll never be the same as you were before cancer. You have to **create a "new" normal**. This might apply to your relationships at school.

Your friends have not had the same experiences as you (thankfully!) and they may have a tough time dealing with your illness. You may lose some of your old "friends" but your true friends will hang in there with you.

Tory, diagnosed with aplastic anemia, said this about returning to high school:

"I was terrified and constantly wondering if people were going to laugh or even reject me for the way I looked. Before I left for school, my father gave me a bit of advice that has stuck with me since. He said, "Throughout your life, you will come to realize that you'll be able to count your true friends with one hand. So, today at school you'll see who's who."

"He was right. People who I had thought were my friends looked at me as if I were a creature from Mars. When all was said and done, however, the few people who spoke to me were and still are my true friends. Every one of them told me it doesn't matter what's on the outside; it's what's on the inside that counts."

> **☞ Remember!!**
>
> Even with a diagnosis of cancer, you still have the same needs as other young people going to school, having friends, and enjoying things that were a part of life before cancer. You can help meet these needs by living as normal a life as possible. Some activities, however, may need to be changed at different times during treatment. After chemotherapy or radiation therapy, you may be very tired and, therefore, need more rest. This tiredness is to be expected. You can find other things to do, such as new hobbies, or ask friends to come over to draw or paint.
>
> Source: Adapted and excerpted from "Life Goes On," *Young People With Cancer: A Handbook for Parents*, January 2001, pages 78–81. Full text is available online at http://www.cancer.gov/cancerinfo/youngpeople.

If you don't have expectations that things will be the "same," it will be easier for you and your friends to deal with things being different.

Life Goes On

Cancer is just one part of your life—a big part, granted—but still just one piece of who you are. You are much more than your cancer.

All the old stuff you used to care about before the big "C"—friends, planning for college or a job, extra-curricular activities—may still be important now. Life goes on, right?

When Jenn, 16, went back to school after treatment for AML (acute myeloid or myelogenous leukemia), she didn't wear anything on her bald head because it wasn't comfortable. She started cheerleading again and simply said,

"People just had to get used to seeing me look different. I was the same old Jenn. I just had a new look."

If your treatment causes you to be in and out of school, try to stay connected, so when you return, you'll know **"who's doing what."**

As Jenn recalls,

"Catching up on the school gossip was hard."

Don't let cancer rule your life. Remember, you are a TLC—a teen living with cancer.

Asking For Help Is OK

Everyone will want to help but might not know how. They might be afraid to offer help because they don't want you to think they are pitying you.

Erin, 15, with non-Hodgkin's lymphoma, told us,

"There is a difference between caring and pity. I hate it when people pity me. I just want them to care."

What's the difference, we asked? Erin answered,

✔ **Quick Tip**

School And Friends

Stay in touch with friends. Keeping contact is easier if you can continue to go to school while being diagnosed and treated, but staying in school is not always possible. If time off from school is needed, it is best for you to return to school as soon as possible. Teens who have cancer need and like to be with others their age, and keeping up with schoolwork makes them feel good about themselves. Some cancer centers offer back-to-school programs, which may help teens and classmates understand the diagnosis and know what to expect. You may ask your doctor, nurse, or child-life specialist to visit your classroom.

Teens often worry about how their friends and classmates will act toward them, especially if they have missed a lot of school or return with obvious physical changes, such as hair loss or a missing limb. Other students are usually accepting, but they may have questions. Try to think of ways to answer their questions and to tell friends and classmates that they cannot "catch" the disease. Your treatment team has had experience helping families with school. Ask them to help you. Ask your nurse if the team or hospital has a school reentry program. Such programs send nurses to the classroom to talk about the your cancer and treatment with classmates and teachers.

You need to know that many people, including other teens, are uneasy about a serious illness. These people may act differently or say hurtful or wrong things to someone who has cancer.

You may want to talk with your teachers and school nurse about the disease, treatment, days missed, and any needed changes in activity. You and your family, the doctor, or members of the treatment team can explain your medical condition and answer questions. Teachers and other school staff may want to use this information to talk with the other students about what to expect when you return to school.

If you cannot return to school right away, a home tutor may be available through the school system to help you keep up with studies, making it easier to return to school.

Source: Adapted and excerpted from "Life Goes On," *Young People With Cancer: A Handbook for Parents*, January 2001, pages 78–81. Full text is available online at http://www.cancer.gov/cancerinfo/youngpeople.

"Caring is treating you as "you", not as someone with cancer. That's pity."

Be straight with your friends about what you need and what you don't. Tell them how they can help—don't accept their pity.

Ask for extra help in your classes and take advantage of tutoring, if it is available. Jenn, 16, said,

"It was hard to catch up with school work. My teachers were very understanding and willing to work with me so that was good and a big help."

Remember, you don't have to go through this alone. Your friends and teachers want to help. Don't be too proud to ask.

Tell Your Teachers What To Expect

Either you or someone from your medical team can talk with your teachers and guidance counselors about what to expect when you return to school. Some hospitals have educational liaisons who help coordinate the transition.

♣ **It's A Fact!!**
Support For You

You are likely to feel uncertain, worried, and afraid at times, but you may find it hard to talk about these fears and may behave differently than usual. For example, you may become loud or bossy, be quieter than usual, have nightmares, have changes in eating habits, not do as well in school, or go back to earlier behaviors.

These common behavior changes are just a few of the ones you may see. You may want to talk about such changes with the doctor, nurse, social worker, teachers, and school counselor, who have helped others who have had experiences like yours.

Source: Adapted and excerpted from "Life Goes On," *Young People With Cancer: A Handbook for Parents,"* January 2001, pages 78–81. Full text is available online at http://www.cancer.gov/cancerinfo/youngpeople.

Your teachers might be able to prepare your classmates so they won't be so shocked.

Erin told her teachers,

"Just tell everyone at the same time what's going on, so everybody knows."

This made it easier for her during treatment and when she returned.

Matt is 13 and recovering from a bone marrow transplant. Because of really bad pancreatitis that kept him in bed for months, he needed to learn to walk all over again.

☞ Remember!!

Teenagers who have cancer have special concerns. They frequently complain that their parents try to protect them too much. Teenagers are at a stage in their lives when they are naturally trying to be their own bosses and do things for themselves, but having cancer forces them to depend on their parents again. Giving teenagers a chance to make their own decisions and choices, when possible, will help.

Although it may not seem like it, your parents' setting limits for behavior and activities is still important and can even be comforting. But it is helpful for them to remember that teens, like adults, have good days and bad days. Ask them to help you feel part of normal life:

- Allow you to make choices as long as they do not cause problems with treatment.
- Use the same rules and level of discipline as before the cancer diagnosis and treatment.
- Ask you to continue doing regular chores around the house, when able.

Source: Adapted and excerpted from "Life Goes On," *Young People With Cancer: A Handbook for Parents*, January 2001, pages 78–81. Full text is available online at http://www.cancer.gov/cancerinfo/youngpeople.

> *"I had a real rough first day of school. I had to use a wheelchair for about three months. I bet some kids wondered why I needed it because I could get up to my desk by myself. But I would never have made it to class on time without it. Even when I was late, they gave me some slack."*

Talk Openly About Your Disease

Most people's natural tendency is to ignore things they either don't understand or are uncomfortable with (read about "The Elephant in the Room," at www.teenslivingwithcancer.org). If you talk openly about your disease, it will make it easier for everyone.

Jenn says,

> *"When I went back to school it was very overwhelming at first. But seeing my friends and talking to them made it a lot easier."*

Often when things are not talked about openly and everything is hush-hush, rumors sometimes get started.

Diane, 17 with Hodgkin's disease, told us that when she returned to school after a long absence,

> *"Some people thought I had been pregnant!"*

She immediately set them straight about that little piece of gossip.

Know Yourself

You might feel ready to jump right back into the swing of things. Don't be surprised if it's not that easy. Some teens find school more difficult—tougher to concentrate, harder to grasp new concepts. Your treatment might have caused some short or long-term learning problems. You might have to work harder than you did in the past to achieve your goals. Maybe your goals will change. That's OK. Just know who you are and what you want. The rest will follow.

Because of your experience with cancer, your motivation to excel in school might be greater. Some kids say that after cancer, life becomes more meaningful and goals come into sharper focus. You may feel new energy at school that will drive you to do incredible things with your life. Others around you will feel that positive energy and will strive to live their lives as fully as you are living yours.

And that's pretty cool, don't you think?

Chapter 34

Counseling For Psychological Issues: Depression, Anxiety, And Post-Traumatic Stress

Psychological Issues

After you have been in treatment for cancer, it is common to experience a wide range of emotions. You may feel relief, anxiety, confusion, fear, anger, and even depression. These feelings may be mild or very strong and may change daily. You can, however, take comfort in the knowledge that, with time, these emotions should subside. You have faced fear and have gained strength, courage, and confidence. This should reassure you that you can handle whatever may come along.

Studies show that cancer survivors are more prepared to adapt to life stresses and seem to be quite resilient.[1] However, it is not uncommon for depression, anxiety and fear, or post-traumatic stress to effect their lives at some point. The following information identifies some feelings or psychological-related symptoms that you may experience and provides suggestions on how you can deal with them. Some of these may be normal, passing experiences,

---

About This Chapter: Excerpted with permission from *The Mountain You Have Climbed: A Young Adult's Guide to Childhood Cancer Survivorship*, © 2003 National Children's Cancer Society, Inc. For information about obtaining a copy of this publication, visit www.children-cancer.com.

others may compromise your life to some extent, while still others may be debilitating or dangerous.

Depression

Disappointment, fatigue, and loneliness are all typical reactions to the crises you have faced. Although sadness may be a common experience for cancer survivors, it is important to know the difference between "normal" levels of sadness and depression. Symptoms of depression include:

- loss of pleasure and interest in most activities;
- changes in eating and sleeping habits;
- nervousness or sluggishness;
- tiredness;
- feelings of worthlessness;
- poor concentration;
- difficulty sleeping or sleeping too much.

You may experience these symptoms now and then, in the years that follow your cancer care, but they should lessen with time. If you find that after a while you are still having difficulty with these symptoms, you may want to contact a professional counselor to talk about how you are feeling. You may want to seek help if symptoms are interfering with social relationships or work performance.

Post-Traumatic Stress Disorder

Cancer patients often undergo repeated and lengthy stays in hospitals and endure painful procedures that may cause fatigue, weakness, and nausea. These experiences may lead to a sense of helplessness. Evidence suggests that they may also lead to an increased risk of post-traumatic stress disorder (PTSD).[2] Symptoms of PTSD include:

- recurring and distressing dreams or recollections about the event;
- avoidance of thoughts, feelings, or conversations associated with the event;

Counseling For Psychological Issues

- inability to recall important aspects of the trauma;
- feelings of detachment from others;
- sleep disturbances;
- irritability or outbursts of anger;
- difficulty concentrating.

If you feel that you are experiencing symptoms of PTSD, you may want to contact a professional counselor or your hospital social worker. For a list of specialists and support groups in your area contact the American Psychological Association (1-800-964-2000).

Anxiety

Cancer survivors may assume that all their anxieties will stop once treatment is completed. Many survivors, however, become even more anxious once treatment ends.[3] There may be many reasons for feeling anxious. For example, your medical team is not following your progress as closely and professionals and friends may not be as available to you. You may also be anxious about cancer reoccurring. Whatever the source of your anxiety, know that it is common and there are things that you can do to feel less anxious. Here are some suggestions to help you reduce your anxiety:[4]

- avoid stimulants like caffeine or decongestants;
- talk about your concerns;
- learn some relaxation techniques;
- get enough sleep;
- exercise regularly;
- learn to pace yourself and set priorities;
- make time to do activities you enjoy;
- join a support group or talk with a friend, counselor, or clergy member.

Fear of recurrence is an understandable source of anxiety for cancer survivors. It is a very real and intense fear for many. Although this reaction is common, it is extremely important that you not allow it to get in the way of your efforts to live a happy and healthy life. You can take steps to cope with fears of recurrence:[5]

- find out about your actual risk of recurrence;
- seek information on how to reduce your chance of recurrence;
- be willing to have potential problems evaluated;
- talk about your fears with others.

Ways To Obtain Emotional Support

You can improve and maintain good emotional balance by taking advantage of these steps, as needed:

- Join a cancer survivors group. Ask your doctor, nurse, or social worker about programs at your local hospital or in your community.
- Consider talking with a psychologist, nurse therapist, clinical social worker, psychiatrist, minister or member of the clergy.
- Talk with your family and friends. Help them to understand how they can help you.
- Support yourself. Draw on your own strength. Read books by other cancer survivors.
- Reach out to others. Helping others not only lessens your isolation but also provides opportunities for you to discuss your feelings which can help you feel stronger and more in control.

References

1. Barakat, Kazak, Meadows, Casey, Meeske, and Stuber, 1997.
2. Kazak, et al., 1997.
3. Schlessel-Harpham, 1994.
4. Schlessel-Harpham, 1994.
5. Schlessel-Harpham, 1994.

Chapter 35

Coping With Cancer's Affect On Appearance

Mirror Mirror On The Wall

"Mirror, mirror on the wall, who's the fairest of them all?"

"Are you kidding? I covered the mirror with a towel the whole time I was in the hospital. I couldn't stand to look at myself."—A teen with cancer

Hair Loss

Quick—what's the first image that comes to your mind when you think of someone with cancer? No hair, bald as a bowling ball, right? That might be cute for little four-year-olds, but not so cute for you.

Losing your hair stinks—there's no better way to say it. At the risk of being politically incorrect and perhaps even sexist, it's often more difficult for girls than guys. Blame it on societal norms and expectations.

> About This Chapter: The information in this chapter is reprinted from "Mirror Mirror on the Wall" and "Dealing With Others: People Who Stare" with permission from Teens Living with Cancer, a co-sponsored project of the Melissa's Living Legacy Foundation and The Children's Oncology Group. © 2003. All rights reserved. The Melissa's Living Legacy Foundation is a non-profit organization providing resources to help teens with cancer have meaningful, life-affirming experiences throughout all stages of their disease. The Children's Oncology Group is a National Cancer Institute-supported clinical trials cooperative group devoted exclusively to childhood and adolescent cancer research. For additional information, visit www.teenslivingwithcancer.org.

Will I Really Lose My Hair?

Maybe yes, maybe no—it depends on your treatment plan. Most, but not all, chemotherapy drugs cause hair loss (alopecia is the medical term). Radiation generally causes hair loss on the part of the body that's being treated.

Your hair cells, like cancer cells, are fast-growing and divide rapidly. That's why chemotherapy affects them. One positive spin is that cancer cells are also being obliterated when your hair falls out.

In most cases, hair loss starts about two weeks after treatment begins. For most teens, it will begin to grow back about six weeks after treatment stops. In very, very rare cases, your hair may not grow back as fully as before or at all. (But don't worry about that possibility now.)

Here's something you might not have thought about. You have hair on other parts of your body besides your head. It too will probably fall out. This includes your eyebrows, eyelashes, hair on your arms and legs (girls—at least you won't have to shave), underarms, and pubic hair. The hair on your head will fall out quicker but the rest will probably follow.

✎ Weird Word
Alopecia: The loss of one's hair.

Getting Ready

Start by visualizing yourself bald. No sense pretending it won't happen. Learn to love and accept yourself bald—it's a new look for a little while. If you are comfortable with it—so will everyone around you.

Think about what, if anything, you might want to wear on your head: wigs, baseball hats, scarves, turbans, cool caps, your dad's toupee. Go shopping with friends and try on every hat in the store. Every person is different—find your own unique style.

Many teens find it helpful to cut their hair short before it falls out. Not only does this save you from finding huge clumps of hair on your pillow, it will also psychologically prepare you for the change.

Coping With Cancer's Affect On Appearance

Some teens dye their hair just for fun. Think of all the possibilities.

Bad Hair Day?

If you're like most teens, you'll be on constant watch for telltale signs.

About two weeks after treatment begins, you will start noticing hairs on your pillow. When you brush or comb your hair, you may notice a few loose strands. In the shower, you might feel your hair becoming a little thinner or see hair on the shower floor.

Things can get kind of messy at this point—hair falling in your cereal and getting in your eyes. A real nuisance. Your head might be itchy and when you scratch it, chunks of hair come out.

This is a good time to consider the next step. Cut or buzz your hair even shorter. Have a Shaving Party with family and friends.

Here's what Diane, 16 with non-Hodgkin's, suggests:

- Pick a date when you and your family can all be home together.
- Have scissors and clippers from a hair salon.
- Call friends that you'd like to invite.
- Order pizza and food.
- Turn on the music and start cutting.
- Try different hairstyles—like a Mohawk, or a shaved head with bangs.

Maybe your friends will want to shave their heads too, to show their support.

OK—Now What?

Even after you've shaved your head, there might still be prickly stubble left behind. Your head may be very sensitive at this point and just laying on a pillow may be uncomfortable. You can help the process by gently massaging your scalp with lotions (rosemary oil smells wonderful). One teen and her mom used "Nair" hair remover to get the last little bit of hair off.

Now, you have to decide—to cover up or not. Make your decision based on comfort, style, and warmth (you'd be surprised how cold it gets with no hair). You might choose different options for different occasions.

Some teens get very creative and decorate their shiny heads with designs. How about the school logo for pep rallies? Just remember to use a mild soap or shampoo on your head. It's very tender.

And if you go out in the sun, be sure to use sunscreen. Sunburn is not a good idea.

And Finally

You may be bald but you are still you.

Keep your sense of humor like one teen, who after losing all her hair, stuck her head out the car window and laughed, *"Oh, how I love the feel of the wind blowing through my hair!"*

This is just temporary. About six weeks after your treatment ends, you will begin to feel your hair beginning to grow again.

Like Melissa, 17, wrote in her journal, *"There is no better feeling than to be able to run your hands through your hair and lather it up in the shower when it grows back."*

Don't be surprised if your hair comes back different. Sometimes it's curly or even a slightly different color. You never know.

Skin Problems

Your skin is dry as a lizard's. Your fingernails are disintegrating. Your skin is turning different colors. *And your friends think a few pimples are a big deal!*

Don't be surprised if your treatment causes some temporary changes to your skin and nails. The good news is that they won't last forever and in the big scheme of things, this is one of the easier things to deal with.

Why Is My Skin Affected?

Chemotherapy destroys "rapidly dividing cells" and your skin cells are innocent by-standers randomly affected by the chemo drugs. You may have

Coping With Cancer's Affect On Appearance

dryness, redness, itching or slight skin color changes (slightly darker along the veins used for chemo).

Radiation can also cause skin changes that can last for several weeks after treatment. Unlike chemo that tends to affect your skin overall, the effects of radiation are limited to the areas that were treated. Your skin in those areas may become dry, itchy, and red.

"Radiation recall" is a reaction that sometimes happens if you also have chemo. The area that received the radiation may turn red, blister, and peel. Make sure you tell your doctor or nurse about this.

If your skin starts to itch or you develop hives or a rash, you may be having an allergic reaction to a new drug. Tell someone immediately because there might be a different drug to use or a medication to help prevent the reaction in the future.

You might also notice changes to your nails. They may become darkened, yellow, brittle, or cracked. Again, these changes will probably be only temporary.

What Can I Do About It?

First, when buying skin care products—deodorant, razors, lotions, moisturizers, make-up, soap, shampoo, laundry detergent, etc.—try to find ones for "sensitive skin". Then, try these tips.

For very dry skin:

- Use a gentle soap (ask your nurse for recommendations).
- Use hypoallergenic products with no artificial colors or fragrances than can irritate your skin.
- Use a moisturizer daily. (Even though it feels a bit greasy, Eucerin Moisturizing Créme is great on rough elbows, heels, and the soles of your feet.) Apply moisturizer right after you bathe while your skin is still a little wet. It will help to hold in some of the moisture.
- Add baby oil to your bath water or squirt a little on a shower sponge.
- Drink lots of fluids to keep your skin hydrated.

- Avoid perfumes, after-shaves, or lotions that contain alcohol (very drying).
- Try to stay cool to avoid sweating and losing more moisture from your skin. *Steam baths and saunas are not a good idea.*

If your face breaks out:

- Keep your face clean and dry, washing frequently with a gentle cleanser.
- Use a fresh, clean towel to gently pat—not rub—your face dry.
- Ask your doc or nurse about using over-the-counter medicated creams. Most are very drying (astringents) and will make your skin even dryer.
- Keep your hands away from your face. This only causes more irritation and increases the chances of making your face dirty (*washing your hands often is a good idea for lots of reasons*).

For cracked, brittle, discolored nails:

- Ask your nurse about using nail-strengthening products. They may irritate your skin, so be careful.
- If you wear nail polish, don't use polish remover with alcohol. Buy an oil-based product.
- Keep your nails short. They will have less tendency to break and chip.
- Use a moisturizer around your cuticles to prevent tearing and bleeding (*tubes of lip balm work great for this*).

If your skin color changes:

- There are only two things to do: cover or camouflage. If the pigment change is really obvious, long sleeves will hide it.
- Some girls use make-up to blend the lighter and darker areas, making them less noticeable. Just be sure to use a hypoallergenic product.

> **❧ Weird Words**
>
> <u>Hypoallergenic</u>: Products made with as few allergens as possible so that allergic reactions are less likely to occur.
>
> <u>Radiation Recall</u>: A reaction that sometimes happens if you have chemotherapy at the same time you have radiation therapy. The area that received the radiation may turn red, blister, and peel.

Coping With Cancer's Affect On Appearance

Steroids

Let's be clear—*there are steroids…and then there are* **steroids**.

We're talking about the kind used in cancer treatment—synthetic derivatives of the natural steroid cortisol. We're not talking about the illegal, anabolic type that bodybuilders use. *Sorry, no chance of killer biceps from prednisone.*

Steroids have many purposes in cancer treatment:

- to control nausea and vomiting
- to kill cancer cells as chemotherapy
- to reduce allergic reactions (before platelet transfusions, as an example)
- to help headaches caused by brain tumors

Oh, Those Side Effects

Increased Appetite And Weight Gain: One of the most difficult side effects of steroids is weight gain. Don't be surprised if you are ravenously hungry—able **and** willing to eat anything in sight.

If you lost a lot of weight during chemo because of nausea, vomiting, mouth sores, diarrhea, etc., it may feel wonderful to eat again. You can use a few extra pounds. Your parents are probably thrilled to see you eating (what is it about parents and food?).

But some teens gain a lot of weight when on steroids and it can be distressing. It's not just the weight gain, but how your body fat gets redistributed that's troubling. You might look like a chipmunk storing nuts for the winter. Fullness in your cheeks or what is sometimes called *"moon face"* is one effect of steroids.

Another is the accumulation of fatty tissue at the back of your neck, creating a hump—sometimes referred to as a "buffalo hump".

But have no fear—this side effect will last only as long as you are taking steroids. This temporary treatment will **not** change your appearance forever. Once you have tapered off the steroids, your body will slowly start to resemble the "old you" again.

Emotional Ups And Downs: Another difficult-to-deal-with side effect is mood swings. Some days you will wonder if you have completely lost your mind—happy one minute, depressed the next. Your family and friends might hide for cover, fearing for their lives, when your *"Don't even look at me"* mood strikes.

The good news: this is one time you can verifiably blame it on "the drugs."

You might also have trouble sleeping (enough to make you irritable all by itself). Try taking your steroids early in the day to not disrupt your sleep patterns.

Hair Growth And Skin Problems: As long as we're talking about outwardly obvious side effects of steroids, there is one more—hair growth in places hair should not be growing. This is especially cruel for girls. You may experience hair growth on your face, usually along your cheekbone.

Trust us—it will go away.

In the meantime, trying to remove it may make it **more** noticeable. Shaving will only leave stubble, and hair removers may irritate your skin. Guys—this might be your best shot at a beard.

Steroids sometimes make your skin sort of thin, causing you to bruise more easily. And you might develop some acne on your face or other parts of your body.

Other Side Effects

These are less obvious, thankfully, but still need to be monitored:

- Increased blood pressure *(don't sweat the small stuff)*
- Increased risk of infection *(be careful around kids with chickenpox)*
- Stomach upsets *(take your steroids with food or a glass of milk)*

Steroids might also be responsible for these long-term side effects:

- Eye problems like cataracts and glaucoma
- Osteoporosis

When your treatment is over, your doctor will recommend a plan to gradually taper off the drugs. This is important—don't stop taking steroids cold turkey.

Coping With Cancer's Affect On Appearance

The Bottom Line

There's not much you can do to prevent the side effects of steroids. If they help you get well, it will seem a small price to pay in the long run. But it's still tough right now, we know.

Don't ever forget — you are still the "same old you" on the inside. That never changes.

To wax philosophical for a minute: Teens on our advisory board said they learned *"that you can't judge people by how they look."* When you look different yourself, you know how it feels to be judged by your appearance.

You will be much more compassionate and understanding of others as a result of this experience. This is a life lesson some people never learn. Maybe you're lucky, in a way.

Dealing With Others: People Who Stare

"His eyes nearly bugged out of his head!" Erin laughed, remembering how he looked.

Erin, 15, had just finished chemotherapy for AML (acute myeloid leukemia) when she and friends went to an amusement park that summer. Even with her fisherman style hat, it was still obvious that she had no hair.

She and her friends were waiting in line for the new roller coaster, reputed to be the scariest ride in the whole park. Next to her was a little boy—about six years old—just tall enough to be able to ride. He stared and stared at Erin's bald head, completely oblivious to the social graces (natural for a little kid).

Now, what would you have done? Become embarrassed and turned away? Try to explain why you had no hair? Just ignore him and get mad? Not Erin!

She looked him square in the eye. Without a trace of laughter to give her away, she pointed to her head and quietly warned, *"I've been on this ride before. This could happen to you, too."*

After the joke, Erin nicely explained to the little boy that she used to be sick and the medicines made her hair come out but that it would grow back soon. He was relieved.

Like Erin, you've probably all experienced people staring at you. Let's face it—having cancer often changes how you look. Hair loss and "steroid-cheeks." Scarring and amputation. Weight gain or loss. Maybe you limp or need a wheelchair or wear a hearing aid.

- Some people stare with that look of pity on their faces. *"Oh, you poor thing,"* you can just hear them saying.
- Others stare with judgment, *"Don't you know you shouldn't wear a hat inside?"*
- Others with ridicule, *"Man, what's wrong with him?"*

All types of staring are difficult. The best advice we can give is: "Don't take it personally." Except for little kids who are curious, people who stare are just rude or ignorant. They obviously never learned good manners. Accept that and hold your head high. Maybe one day they'll get it.

> **☞ Remember!!**
>
> Even with all the visible exterior changes your body is going through, inside you are still the same old you. *That will never change—no matter what.*

Chapter 36

Sexuality And Dating: Special Concerns For Teens With Cancer

Afraid To Ask?

Want straight answers to questions you're uncomfortable asking your parents or medical team? Want to talk openly about dating, sex, and life in general?

This chapter has one primary objective: to give you information to protect your physical and emotional well-being during these rough times. Answers will be medically sound and non-judgmental. The goal is to help you make the best decisions for yourself.

Many teens have questions about four major areas of concern. They are:

> About This Chapter: The information in this chapter is reprinted from "Afraid to Ask?" with permission from Teens Living with Cancer, a co-sponsored project of the Melissa's Living Legacy Foundation and The Children's Oncology Group. © 2003. All rights reserved. The Melissa's Living Legacy Foundation is a non-profit organization providing resources to help teens with cancer have meaningful, life-affirming experiences throughout all stages of their disease. The Children's Oncology Group is a National Cancer Institute-supported clinical trials cooperative group devoted exclusively to childhood and adolescent cancer research. For additional information, visit www.teenslivingwithcancer.org. Text on "Peer Relationships and Dating" excerpted with permission from *The Mountain You Have Climbed: A Young Adult's Guide to Childhood Cancer Survivorship*, © 2003 National Children's Cancer Society, Inc. For information about obtaining a copy of this publication, visit www.children-cancer.com.

- Sexuality
- Body Issues
- Relationships
- Reproduction

Sexuality

We know that many of you are sexually active or at least curious. You, like many other teens, may have important questions that you are hesitant to ask your parents or medical team. So, we asked them for you.

Question: How do you, the experts, handle the issue of teens being sexually active while in treatment?

First, we ask them if they are sexually active. If they say they're not, we say, "OK, but if you are, we need to discuss it because it's important to your care. No judgment. It's not up to me—it's your personal choice. But if you are sexually active, you need to do certain things to protect yourself."

Some kids will openly say that they are sexually active. You usually get better information when their parents aren't around. Sometimes kids going off to college will say they're not having sex yet. Our usual response is, "Well, someday you probably will be, so listen up."

They usually laugh—but they listen. Hormones are raging, you know?

Then, we educate them about the important ways they can protect themselves. One is birth control. We don't want girls getting pregnant. If girls are still ovulating, they could get pregnant. Some girls go on the pill for reasons other than birth control, but if they continue to menstruate on therapy and are sexually active, we would prescribe birth control pills.

We also advocate safe sex and use of condoms for guys to prevent sexually transmitted diseases (STDs). Another reason to use condoms is not to impregnate someone with sperm that's been affected by chemotherapy. We don't know what it would do to an unborn fetus. There could be congenital abnormalities, prematurity, and many other problems.

Sexuality And Dating

We advise them not to have sex when their blood counts are low for a couple of reasons. With low white counts (neutropenia), they are very susceptible to infection, and with a low platelet count, there's the risk of bleeding. Some kids ask about having anal sex. First, we tell them they probably won't feel like it. But if they're determined to have sex and given the choice, there's less risk of infection and bleeding with vaginal vs. anal intercourse.

We also remind them that there are lots of other ways to express affection and be close. There's more to love than sex.

Body Issues

Question: Do I lose all my hair during chemo?

> **Weird Word**
> Neutropenia: Low white blood cell counts.

Most teens will lose all their body hair during chemotherapy, including pubic hair (considered cool by some), hair on their arms and legs, axillary (armpit) hair, and chest hair for boys. The good news is girls don't have to shave their legs and underarms. Lack of chest hair for guys is very "in" now.

A note of caution: For girls, when the hair on your legs and underarms starts coming back in, be very careful shaving if you are still neutropenic. The slightest cut could cause a serious infection. You might use a hair remover like "Nair" instead of a razor or wait until your counts are normal again. For you guys, facial shaving presents the same risk.

Question: Can I get a tattoo or pierce my navel, or eyelid, or anything else when I'm getting chemo?

Well, you could, but there are risks. Even if your counts are good, you are still immunocompromised. Your immune system is not up to snuff, so we suggest you wait until after therapy. You never really know how sterile the procedure is, even in a reputable place. It's just not a good idea and not worth the risk. Just wait.

But if you absolutely must, make sure you go to a reputable place when your counts are high. That would mean just before your next course of chemotherapy. At least a couple of days before, so there is some time to heal before your counts drop again.

Relationships

Question: I'm concerned that my boy/girlfriend will be grossed out by my baldness, scars, or central line. What should I do?

Get a new boyfriend or girlfriend. You deserve it. Easy to say, but bald is beautiful. Most teens who lose their hair have great heads, and their facial features, especially their eyes, really stand out. They're beautiful.

One teen chose a medi-port (Port-a-Cath) implanted under the skin instead of an external catheter so it wouldn't show. This made the teen feel less self-conscious and her boyfriend was comfortable as well. But getting the best possible treatment should always be your first consideration.

About scarring: often teens are more conscious about their scars than are others. If your girlfriend or boyfriend can't see the real you beneath a scar, then who needs him or her? You can do much better.

Question: What if my boy/girl friend touches my central line? Should I "show and tell"?

Absolutely. If you are close enough that he or she would be checking out the central line in your chest, I would say be very honest and by all means "show and tell." Describe how it works and that it saves you from getting poked with needles. It's the way you get your chemotherapy. It's part of your treatment. And it's not forever. But be careful to keep it securely taped in place. You don't want it getting caught up in the activity.

Reproduction

Question: If I have sex with my boyfriend, can I still get pregnant even if I don't get my period any more?

Yes, you can although it's unlikely. If you've really stopped menstruating, you've probably also stopped ovulating. But it's completely unpredictable. You could happen to ovulate at that time, so the risk is not zero for pregnancy.

We strongly advise that you continue using birth control and condoms not only to prevent possible pregnancy but to prevent STDs (sexually transmitted

Sexuality And Dating

diseases). Safe sex is especially important when you are being treated for cancer.

Peer Relationships And Dating

As a survivor of childhood cancer, you have persevered medically and in many other ways. Socially, you may be concerned about forming new relationships outside your family. An experience with cancer is trying and absorbing. Treatment may have caused you to withdraw from many social activities. It is important, however, to form and maintain relationships with both friends and potential dating partners. You may be asking yourself when the proper time is to disclose information about your cancer to those with whom you have relationships. You may be concerned that your friends and potential dating partners will not understand or accept what you have experienced.

If you find it difficult to meet new people, or if social experiences seem overwhelming, rest assured that there are steps you can take to make yourself more comfortable. Try not to let fear of rejection prevent you from seeking new relationships or continuing to build and maintain existing relationships.

If you feel anxious, awkward, or shy socially, set small goals for yourself to make the task of meeting people easier. Here are some suggestions that may help you:

- Learn to smile or compliment one person each day. When you feel more comfortable, increase the communication.
- Join a community interest group, club, support group, recreational activity, or sport team.
- Consider volunteering.
- Look into classes that interest you.
- Build on relationships you already have. Friends offer great support and can also help you meet new people.

After meeting someone new, many cancer survivors wonder how long they should wait before disclosing information about their cancer. This will depend on your personality, the personality of your friend, and the level and type of relationship. Some cancer survivors wish to be completely open and up-front. Others may wait until they feel trust and friendship. Waiting too long to disclose information, however, may result in feelings of betrayal on the part of the person who learns of this medical history.

If you are nervous about discussing your cancer, try these techniques to make you feel more comfortable:

- Role-play with a family member, counselor, or trusted friend.
- Prepare ahead of time how you will express the things you want to share.
- Pick a place that is comfortable for you.
- Be honest about the risk of recurrence and long-term effects.
- Help your friend to understand the facts and to avoid confusion from cancer myths.
- Tell the other person that you are a survivor.

Discussing your feelings will allow your friend to ask questions and discuss any concerns.

☞ Remember!!

Many survivors fear rejection after talking about the fact they had cancer. If friends or partners have a problem with your past history of cancer, realize they may need more information or have something in their own past that concerns them. Even though it is difficult and disappointing to deal with rejection from a "friend" who is frightened of the fact that you are a cancer survivor, it is better to know this at an early point in a relationship, rather than later on.

Chapter 37

When Friends Don't Call: Coping With Isolation And Loneliness

Anyone who has been affected intimately by cancer knows that it can change the pattern of our relationships outside the family as well as those within. Friends react as they do to other difficult situations. Some handle it well; others are unable to maintain any association at all. Casual acquaintances, and even strangers, can cause unintended pain by asking thoughtless questions about visible scars, artificial devices, or other noticeable changes in appearance.

One or two people within your circle may be gratifying in their devotion and in the sensitivity they show toward your needs. One woman said her mother-in-law found one or two close friends with whom she felt truly relaxed. They were not startled when she laughed nor ill at ease when she cried. With others she maintained an outward calm.

"I have three really good friends with whom I can talk about my cancer," explained another. "I have talked about dying with my sister, and she does understand a lot more than I thought a person without cancer could."

> About This Chapter: Text in this chapter is excerpted and adapted from "Taking Time: Support for People with Cancer and the People Who Care About Them," National Cancer Institute (NCI), April 1999. Full text available online at http://cancer.gov/cancerinfo/takingtime.

When Friends Don't Call

Lost friendships are one of the real heartbreaks people with cancer face. Friends do not call for a variety of reasons. They might not know how to respond to a change in your appearance. They might be avoiding you in order to avoid facing the possibility of your death and the eventuality of their own. Their absence does not necessarily mean they no longer care about you. Still, it is little comfort to know that "out there" you have friends if they have so little confidence in their worth as companions that they would rather say nothing than risk saying the wrong thing.

If you believe discomfort rather than fear is keeping a particular friend from visiting, you might try a phone call to dissolve the barrier. Yet you cannot combat all the reasons why people avoid you; some still believe that cancer is contagious.

Knowing that others are ignorant does little to lessen the hurt and frustration of being needlessly isolated. You only can change the attitudes of others if you are among them. Examine carefully whether friends shun you or whether you have withdrawn from your usual social contacts to protect your own feelings. You can neither enlighten nor draw comfort from an empty room. If possible, the best place to be is out in the world with other people.

> ♣ **It's A Fact!!**
> - Some friends will deal well with your illness and provide gratifying support.
> - Some will be unable to cope with the possibility of death and will disappear from your life.
> - Most will want to help but may be uncomfortable and unsure of how to go about it.

Easing The Way For Others

Most people fall into a middle group, somewhere between the staunch friends and the "avoiders." They are groping for an approach to cancer with which they can be comfortable. These people may say things which sound inane, insincere, or hurtful. You have to keep reminding yourself that they are trying their best. If you are open about cancer, they may relax, too.

A perceptive high school student explained, "I guess what I'm trying to say boils down to this. One of these days people may not feel so uneasy around a disabled person. I'm not bitter with people; I'm really quite at ease with them and strive to make them feel at ease with me. They feel afraid of me, and consequently trip over their tongues. I have learned a lot by living in a disabled person's world and am quite willing to share it. One of these days, I may be given the chance."

A woman who had had extensive surgery for oral cancer explained how she tried to lessen the discomfort of others without causing discomfort for herself. She focused on her disability rather than its cause.

"I am determined to put people at ease, so when I speak on the telephone, or to someone for the first time, I immediately say, 'I have a speech defect, so please don't hesitate to tell me if you don't understand me.' I also carry a pencil and paper and offer to write what can't be understood. I find it much more frustrating to have people try to save my feelings by pretending to understand me when they don't."

A man we know startled his fishing buddies, who were paying a group visit to his hospital room. He positively threw open the door to honest communication when he boomed out, "You know, I've learned a lot about cancer since I became a member of the club."

We can't all be that direct. He had been a straight forward man all his life. But he had let his friends know that he preferred talking about his cancer to pussyfooting around it.

Helping Friends Help

Many times friends are waiting for some clue as to what behavior is appropriate. They might not be sure you want company. They might call to "see how things are going," then add as they hang up the phone, "Let me know if there's anything I can do to help."

These friends are asking for more than a job to do. They are asking for direction, giving you clues that they will not desert you if only they have some guidance on how to proceed. The next time friends or relatives offer assistance, try to look at the offer in that light. If you can think of one specific errand they can run, one chore they can take off your hands, you have done them and yourself a favor.

Most people are grateful if there is something concrete they can do to show their continuing friendship. If such tasks bring them into your home, it gives them a chance to see that you are still living and functioning—not a funeral waiting to happen. Their next visit might be easier, and then they may be able to stop by without a "reason."

Choosing to help friends in this way is no easy undertaking. When you feel stretched to breaking just keeping your own life going, it is difficult to extend your energies further to make others feel at ease. It can be a new and difficult experience for some, this reaching out, but the rewards can be exhilarating. We all feel better giving than receiving, so it might be easier if you think of your requests for assistance as letting others feel useful, rather than as petitions for help.

> ✔ **Quick Tip**
>
> Help your friends support you.
>
> - Ask yourself, "Have friends deserted me or have I withdrawn from them?"
> - Telephone those who don't call you.
>
> Ask for simple assistance—to run an errand, prepare a meal, or visit. These small acts bring friends back into contact and help them feel useful and needed.
>
> If you are alone, ask your physician, social worker or pastor to "match" you with another patient. Someone else needs friendships, too.
>
> Groups of other cancer patients can offer new friendships, understanding, support, and companionship.

Fighting Loneliness

Regardless of what you do, your friends might desert you. This is a special, awful loneliness. There are no easy answers, no pat solutions. The mutual support of other people with cancer might provide some solace and comfort. There probably are others in your community who need your companionship as much as you need theirs. A physician, social worker, visiting nurse, or member of the clergy should be able to help you contact another cancer patient or shut-in who could use company.

Chapter 38

What If The Cancer Comes Back?

Meeting The Challenge Again

In the back of every cancer patient's mind is the possibility that the disease may return. Yet if it does, most patients think, "How can this be happening to me again?"

The shock is back. The fears are back—of telling your family and friends, of more treatment, and possibly of death. The anger is there, too. You've been told you have cancer again. You may feel that after all you've been through, it should have been enough. And the unanswered question is, "Will the treatment work this time?"

Even though you may feel some of the same things you felt when you were first diagnosed, now there is a difference. You've been through this before. You've faced cancer and its treatment and the changes that came to your life. You know that medical care and emotional support are available to you. Facing cancer again is difficult, but it's a challenge you can handle.

As you read this, remember that there are more than 100 different types of cancer. Each is different, and each person responds to treatment differently.

> About This Chapter: Text in this chapter is excerpted and adapted from "When Cancer Recurs: Meeting the Challenge," National Cancer Institute (NCI), Revised, April 1997. Full text available online at http://cancer.gov/cancerinfo/when-cancer-recurs. Reviewed by David A. Cooke M.D. on January 24, 2004

One piece of information can't cover every situation for every person. For this reason, the information here is general, and some of it may not apply to you. Still, a lot of people have found ways to handle recurring cancer in similar ways, and their experiences may help you.

Many people who have faced the return of cancer will tell you that learning more about your illness and its treatment helps you take part in your care. Having a positive attitude toward treatment may help you control some of your emotional and physical reactions to it. Drawing on your own strengths and support from the people and resources around you can help you meet this challenge again. Many resources are available from the National Cancer Institute's Cancer Information Service (1-800-4-CANCER) or the American Cancer Society (www.cancer.org).

Why Cancer Can Recur

A cancer recurrence is the reappearance of disease that was thought to be cured or inactive (in remission). Cancer may recur after several weeks, several months, a few years, or many years.

Recurrent cancer starts from cancer cells that were not removed or destroyed by your original therapy. You may have had previous treatment that was meant to destroy the original cancer, as well as any cancer cells that may have moved to another part of your body. Sometimes, no matter what treatment is used, a small number of cancer cells survive, and it may take a while for them to grow into tumors that are large enough to be detected.

A cancer recurrence is not the same thing as a new cancer, even if it appears in a new place in your body. A recurrence has the same type of cancer cells as the original tumor—no matter where it is found. For example, if you had colon cancer and it recurs in your liver, it is not liver cancer; colon cancer cells have spread to the liver, and the disease is still colon cancer. (The spread of cancer cells to a new part of the body is called metastasis.) This point is important because there are different treatments for different types of cancer.

Although it's possible to develop a second, entirely new tumor that is not related to your original cancer, this situation is more unusual than a recurrence.

What If The Cancer Comes Back?

Where Cancer Can Recur

Not every cancer cell that breaks away from a tumor is able to grow elsewhere. Most are stopped by the body's natural defenses or destroyed by treatment. Cancers differ in their ability to recur and in the places where they are likely to show up.

Recurrent cancers are classified by location: local, regional, or distant.

- Local recurrence means that the cancer has come back in or very close to the same place as the original cancer. For instance, a woman who has had a mastectomy could later have a local recurrence of breast cancer in the area of her surgery. The term "local" also means that there is no sign of cancer in nearby lymph nodes or other tissues.

- A regional recurrence involves growth of a new tumor in lymph nodes or tissues near the original site but with no evidence of cancer at distant places in the body. A person who has had a melanoma removed from an arm, for instance, might have a regional recurrence in the lymph nodes under that arm.

- In distant recurrence, the original cancer has spread (metastasized) to organs or other tissues far from the site of origin. For example, a man who had prostate cancer could have a recurrence of that cancer in his bones. This man does not have bone cancer; he has prostate cancer that has spread to his bones.

♣ **It's A Fact!!**
Recurrent cancers are classified by location: local, regional, or distant.

Diagnosing Recurrent Cancer

Over the past several months or years, you may have had a number of tests and checkups. Most likely, your doctor told you to watch for changes in your body and to report any unusual symptoms. You may have noticed a weight change, bleeding, or pain (these changes don't always mean that you have cancer), or your doctor may have found signs of illness while examining you.

In either case, specific procedures and tests are used to find the exact cause of the problem and decide on the best treatment. These procedures and tests, which you may be familiar with from your original cancer, help your doctor answer these questions:

- Are the signs and symptoms caused by cancer or by some other medical problem?
- If cancer is present, is it a recurrence or is it a new type of cancer?
- Has the cancer spread to more than one place?

Because certain types of cancer tend to recur in certain parts of the body, your doctor is likely to check those places first. Information from physical exams and tests helps the doctor make an accurate diagnosis. If your cancer has recurred, an accurate diagnosis is the first step in determining the best course of treatment and getting the disease under control again.

> ♣ It's A Fact!!
>
> Your doctor may use one or more of the following to diagnose recurrent cancer:
>
> - physical exam
> - lab tests
> - imaging tests
> - biopsy

Physical Exams

In addition to your routine physical exam, which includes feeling for lumps and swelling, your doctor may need to look inside your colon, stomach, bladder, breathing passages, or other organs for recurrent cancer. Special instruments are used for viewing different parts of the body. The names of most of these instruments end in "scope." For example, a bronchoscope is used to view the air passages of a lung. In some cases, the doctor may even take a tissue sample (biopsy) through the scope and for viewing under a microscope.

Laboratory Tests

A number of laboratory tests are used to help diagnose recurrent cancer. For example, blood samples can be tested to check the levels of certain tumor marker, such as carcinoembryonic antigen (CEA), that may change when cancer recurs.

What If The Cancer Comes Back?

Other tests, such as the examination of a stool smear (fecal occult blood test), can detect internal bleeding that may be too slight for you to notice. If blood is found, a series of x-rays or another type of test is done to learn if the bleeding is caused by cancer or some other problem.

These are only a few examples of laboratory tests used to diagnose cancer and other health problems. Your doctor will select those that may be helpful in your case.

Imaging

To learn the location and size of suspected cancer, the doctor can use x-rays, computed tomography (CT) scans, magnetic resonance imaging (MRI), nuclear scanning, or ultrasonography. These tests are often done someplace other than your doctor's office.

These tests may use radiation, computers, magnets, and other sophisticated equipment. If you have questions about how they're used, their risks or benefits, or what you should expect during the procedure, be sure to talk with your doctor, nurse, or technician about your concerns. It may be possible for you to see the equipment and how the test will be done in advance. Most CT and MRI equipment requires you to be in a tight space, sometimes for an hour or more. It also may be noisy. If you feel extremely uncomfortable in small spaces, discuss this with your doctor before your test is scheduled. The CT or MRI technician also may have suggestions.

X-Ray. Tumors can often be seen with a standard x-ray. Other tests use x-rays and a barium solution, dye, or air to give sharp pictures of organs such as the stomach, kidney, and colon that cannot be seen clearly with x-rays alone. An example of this kind of test is the "lower GI series" (barium enema followed by an x-ray of the gastrointestinal tract). Barium is a white, chalky substance that outlines the colon and rectum on the x-ray.

CT Scan (also called *CAT scan*, for computed axial tomography). In a CT scan, x-rays are taken from many directions and combined into one cross-sectional picture with the aid of a computer. The CT scan gives more detailed pictures than standard x-rays for certain body parts and often is used for tissues such as the liver and brain. In some cases, a special dye is injected into a vein before the scan to improve the details of the pictures.

MRI. Instead of x-rays, MRI uses radio waves and a powerful magnet to create detailed pictures of areas inside the body. Like a CT scan, MRI uses a computer to combine many images into a single picture. That picture may include organs, muscles, blood vessels, and other parts of the body that are hard to see with other equipment. For MRI, you'll be asked to lie very still in a tunnel-like machine. Headphones are often available to help block the machine's rather loud clicking sounds.

Nuclear Scan. Nuclear scans often are used to see areas inside the body. A special substance is swallowed or injected into the bloodstream. It contains a

---

❧ Weird Words

Biofeedback: A method of learning to voluntarily control certain body functions such as heartbeat, blood pressure, and muscle tension with the help of a special machine. This method can help control pain.

Biological Therapy: Treatment to stimulate or restore the ability of the immune system to fight infections and other diseases. Also used to lessen side effects that may be caused by some cancer treatments. Also known as immunotherapy, biotherapy, or biological response modifier (BRM) therapy.

Cancer: A term for diseases in which abnormal cells divide without control. Cancer cells can invade nearby tissues and can spread through the bloodstream and lymphatic system to other parts of the body.

Clinical Trial: A type of research study that tests how well new medical treatments or other interventions work in people. Such studies test new methods of screening, prevention, diagnosis, or treatment of a disease. The study may be carried out in a clinic or other medical facility. Also called a clinical study.

Complementary and Alternative Medicine (CAM): Forms of treatment that are used in addition to (complementary) or instead of (alternative) standard treatments. These practices generally are not considered standard medical approaches. CAM may include dietary supplements, megadose vitamins, herbal preparations, special teas, acupuncture, massage therapy, magnet therapy, spiritual healing, and meditation.

What If The Cancer Comes Back?

small amount of radioactivity, similar to the amount used in a chest x-ray, so it can be seen inside the body. A machine called a scanner then takes pictures of the areas of the body where the substance shows up. In the pictures, a cancer can appear as an area of more or less radioactivity than the tissue around it.

Ultrasonography. In ultrasonography, a microphone-like device sends sound waves that bounce off internal organs, like the brain or lung. A computer converts the echoes made by the sound waves into pictures called sonograms. The pictures are shown on a monitor like a TV screen. Tissues of different densities look different in the picture because they reflect sound waves

---

Fecal Occult Blood Test: A test to check for blood in stool. (Fecal refers to stool; occult means hidden.)

Gastrointestinal Tract: The stomach and intestines.

Hormone Therapy: Treatment with hormones to replace or block other hormones. For certain conditions (such as diabetes or menopause), hormones are given to adjust low hormone levels. To slow or stop the growth of certain cancers (such as prostate and breast cancer), hormones may be given to block the body's natural hormones. Also called hormonal therapy, hormone treatment, or endocrine therapy.

Local Therapy: Treatment that affects cells in the tumor and the area close to it.

Recurrence: The return of cancer, at the same site as the original (primary) tumor or in another location, after the tumor had disappeared.

Remission: A decrease in or disappearance of signs and symptoms of cancer. In partial remission, some, but not all, signs and symptoms of cancer have disappeared. In complete remission, all signs and symptoms of cancer have disappeared, although cancer still may be in the body.

Surgery: A procedure to remove or repair a part of the body or to find out whether disease is present. An operation.

Systemic Therapy: Treatment using substances that travel through the bloodstream, reaching and affecting cells all over the body.

differently. For example, a sonogram can often show whether a breast lump is a fluid-filled cyst or a recurrent cancer.

Biopsy

Biopsy is the removal of a tissue sample so it can be examined under a microscope to establish a precise diagnosis. Although an abnormal area of the body may be seen on physical exam or imaging, a biopsy is the only way to tell for sure whether the tissue contains cancer cells.

For some suspected cancers, the doctor uses a needle to withdraw fluid (aspirate) or remove small tissue samples (needle biopsy). A surgical biopsy, done under local or general anesthesia, removes the entire tumor or a piece of it.

Treatment Methods

Many of the same factors that affected treatment decisions for your original cancer will be taken into account in planning treatment for recurrent cancer. Some of those factors include the type, size, and location of the cancer, your general health, and other treatments you've had.

Your doctor may recommend surgery, radiation, anticancer drugs (chemotherapy), or a combination of these treatments. For certain cancers, such as those in the breast or reproductive organs, the doctor may suggest hormone therapy. In other cases, biological therapy may be considered.

> ♣ **It's A Fact!!**
>
> Treatment plans can include any of these:
>
> - surgery
> - radiation therapy
> - chemotherapy
> - hormone (or endocrine) therapy
> - biological therapy (also known as immunotherapy or biotherapy)
> - bone marrow transplant
> - supportive therapy
> - nutritional support
> - pain management

Before you and your doctor agree on a treatment plan, you should understand why one treatment is recommended over others. Talk to your doctor

What If The Cancer Comes Back?

about treatment goals, methods, and side effects. Compare the recommended treatment with other treatments. Do this by looking at the possible benefits, risks, side effects, and impact on the quality of your life. NOTE: If you're having radiation therapy or chemotherapy, be sure to check with your doctor before taking any medicines—even those you can buy without a doctor's prescription for colds or headaches. Some of these products can interfere or interact with your other treatments.

As with other important medical decisions, a second opinion about treatment for recurrent cancer is a good idea. Some insurance companies require a second opinion; others will pay for a second opinion at the patient's request. You can find another doctor to consult by asking your doctor or calling a local medical society, nearby hospital, or medical school. The Cancer Information Center (1-800-4-CANCER) also can tell you about treatment facilities, including cancer centers and other programs supported by the National Cancer Institute (NCI).

You can take an active part in your treatment by asking questions and expressing your feelings. Questions that patients often ask are included throughout this section. You may want to add your own questions to discuss with your doctor, nurse, social worker, or other member of your health care team. Family members or others close to you may have questions, too.

Questions to ask about any recommended treatment:

- What is the goal of this treatment? Is it a cure, or will it shrink the tumor and relieve the symptoms only for a period of time?
- Why do you think this treatment is the best one for me?
- Is this the standard treatment for my type of cancer?
- Are there other treatments? What are they?
- Am I eligible for any clinical trials?
- Where is the best place to receive treatment?
- What benefits can I expect from the treatment?
- Are there side effects with this treatment? What are they? Are they temporary or permanent?

- How can the side effects be treated or relieved?
- How safe is this treatment? What are the risks?
- How will I know if the treatment is working?
- Will I need to be in the hospital?
- What will happen if I don't have the treatment?
- Will I lose time from school or work or need help at home?
- What does my family need to know about the treatment? Can they help?
- How long will I be on this treatment?
- How much will the treatment cost?
- How is this treatment similar to or different from my last treatment?

The remainder of this section describes some of the newer methods now under study and unconventional treatments that may not be familiar to you.

New Cancer Treatments

Clinical Trials

Clinical trials are studies of new methods for treating disease that are used under strict scientific conditions. These methods have been tested on animals and have shown promise for treating humans. Doctors test the value of new treatments with the help of cancer patients who take part in these studies.

> ☞ **Remember!!**
> New cancer treatments may include clinical trials or complementary and alternative medicine.

Patients who take part in clinical trials may be the first to benefit from improved treatment methods. They also can make an important contribution to medical care because the results of the studies may help many people. Patients participate in clinical trials only if they so choose and are free to leave the trial at any time. More information about these studies is available from the Cancer Information Service. NCI's booklet *Taking Part in Clinical Trials: What Cancer Patients Need to Know* also provides information.

What If The Cancer Comes Back?

Right now, cancer clinical trials are studying several new treatments. If proven effective, these treatments could become the standard treatments of the future.

Questions to ask about clinical trials:

- What trials are available for my type of cancer?
- What is the purpose of these trials?
- Who is sponsoring the study?
- How are the study data and patient safety being checked?
- Where will the information from the study go?
- What benefits can I expect from the treatment?
- Is there scientific evidence that the treatment can help?
- What are the known or potential risks?
- What are the possible side effects?
- Will I have to get the new treatment from a different doctor?
- Will my insurance cover the costs of treatment?
- Will I have to travel to get the treatment? How often?

Complementary and Alternative Medicine

Complementary and alternative medicine (CAM) includes many healing philosophies, approaches, and therapies. A therapy is usually called complementary when it is used in addition to conventional treatments; it is often called alternative when it is used instead of conventional treatment. (Conventional treatments are those that are widely accepted and practiced by the mainstream medical community.) Depending on how they are used, some therapies can be considered either complementary or alternative.

Conventional approaches to cancer treatment are usually studied for safety and effectiveness through a strict scientific process, including clinical trials with large numbers of patients. Often, less is known about the safety and effectiveness of complementary and alternative methods. Some of these methods have not undergone scientific evaluation. Others, once considered unorthodox, are finding a place in cancer treatment as complementary therapies that may help patients feel better and recover faster. One example is acupuncture. In 1997, a panel of experts found acupuncture to be effective in managing nausea and vomiting caused by chemotherapy and in controlling pain associated with surgery.

If you have questions about complementary or alternative therapies, discuss them with your doctor or treatment team.

Questions to ask about complementary and alternative therapies:
- What benefits can be expected from this therapy?
- What are the risks associated with this therapy?
- Do the known benefits outweigh the risks?
- What side effects can be expected?
- Will the therapy interfere with conventional treatment?
- Is this therapy part of a clinical trial? If so, who is sponsoring the trial?
- Will the therapy be covered by health insurance?

Helping Yourself

You may remember that much of the fear and anxiety that you felt the first time cancer appeared in your life was "fear of the unknown." You can help yourself again by gathering information, taking part in your treatment as actively as possible, and finding the support you need to deal with your feelings.

Gathering Information

Learn as much as you can about what's happening to you. If you have questions, ask your doctor, nurse, and other members of your treatment team. Your pharmacist is a good person to talk to if you have questions about your medicines. Your nurse can discuss ways to handle the side effects of your treatment. If you don't understand the answer to a question, ask again.

Some patients hesitate to ask their doctors about their treatment options. They may think that doctors don't like to have their recommendations questioned. Most doctors, however, believe that the best patient is an informed patient. They understand that coping with treatment is easier when patients understand as much as possible, and they encourage patients to discuss their concerns.

Here are some ideas that other people have found helpful:

- Write down your questions about possible treatments or anything else related to treatment. When you see your doctor, bring the questions with you so you don't forget something you wanted to ask.

> ☞ **Remember!!**
>
> You can help yourself through a recurrence of cancer in the following ways:
>
> - gather information
> - take part in your treatment: eat well, get extra rest, and adjust your activities as necessary.
> - manage your emotions

- Ask a friend or relative to go with you. This can be an emotional time, and you may not be able to focus on what the doctor says. It can be easier for someone else to write down information and help you remember later what was discussed. Or use a tape recorder instead of notes.
- Speak openly with the doctor about your needs, expectations, wishes, and concerns, to get the most useful advice. And don't be embarrassed to ask the doctor to repeat or explain something or spell unfamiliar words.

Taking Part In Your Treatment

Taking an active part in your care can help you have a sense of control and well-being. You can be involved in many ways. One is to follow your doctor's recommendations about caring for yourself, such as staying on a special diet.

Another way you can help is to keep your doctor informed. Report honestly how you feel, and if problems arise, describe them as specifically as possible. Don't ever hesitate to report symptoms to your doctor or to ask advice about what to do about them. Although many health-related signs and symptoms may not seem important to you, they could provide valuable information to your doctor. Make sure you know what signs you should look for, and if any of them appears, tell your doctor promptly.

Take care of yourself. Some things you can do to keep up your strength are to:

- **Eat well.** Ask about nutrition recommendations for cancer patients. They can be very different from usual suggestions about healthy eating. Learn when your appetite is best and try to eat well at that time.
- **Get extra rest.** Your body will use a lot of extra energy during treatment. Get more sleep at night, and take naps whenever you feel the need.
- **Adjust activities.** Try to stay active, but don't demand too much of yourself. Ask other people to take over some of your tasks if necessary. If your energy level is low, do the things that are most important to you and cut back on the others. Talk to your doctor if you have questions about doing specific activities.

Managing Your Emotions

The diagnosis of cancer, whether for the first time or when it recurs, can threaten anyone's sense of well-being. Some people feel shock and denial when they first find out that cancer has returned. Many had put their experiences with cancer completely behind them, and the new diagnosis hits them as hard as it did the first time—or even harder. Others are not surprised, as if they had been expecting it all along.

Starting cancer treatment again can place demands on your spirit as well as your body. Your attitudes and actions really can make a difference. Remember that you've coped with this situation before. Keeping your treatment goals in mind may help you keep your spirits up during therapy. As you go through treatment, you're bound to feel better about yourself on some days than on others. When a bad day comes along, try to remember that there have been good days, and there will be more. Feeling low today doesn't mean you'll feel that way tomorrow or that you're giving up. At these times, try distracting yourself with a book, a hobby, or plans for a new garden.

What If The Cancer Comes Back?

Many people say it helps to have something to look forward to—even simple things like a drive, a visit from a friend, or a telephone call.

Sometimes, however, you may feel overcome by fear, anxiety, anger, or depression, and you may just want to cry. That's okay, too. These emotions are common ways to cope with a difficult situation like recurrent cancer. Feel free to express these feelings if they occur. None of these reactions is wrong, and letting them out can help you deal with them.

During your treatment, you may need to rely more on the people closest to you, but this may be difficult at first. You may not want to accept help, and some people may have trouble giving it. Many people don't understand cancer, and some may avoid you because they're afraid of your illness. Others may worry that they'll upset you by saying the wrong thing. You may have to make the first move. Try to be open in talking with others about your illness, your treatment, your needs, and your feelings. Once people know that you can discuss these things, they may be more willing to open up and help. By sharing your feelings, you and your loved ones will be better able to help each other through a difficult time.

Sometimes it's easier to talk to someone other than your family or your friends. Try talking to your doctor, nurse, social worker, or a member of the clergy with whom you feel comfortable. You may want to consider a counselor trained to help cancer patients deal with their feelings. These counselors understand the special problems that go along with serious illness as well as the various ways of coping that others have found useful. If you think this kind of professional support could help you, ask your doctor or nurse for the name of an appropriate counselor, such as an oncology social worker or psychologist.

Many people also find that hospital-sponsored or other support groups, where they can meet others who have been through similar experiences, are helpful places to express their thoughts and feelings. Your hospital, as well as the Cancer Information Service and American Cancer Society, can help you find local support groups.

Although feeling stressed by the continuing changes in your life is normal, too much stress can harm your health and make you feel like you're losing control. You may not be able to remove all the stress around you, but you can try to limit it. Relaxation techniques help you reduce stress and cope better with your illness. Rhythmic breathing, imagery, and distraction are among the techniques that are easy to learn and use whenever you need them. If you're interested, ask your doctor or nurse to refer you to someone trained to teach these techniques. The local library and bookstore also have useful books on relieving stress.

Chapter 39

Follow-Up Care For Childhood Cancer Survivors

When you beat cancer, you will probably feel many emotions. You might feel relieved, happy, and excited. But you might also feel scared. You might be scared that cancer will come back. Or, you might be scared to return to your "normal" life. It might help to talk about how you feel to others—to your parents, a doctor, nurse, or to other childhood cancer survivors.

Your Doctor

Some types of cancer and its treatments may still affect your body after the cancer is gone. This is why it's very important for you to see a doctor for check-ups every year for the rest of your life. You should try to see a doctor who knows about the effects of childhood cancer. You might continue to see the doctor who treated you. Or, you might join a long-term follow-up program at the hospital where you were treated. There, you can see doctors who are familiar with the kinds of health problems you could develop. You should discuss a plan for long-term follow-up care before your treatment is completed. It is important that your long-term follow-up care is with a doctor with experience in treating kids with cancer.

> About This Chapter: The information in this chapter is reprinted with permission from CancerSource. For additional information on childhood cancer and other cancers, visit the CancerSource website at www.cancersource.com. © 2003 CancerSource. All Rights Reserved.

Your Medical History

Chances are, you will not have the same doctor for the rest of your life. You or your doctor may move, you may need to see other doctors who specialize in certain types of medicine or conditions, or you may just want to see a new doctor. When you see a new doctor, it will be very important for you to have copies of your medical records. You should also have copies of x-rays and procedure reports. Your parents may have copies of these records. If they don't have these records, they should contact your medical team for them. These records show:

- the type of cancer you had
- where it was in your body
- the type(s) of treatments you received
- problems, such as side effects
- schedules for future follow-up tests

Special Tests

During your yearly visit to the doctor, you may have to get special tests. These tests will depend on the type of cancer you had and the cancer treatments you received. For example, if you had radiation to your back, your doctor may check your spine to see if it is straight or curved. There are also special tests for males and females. You may have to do some of these tests yourself.

Male Tests

- **Testicular self-exams:** When you turn 14, you will have to examine your testicles regularly. Your doctor will tell you how to do this, what to look for, and how often to do it. You need to do this because certain cancers recur in the testes, like leukemia.

Female Tests

- **Breast self-exams:** When you start your period, you will have to examine your breasts for lumps regularly. Your doctor will tell you how to do this, what to look for, and how often to do it.

Follow-Up Care For Childhood Cancer Survivors

- **Breast exams:** When you turn 18, your doctor will check your breasts for lumps or changes every year. If you had radiation to your chest, your doctor will check your breasts every year during puberty.

- **Mammograms:** If your doctor says that you are at risk for developing breast cancer later in life because you had radiation to your chest, you will have to have a mammogram ten years after treatment or when you turn 25 and regularly after that. A mammogram is like an x-ray of your breasts. It can hurt a little. Your doctor will tell you what to expect.

- **Pap smears and pelvic exams:** A Pap smear is when your doctor scrapes some tissue from an area inside your vagina with an instrument. This can hurt a bit. The doctor then looks at the tissue under a microscope. A pelvic exam is when your doctor puts his or her hand into your vagina to check that your ovaries and uterus are normal. The doctor will wear a glove when checking. This can hurt a bit too. You will have to start these tests when you turn 18 and continue regularly after that.

Stay Healthy

When you survive childhood cancer, it's important for you to stay healthy. Your teenage years are a time when you will be tempted to try many new things. As a cancer survivor, some of these "new things" can harm you more than other teens who have not had cancer.

- **Don't smoke.** Smoking causes cancer. All teens are told not to smoke, but as a cancer survivor, you have a higher risk of developing another cancer if you smoke.

- **Use sun protection.** Not wearing sunscreen can increase your chances of developing skin cancer. Wear sunscreen or sun block with at least SPF (sun protective factor) 15. Certain medications can also make your skin extra sensitive to the sun. Ask your doctor if any of the medicine you took as a cancer patient or are taking now could make your skin extra sensitive to the sun.

- **Eat well.** Eating a well-balanced, healthy diet can help you reduce your risk of developing cancer. Eat lots of fruits and vegetables and try to eat foods that are low in fat, sugar, and salt.

- **Stay active.** Exercise is good for you and it also helps reduce your risk of developing cancer as an adult. If you have heart problems due to childhood cancer, exercise can help your heart stay healthy. You should talk to your doctor about the kinds of exercise you should do.

- **Don't drink alcohol or take drugs.** As a teen, you may be tempted to try alcohol and drugs. However, the treatments you received for cancer may have damaged your organs. By drinking or taking drugs, you could make this damage worse. Plus, alcohol and drugs can also cause other health problems.

- **If you have sex, practice safer sex.** Having sex is an important life decision. Depending on the type of cancer you have and the treatments you receive, your doctor might tell you that it will be hard for you to have children or that you may not ever be able to have children. Only by seeing a doctor or nurse who specializes in reproduction (a fertility specialist) can you be sure of your ability to have children. That's one of the reasons why, if you decide to have sex, you should practice safer sex. If you have sex, you can also pass and catch STDs (sexually transmitted diseases). Certain types of STDs can lower your chances of having children and cause other, permanent damage. And, HPV (human papillomavirus), an STD, can cause cervical and penis cancer. Only by using condoms with sex can you prevent pregnancy and STDs.

Emotional Wellness

As you make the change from childhood to adulthood, there will be some bumps along the way. As a teen, you will be dealing with everyday teen worries: grades, dates, friends, and finding your place in the world. As a teen who has survived cancer, you may have other worries as well. These can include:

- fear of cancer coming back.
- fitting in with other teens now that you've survived cancer.
- guilt that you survived cancer and some of your friends did not.
- mixed feelings as you celebrate each anniversary of your cancer diagnosis. You may feel happy, angry, or nervous.

Follow-Up Care For Childhood Cancer Survivors

- having emotional problems like depression.

If you have any of these worries, talk to your parents, a teacher, or a friend. You may need to see a counselor to feel better about yourself. It may also help to talk to others who have survived childhood cancer. Talk to older teens or young adults about how they adjusted to life as "normal" teens. It may also help you to talk to kids who are currently in treatment. You may feel better about yourself by helping others. Surviving cancer is a big deal. Remember that you will need to see your doctor once a year and stay healthy. And if you feel that you need help adjusting to life as a cancer survivor, talk to someone who's been there or someone who is trained to help you like a nurse or psychologist.

> **☞ Remember!!**
>
> Keys to staying healthy include:
>
> - don't smoke
> - use sun protection
> - eat well
> - stay active
> - don't drink alcohol or take drugs
> - practice safer sex, if you have sex

Part 5

When A Family Member Or Friend Has Cancer

Chapter 40

If Someone You Know Has Cancer

If You Or Someone You Know Has Cancer

If you're like most teens, life can be pretty good. You're old enough to have earned your parents' trust and with it, some new freedom. Maybe you belong to a circle of close friends. You may feel so good that you actually feel invincible. But when you or someone you know is diagnosed with cancer, everything can change.

Suddenly, your familiar world can take on a sense of urgency. Instead of worrying about grades, you may worry about medical tests. Instead of rushing to a football game, you may find yourself hurrying to the hospital to visit a friend—or to your own doctor's appointment.

But as scary as the word cancer may sound, it is simply the name of an illness. Like many medical conditions, cancer **can** be treated. And although some teens with cancer don't recover, many not only survive, but return to their everyday lives. Read on to learn about how to cope if you or someone you know has cancer.

> About This Chapter: "If You Or Someone You Know Has Cancer" was provided by TeensHealth, one of the largest resources online for medically reviewed health information written for parents, kids, and teens. For more articles like this one, visit www.TeensHealth.org, or www.KidsHealth.org. © 2001 The Nemours Center for Children's Health Media, a division of The Nemours Foundation. Text under "When Someone in Your Family Has Cancer," was excerpted and adapted from a document prepared by the National Cancer Institute (NCI), February 1995. Full text available online at http://www.cancer.gov/cancerinformation/whensomeoneinyourfamily.

Learning About Cancer

You may be wondering what cancer is and how teens get it. If so, you're not alone because most people don't usually associate cancer with kids and teens. Cancer is actually the name given to many diseases in which cells (tiny units found in all living things) behave abnormally. In someone who has cancer, cells uncontrollably grow and divide and eventually form tumors, lumps that can destroy normal tissue. Cancer is a common disease, so it's likely that you know someone who has had it, such as an older relative or someone in a friend's family.

Many people find that learning more about cancer is important to their recovery. Suppose you were watching a play on stage and the actors were speaking a foreign language. Even though you might be able to figure out the plot by watching their movements, you would definitely miss a great deal of information. The same is true for cancer.

Whether it is you or a friend who has been diagnosed, it's good to learn as much as you can about cancer. If a friend has cancer, you can be a sounding board for his concerns. If you are the patient, you will be knowledgeable enough to ask relevant questions, give informed opinions, and take control of your medical options.

Cancer has its own language, and doctors can sometimes forget that you may not understand unfamiliar terms and phrases. If not, ask for explanations. Most doctors are happy to explain things in a way that makes sense to you. Or find someone such as a nurse who can help you understand.

Another way to make sense of cancer is to read. You can find tons of information and resources in public libraries, bookstores, and on the Internet. Remember, though, that you may come across information (especially on the Internet) that is incorrect or outdated. If you find information in your research that is different from what your doctor is telling you, be sure to ask your doctor about it.

There are also Internet chat areas for people with cancer and their families and friends. They provide a convenient place to talk with people who have had similar experiences.

If Someone You Know Has Cancer

You can also ask your doctor to put you in touch with another teen who has cancer. You may find it helpful and comforting to share your experiences. And although no two patients have the exact same cancer experiences, it's good to know you're not alone.

How Can I Take Care Of Myself Physically?

Since you were a little kid, you've probably heard again and again that eating right and getting rest are two of the most important things you can do to stay healthy. If you've been diagnosed with cancer, getting healthy is your first priority. Now it is more important than ever to pay attention to your diet and your sleep schedule.

If you're undergoing chemotherapy or radiation therapy as part of your treatment, you may need help with your diet because side effects can include loss of appetite and nausea. It may help to consult with a dietitian, a professional who can create a nutrition plan geared to your specific needs.

Your doctor will let you know whether you should exercise, how much, and whether physical therapy might help. Once you are able to exercise, find out which types will help to increase your strength and stamina.

How Can I Take Care Of Myself Emotionally?

It is natural to feel many emotions when you learn you have cancer. Anger, fear, sadness, and anxiety are all common reactions to serious illness.

It's important to get help from trusted adults in sorting out your emotions. Some possibilities include social workers, clergy, close relatives, art or music therapists, and psychologists and psychiatrists.

Your doctor can help, too. Ask to meet another teen who has cancer. It can really help to exchange information and ideas and to learn how others your own age have managed to cope. There are also many medical organizations devoted to cancer support, and some have websites as well as toll-free telephone numbers to make it easy to contact them.

Above all, remember that although you may have cancer, you are a person first and a patient second. Cancer is not your identity; it is simply an illness you are trying to overcome.

How Can I Help Someone Who Has Cancer?

If a friend or relative has cancer, the most important thing you can do is to be yourself! Many people who have cancer report that the people they love suddenly treat them differently or stay away completely.

It's natural to feel frightened, anxious, or even angry when someone you know has cancer, but don't let that keep you from being there for your friend or loved one. You may need help with your strong emotions and there are many places you can turn. Many hospitals conduct counseling groups for families and friends of people with cancer. Or you can identify an adult whom you trust for support and reassurance. You can also visit websites related to cancer. Another way you might help a person with cancer is to consider volunteering at a hospital or clinic that treats people with cancer. Volunteering is an excellent way to show your support.

Try to remember that the person with cancer is on an emotional roller coaster. Being in the hospital or having to stay home a lot to rest can be isolating and cause loneliness. Most people with cancer like having their friends and family around, even if the visits are short and there may not be much to say. If you're not sure whether to visit, ask. Even if your schedule is very busy, you can keep in touch in other ways, like sending cards, talking on the phone, or using e-mail. It will do a lot to lift the spirits of someone you know who is dealing with cancer.

Keep in mind that the person you care about is simply sick. Despite the cancer, he or she is still the same person you loved or knew before.

When Someone In Your Family Has Cancer

Cancer Changes Things

When someone in your family has cancer, things can change for everyone. These changes can be large or small. What it is like to have a parent or a brother or sister with cancer depends on a lot of things such as:

- Who in your family has cancer.
- What kind of cancer the person has and how it's treated.

If Someone You Know Has Cancer

- How old you are.
- If you have other people in your family or close friends nearby who can help.
- Whether you live with two parents or with one.
- If you have brothers and sisters at home and how old they are.
- How far the person with cancer goes for treatment—across town or to another city or state—and if you can visit or call them.
- How long the person has to stay in the hospital.
- How well or sick the person with cancer feels.
- Whether you can get the answers to your questions about cancer.
- How easy it is for your family or friends to talk with you about cancer.
- How easy it is for you to talk about cancer.
- Whether your friends know what is happening to your family.
- How your friends treat you.

Any of these can make a difference, and only you know how cancer has changed your life. One piece of information can't answer all your questions. This information was written to help you understand more about cancer and how it is treated. It may help you to understand the changes that may happen in your life. It also may help you understand and deal with feelings you have about cancer and about the person in your family who has it.

Cancer And The Family

Any illness changes family life for a while. A parent or a brother or sister who is home sick with the flu can't spend as much time with the family as usual. The sick person may get special attention, and you may need to help around the house. But most times, the person is not sick for very long, and family life soon goes back to normal.

But when someone has cancer, it is different. He or she needs special medical treatment and may go to the hospital or clinic a lot. People in the family may worry. They worry for the person who has cancer and for themselves.

Cancer is a serious illness, and it can be scary if you don't know for sure if the person will get well or not.

People in your family may react differently. They may be afraid or angry that their life has changed. They may be tired, or they may be nervous about the future. They may be tense and not as easy to talk to as before, because they are worried. Some people may go on just as if nothing has happened, and they may not seem different at all. If you are upset, you may wonder if they care about the family member who has cancer. It's important to remember that each person reacts in his or her own way. You may get mad at other members of your family for the way they are acting. It is better to talk with them than to stay mad. If you talk, you can understand why they are acting that way.

Cancer In The Family: What It's Like For You

When someone in your family has cancer, it may mean many things to you. Other people who have been through it say it can be a lot of things: confusing, scary, lonely, and much more. You may find that you have feelings that are hard to understand and sometimes hard to share.

This section tells about the experiences of others who have had a family member

> ✔ **Quick Tip**
>
> **People To Help You, Besides Your Parents**
>
> *For Support And Sharing Feelings*
>
> - Grandparents, aunts, uncles
> - Neighbors
> - Teachers, guidance counselors
> - Ministers, rabbis, priests
> - Coaches, youth or scout leaders
> - Special adult friends
> - Older brother or sister
> - Friends your own age
>
> *For Support And Information About Cancer*
>
> - Someone at the hospital—a doctor, nurse, social worker, or other person treating your family member
> - Family doctor
> - School nurse

If Someone You Know Has Cancer

with cancer. Some of what you read, especially about feelings, may not make sense or seem right to you. It may even seem silly. Or it may seem a lot like what you've felt and what has happened to you.

Remember, feelings aren't "good" or "bad." They are just feelings and are normal and shared by many others. And even if you try to wish them away or ignore them, or if you feel guilty or ashamed of them, they'll still be there.

A good way to handle feelings is to admit you have them and talk about them. Talk with your parents, other adults, or your friends. Or you can talk with others who have had a family member with cancer. You'll be surprised how much better you feel once you have talked about your feelings.

It May Be Hard to Talk About Cancer

Sometimes it's not easy to talk about what you feel or about problems. Not only is it hard to say what you feel, but other people may not be ready or able to listen or to be helpful. Some of your questions may upset your parents because they don't know how to answer or because your worries remind them of their own. It's possible that your parents may not be ready to talk when you are. They may need more time to sort things out in their own minds before they can talk with you. Some parents, no matter how much they love their children, don't know how to talk about upsetting things with them. If your parents aren't able to talk with you about your feelings, they may be able to help you find someone you can talk to, like someone at the hospital, a relative or friend, or a teacher or school counselor.

Here is what some others who have had a parent or brother or sister with cancer have said about what they felt.

Being Scared

> "I really didn't understand much at first. Mostly I was afraid that she might die, because my sister and I are pretty close. I was really scared, and I also thought it might be catching or something." —Laura, age 13

The girl who said this had a sister with cancer, but it can be just as scary when a parent has cancer. When someone is first diagnosed with cancer, it may seem as though your whole world has fallen apart. You may not know much about it, so you may remember what you've heard about cancer before. Being afraid someone might die from cancer is normal, especially if the only people with cancer that you have known have died. And being afraid that you or another person in the family might catch it is normal, too. Why? Because there are so many things you can catch from someone else such as a cold or the flu. It's easy to think cancer may be the same, but doctors and other scientists know that you cannot catch cancer from anyone. Learning about cancer can help you. You will feel less afraid when you know more about the disease.

Hearing about treatments and tests can be hard. Some people find it's scary just to think about the needles and blood tests and radiation treatments. Sometimes, learning about these things and talking to the person with cancer (or someone else) about what it's really like is the best way to deal with these fears. If a trip to the hospital is possible, it might help.

"One day I went to the clinic with my brother for his treatment. I saw the machine that he gets radiation from and how IVs work, and I met his doctor and the nurses. I saw lots of other kids who didn't have any more hair than he does. Now, when he goes to the clinic, I don't have to wonder what he's going through. I know what it's like. It's no fun for a little kid like him, but it's not as bad as I thought." —Matthew, age 14

Sometimes, when one parent has cancer, the other one spends a lot of time at the hospital and away from the rest of the family. Having their parents at the hospital instead of at home can be scary to some young people. They may worry about their parents and need to have someone special to call to make sure that things are all right.

"When dad's in the hospital, mom goes too, and I stay with my aunt, Emily. She's nice, but sometimes, I get scared because I don't know how dad is, or I miss them. So now mom and dad call me every night before dinner, and they tell me what's happening, and I can tell them about my day, and I know they're all right." —Erin, age 9

Feeling Guilty

"I got really mad at Chrissy one day. She wouldn't let me go bike riding with her and my cousin, and I got mad and said 'I wish you were dead.' Now she

has leukemia, and she could die, and I think maybe it's my fault. I was scared to tell anyone because then they'd all know what I did and be mad. But my dad heard me crying one night, and he got me to tell him why. He says it isn't my fault or anybody else's that Chrissy has cancer, and you can't make somebody get cancer just by what you say." —Katy, age 10

Until you understand what does and doesn't cause cancer, it's easy to think that anything could have done it—even words or a fall.

"I left my junk all over the floor one night instead of putting it away, and the next morning, mom fell over it. She was mad and had a lot of bruises. A little later, the doctor told her she had cancer. She's in the hospital now. Maybe if she hadn't fallen down because of me, she'd be okay." —Tom, age 11

Just as words can't cause cancer, neither can bruises or bumps or even broken bones. Never forget: It was nothing you did, said, or thought that caused the cancer.

Some people are afraid to tell any one what they are thinking and may feel guilty for a long time. Even if your parents can see that something is worrying you, they may not be able to guess what it is. It's hard to talk about, especially if you think you've done something wrong, and everyone will be mad at you. But it is best to get it out in the open so you and your parents or someone at the hospital can talk it over.

People sometimes feel guilty because they are well, and their parent or sibling is sick. Young people may feel that it's not right for them to enjoy things they like to do when the person with cancer can't do what he or she likes. These feelings show that you care about your family, but it's important to care not only for the person with cancer but also for yourself. It's best for everyone if you keep being you and doing things that are important to you.

"Last year, mom and dad always drove me to play softball, but now dad's sick and mom's always at the hospital or busy at work or at home. I didn't think I'd be able to play this year, and I wasn't sure I should, with my dad so sick. I told my grandmom, and she said I should play, and she'd take me. She likes to come, and she tells my folks all about the game and how I played. Next year, maybe, they'll all be able to come." —Dave, age 11

Getting Mad

> *"Sometimes, I feel mad at my brother for having cancer. I know that's not right, and he can't help it. But it has changed everything. My mom and dad don't talk about anything but him and neither does anyone else. It's just not fair."* —Sharon, age 13

People who have a brother or sister or a parent with cancer can feel angry at that person for getting sick and changing their lives. This may seem wrong, and people sometimes feel guilty about getting mad. But, if having someone with cancer in your family means you can't be with your parents as much or have to stay somewhere else or give up things you like, it can be hard. Even if you understand why it's happening, you don't have to like it. Others who have been through it say it's important to remember that things won't always be this way. And when you get mad, remember that it doesn't mean you are a bad person or don't love the person with cancer. It just means you're mad.

Feeling Neglected

One of the things that young people get mad about is feeling left out or neglected. Some feel that they don't get as much attention as before, and they often are right. Family members, including your parents, all have a lot on their minds, and they may have to put all their energy into helping the person with cancer. This may not leave much time for you, especially if they are going back and forth to the clinic or hospital.

Young people often feel that the brother or sister with cancer gets more attention from their parents.

> *"At night my parents go in and turn on my sister's light and kiss her good night, and they don't come in my room—well, sometimes mom will. She tells me, 'Don't think we are partial to her.'"* —Maria, age 15

Young people may feel that their sibling with cancer gets away with a lot of things that they can't do.

> *"If I do something wrong, mom yells. If my brother does, she lets it pass."* —Dennis, age 13

Why do some parents do this? It's not because they don't love all their children. This is a confusing time for them, just as it is for you. They have to learn a lot about cancer and hospitals very fast. They are tired and worried. They see one of their children sick and may try to make up for it by giving that child a little more attention. Parents know, as you do, that some people die from cancer, and they could be afraid of that and want to do all they can for your brother or sister who has cancer. Sometimes they give a young person with cancer special treatment that isn't wanted.

> *"I have a sister who has cancer. She gets upset because she's treated differently now. She doesn't want to be babied, just treated normally as she was before. She and mom always used to fight, and now mom is really sweet all the time, and it's weird. Not that my sister likes to fight, but it's just not normal."* —Peggy, age 15

For whatever reason, and whether your brother or sister likes it or not, your parents may give special treatment to the one who has cancer. At times like this, it's normal to feel jealous, even if people tell you that you shouldn't because you're not sick. But it's natural for you to want time with your parents and some special attention, too.

Young people who have a parent with cancer also may feel neglected.

> *"Now that mom's sick, everything at our house is different. We hardly ever eat together as a family anymore, and there's never anyone to help me with my homework or to listen to me. Mom used to do that. I feel like it's sort of being left up to me to take care of myself."* —Martha, age 13

When one parent has cancer, the other one may be so busy that neither one of them can spend much time with the rest of the family.

> *"Sometimes, my father feels like he is neglecting us because he is with mom so much. And, in a way, it's true. I know he can't help it. He has to work and wants to see mom, but he's not around like he used to be, and he doesn't do things with us like he did. He's just too busy."* —Barry, age 16

If you feel like you're not getting much attention, whether you have a parent or a brother or sister with cancer, remember that the person with cancer is getting more attention because they need special care not because you are loved less.

Feeling Lonely

You may be lucky and have a special friend and friends who treat you the same as before your family member was diagnosed with cancer. But many young people with cancer in their families have found that they've lost some of their friends. Sometimes this happens because friends may not know much about cancer and may be afraid of catching it from you. Or they may not know what to say and find it easier to stay away than to be embarrassed. Having cancer in your family may make you act a little different because you're upset or scared or embarrassed or because you want to be with your family.

> *"Sometimes, my friends wonder why I act strange. I wish they understood that, sometimes, I don't want to do what they're doing, I really want to be with my sick sister."* —Nan, age 12

If your friends don't understand, they may think that you don't want to see them anymore. It can be a hard time for all of you.

What can you do? You may need to reach out to your friends, even if that's hard to do. Maybe everyone won't respond as you'd like, but it helps if you give them a chance. Often friends just don't know how to act and need you to tell them how you want to be treated. They also may need you to show that you still need them, even if you seem a little different because you're upset. You may want to invite them over to watch TV, play video games, or just to

☞ **Remember!!**

If this is a hard time for you, remember that it won't last forever. Old friends may become close to you again. And people who have lost friends have found that they also made new ones. There may be someone at school who has had a sick person in the family and will understand how you feel. That person could be a special new friend.

If Someone You Know Has Cancer

talk. Let them know that you still enjoy talking with them on the phone or going to the movies—just as you did before.

Answering Questions

When your friends do talk to you, some of them may not say what you want to hear. Sometimes, especially in the beginning, people ask a lot of questions that are hard to answer.

> *"People asked me questions all the time. They'd say things like 'I heard Jean is in a coma' or 'I heard you were hysterical.' Whenever I told them the truth, they didn't believe me. And they'd ask dumb questions like 'Can Jean walk? Can she write?' They didn't know what was going on, and I didn't know how to answer them. I got sick of it."* —John, age 14

One way to answer your classmates' questions is for you and your parents to talk to your teacher and see if the teacher or someone who knows about cancer and its treatment can talk to your class. Ask the doctor, nurse, or social worker about a school conference or classroom presentation. This will give your friends a chance to ask their questions and be sure they're getting the right answers—not about your family member but about cancer in general.

Other people ask questions, and they may not know that some of them are hard for you to answer or make you feel bad. If you want to answer their questions, it's a good idea to think of what people might ask and have an answer ready. People may ask you how the person with cancer is feeling or how long the person will be in the hospital. And they also may ask questions like these:

- "Are you going to get cancer from your mother?"
- "Why does your brother always wear that cap? Did his hair really fall out?"

"Is your dad going to die?"

- "What did your sister do to get cancer?"

You may want to get help finding answers to questions like these. There may be several people to ask such as your parents, teacher, or school counselor, an adult friend, or the doctor, nurse, or social worker. And remember, you always can tell people that you don't want to talk about something or that you don't know. You don't have to answer their questions. Sometimes, though, trying to answer a few questions and talking about your feelings can help others understand what you are experiencing.

Feeling Embarrassed

> *"Since my brother lost his hair and got so pale and thin, I don't want to bring my friends home anymore. I don't want them to see how different Tim looks now, and I don't think he likes to see them. Besides, it's not easy to laugh and giggle at home when someone is sick."* —Caroline, age 12

Sometimes people who have a person with cancer in their family may feel embarrassed because now their family is different. It is different from what it used to be, and it is different from their friends' families. And people who ask them questions they can't answer just embarrass them more. So sometimes they want to try to leave the cancer at home and hope that none of their friends learn about it. Of course, you can't really do that because when someone you love is sick, you need people you can talk to and who understand if you're upset. If you feel a little embarrassed around people because someone in your family has cancer, remember that others have felt this way also and that this feeling often goes away once everyone has gotten used to what is happening.

Even though others feel all right about asking a lot of questions, some people with a family member who has cancer find that it embarrasses them to ask questions. Just remember: No question is a dumb question if you don't understand it.

> *"At first I didn't ask any questions, although I had a lot of them. I thought people would think I was really dumb, but now I know it really helps to ask."* —Brad, age 14

Dealing With Side Effects

> *"Diane had all this hair, and some nights it would fall out and be all over her pillow when she woke up, or fall out in her comb, or when she washed*

her hair. It really kind of scared me to see that happen at first, but she took it pretty well." —Lois, age 16

When someone you love has side effects from cancer treatments, you too have to learn to live with these changes. It may seem a little strange at first, or scary, but other people have found that they soon got used to it. Some people outside the family may not understand, and they may hurt the feelings of the person with cancer.

"When my little brother, James, went back to school, he was still on chemo and had lost all his hair, so he wore a baseball cap. One day a kid pulled the cap off and teased him. James said everybody stared at him. Mom says we should feel sorry for that kid because he doesn't know any better. But I don't, I feel sorry for James." —Amy, age 12

It's hard to imagine why anyone would want to tease James, but it's not as important to know why someone did it as it is to know that these things may happen, and that you can't always protect your brother or sister. What you can do for people with cancer is try to understand how they feel and help them see that they still have friends. And, if you tease them from time to time, like you did before they had cancer, it's not a bad thing, as long as you don't keep it up for long or keep doing it when you see that it really hurts their feelings. Brothers and sisters all tease each other, and it's important that, even when your brother or sister has cancer, you treat each other as much like before as you can.

You may be shocked if the person who has cancer looks different after coming home.

"My dad has cancer, and he was in the hospital for a long time. When he finally got to come home, he was still really sick. I had to help him up the stairs because he was so weak. It was strange, because he had always been so big and strong, and now he was weak. It bothered me." —Richard, age 16

Even if someone tells you that your family member won't look the same, you may not be prepared for the changes. Try to find out what type of changes to expect. It may be hard for you, but it's important to remember that, even if they look different, they're still the same person.

Changing

Some young people who have a family member with cancer may change a little themselves. Sometimes they don't realize it or don't know why. But, with all the new and different experiences and feelings, it's not surprising that people change. They may have trouble at school or be unable to concentrate or to get along with other people as well as they did before.

They may start to be a little less careful or do things that are dangerous, maybe getting hurt more often.

They may worry a lot about getting sick themselves and may even get sick more often. Their school grades may fall, or they may become more involved in school than they were before and make better grades.

> ✔ **Quick Tip**
> If you haven't noticed that you have changed, someone else may notice and want to talk to you about it. If they do, it's because they want to help. Your parents or teachers or social workers at the hospital or clinic all may be able to help if you've changed in a way that isn't good for you or that makes you sad and uncomfortable.

Any of these changes can happen because young people who are scared or worried or whose lives have changed may need more attention at home. Just as with other problems or worries, it helps to talk with people who care and understand what's happening.

Not all of the changes are bad; some may be good. Many young people who have had cancer in the family felt it has helped them grow up. Others say it also has brought their family closer together.

> *"My brother is in remission now. Things were pretty bad at first. Then, after a while, things sort of settled down and got back to the way they were before. I think Billy's cancer brought us all closer together. I get along better with him and my sister and even with my older brother now. I'm closer to mom and dad. And I think we all grew up a lot while he was sick."* —Alice, age 15

How Your Parents Feel

If someone in your family has cancer, you may wonder how your parents feel. There's no one answer to this question. Just like everyone else, parents may feel many different things when they have cancer themselves or when another member of their family does. They may be worried, scared, tired, or a little confused by all the decisions they need to make and all the changes that cancer can bring. Along with this, parents want to be strong so they can help everyone else, and they want to keep the family together during this time. They may feel that they don't have enough energy to do all the things they would like to do or share all they'd like to with other family members. This section tells some things parents have said about how they feel.

A parent who has cancer may worry that by being sick they are upsetting the family's life.

> *"I feel bad because now that I'm sick my husband tries to be with me a lot. I think my children's feelings are hurt but they won't say so. I just wish we could talk about it as a family."*

Or parents may know that being sick means that they can't do some things with their children that other parents do. They may wish they could, and they feel guilty.

> *"I feel like I'm letting my son down, like I'm not being a real father because I can't run around with him the way other fathers do."*

When this happens, parents find they need to look for something they can do with their children that they'll all enjoy.

A parent whose husband or wife has cancer often needs to learn to do new things for their family and may be concerned about how well they'll do.

> *"Now that my wife is sick, I need to be both mother and father while she's in the hospital. I'm afraid I don't do as good a job at some things as she does. The other day, our youngest son said 'Mommy never scrambled eggs like that.' I don't blame him, I'd rather eat her cooking, too. I asked her how she scrambles eggs and now at least breakfast tastes a little better."*

Parents don't expect their children to pretend that everything is all right or tastes great when it doesn't. Even if they get mad for a while, most parents would rather hear what other family members feel than not know when others are upset.

Parents may know when they've been treating a child with cancer differently than they treat the others or when they've been short-tempered. They may feel like they can't help it but still wish it didn't happen.

> *"After I spend a day in the pediatrics clinic with Lisa, I'm so drained when I get home that I yell at my other kids over little things. Then they get upset, and I get more upset because I know that I shouldn't have done that."*

Some parents worry that their children are upset, and even though they want to help their children, they don't know what to do. Sometimes this is because young people don't want to talk to their parents about cancer. They may be afraid that their parents will worry or won't understand. In fact, most parents worry more if they feel you are upset, but they don't know why, or you won't discuss it with them.

> *"Since I've been sick, my kids have changed. I know something is bothering them, but when I ask what it is, they say it's nothing I just wish they would talk about it. I want to help them."*

Often, one thing young people can do to help is to talk about how they feel and give their parents a chance to say how they feel, too.

Parents say that they want their children to know that the family is there to help even when one of its members has cancer. Your family life may change when someone has cancer. The important thing, however, is that you're a family, and families solve problems together. If you need some extra help, talk with the doctor, nurse, or social worker. And remember: even if life is a little different, you're still a family, and your family is still there for you.

☞ Remember!!

There are many different ways to think and feel about having a person with cancer in your family. It's important to remember that people can learn to adjust to changes in their lives. Sometimes it takes a little work, but you can almost always find some thing or someone who can help you when you need it. Keep trying and don't be afraid to ask for help.

Chapter 41

Helping Family Members Cope With Cancer

Although cancer has "come out of the closet," much of what we read in newspapers and magazines is about the disease itself—its probable causes or new methods of treatment. There is little information about how families deal with cancer on a day-to-day basis. This gap reinforces feelings that families coping with cancer are isolated from the rest of the world: that everyone else is managing nicely while you flounder with your feelings.

Cancer is a blow to every family it touches. How you handle it is determined to a great extent by how you have functioned as a family in the past. Families who are used to sharing their feelings with each other usually are able to talk about the disease and the changes it brings. Families in which each member solves problems alone or in which one person has played the major role in making decisions might have more difficulty coping.

Not Everyone Can

Problems within the family can be the most difficult to handle simply because you cannot go home to escape them. Some family members may deny the reality of cancer or refuse to discuss it.

About This Chapter: Text in this chapter is excerpted and adapted from "Taking Time: Support for People with Cancer and the People Who Care About Them," National Cancer Institute (NCI), April 1999. Full text available online at http://cancer.gov/cancerinfo/takingtime.

In these situations individual counseling or cancer patient groups can provide needed support and reinforcement. Moreover, these resources provide an outlet for the frustrations you are facing within the family.

Changing Roles

Families may have difficulty adjusting to the role changes that are sometimes necessary. Changes can cause great upheavals in the ways members of the family interact. The usual patterns are gone. Parents might look to children for emotional support at a time when the children themselves need it most. Teenagers might have to take over major household responsibilities. Young children can revert to infantile behavior as a way of dealing with the impact of cancer on the family as a unit and on themselves as individuals. The sheer weight of responsibility can become insurmountable, destroying normal family associations, devouring time needed for rest and recreation,

---

✔ Quick Tip
Coping Within The Family

- Cancer is a blow to every family it touches. How it is handled is determined to a great extent by how the family has functioned as a unit in the past.

- Problems within the family can be the most difficult to handle; you cannot go home to escape them.

- Adjusting to role changes can cause great upheavals in the way family members interact.

- Performing too many roles at once endangers anyone's emotional well-being and ability to cope. Examine what tasks are necessary and let others slide.

- Consider hiring professional nurses or homemakers. Financial costs need to be compared with the physical and emotional cost of shouldering the load alone.

- Children may need special attention. They need comfort, reassurance, affection, guidance, and discipline at times of disruption in their routine.

and depriving family members of wholesome opportunities for expressing anxiety and resentment.

Help For The Children

Children might have difficulty coping with cancer in a parent. Mother or Dad may be gone from the house—in a hospital that may be hundreds of miles from home—or home in bed, in obvious discomfort, and perhaps visibly altered in appearance.

In the face of this upheaval, children often are asked also to behave exceptionally well: to "play quietly," to perform extra tasks or to be understanding of others' moods beyond the maturity of their years. The children may resent lost attention. Some fear the loss of their parent or begin to imagine their own death. Some children, formerly independent, now become anxious about leaving home and parents. Discipline problems can arise if children attempt to command the attention they feel they are missing.

It may help if a favorite relative or family friend can devote extra time and attention to the children, who need comfort and reassurance, affection, guidance, and discipline. Trips to the zoo are important, but so is regular help with homework and someone to attend the basketball awards banquet. If your efforts to provide support and security fail, professional counseling for a child, or child and parent together, may be necessary and should not be overlooked.

Emotional Assistance

It is said that we cope with cancer much as we cope with other problems that confront us. Many do come to terms with the reality of cancer. After initial treatment, they find somehow they are able to continue their normal working and social relationships. Or, as one psychologist put it, they learn to get up in the morning and pour the coffee, even knowing that they have cancer. They find, sometimes to their amazement, that they can laugh at bad jokes, or become totally absorbed in a good movie, or a hard-fought football game.

At other times, strength deserts them. They feel overwhelmed by this new world of uncertainties. Some lose interest in favorite hobbies or activities, viewing them as painful reminders of what will be lost if treatment is unsuccessful. They want to cope, but they need help, some support systems beyond their own. Where does one look for such support?

At The Hospital

It was not very long ago that emotional assistance for the cancer patient or family was impossible to find. Attention to emotional needs is a relatively recent addition to standard cancer treatment. Growing numbers of hospitals routinely include a mental health professional as a member of the cancer treatment team or offer group counseling programs. This is a hopeful sign; it says, "This diagnosis does not mean imminent death. We have a whole person to treat here, one with a future and a life to live. This person should be able to live as normally as possible. We must provide the emotional tools to get the job done."

Counseling also is now available for health professionals to help them face feelings of frustration and uncertainty in their work. They have recognized the awesome degree of stress that cancer can create in those it touches. You should have no feelings of shame or hesitancy, then, if you feel the need to seek professional help.

Some hospitals consider some form of group counseling as part of the standard treatment—as necessary as an exercise class, for example. Programs are organized in a variety of ways. Some are just for patients; others include spouses, family, or other special people.

Groups can incorporate music, poetry, or role playing in attempts to help members explore their feelings. Some are action-oriented with "veteran" patients helping others now facing the same problem. All counseling groups should be run by trained professionals so that the direction of exploration is truly helpful to each participant.

In The Community

If you want to explore your feelings in individual therapy, you will find a growing number of psychologists, psychiatrists, or licensed clinical social workers specializing in counseling people affected by cancer. Many find it helpful to

Helping Family Members Cope With Cancer

explore feelings—especially those they don't want to accept, such as guilt, resentment, and intense anger—with a nonjudgmental person who, will help them understand these feelings and find ways to channel them constructively.

Often the problem is not an individual one. The family is a unit, and when one member is stricken with cancer all members are affected. Family counseling can help absorb the shock and deal with the stresses of cancer.

It can be difficult for persons with cancer and their family members to discuss their emotions. Cancer patients themselves have tagged the absence of open communication within their families as a major problem. People are particularly hesitant to express negative feelings when no one is "at fault." Yet major shifts in responsibilities such as those cancer brings to a family can cause great resentment by those shouldering (or incapable of shouldering) extra burdens. A loss of accustomed responsibility or authority also can cause resentment mingled with anxiety over a loss of power.

Children, especially, find that their usual roles no longer are defined clearly. Parents may not have the emotional energy to provide the usual support, love, and authority. Teenagers can feel torn between expressing independence and a need to remain close to the sick parent.

Your physician, a hospital social worker or hospital psychologist are good sources for referrals to psychologists, psychiatrists, or other mental health professionals trained to counsel individuals and families affected by cancer.

Helping Each Other

There are numerous self-help groups organized by people like you and designed to help you overcome both the practical problems of cancer and the feelings these changes cause. Some groups are local chapters of national organizations; others are strictly "grass roots." Some are only for patients; others include family members.

These organizations shun a "pity me" approach. They exist to help you work through your feelings and frustrations. Whether you accept them or change them, you can do so within the framework of a supportive group of people who know your problems firsthand.

✔ Quick Tip

When cancer develops, many people need to learn to ask for and accept outside help for the first time. These are good ways to begin:

- Take time to ask medical questions of your doctor, nurse specialists, therapists, and technologists.

- Make lists of questions. Write or tape record the answers. Take someone else along as a second listener.

- Ask your physician to suggest other doctors if you wish a second opinion on your diagnosis before deciding on treatment.

- Ask your physician about alternative treatments if you have questions about them.

- Physicians wait for clues from their patients to determine how much to say. Let your doctor know whether you want to know everything at once or in stages.

- Remember that there is a difference between a physician who does not know that cancer need not be fatal and one who will not promise you a miracle.

- Trust and rapport between patient and physician are important; you must be able to work together to treat the cancer most effectively.

- Your physician, hospital, library, the National Cancer Institute or affiliated Cancer Information Service offices, and local chapters of the American Cancer Society are good sources of facts about cancer. Many also can provide the names of local support and service organizations established to help you cope with the emotional stresses of the disease.

- Emotional assistance takes many forms. Counseling or psychiatric therapy for individuals, for groups of patients, and for families often is available through the hospital or within the community.

- Many groups have been established by patients and their families to share practical tips and coping skills. One may be right for you.

- Your minister or rabbi, a sympathetic member of the congregation, or a specially trained pastoral counselor may be able to help you find spiritual support.

Some offer family members an opportunity to share feelings, fears, and anxieties with others bearing similar burdens. Some provide patients a place to express negative feelings that they don't want to unload on their families. Patients without families can speak openly and release their pent-up emotions without fear of taxing existing friendships.

Spiritual Support

Religion is a source of strength for some people. Some find new faith in a divine being and new hope from sacred writings when cancer enters their lives. Others find the ordeal of disease strengthens their faith, or that faith gives them new-found strength. Others never have had strong religious beliefs and feel no urge to turn to religion at such at time.

Individual pastors can provide hope and solace, but they vary, as do physicians and lay people, in their capacity to cope with life-threatening illnesses and the possibility of death. A religious leader untrained in illness counseling may refer you to an associate trained to work with people with cancer. He or she also might introduce you to another member of the congregation who can provide comfort.

Living Each Day

Whether the outlook for recovery is good or poor, the days go by, one at a time, and patient and family must learn to live each one. It's not always easy. On learning the diagnosis, some decide that death is inevitable, and there is nothing to do but give up and wait. They are not the first to feel that way.

Orville Kelly, a newspaperman, described his initial battle with the specter of death. "I began to isolate myself from the rest of the world. I spent much time in bed, even though I was physically able to walk and drive. I thought about my own impending funeral and it made me very sad."

These feelings continued from his first hospitalization through the first outpatient chemotherapy treatment. On the way home from that treatment, he was haunted by memories of the happy past, when "everything was all right." Then it occurred to Kelly, "I wasn't dead yet. I was able to drive my automobile. Why couldn't I return home to barbecue ribs?"

He did, that very night. He began to talk to his wife and children about his fears and anxieties. And he became so frustrated at the feelings he had kept locked up inside himself that he wrote the newspaper article that led to the founding of Make Today Count, the mutual help organization for cancer patients and their families.

Each person must work through individual feelings of possible death, fear and isolation in his or her own good time. It is hard to overcome these feelings if they are never confronted head on, but it is an ongoing struggle. One day brings feelings of confidence, the next day despair. Many people find it helps considerably if they strive to return, both as individuals and as a family, to their normal lives.

Each day brings pleasures and responsibilities totally outside the realm of cancer. We should try to give each the attention it deserves. These are the threads of the fabric that enfolds our lives. They give it color and meaning.

> ✔ Quick Tip
> # How To Live For Each Day
>
> - Each person must work through, in his or her own way, feelings of possible death, fear, and isolation. Returning to normal routines as much as possible often helps.
>
> - Give the pleasures and responsibilities of each day the attention they deserve.
>
> - Responsible pursuits keep life meaningful; recreation keeps it zesty. Fill your life with both.
>
> - Remember the difference between "doing" and "overdoing." Rest is important to both physical and emotional strength.
>
> - It's harder to bolster one's will to live if you are alone. Yet many have acted as their own cheering squad and have found ways to lead meaningful lives.
>
> - Family members must not make an invalid of a person with cancer who is fully capable of physical activity and responsible participation in the family.
>
> - Family members should not equate physical incapability with mental failing. It is especially important that an ill patient feel a necessary part of the family.
>
> - Families must guard against "rehearsing" how they will act if the patient dies by excluding him or her from family affairs now.

Helping Family Members Cope With Cancer

Support From The Family

The desire to "do something" is common among nearly everyone with a family member or dear friend who has cancer. There is nothing you can do to change the course of cancer, so you do everything you can for the person. Sometimes, doing everything is the worst course to follow.

People with cancer still have the same needs and often the same capabilities as they did before. If they are physically able, they need to participate in their normal range of activities and responsibilities—right down to taking out the garbage. Helplessness, or worse, an unnecessary feeling of helplessness, is one of the great woes of the person with cancer. In the words of one:

> *"I am deeply angry over the way patients (not only cancer patients but any patient with a life-threatening diagnosis) are automatically treated as if we were mentally incompetent. Our relatives have RIGHTS; we have none. This is by a sort of mutual consent, an unconscious conspiracy which seems to be part of our culture. Let an individual become a patient . . . and he is treated, without any 'competency hearing,' as if he had been found in a court of law to be incompetent. Only the relatives are consulted or empowered to make decisions..."*

There is great bitterness in this woman's words, and they can stand as a lesson to all. Although bedridden, a patient probably still is able to discuss treatment options, financial arrangements, and the children's school problems. The rest of the family must make every effort to preserve as much as possible the patient's usual role within the family.

The least you can do is to keep the patient informed of necessary decisions. You can help the seriously ill patient ward off feelings of helplessness or abandonment if you continue to share your activities, goals, and dreams as before.

Few of us who are well know what it is like to be placed in a position of dependency. Cancer attacks one's self concept as a whole person as well as threatening one's life. Feelings of helplessness are real enough when one is flat on one's back. Make every effort not to compound them by ignoring the wishes of the patient, or worse, by trying to make an invalid of a person who is up and around. Pulling one's weight is good exercise.

How The Family Copes

The needs of the family as a unit are important, too. Maintain normal living patterns within the family as well as possible. This is important for long-range as well as day-to-day coping. Sometimes, when the patient is in active treatment, family life becomes totally disrupted. If that happens, it is harder to resume functioning as a unit during periods of extended remission or permanent control.

"My worst emotional problem," one patient said, "was finding that my improved health posed inconveniences and threw my family's plans all out of line."

Understanding such a situation might help prevent it. There are many ways we cope with fear, anxiety and the threat of loss or death. One way is to begin preparing ourselves for an event by thinking about it, without being aware that we are doing so, as if it had already happened. Thus, we "rehearse" life as it will be so that we can assume our new roles more easily when the time comes. People do this throughout their lives, although usually they are unaware of it. For example, teenagers spend increasing amounts of time with friends rather than with family, "rehearsing" for the time when they will go out on their own.

When a family member has cancer, you may be "rehearsing" the future in your own mind. You might begin to "practice" how the family will function if that person dies. Watch for signs that you are excluding the patient and turn the routine back toward normal if you are. Knowing that these things happen, however, try not to feel guilty if you find yourself emotionally out of step with remission or recovery.

♣ **It's A Fact!!**
Problems become less difficult to face if the family can discuss them.

Chapter 42

Coping With Death, Traumatic Events, And Feelings

Coping With Loss—Bereavement And Grief

The loss of a loved one is life's most stressful event and can cause a major emotional crisis. After the death of someone you love, you experience bereavement, which literally means "to be deprived by death."

Knowing What To Expect

When a death takes place, you may experience a wide range of emotions, even when the death is expected. Many people report feeling an initial stage of numbness after first learning of a death, but there is no real order to the grieving process.

Some emotions you may experience include:

- Denial
- Disbelief
- Confusion
- Shock

About This Chapter: "Coping With Loss—Bereavement And Grief" is copyrighted and published by the National Mental Health Association, no part of this document may be reproduced without written consent, © 2003; reprinted with permission. "Coping With Loss And Grief Through Online Support Groups" was taken from Document #ED446331, ERIC Counseling and Student Services Clearinghouse, July 2000, located online at http://www.ericfacility.net/ericdigests/ed446331.htm.

♣ It's A Fact!!

Q: My mom died yesterday in the hospital and I don't know what to do with myself. I feel shocked, drained and empty. My friends have been brilliant but it isn't helping. My dad has been amazing but has been bottling up his feelings for my sister and me. Everything has changed and I don't feel like I have a reason to live anymore. Please help me, I can't cope.

A: We are so very sorry to hear about your mother's death. We send our sincere sympathy to you, your father, and your family for such a deeply painful loss. Your mother must have been a wonderful woman and you will carry her memory and her love for you in your heart forever.

In these first days following your mom's passing, it is completely normal to feel the way you do. To feel numb, shocked, drained and terribly sad is inevitable. You have begun the process called grieving, and it will last many months, perhaps a year or more, as your mind works through all the emotions involved with the loss of such an irreplaceable and special person in your life. You will be coping with many feelings as you go through the different stages of grieving. You will feel fear, anger, and depression, but eventually comes understanding, acceptance, and a readiness to move on with life. Allow the feelings to come, embrace them, and experience them even though they hurt, because that's how you will recover. The healing process takes time when the loss is so great, but you will survive and learn to be happy again, as your mother would so much wish for you.

We are grateful to know that your father is a strong part of your family and that you have very supportive friends. Let them help you in whatever way they wish. Your dad and your sister have to go through their own grieving too, however. And they will do it in the ways that work for them. Find someone comfortable to talk with about your feelings, preferably a trusted adult such as a school counselor or clergy person. Talking through the many different emotions that will come up over these next months is very important for the healing process. If possible, some short-term family counseling might be very helpful too. Loss is a part of life, but the pain and hurt will at moments seem unbearable. Those moments pass. Time does heal. Our thoughts are with you.

Source: This information is reprinted with permission from www.Teen Growth.com. © 2003. All rights reserved.

- Sadness
- Anger
- Despair
- Yearning
- Humiliation
- Guilt

These feelings are normal and common reactions to loss. You may not be prepared for the intensity and duration of your emotions or how swiftly your moods may change. You may even begin to doubt the stability of your mental health. But be assured that these feelings are healthy and appropriate and will help you come to terms with your loss.

Remember—It takes time to fully absorb the impact of a major loss. You never stop missing your loved one, but the pain eases after time and allows you to go on with your life.

Mourning A Loved One

It is not easy to cope after a loved one dies. You will mourn and grieve. Mourning is the natural process you go through to accept a major loss. Mourning may include religious traditions honoring the dead or gathering with friends and family to share your loss. Mourning is personal and may last months or years.

Grieving is the outward expression of your loss. Your grief is likely to be expressed physically, emotionally, and psychologically. For instance, crying is a physical expression, while depression is a psychological expression.

It is very important to allow yourself to express these feelings. Often, death is a subject that is avoided, ignored, or denied. At first it may seem helpful to separate yourself from the pain, but you cannot avoid grieving forever. Someday those feelings will need to be resolved or they may cause physical or emotional illness.

Many people report physical symptoms that accompany grief. Stomach pain, loss of appetite, intestinal upsets, sleep disturbances, and loss of energy are all common symptoms of acute grief. Of all life's stresses, mourning can seriously test your natural defense systems. Existing illnesses may worsen or new conditions may develop.

♣ It's A Fact!!

Q: I am 15 years old and recently I had to deal with something I don't think I'm ever going to be able to get over—my dad died. My mom has three children and is trying to move on and raise us. It's really hard for us and sometimes I want to help her, but I don't feel like I can help myself. I just want OUT of everything. I miss my dad and I don't know what to do.

A: We are deeply sorry for the loss of your father. This is a very difficult time for you. All of the emotions (depression, anger, and confusion) you're going through are completely normal.

The grieving process is something we all go through when we've lost someone special. However, everyone goes through this process at different speeds and with different emotions. Your mother, for example, may be using her determination and strong spirit to help her through this difficult time. She's using her energy to focus on you and your siblings. Your feelings (emotions) of wanting to get away from everything and being confused about what's the "right thing" to do are part of your grieving process. Mourning the death of a parent and coming to terms with the loss will take time, but slowly you will adapt.

While everyone experiences grief in his or her own way, one thing is for certain—it helps to talk to someone. If you're sad and confused, tell your mother (or another trusted adult). Don't be afraid to show your emotions. Keeping things bottled-up inside to be strong for other people won't help you and it won't help the people you care about. It sounds like your mother is a wonderful person and we don't think she would want you to suffer alone because you were afraid to talk to her about this. Just knowing that someone else is listening and is there when you need support can make all the difference in the world.

We know you miss your dad. It's completely natural. Your father may have passed on, but we're sure you have many special memories that will live on in your heart. As long as you have those memories, you'll always have a part of your dad with you.

Source: This information is reprinted with permission from www.TeenGrowth.com. © 2003. All rights reserved.

Profound emotional reactions may occur. These reactions include anxiety attacks, chronic fatigue, depression and thoughts of suicide. An obsession with the deceased is also a common reaction to death.

Dealing With A Major Loss

The death of a loved one is always difficult. Your reactions are influenced by the circumstances of a death, particularly when it is sudden or accidental. Your reactions are also influenced by your relationship with the person who died.

A child's death arouses an overwhelming sense of injustice—for lost potential, unfulfilled dreams and senseless suffering. Parents may feel responsible for the child's death, no matter how irrational that may seem. Parents may also feel that they have lost a vital part of their own identity.

A spouse's death is very traumatic. In addition to the severe emotional shock, the death may cause a potential financial crisis if the spouse was the family's main income source. The death may necessitate major social adjustments requiring the surviving spouse to parent alone, adjust to single life and maybe even return to work.

Elderly people may be especially vulnerable when they lose a spouse because it means losing a lifetime of shared experiences. At this time, feelings of loneliness may be compounded by the death of close friends.

A loss due to suicide can be among the most difficult losses to bear. They may leave the survivors with a tremendous burden of guilt, anger and shame. Survivors may even feel responsible for the death. Seeking counseling during the first weeks after the suicide is particularly beneficial and advisable.

Living With Grief

Coping with death is vital to your mental health. It is only natural to experience grief when a loved one dies. The best thing you can do is allow yourself to grieve. There are many ways to cope effectively with your pain.

- **Seek out caring people.** Find relatives and friends who can understand your feelings of loss. Join support groups with others who are experiencing similar losses.

♣ It's A Fact!!
Feeling Mad Or Sad

"One of the biggest lessons I learned," says Jon Wagner-Holtz, son of a breast-cancer survivor, *"is that you will feel mad or sad. But other people can help."*

It's natural to feel sad or mad or angry. And it's okay to share your feelings with your parents. They can help you try to understand why you are feeling this way.

It is natural to feel sad when we lose something—whether that loss is temporary or permanent. In life, you are constantly gaining and then losing certain things. And it's natural to be sad about these losses. Talking about loss helps us accept it and move forward.

For example, you can feel sad about losing a game. You may feel that way if you fail a test or can't go somewhere because you're sick. You can be feeling that way now, because your mom can't do things with you the way she used to.

You might feel angry too. Anger is another normal reaction to change—because sometimes we resist change. It's okay to feel angry and to talk to someone about it. What's not okay is to hold anger in and not let it out. It's also not okay to act it out in a way that hurts yourself or someone else. Many families don't allow themselves or their children to express anger. But anger is a feeling that lets us know that things aren't right. It needs to be expressed and acknowledged. Talk to your parents or another caring adult about the sad and angry feelings you have.

Source: Reprinted with permission from The Gillette Women's Cancer Connection website, www.gillettecancerconnect.org. © 2003 The Gillette Company. All rights reserved.

- **Express your feelings.** Tell others how you are feeling; it will help you to work through the grieving process.
- **Take care of your health.** Maintain regular contact with your family physician and be sure to eat well and get plenty of rest. Be aware of the danger of developing a dependence on medication or alcohol to deal with your grief.
- **Accept that life is for the living.** It takes effort to begin to live again in the present and not dwell on the past.
- **Postpone major life changes.** Try to hold off on making any major changes, such as moving, remarrying, changing jobs, or having another child. You should give yourself time to adjust to your loss.
- **Be patient.** It can take months or even years to absorb a major loss and accept your changed life.
- **Seek outside help when necessary.** If your grief seems like it is too much to bear, seek professional assistance to help work through your grief. It's a sign of strength, not weakness, to seek help.

Helping Others Grieve

If someone you care about has lost a loved one, you can help them through the grieving process.

- **Share the sorrow.** Allow them—even encourage them—to talk about their feelings of loss and share memories of the deceased.
- **Don't offer false comfort.** It doesn't help the grieving person when you say "it was for the best" or "you'll get over it in time." Instead, offer a simple expression of sorrow and take time to listen.
- **Offer practical help.** Baby-sitting, cooking, and running errands are all ways to help someone who is in the midst of grieving.
- **Be patient.** Remember that it can take a long time to recover from a major loss. Make yourself available to talk.
- **Encourage professional help when necessary.** Don't hesitate to recommend professional help when you feel someone is experiencing too much pain to cope alone.

Helping Children Grieve

Children who experience a major loss may grieve differently than adults. A parent's death can be particularly difficult for small children, affecting their sense of security or survival. Often, they are confused about the changes they see taking place around them, particularly if well-meaning adults try to protect them from the truth or from their surviving parent's display of grief.

Limited understanding and an inability to express feelings puts very young children at a special disadvantage. Young children may revert to earlier behaviors (such as bed-wetting), ask questions about the deceased that seem insensitive, invent games about dying or pretend that the death never happened.

Coping with a child's grief puts added strain on a bereaved parent. However, angry outbursts or criticism only deepen a child's anxiety and delays recovery. Instead, talk honestly with children, in terms they can understand. Take extra time to talk with them about death and the person who has died. Help them work through their feelings and remember that they are looking to adults for suitable behavior.

Looking To The Future

Remember, with support, patience and effort, you will survive grief. Some day the pain will lessen, leaving you with cherished memories of your loved one.

Coping With Loss And Grief Through Online Support Groups

The death of a loved one is a natural and inevitable life experience. Those who must cope with the loss experience various grief reactions. Typically, people discuss their grief reaction with someone they know or do not discuss it at all. Current technology now enables people to cope with grief through participation in online support groups from the comfort and privacy of their home.

Grief And Healing

The grief process is typically nonlinear, repetitive and painful to transcend. It involves adaptation to many changes, and it is marked by repetitive

Coping With Death, Traumatic Events, And Feelings

cycles of progression followed by stagnation or regression. The three aspects of grief are emotional, physical and behavioral.

- Emotional reactions include fear, anxiety, depression, confusion, search for meaning and anger.

- Physical symptoms include changes in eating and/or sleeping patterns, fatigue, increased risk for illness and weight increase/decrease.

- Behavioral responses include diminished interest in usual activities, acting out or withdrawal from and/or rejection of support systems.

Online Support

Online support groups for loss assist members in facing the void left by the loss of a loved one and help to reduce members' feelings of isolation and their sense of feeling overwhelmed. These are common reactions during the grieving process. Members in an early phase of grief can share their reactions with others in the group while members in a later phase can offer support and problem solving. Facing holidays and special occasions are considered difficult for most members, especially if this will be their first occasion or holiday since the loss of a loved one. Likewise, those who are terminally ill and/or their loved ones face similar anxieties if they anticipate that approaching holidays and special occasions may be the last ones they celebrate together.

Online support groups are a relatively new and growing cyber service. They can be accessed through use of a computer and modem in conjunction with an Internet service provider (ISP) such as America Online (AOL). Once connected through an ISP, online support groups may also be reached through Internet portals (for example, Yahoo) or through specialized websites (for example, http://www.death-dying.com). Each ISP, website or portal sets its own standards and procedures regarding regulations, quality control, crisis management, disclaimers and training of group leaders.

Benefits Of Online Support Groups For Loss

- **Increased Access to Support.** Intimate, honest dialogues and expressions of grief can be stigmatizing. Relatives and neighbors may be overwhelmed or unable to offer support and avoid the subject, pushing the frustrated and grieving person into isolation. Online support groups reduce their sense of isolation and loneliness, a predominant reaction for most people in the midst of the grief process or for those who might otherwise grieve alone and not seek a face-to-face support group or support person.

- **Specialized Online Support Groups.** Some loss groups may need to be age- and/or gender-specific or focus on specific needs or characteristics of loss. Specialized online support groups can be formed more successfully than traditional support groups that are limited by geographic boundaries. For example, teens and children may need age-specific groups in order to discuss loss issues based on their developmental level. They may be encountering their first experience with death, may be uncomfortable seeking help from adults or may be unable to relate to adult issues about loss in adult online support groups. Similarly, adults may encounter difficulty helping teens and children cope with grief. Youth can access online support groups as long as a parental security block has not been imposed. Parents, however, should be aware of their child's Internet use and should be encouraged to capitalize on the youth's participation in online support groups to strengthen family communication.

> **Remember!!**
> Some of the benefits of online support are:
> - Increased access to support.
> - Specialized online support groups.
> - Knowledge of the universality of grief. Grief is normal.
>
> Some of the limitations of online support groups include:
> - Anonymity breaches
> - Differing stages of group development and phases of grief
> - Hoax perpetuations
> - Lack of accountability

- **Universality of Grief.** Others struggle, too, and this is not always evident to grieving people who tend to isolate themselves. Universality unites people as they share similar thoughts, feelings, fears, and/or reactions with their cybercommunity. They realize that grief is normal, they feel validated, and they heal as they complete the grief process.

Limitations Of Online Support Groups For Loss

- **Anonymity Breaches.** Limit the disclosure of personal and identifying information when registering for and participating in on-line support groups. Personal communication between members is discouraged as it can culminate in the exchange of identifying information, thus placing a vulnerable member at risk for cyberstalking or at risk for one's physical safety and privacy.

- **Differing Stages of Group Development and Phases of Grief.** Online support groups for loss are open continuously to new membership. Fluctuations in membership make it difficult for online support groups to maintain the working stage of group development for extended periods. Group cohesion is also diluted by each member's individual grief reactions, resulting in a diverse membership that needs support throughout the grief process. These limitations reduce the efficacy of online support groups as a sole support source for some members.

- **Hoax Perpetuations.** People with unscrupulous motives can deceive an online support group; however, online support groups for loss do not attract many hoaxes.

- **Limited Feedback.** Those with cultural or familial barriers that inhibit open discussions about death or emotional expressions of grief may perceive less personal feedback, absence of face-to-face contact, decreased intimacy, and reduced intensity as incentives to participate.

- **Accountability.** Participation in online support groups raises some accountability, ethical, and legal questions that currently remain unanswered. Accountability is unclear and confusing because online support groups function without regard to geographic borders or local or national laws. Furthermore, professional requirements (or lack of) for hosts are inconsistent.

Conclusion

Online support groups provide assistance by linking grieving people who seek support, especially if support is not available in their local community. However, they are not appropriate for everyone and should not be considered a panacea.

✔ Quick Tip
Tips For Dealing With Traumatic Events

1. Write down your feelings and observations in a journal.
2. Draw.
3. Help out someone or volunteer for something.
4. Build on your "support system"—hang out with friends and family.
5. Learn from the traumatic event. Has anything positive come out of it (like patriotism)?
6. Try not to let it interfere—try to do all your normal activities.
7. Exercise.
8. Meditate.
9. Eat well.
10. Get plenty of sleep.
11. Turn to your religion for comfort (pray, meditate).
12. Have fun and try to "escape" sometimes (like going to the movies, working on a hobby).
13. Don't rely on alcohol or drugs.
14. Make a plan with your family and friends about what you would do in the event of a tragedy.

Source: Excerpted with permission from the TeenHealthFX website, www.teenhealthfx.com. Copyright © 2002 Atlantic Health System. All Rights Reserved.

Part 6

If You Need More Information

Chapter 43

Sources Of Cancer Information, Advocacy, And Support

People with cancer and their families sometimes need assistance coping with the emotional as well as the practical aspects of their disease. This chapter includes some of the national organizations that provide this type of support. It is not intended to be a comprehensive listing of all organizations that offer these services in the United States, nor does inclusion of any particular organization imply endorsement. The intent of this chapter is to provide information useful to individuals nationally. For that reason, it does not include the many local groups that offer valuable assistance to patients and their families in individual states or cities.

Doctors, nurses, or hospital social workers who work with cancer patients may also have information about support groups, such as their location, size, type, and how often they meet. Most hospitals have social services departments that provide information about cancer support programs. Additionally,

---

About This Chapter: Text in this chapter is excerpted and adapted from the following documents: "Guide to National Cancer Institute Information Resources for Patients and the Public," Cancer Facts Fact Sheet 2.9, National Cancer Institute (NCI), April 25, 2003; "Cancer Support Groups: Questions and Answers," Cancer Facts Fact Sheet 8.8, NCI, February 25, 2002; "National Organizations That Offer Services to People With Cancer and Their Families," Cancer Facts Fact Sheet 8.1, NCI, August 8, 2003; and compiled from other sources deemed accurate. All contact information was updated and verified in December 2003.

many newspapers carry a special health supplement containing information about where to find support groups.

Guide to National Cancer Institute Information Resources for Patients and the Public

Cancer.gov Website

The cancer information section of the National Cancer Institute's (NCI) Cancer .gov website provides access to PDQ®, the Institute's comprehensive cancer information database. Additional resources available on this website include publications for cancer patients, clinical trial results, a dictionary of cancer terms, and prepared literature searches on specific cancer topics. Links to other websites that have been reviewed for quality and reliability can also be found on Cancer.gov. These resources are available at http://cancer.gov/cancerinformation on the Internet.

✔ **Quick Tip**

- The National Cancer Institute's (NCI) Cancer.gov website provides access to cancer information, clinical trial results, and prepared literature searches on specific cancer topics (see the Cancer.gov website section).

- NCI's PDQ database contains cancer information summaries and abstracts of ongoing cancer clinical trials (see the PDQ section).

- NCI's Cancer Information Service staff provide the latest cancer information (see the Cancer Information Service section).

Cancer Information Service

The NCI's Cancer Information Service (CIS) is a national information and education network for patients, the public, and health professionals. From 14 regional offices covering the entire United States, including Puerto Rico, the U.S. Virgin Islands, and the Pacific Islands, trained staff provide the latest cancer information and smoking cessation counseling through a toll-free telephone service. Staff can respond to calls in either English or Spanish.

The CIS's toll-free number is 1-800-4-CANCER (1-800-422-6237). For deaf and hard of hearing callers with TTY equipment, the number is 1-800-332-8615. Hours of operation are Monday through Friday, 9:00 a.m. to 4:30 p.m., local time. Callers also have the option of listening to recorded information about cancer 24 hours a day, 7 days a week.

The CIS also provides live, online assistance through the LiveHelp link on the NCI's website. Through LiveHelp, an instant messaging service, information specialists provide Internet users with help in navigating NCI websites, searching for clinical trials, and finding answers to questions about cancer. LiveHelp is available Monday through Friday, 9:00 a.m. to 10:00 p.m. Eastern time.

Additional Government Sources of Cancer Information

The following agencies include information on cancer within their websites.

Centers for Disease Control and Prevention (CDC)
1600 Clifton Rd.
Atlanta, GA 30333
Toll-Free: 800-311-3435
Phone: 404-639-3311
TTY: 404-639-3312
Website: http://www.cdc.gov

Environmental Protection Agency
Ariel Rios Building
1200 Pennsylvania Ave., NW
Washington, DC 20460
Phone: 202-272-0167
Website: http://www.epa.gov
E-Mail: public-access@epa.gov

National Institutes of Health (NIH)
Bethesda, MD 20892
Toll-Free: 800-729-6686; TTY: 888-889-6432
Phone: 301-496-4000
Website: http://www.nih.gov
E-mail: NIHInfo@od.nih.gov

U.S. Food and Drug Administration (FDA)
5600 Fishers Lane
Rockville, MD 20857
Toll-Free: 888-463-6332
Website: http://www.fda.gov

Cancer Support Groups: Questions and Answers

People diagnosed with cancer and their families face many challenges that may leave them feeling overwhelmed, afraid, and alone. It can be difficult to cope with these challenges or to talk to even the most supportive family members and friends. Often, support groups can help people affected by cancer feel less alone and can improve their ability to deal with the uncertainties and challenges that cancer brings. Support groups give people who are affected by similar diseases an opportunity to meet and discuss ways to cope with the illness.

How can support groups help?

People who have been diagnosed with cancer sometimes find they need assistance coping with the emotional as well as the practical aspects of their disease. In fact, attention to the emotional burden of cancer is sometimes part of a patient's treatment plan. Cancer support groups are designed to provide a confidential atmosphere where cancer patients or cancer survivors can discuss the challenges that accompany the illness with others who may have experienced the same challenges. For example, people gather to discuss the emotional needs created by cancer, to exchange information about their disease—including practical problems such as managing side effects or returning to work after treatment—and to share their feelings. Support groups have helped thousands of people cope with these and similar situations.

Can family members and friends participate in support groups?

Family and friends are affected when cancer touches someone they love, and they may need help in dealing with stresses such as family disruptions, financial worries, and changing roles within relationships. To help meet these needs, some support groups are designed just for family members of people diagnosed with cancer; other groups encourage families and friends to participate along with the cancer patient or cancer survivor.

What types of support groups are available?

Several kinds of support groups are available to meet the individual needs of people at all stages of cancer treatment, from diagnosis through followup care. Some groups are general cancer support groups, while more specialized groups may be for teens or young adults, for family members, or for people affected by a particular disease. Support groups may be led by a professional, such as a psychiatrist, psychologist, or social worker, or by cancer patients or survivors. In addition, support groups can vary in approach, size, and how often they meet. Many groups are free, but some require a fee (people can contact their health insurance company to find out whether their plan will cover the cost). It is important for people to find an atmosphere that is comfortable and meets their individual needs.

National Organizations That Offer Services to People With Cancer and Their Families

American Brain Tumor Association
2720 River Road
Des Plaines, IL 60018
Toll-Free: 800-886-2282
Phone: 847-827-9910
Fax: 847-827-9918
Website: http://www.abta.org
E-mail: info@abta.org

The American Brain Tumor Association provides patient information and supports researchers in the United States and Canada.

American Cancer Society (ACS)
1599 Clifton Road, NE.
Atlanta, GA 30329-4251
Toll-Free: 1-800-227-2345 (1-800-ACS-2345)
Phone: 404-320-3333
Website: http://www.cancer.org

The ACS is a voluntary organization that offers a variety of services to patients and their families. The ACS also supports research, provides printed materials, and conducts educational programs. Staff can accept calls and distribute publications in Spanish. A local ACS unit may be listed in the white pages of the telephone directory under "American Cancer Society."

American Cancer Society (ACS) Supported Programs

Cancer Survivors Network (http://www.acscsn.org): This is both a telephone and Web-based service for cancer survivors, their families, caregivers, and friends. The telephone component (1-877-333-HOPE) provides survivors and families access to pre-recorded discussions. The Web-based component offers live online chat sessions, virtual support groups, pre-recorded talk shows, and personal stories.

I Can Cope: I Can Cope is a patient education program that is designed to help patients, families, and friends cope with the day-to-day issues of living with cancer.

Look Good...Feel Better (http://www.lookgoodfeelbetter.org): This program was developed by the Cosmetic, Toiletry, and Fragrance Association Foundation in cooperation with ACS and the National Cosmetology Association. It focuses on techniques that can help people undergoing cancer treatment improve their appearance. The entire program is also available in Spanish.

Reach to Recovery: The Reach to Recovery Program is a rehabilitation program for men and women who have or have had breast cancer. The program helps breast cancer patients meet the physical, emotional, and cosmetic needs related to their disease and its treatment.

Sources Of Cancer Information, Advocacy, And Support

American Institute for Cancer Research (AICR)
1759 R Street, NW.
Washington, DC 20009
Toll-Free: 1-800-843-8114
Phone: 202-328-7744; Fax: 202-328-7336
Website: http://www.aicr.org; E-mail: aicrweb@aicr.org

The AICR provides information about cancer prevention, particularly through diet and nutrition. They offer a toll-free nutrition hotline and funding of research grants. The AICR also has a wide array of consumer and health professional brochures, plus health aids about diet and nutrition and their link to cancer and cancer prevention. The AICR also offers the AICR CancerResource, an information and resource program for cancer patients. A limited selection of Spanish-language publications is available.

Blood and Marrow Transplant Information Network
2900 Skokie Valley Road, Suite B
Highland Park, IL 60035
Toll-Free: 888-597-7674
Phone: 847-433-3313; Fax: 847-433-4599
Website: http://bmtinfonet.org; E-mail: help@bmtinfonet.org

Blood and Marrow Transplant Information Network (BMTinfonet) provides medical information to patients facing bone marrow, blood stem cell, or umbilical cord blood transplant.

Cancer Care, Inc.
National Office
275 Seventh Avenue
New York, NY 10001
Toll-Free: 1-800-813-4673 (1-800-813-HOPE)
Phone: 212-712-8080; 212-712-8400 (Administration)
Fax: 212-712-8495
Website: http://www.cancercare.org; E-mail: info@cancercare.org

Cancer Care is a national nonprofit agency that offers free support, information, financial assistance, and practical help to people with cancer and their loved ones. Services are provided by oncology social workers and are available in person, over the telephone, and through the agency's Website. Cancer Care's reach also extends to professionals—providing education, information, and assistance.

A section of the Cancer Care Website and some publications are available in Spanish, and staff can respond to calls and e-mails in Spanish.

Cancer Hope Network
Two North Road
Chester, NJ 07930
Toll-Free: 1-877-467-3638 (1-877-HOPENET)
Website: http://www.cancerhopenetwork.org
E-mail: info@cancerhopenetwork.org

The Cancer Hope Network provides individual support to cancer patients and their families by matching them with trained volunteers who have undergone and recovered from a similar cancer experience. Such matches are based on the type and stage of cancer, treatments used, side effects experienced, and other factors.

Candlelighters Childhood Cancer Foundation (CCCF)
Post Office Box 498
Kensington, MD 20895-0498
Toll-Free: 1-800-366-2223 (1-800-366-CCCF)
Phone: 301-962-3520
Fax: 301-962-3521
Website: http://www.candlelighters.org
E-mail: info@candlelighters.org

The CCCF is a nonprofit organization that provides information, peer support, and advocacy through publications, an information clearinghouse, and a network of local support groups.

A financial aid list is available that lists organizations to which eligible families may apply for assistance.

Children's Brain Tumor Foundation

274 Madison Avenue, Suite 1301
New York, NY 10016
Website: http://www.cbtf.org
E-mail: info@cbtf.org

The Children's Brain Tumor Foundation provides medical and quality-of-life information for patients with brain tumors and their families. The foundation also funds clinical research.

Children's Hospice International®

901 North Pitt Street, Suite 230
Alexandria, VA 22314
Toll-Free: 1-800-242-4453 (1-800-2-4-CHILD)
Phone: 703-684-0330
Website: http://www.chionline.org
E-mail: info@chionline.org

Children's Hospice International provides a network of support for dying children and their families. It serves as a clearinghouse for research programs and support groups, and offers educational materials and training programs on pain management and the care of seriously ill children.

Colon Cancer Alliance (CCA)

175 Ninth Avenue
New York, NY 10011
Toll-Free: 1-877-422-2030 (Helpline)
Phone: 212-627-7451 (Main office)
Fax: 425-940-6147
Website: http://www.ccalliance.org
E-mail: info@ccalliance.org

The CCA is an organization of colon and rectal cancer survivors, their families, caregivers, and the medical community. The Alliance provides patient support and public education, supports research, and advocates for the needs of cancer patients and their families. The CCA offers information including brochures and booklets, a newsletter, a toll-free Helpline, and weekly online chats. It also offers the CCA Buddies Network, which matches survivors and caregivers with others in a similar situation for one-on-one emotional support. The CCA has volunteers who speak Spanish.

International Myeloma Foundation (IMF)
12650 Riverside Drive
Suite 206
North Hollywood, CA 91607-3421
Toll-Free: 1-800-452-2873 (1-800-452-CURE)
Phone: 818-487-7455
Fax: 818-487-7454
Website: http://www.myeloma.org
E-mail: TheIMF@myeloma.org

The IMF supports education, treatment, and research for multiple myeloma. They provide a toll-free hotline, seminars, and educational materials for patients and their families. Although the IMF does not sponsor support groups, they do keep a list of other organizations' support groups and provide information on how to start a support group. A section of the IMF Website and some printed materials are available in Spanish.

Lance Armstrong Foundation (LAF)
Post Office Box 161150
Austin, TX 78716-1150
Phone: 512-236-8820
Fax: 512-236-8482
Website: http://www.laf.org

The LAF, a nonprofit organization founded by cancer survivor and cyclist Lance Armstrong, provides resources and support services to people diagnosed with cancer and their families. The LAF's services include Cycle of Hope, a national cancer education campaign for people with cancer and those at risk for developing the disease, and the Cancer Profiler, a free interactive treatment decision support tool. The LAF also provides scientific and research grants for the better understanding of cancer and cancer survivorship.

Sources Of Cancer Information, Advocacy, And Support

The Leukemia and Lymphoma Society
1311 Mamaroneck Avenue
White Plains, NY 10605-5221
Toll-Free: 1-800-955-4572
Phone: 914-949-5213
Fax: 914-949-6691
Website: http://www.leukemia-lymphoma.org
E-mail: infocenter@leukemia-lymphoma.org

The goal of The Leukemia and Lymphoma Society is to find cures for leukemia, lymphoma, Hodgkin's disease, and multiple myeloma and to improve the quality of life of patients and their families. The Society supports medical research and provides health education materials, as well as the following services: patient financial aid for specified treatment expenses and transportation, family support groups, First Connection (a professionally supervised peer support program), referrals, school re-entry materials, and public and professional education. The Society also provides audiotapes in English and some Spanish-language publications.

Living Beyond Breast Cancer (LBBC)
10 East Athens Avenue, Suite 204
Ardmore, PA 19003
Toll-Free: 1-888-753-5222 (1-888-753-LBBC) (Survivors' Helpline)
Phone: 610-645-4567; Fax: 610-645-4573
Website: http://www.lbbc.org
E-mail: mail@lbbc.org

The LBBC is an educational organization that aims to empower women with breast cancer to live as long as possible with the best quality of life. The LBBC offers an interactive message board and information about upcoming conferences and teleconferences on its Website. In addition, the organization has a toll-free Survivors' Helpline, a Young Survivors Network for women diagnosed with breast cancer who are age 45 or younger, and outreach programs for medically underserved communities. The LBBC also offers a quarterly educational newsletter and a book for African American women living with breast cancer.

Locks of Love
2925 10th Avenue N., Suite 102
Lake Worth, FL 33461
Toll Free: 888-896-1588
Phone: 561-963-1677; Fax: 561-963-9914
Website: http://www.locksoflove.org; E-mail: info@locksoflove.org

Locks of Love was founded in 1997 to provide hairpieces to children under the age of 18 who have experienced hair loss as a result of medical concerns. Hairpieces are created with donated hair and made available on a sliding scale based on financial need.

Lymphoma Research Foundation (LRF)
For patient services:
8800 Venice Boulevard, Suite 207
Los Angeles, CA 90034
Toll-Free: 1-800-500-9976
Phone: 310-204-7040
Fax: 310-204-7043
Website: http://www.lymphoma.org/
E-mail: LRF@lymphoma.org (general information);
helpline@lymphoma.org (patient services)

For research and advocacy:
19th Floor
111 Broadway
New York, NY 10006
Toll-Free: 1-800-235-6848; Phone: 212-349-2910
E-mail: researchgrants@lymphoma.org (research program); advocacy@lymphoma.org (advocacy)

In 2001, the Lymphoma Research Foundation of America (LRFA) and the Cure For Lymphoma Foundation (CFL) merged to become the Lymphoma Research Foundation (LRF). The LRF's mission is to eradicate lymphoma and serve those touched by this disease. The LRF funds research, advocates for lymphoma-related legislation, and provides educational and support programs for patients and their families.

The Multiple Myeloma Research Foundation (MMRF)
Three Forest Street
New Canaan, CT 06840
Phone: 203-972-1250
Website: http://www.multiplemyeloma.org
E-mail: themmrf@themmrf.org

The MMRF supports research grants and professional and patient symposia on multiple myeloma and related blood cancers. The MMRF publishes a quarterly newsletter, and provides referrals and information packets free of charge to patients and family members.

National Alliance of Breast Cancer Organizations (NABCO)
Nine East 37th Street
10th Floor
New York, NY 10016
Toll-Free: 1-888-806-2226 (1-888-80-NABCO)
Phone: 212-889-0606; Fax: 212-689-1213
Website: http://www.nabco.org; E-mail: NABCOinfo@aol.com

NABCO is a nonprofit organization that provides information about breast cancer and acts as an advocate for the legislative concerns of breast cancer patients and survivors. NABCO maintains a list, organized by state, of phone numbers for support groups.

National Asian Women's Health Organization (NAWHO)
250 Montgomery Street, Suite 900
San Francisco, CA 94104
Phone: 415-989-9747; Fax: 415-989-9758
Website: http://www.nawho.org
E-mail: nawho@nawho.org

The NAWHO is working to improve the health status of Asian women and families through research, education, leadership, and public policy programs. They have resources for Asian women in English, Cantonese, Laotian, Vietnamese, and Korean. Publications on subjects such as reproductive rights, breast and cervical cancer, and tobacco control are available.

National Bone Marrow Transplant Link (nbmtLink)
20411 West 12 Mile Road, Suite 108
Southfield, MI 48076
Toll-Free: 1-800-546-5268 (1-800-LINK-BMT)
Phone: 248-358-1886
Website: http://www.nbmtlink.org; E-mail: info@nbmtlink.org

The nbmtLink motto is "A Second Chance at Life is Our First Priority." The nbmtLink operates a 24-hour, toll-free number and provides peer support to bone marrow transplant (BMT) patients and their families. It serves as an information center for prospective BMT patients as well as a resource for health professionals. Educational publications, brochures, and videos are available. Staff can respond to calls in Spanish.

National Children's Cancer Society
1015 Locust, Suite 600
St. Louis, MO 63101
Toll-Free: 1-800-5-FAMILY (1-800-532-6459)
Phone: 314-241-1600
Fax: 314-241-1996; Program Services Fax: 314-241-6949
Website: http://www.children-cancer.org

The NCCS helps children with cancer get the care and support they deserve. They provide emotional support, advocacy, education and financial assistance. The website contains links to organizations which provide scholarships for survivors.

National Childhood Cancer Foundation (NCCF)
440 East Huntington Drive
Post Office Box 60012
Arcadia, CA 91066-6012
Toll-Free: 1-800-458-6223
Phone: 626-447-1674; Fax: 626-447-6359
Website: http://www.nccf.org; E-mail: webinfo@nccf.org

The NCCF supports research conducted by a network of institutions, each of which has a team of doctors, scientists, and other specialists with the

Sources Of Cancer Information, Advocacy, And Support

special skills required for the diagnosis, treatment, supportive care, and research on the cancers of infants, children, and young adults. Advocating for children with cancer and the centers that treat them is also a focus of the NCCF. A limited selection of Spanish-language publications is available.

National Marrow Donor Program® (NMDP)
3001 Broadway Street, NE, Suite 500
Minneapolis, MN 55413-1753
Toll-Free: 1-800-627-7692 (1-800-MARROW-2);
1-888-999-6743 (Office of Patient Advocacy)
Phone: 612-627-5800
Website: http://www.marrow.org

The National Marrow Donor Program (NMDP), which is funded by the Federal Government, was created to improve the effectiveness of the search for bone marrow donors. It keeps a registry of potential bone marrow donors and provides free information on bone marrow transplantation, peripheral blood stem cell transplant, and unrelated donor stem cell transplant, including the use of umbilical cord blood. The NMDP's Office of Patient Advocacy assists transplant patients and their physicians through the donor search and transplant process by providing information, referrals, support, and advocacy.

National Mental Health Association
2001 N. Beauregard St.
12th Floor
Alexandria, VA 22311
Toll-Free: 800-969-6642
Toll-Free TTY: 800-433-5959
Phone: 703-684-7722
Fax: 703-684-5968
Website: http://www.nmha.org

The National Mental Health Association has several resources available to help cope with tragic events, loss and other topics.

National Patient Travel Center (NPTC)
4620 Haygood Road, Suite One
Virginia Beach, VA 23455
Toll-Free: 1-800-296-1217
Phone: 757-318-9174; Fax: 757-318-9107
Website: http://www.patienttravel.org; E-mail: mercymedical@erols.com

The NPTC provides the National Patient Travel Helpline, a telephone service which facilitates patient access to charitable medical air transportation resources in the United States. The NPTC also offers information about discounted airline ticket programs for patients and patient escorts, operates Special-Lift and Child-Lift programs, and brings ambulatory outpatients to the United States from many overseas locations.

The Oral Cancer Foundation
Number 205
3419 Via Lido
Newport Beach, CA 92663
Phone: 949-646-8000; Fax: 949-496-3331
Website: http://www.oralcancerfoundation.org
E-mail: info@oralcancerfoundation.org

The Oral Cancer Foundation is a nonprofit organization that is dedicated to saving lives through education, research, prevention, advocacy, and support for persons with oral cancer. The Foundation provides an online Oral Cancer Forum, which includes a message board and chat room that connect newly diagnosed patients, family members, and the public.

Patient Advocate Foundation (PAF)
700 Thimble Shoals Boulevard, Suite 200
Newport News, VA 23606
Toll-Free: 1-800-532-5274
Phone: 757-873-5274; Fax: 757-873-8999
Website: http://www.patientadvocate.org; E-mail: help@patientadvocate.org

The PAF provides education, legal counseling, and referrals to cancer patients and survivors concerning managed care, insurance, financial issues, job discrimination, and debt crisis matters.

Sisters Network®, Inc.
8787 Woodway Drive, Suite 4206
Houston, TX 77063
Toll-Free: 1-866-781-1808
Phone: 713-781-0255
Fax: 713-780-8998
Website: http://www.sistersnetworkinc.org
E-mail: sisnet4@aol.com

Sisters Network seeks to increase local and national attention to the impact that breast cancer has in the African American community. All chapters are run by breast cancer survivors and receive volunteer assistance from community leaders and associate members. The services provided by Sisters Network include individual/group support, community education, advocacy, and research. The national headquarters serves as a resource and referral base for survivors, clinical trials, and private/government agencies. Teleconferences are held to update chapters with the latest information and share new ideas. An educational brochure designed for underserved women is available. In addition, a national African American breast cancer survivors newsletter is distributed to survivors, medical facilities, government agencies, organizations, and churches nationwide.

The Skin Cancer Foundation
245 Fifth Avenue, Suite 1403
New York, NY 10016
Toll-Free: 1-800-754-6490 (1-800-SKIN-490)
Phone: 212-725-5176
Fax: 212-725-5751
Website: http://www.skincancer.org
E-mail: info@skincancer.org

Major goals of The Skin Cancer Foundation are to increase public awareness of the importance of taking protective measures against the damaging rays of the sun and to teach people how to recognize the early signs of skin cancer. They conduct public and medical education programs to help reduce skin cancer.

STARBRIGHT Foundation
1850 Sawtelle Blvd., Suite 450
Los Angeles, CA 90025
Toll-Free: 1-800-315-2580
Phone: 310-479-1212
Fax: 310-479-1235
Website: http://www.starbright.org
E-mail: ford@starbright.org

The STARBRIGHT Foundation creates projects that are designed to help seriously ill children and adolescents cope with the psychosocial and medical challenges they face. The STARBRIGHT Foundation produces materials such as interactive educational CD-ROMs and videos about medical conditions and procedures, advice on talking with a health professional, and other issues related to children and adolescents who have serious medical conditions. All materials are available to children, adolescents, and their families free of charge. Staff can respond to calls in Spanish.

The Susan G. Komen Breast Cancer Foundation
5005 LBJ Freeway, Suite 250
Dallas, TX 75244
Toll-Free: 1-800-462-9273 (1-800-I'M AWARE®)
Phone: 972-855-1600
Fax: 972-855-1605
Website: http://www.komen.org
E-mail: helpline@komen.org

The Susan G. Komen Breast Cancer Foundation's mission is to eradicate breast cancer as a life-threatening disease by advancing research, education, screening, and treatment. This organization operates a national toll-free breast cancer helpline (1-800-I'M AWARE®) that is answered by trained volunteers whose lives have been personally touched by breast cancer. Breast health and breast cancer materials, including pamphlets, brochures, booklets, posters, videos, CD-ROMs, fact sheets, and community outreach materials are available. Staff can respond to calls in Spanish, and some publications are available in Spanish.

TeensHealth
The Nemours Foundation
1600 Rockland Rd.
Wilmington, DE 19803
Phone: 302-651-4046
Website: http://www.teenshealth.com; http://www.kidshealth.org
E-mail: info@KidsHealth.org

Information on a variety of health topics for children and teens, including cancer.

US® TOO! International, Inc.
5003 Fairview Avenue
Downers Grove, IL 60515
Toll-Free: 1-800-808-7866 (1-800-80-US TOO)
Phone: 630-795-1002; Fax: 630-795-1602
Website: http://www.ustoo.org
E-mail: ustoo@ustoo.com

US TOO is a prostate cancer support group organization. Goals of US TOO are to increase awareness of prostate cancer in the community, educate men newly diagnosed with prostate cancer, offer support groups, and provide the latest information about treatment for this disease. A limited selection of Spanish-language publications is available.

Vital Options® International TeleSupport® Cancer Network
15821 Ventura Boulevard, Suite 645
Encino, CA 91436-2946
Toll-Free: 1-800-477-7666 (1-800-GRP-ROOM)
Phone: 818-788-5225
Fax: 818-788-5260
Website: http://www.vitaloptions.org
E-mail: info@vitaloptions.org

The mission of Vital Options is to use communications technology to reach people dealing with cancer. This organization holds a weekly syndicated call-in cancer radio talk show called "The Group Room®," which provides a forum for patients, long-term survivors, family members, physicians, and therapists to discuss cancer issues. Listeners can participate in the show during its broadcast every Sunday from 4 p.m. to 6 p.m. Eastern time by calling the toll-free telephone number. A live Web simulcast of "The Group Room" can be heard by logging onto the Vital Options Website.

The Wellness Community
919 18th Street, NW, Suite 54
Washington, DC 20006
Toll-Free: 1-888-793-9355 (1-888-793-WELL)
Phone: 202-659-9709
Fax: 202-659-9301
Website: http://www.thewellnesscommunity.org
E-mail: help@thewellnesscommunity.org

The Wellness Community provides free psychological and emotional support to cancer patients and their families. They offer support groups facilitated by licensed therapists, stress reduction and cancer education workshops, nutrition guidance, exercise sessions, and social events.

Chapter 44

Finding Cancer Information On The Internet

How To Evaluate Health Information on the Internet: Questions and Answers

The growing popularity of the Internet has made it easier and faster to find health information. However, the Internet also allows rapid and widespread distribution of false and misleading information. It is important for people to carefully consider the source of information and to discuss the information they find with their health care provider. This chapter can help people decide whether the health information they find on the Internet or receive via e-mail from a website is likely to be reliable.

1. Who runs the website?

Any website should make it easy for people to learn who is responsible for the site and its information. On the National Cancer Institute's (NCI) Cancer.gov

---

About This Chapter: Text in this chapter is excerpted and adapted from the following documents: "How to Evaluate Health Information on the Internet," Cancer Facts Fact Sheet 2.10, National Cancer Institute (NCI), August 28, 2002; "Cancer Information Sources," Cancer Facts Fact Sheet 2.1, NCI, June 19, 2003; and compiled from other sources deemed accurate. All contact information was updated and verified in December 2003.

website, for example, the NCI is clearly noted on every major page, along with a link to the site's homepage.

2. Who pays for the website?

It costs money to run a website. The source of a website's funding should be clearly stated or readily apparent. For example, Web addresses ending in ".gov" are Federal Government-sponsored sites, ".edu" indicates educational institutions, ".org" is often used by non-commercial organizations, and ".com" denotes commercial organizations. The source of funding can affect what content is presented, how the content is presented, and what the owners want to accomplish on the site.

3. What is the purpose of the website?

The purpose of the website is related to who runs and pays for it. Many websites have a link to information about the site. The link, which is often called "About This Site," should clearly state the purpose of the site and help users evaluate the trustworthiness of the information on the site.

4. What is the original source of the information on the website?

Many health and medical websites post information collected from other websites or sources. If the person or

> ✔ **Quick Tip**
> - Any website should make it easy for people to learn who is responsible for the site and its information (see Question 1).
>
> - If the person or organization in charge of the website did not write the material, the original source should be clearly identified (see Question 4).
>
> - Health-related websites should give information about the medical credentials of the people who prepare or review the material on the site (see Question 6).
>
> - Any website that asks users for personal information should explain exactly what the site will and will not do with that information (see Question 9).
>
> - The Federal Trade Commission and the Food and Drug Administration are Government agencies that help protect consumers from false or misleading health claims on the Internet (see Question 12).

Finding Cancer Information On The Internet 395

organization in charge of the site did not write the material, the original source should be clearly identified.

5. How is the information on the website documented?

In addition to identifying the original source of the material, the site should identify the evidence on which the material is based. Medical facts and figures should have references (such as citations of articles in medical journals). Also, opinions or advice should be clearly set apart from information that is "evidence-based" (that is, based on research results).

6. How is information reviewed before it is posted on the website?

Health-related websites should give information about the medical credentials of the people who prepare or review the material on the website. For example, Cancer.gov contains cancer information summaries from the Institute's PDQ® database. All PDQ cancer information summaries are peer-reviewed and updated regularly by six editorial boards of cancer specialists in adult treatment, pediatric (childhood) treatment, supportive care, screening and prevention, genetics, and complementary and alternative medicine. The editorial boards review current literature from more than 70 biomedical journals, evaluate its relevance, and synthesize it to write the PDQ summaries.

7. How current is the information on the website?

Websites should be reviewed and updated on a regular basis. It is particularly important that medical information be current, and that the most recent update or review date be clearly posted. Even if the information has not changed, it is helpful to know that the site owners have reviewed it recently to ensure that the information is still valid.

8. How does the website choose links to other sites?

Reliable websites usually have a policy about how they establish links to other sites. Some medical websites take a conservative approach and do not link to any other sites; some link to any site that asks or pays for a link; others link only to sites that have met certain criteria.

9. What information about users does the website collect, and why?

Websites routinely track the path users take through their sites to determine what pages are being used. However, many health-related websites ask the user to "subscribe" or "become a member." In some cases, this may be done so they can collect a user fee or select relevant information for the user. In all cases, the subscription or membership will allow personal information about the user to be collected by the website owners.

Any website asking users for personal information should explain exactly what the site will and will not do with the information. Many commercial sites sell "aggregate" data about their users to other companies—information such as what percent of their users are women with breast cancer. In some cases, they may collect and reuse information that is "personally identifiable," such as the user's ZIP Code, gender, and birth date. Users should be certain they read and understand any privacy policy or similar language on the site, and not sign up for anything they do not fully understand.

10. How does the website manage interactions with users?

There should always be a way for users to contact the website owners with problems, feedback, and questions. If the site hosts a chat room or other online discussion areas, it should tell users about the terms of using the service. Is the service moderated? If so, by whom, and why? It is always a good idea to spend time reading the discussion without joining in, to feel comfortable with the environment before becoming a participant.

11. How can people verify the accuracy of information they receive via e-mail?

Any e-mail messages should be carefully evaluated. The origin of the message and its purpose should be considered. Some companies or organizations use e-mail to advertise products or attract people to their websites. The accuracy of health information may be influenced by the desire to promote a product or service.

Finding Cancer Information On The Internet 397

12. How does the Federal Government protect consumers from false or misleading health claims posted on the Internet?

The Federal Trade Commission (FTC) enforces consumer protection laws. As part of its mission, the FTC investigates complaints about false or misleading health claims posted on the Internet. The FTC's Operation Cure-All page, located at http://www.ftc.gov/bcp/conline/edcams/cureall/ on the Internet, has information to help users evaluate health product claims.

Federal Trade Commission
Consumer Response Center
CRC-240
Washington, DC 20580
Toll-Free: 1-877-382-4357 (1-877-FTC-HELP)
Toll-Free TDD/TTY: 1-866-653-4261
Phone: 202-326-2222
TTY: 202-326-2502 (for deaf and hard of hearing callers)
Website: http://www.ftc.gov

The Food and Drug Administration (FDA) regulates drugs and medical devices to ensure that they are safe and effective. The FDA's Buying Medicines and Medical Products Online webpage is located at http://www.fda.gov/oc/buyonline/ on the Internet. Buying Prescription Medicines Online: A Consumer Safety Guide is available at http://www.fda.gov/cder/drug/consumer/buyonline/guide.htm on the Internet.

Food and Drug Administration
5600 Fishers Lane
Rockville, MD 20857-0001
Toll-Free: 1-888-463-6332 (1-888-INFO-FDA)
Website: http://www.fda.gov

Cancer Information Sources Online

Information about cancer is available in libraries, on the Internet, and from many Government and private sector organizations. Most libraries have resources to help people locate cancer-related articles in the medical and scientific literature, as well as cancer information written specifically for patients and the public. Many libraries also offer public access to computer databases, allowing users to obtain information electronically. Information may also be accessed through the Internet using a computer.

The Internet is a worldwide system of computer networks containing information on a wide variety of subjects, including cancer. Internet users can find information through the World Wide Web (WWW) and electronic mail (e-mail). The WWW allows access to information that may include text and graphics or text only. E-mail can be used to order documents and communicate with other people who can answer questions and offer technical support.

National Cancer Institute

The National Cancer Institute's (NCI) website, Cancer.gov (http://cancer.gov), is a one-stop resource for cancer information. This website provides immediate access to critical information and resources on cancer, helping people with cancer become better informed about their disease and play

---

✔ Quick Tip

- The National Cancer Institute's Cancer.gov website provides access to information about cancer (see the National Cancer Institute section).

- Books and articles about cancer can be found in public, university, hospital, and medical school libraries (see the Public, University, and Medical Libraries section).

- The National Library of Medicine is the world's largest medical library. It is open to the public, and its databases can be accessed on the Internet (see The National Library of Medicine section).

- Cancer information is also available through the National Network of Libraries of Medicine and on the Healthfinder website (see the National Network of Libraries of Medicine and Healthfinder sections).

Finding Cancer Information On The Internet

a more active role in their treatment and care. The site's information is logically arranged by topic, and a search function allows convenient keyword searching across all NCI webpages. The search engine displays the most pertinent information retrieved on many topics under the "Best Bets" feature. Cancer.gov is a comprehensive resource that enables users to quickly find accurate and up-to-date information on all types of cancer, clinical trials (research studies), research programs, funding opportunities, cancer statistics, and the Institute itself.

Many of the NCI's cancer information resources are accessible through the cancer information page of the Institute's website at http://cancer.gov/cancerinformation. The page contains selected information from PDQ®, NCI's cancer information database, including information about ongoing clinical trials. Over 100 PDQ information summaries about cancer treatment, screening, prevention, supportive care, genetics, and complementary and alternative medicine are available. Written by experts and updated regularly, these summaries are based on current standards of care and the latest research. Most of the cancer information summaries are available in both a technical version for health professionals and a nontechnical version for patients, their families, and the general public. In addition, the cancer information page offers links to fact sheets on a range of topics.

Cancer.gov also provides comprehensive information about clinical trials (research studies with people) at http://cancer.gov/clinicaltrials. This webpage provides information on recent advances in cancer research, and materials to help people understand and decide whether to participate in clinical trials. A simple-to-use search tool is available for those interested in finding trials for a specific type of cancer, in a certain geographic region, or for a particular type of treatment.

Up-to-date, accurate cancer information is also available to patients and their families, the public, and health professionals through the NCI's Cancer Information Service (CIS). The CIS website provides background information on the CIS and links to NCI resources and other cancer-related Government websites. It also has a Frequently Asked Questions section that addresses a variety of cancer topics. The CIS website is located at http://cancer.gov/cis.

The NCI also offers additional websites and services that are accessible directly or through NCI's main website at http://cancer.gov:

- The NCI's Publications Locator website can be used to order or view publications online at http://cancer.gov/publications. NCI materials may be identified by topic or searched by keyword, type of cancer, subject, audience, and/or language.

- The NCI's *LiveHelp* service, which is available through the *LiveHelp* link on the NCI's website, provides Internet users with the ability to chat online with an information specialist in English. The service is available Monday through Friday, 9:00 a.m. to 10:00 p.m. Eastern time.

The National Library of Medicine

The National Library of Medicine (NLM) is the world's largest medical library. The NLM is open to the public, and its databases can be used to search for journal article references and abstracts (summaries of articles) without charge or registration. The NLM's databases can be accessed on the Internet and may also be available through some local university, public, and medical libraries.

MEDLINE®, the NLM's premier bibliographic database, contains over 12 million references to articles published since 1966. By searching MEDLINE, readers can find journal articles about specific topics (such as cancer) and, in many cases, can retrieve abstracts of the articles included in the databases.

The NLM allows free access to MEDLINE through PubMed®, an easy-to-use search tool. PubMed provides links to the full text of articles and other resources at the websites of participating publishers. User registration, a subscription fee, or other fees may be required to access the full text of articles in some journals. PubMed can be found at http://www.ncbi.nlm.nih.gov/PubMed.

MEDLINE*plus* is the NLM's website for consumer health information. This site includes links to information about a number of health topics, a

Finding Cancer Information On The Internet

medical encyclopedia, medical dictionaries, databases (including MEDLINE), interactive health tutorials, drug information, directories, organizations, publications and health news, and consumer health libraries. People can access MEDLINE*plus* at http://medlineplus.gov on the Internet.

Loansome Doc® is an NLM service that allows users to order full-text copies of articles found in MEDLINE. Users must establish an agreement with a library that uses DOCLINE®, the NLM's automated interlibrary loan request and referral system, and register to use Loansome Doc. A fee is usually charged by the ordering library.

For more information on NLM programs, services, and hours of operation, individuals may contact the Office of Communications and Public Liaison at 1-888-FIND-NLM (1-888-346-3656) or 301-594-5983. The address is 8600 Rockville Pike, Bethesda, MD 20894. Online assistance is available on the NLM's website at http://wwwns.nlm.nih.gov on the Internet, and by e-mail from custserv@nlm.nih.gov.

National Network of Libraries of Medicine

The National Network of Libraries of Medicine (NN/LM) directs health professionals, educators, and the general public to health care information resources. Inquirers are directed to medical libraries in their region, which can provide assistance with research. Further information about the Network is available by calling 1-800-338-7657, or by visiting the NN/LM Website at http://nnlm.gov on the Internet.

Healthfinder

Healthfinder® is a website created by the U.S. Department of Health and Human Services to provide a free gateway to reliable online consumer health information. It offers information from selected online publications, clearinghouses, databases, and websites, as well as support and self-help groups. Healthfinder also provides links to the websites of Government agencies and nonprofit organizations that provide health information for the public. Healthfinder is located at http://www.healthfinder.gov.

Chapter 45

Additional Reading On Cancer

To make topics easier to identify, the books, magazine and journal articles, and webpages listed in this chapter are alphabetized by title within each section.

Books

At Face Value: My Struggle With A Disfiguring Cancer
By Terry Healey
Published by Xlibris Corporation, August 2001
ISBN: 073886658X

Cancer
By Kirsten Lamb and Wendy Lamb
Published by Raintree Publishers, October 2002
ISBN: 0739852191

Cancer Patient Workbook: Everything You Need To Stay Organized And Informed
By Joanie Willis and Diane Blumenson
Published by DK Publishing, Inc., March 2001
ISBN: 0789467828

About This Chapter: The documents listed in this chapter are intended to serve as a starting point for further research and information. They represent a sampling of available material. Inclusion does not constitute endorsement.

Childhood Cancer Survivors: A Practical Guide To Your Future
By Nancy Keene, Wendy L. Hobbie, and Kathy Ruccione
Published by O'Reilly & Associates, Inc., April 2000
ISBN: 1565924606

The Human Side Of Cancer: Living With Hope, Coping With Uncertainty
By Jimmie C. Holland and Sheldon Lewis
Published by HarperCollins Publishers, 2000
ISBN: 006093042X

Informed Decisions: The Complete Book Of Cancer Diagnosis, Treatment, And Recovery, Second Edition
By Harmon J. Eyre, Lois B. Morris, and Dianne Lange
Published by the American Cancer Society, Inc., October 2001
ISBN: 0944235271

It's Always Something
By Gilda Radner
Published by William Morrow & Co., March 2000
ISBN: 038081322X

It's Not About The Bike: My Journey Back To Life
By Lance Armstrong, with Sally Jenkins
Published by Berkley Trade, September 2001
ISBN: 0425179613

Living With Childhood Cancer: A Practical Guide To Help Families Cope
By Leigh A. Woznick and Carol D. Goodheart
Published by the American Psychological Association, October 2001
ISBN: 1557988722

Surviving Childhood Cancer
By Margot Joan Fromer
Published by New Harbinger Publications, March 1998
ISBN: 1572241020

Additional Reading On Cancer

Women At Risk: The HPV Epidemic And Your Cervical Health
By Gregory Henderson with Allan Warshowsky and Batya Yasgur
Published by Avery, May 2002
ISBN: 158333128X

Magazine And Journal Articles

"Cervical Cancer Screening," by Linda Bren, *FDA Consumer*, January-February 2004 (available online at www.fda.gov/fdac).

"Chronic-Leukemia Drug Clears A Big Hurdle," by N. Seppa, *Science News*, December 14, 2002, p. 371(2)

"Dangerous Tans," by Jaime deBlanc-Knowles and Kim Allen, *E*, September-October 2003, p. 11(2).

"Facts About Teens And Cancer," by Michelle Mueller, *Current Health 2*, a Weekly Reader publication, February 2003, p. 22(3).

"LISA Set To Transform Children's Cancer Care," *Cancer Weekly*, January 20, 2004. p. 84.

"Model Program Monitors Late Effects Of Cancer Treatment In Young Adults," *Cancer Weekly*, September 16, 2003, p. 43.

"New Hope For Children With Eye Tumors, Cancer," *Cancer Weekly*. July 15, 2003, p. 147.

"Preventing Colon Cancer: Screening And Early Detection Save Lives," by Lynne L. Hall, *FDA Consumer*, November-December 2000 (available online at www.fda.gov/fdac).

"Salon Tans Called Cancer Risk," *Current Science* (a Weekly Reader publication), September 14, 2001, p. 12.

"Speedy Approvals For New Cancer Treatments," *FDA Consumer*, July-August 2003 (available online at www.fda.gov/fdac).

"Therapies For Cancer In Children—Past Successes, Future Challenges," by Robert E. Wittes, *The New England Journal of Medicine*. February 20, 2003, p. 747(3).

"What Almost Dying Taught Me About Living," by Sandy Fertman Ryan, *Girls' Life*, October-November 2002, p. 72(3).

Further Reading On The Internet

2bMe
(augments *Look Good... Feel Better for Teens* program)
http://www.2bme.org

Ask NOAH About: Cancers in Children
(links to sources of information)
New York Online Access to Health (NOAH)
http://www.noah-health.org/english/illness/cancer/childcancer.html

Cancer Facts And Figures 2003
American Cancer Society
http://www.cancer.org/downloads/STT/CAFF2003PWSecured.pdf

Choose Your Cover
(series on skin cancer risks)
Centers for Disease Control and Prevention (CDC)
http://www.cdc.gov/chooseyourcover

Getting Ready To Go Back To School
Suite 101.com, Inc.
http://www.suite101.com/article.cfm/8314/76090

Go Ask Alice!
(health questions and answers)
Columbia University
http://www.goaskalice.columbia.edu

Grief During Childhood
American Cancer Society
http://www.cancer.org/docroot/MBC/content/MBC_4_1x_Grief_During_Childhood.asp

Additional Reading On Cancer

History Of Cancer
American Cancer Society
http://www.cancer.org/docroot/CRI/content/
CRI_2_6x_the_history_of_cancer_72.asp

Home Care Guide—Helping Brothers And Sisters Cope
Penn State University Children's Hospital
http://www.hmc.psu.edu/pedsonco/Chapter16.html

How You Can Help A Family Who Has A Child With Cancer
National Children's Cancer Society
http://www.children-cancer.com/pfs/helpinfo/youhelp.html

Interactions With Friends
Childhood Leukemia Center
http://www.patientcenters.com/leukemia/news/friends.html

OncoLink
Abramson Cancer Center of the University of Pennsylvania
http://www.oncolink.org

Pediatric Cancer Care: For Teens Only
Memorial Sloan-Kettering Cancer Center
http://www.mskcc.org/mskcc/html/8228.cfm

TeenHealthFX
Atlantic Health System
http://www.teenhealthfx.com

Teens Living With Cancer
(cancer facts series)
Melissa's Living Legacy Foundation
http://www.teenslivingwithcancer.org/cancerFacts

Tips 4 Youth
(series on tobacco risks)
Centers for Disease Control and Prevention (CDC)
http://www.cdc.gov/tobacco/tips_4_youth

When Your Child Goes Back To School
American Cancer Society
http://www.cancer.org/docroot/CRI/content/
CRI_2_6x_When_Your_Child_Goes_Back-to_School.asp

Young People With Cancer: A Handbook For Parents
National Cancer Institute (NCI)
http://www.cancer.gov/cancerinfo/youngpeople

Index

Index

Page numbers that appear in *Italics* refer to illustrations. Page numbers that have a small 'n' after the page number refer to information shown as Notes at the beginning of each chapter. Page numbers that appear in **Bold** refer to information contained in boxes on that page (except Notes information at the beginning of each chapter).

A

ABNOBAviscum *see* mistletoe
abortion, cancer study **144**
absolute neutrophil count (ANC) 192
ACS *see* American Cancer Society
actinic keratoses, described 89
acute lymphoblastic leukemia (ALL), defined **24**
acute lymphocytic leukemia (ALL)
　described 14
　overview 26–27
acute myelogenous leukemia (AML)
　defined **24**
　described 14
　overview 27–228
addiction, tobacco 74
adenocarcinoma
　defined **112**
　described 58
adenosquamous carcinoma, described 58
adjuvant therapy
　defined **206**
　described 41
Adriamycin (doxorubicin) 244
"Afraid to Ask?" (Teens Living with Cancer) 297n

age factor
　breast cancer **50**
　colon cancer **55**, **56**
　testicular cancer **176**
AICR *see* American Institute for Cancer Research
alcohol use
　breast cancer **50**
　cancer 9
　recurrent cancer 326
Alkeran (melphalan) 245
ALL *see* acute lymphoblastic leukemia; acute lymphocytic leukemia
"All Drugged Up: Understanding Your Medications" (Teens Living with Cancer) 241n
allogeneic transplant, described 33, 215
alopecia, defined **288**
alternative therapies, described **232**
alveoli, described *see* trachea
American Academy of Family Physicians, described 79
American Brain Tumor Association, contact information 377
American Cancer Society (ACS), contact information 378
American Institute for Cancer Research (AICR), contact information 379

amino acids, defined **106**
AML *see* acute myelogenous leukemia
amputate, defined **12**
amygdalin 233
ANC *see* absolute neutrophil count
anemia
  defined **12**
  leukemia 14, 25
anesthesiologists, described 197
angiogenesis inhibitor, defined **230**
anorexia
  cancer treatment 224–25
  defined **224**
anthracyclines 185, 247–49, **268**
antibiotic medications
  cancer treatment 221
  leukemia 26
anti-cancer medications, cancer treatment 7
anti-depressant medications, cancer treatment 250–51
antiemetic medications
  cancer treatment 224, 249, 255
  defined **224, 254**
antigens, defined **212**
antioxidants, defined **230**
antiperspirants, breast cancer 142, 145
"Antiperspirants/Deodorants and Breast Cancer" (NCI) 139n
anxiety, counseling 285–86
appearance, cancer treatment 287–96
ARA-C (cytarabine) 243
Armstrong, Lance 175, 179
  see also Lance Armstrong Foundation
artificial sweeteners
  cancer risk 133–35
  described **134**
  regulation **136**
"Artificial Sweeteners" (NCI) 133n
artificial tanning, recommendations **94**
asbestos, breast cancer 146–47
Askin's tumor, described 38
asparaginase 241
aspartame, cancer risk 134–35
astrocytomas, described 15
audiogram, cancer diagnosis 186
autologous transplant, described 33, 215

B

Bactrim 221
barium enema, colon cancer 57, 162
Barrett's esophagus 113
basal cell carcinomas
  defined **88**
  described 45, 88, 164
BCNU (carmustine) 242
benign prostatic hyperplasia (BPH), described 62
bereavement, described 359–70
bichloroacetic acid 103
biofeedback, defined **312**
biological response modifiers (BRM), defined **212**
biological response modifier (BRM) therapy *see* biological therapy
biological therapy
  defined **312**
  overview 211–12
biopsy
  breast cancer 51–52
  cancer diagnosis 187–89
  cervical cancer 102
  colon cancer 57
  defined **188**
  described 5
  leukemia 25
  lung cancer 61
  prostate cancer 63
  recurrent cancer 314
blasts, leukemia 24, 29
Blenoxane (bleomycin) 242
bleomycin 242
blessed thistle **231**
Blood and Marrow Transplant Information Network, contact information 179
blood counts, leukemia 25
blood count summary chart **190**
blood tests, cancer diagnosis 189–94
blood transfusions, cancer treatment 219–21
BMI *see* body mass index
body mass index (BMI)
  defined **110**
  described 111
Bond, John H. **161**
bone cancer *see* Ewing's sarcoma; osteosarcoma

Index

bone marrow, described 23, 214–15
bone marrow aspiration, cancer diagnosis 187–89
bone marrow transplantation (BMT)
  coping strategies 218
  defined 214
  leukemia 28
  lymphoma 32, 36
  overview 213–18
bone scanning, cancer diagnosis 184
bovine cartilage, cancer treatment 229
boys *versus* girls *see* gender factor
BPH *see* benign prostatic hyperplasia
brachytherapy, defined 206
brain tumors, described 15
breast cancer
  exercise 113
  male 52–54
  missed diagnosis 140–41
  myths 139–45
  oral contraceptives 119–21
  overview 49–52
  screening tests 158, 158–59, 165–67
"Breast Cancer (PDQ): Screening-Patient" (NCI) 157n
"Breast Cancer (PDQ): Treatment-Patient" (NCI) 49n
breast self examination (BSE)
  described 158
  overview 169–73
  recurrent cancer 324
BRM *see* biological response modifiers
BRM therapy *see* biological therapy
bronchi, described 58
bronchitis 68
bronchoscopy, described 61
BSE *see* breast self examination
Bunin, G.R. 20
burdock 231
Burkitt's lymphoma, described 35
busulfan 242

C

cachexia
  cancer treatment 224–25
  defined 224
CAM *see* complementary and alternative medicine
cancell/entelev
  cancer treatment 229
  described 229
Cancell/Entelev (PDQ): Treatment-Patient (NCI) 227n
cancer
  abortion study 144
  causes 4–5, 8–10
  defined 312
  described 10
  diagnostic procedures 181–94
  drug categories 243
  friends 331–48
  overview 3–10, 331–48
  recurrent 307–22
  risk factors 111, 118
  statistics 17–22
"Cancer Among Adolescents 15-19 Years Old" (Ries, et al.) 20
Cancer Care, Inc., contact information 379
Cancer Facts and Figures 2003 (ACS), Web site address 406
"Cancer.gov Dictionary" (NCI) 6, 18, 24, 32, 38, 44, 88, 112, 189, 202, 214, 230, 254
Cancer.gov Web site, described 374
Cancer Hope Network, contact information 380
Cancer Incidence and Survival among Chilren and Adolescents: United States SEER Program 1975-1995 (NCI) 20
Cancer Information Service, contact information 122
"Cancer Information Sources" (NCI) 393n
cancer myths 139–54
CancerSource, cancer treatment side effects publication 267n
"Cancer Support Groups: Questions and Answers" (NCI) 373n
cancer survivors, follow-up care 323–27
Cancer Survivors Network, described 378
cancer treatment
  long-term side effects 267–72
  overview 219–25
  side effects 13, 253–66
Candlelighters Childhood Cancer Foundation (CCCF), contact information 380
cantron *see* cancell/entelev
carboplatin 242
carcinoembryonic antigen (CEA) 310

carcinogens
  defined **78, 135**
  environmental tobacco smoke 83, 85
  smokeless tobacco 76
carmustine 242
cartilage, cancer treatment 229
Cartilage (Bovine and Shark) (PDQ): Treatment-Patient (NCI) 227n
cataracts, sun overexposure 89
catheters, chemotherapy 7
CAT scan *see* computed tomography
"Causes and Symptoms Of Cancer" (Cherath) 3n
CBE *see* clinical breast examination
CCA *see* Colon Cancer Alliance
CCCF *see* Candlelighters Childhood Cancer Foundation
CCNU (lomustine) 245
CEA *see* carcinoembryonic antigen
CeeNU (lomustine) 245
cell phones *see* cellular telephones
cells, described 3
cellular telephones
  cancer risk 125–31
  statistics **126**
"Cellular Telephone Use and Cancer" (NCI) 125n
Centers for Disease Control and Prevention (CDC)
  contact information **68,** 375
  described 78
  publications
    skin cancer 45n, **92**
    tobacco use 67n
central nervous system (CNS) prophylaxis, leukemia 26, 27
central venous access catheter, defined **202**
cervical cancer
  environmental tobacco smoke 83
  oral contraceptives 122–23
  unprotected sex 99–104
cervical intraepithelial neoplasia (CIN)
  defined **100**
  described 101
chaplains, described 199
chemotherapy
  cancer treatment 7
  defined **206**
  Ewing's sarcoma 13

chemotherapy, continued
  germ cell tumors 44
  hematocrit 191
  Hodgkin's disease 34
  leukemia 25, 27
  lymphoma 32–33, **36**
  medications, described 241–47
  non-Hodgkin's lymphoma 36
  osteosarcoma 12–13, 40–41
  overview 205–8
Cherath, Lata 3n, 227n
chewing tobacco, defined **78**
  see also smokeless tobacco
child life specialists, described 198
Children's Brain Tumor Foundation, contact information 381
Children's Hospice International, contact information 381
Choose Your Cover (CDC), Web site address 406
"Choose Your Cover: Facts and Statistics About Skin Cancer" (CDC) 45n
"Choose Your Cover: Questions and Answers" (CDC) **92**
cigarette smokers, cancer risk 67–79
  see also environmental tobacco smoke; tobacco use
"Cigarette Smoking-Related Mortality" (National Center for Chronic Disease Prevention and Health Promotion) 67n
cigar use
  overview 71–75
  statistics **75**
  see also environmental tobacco smoke; tobacco use
CIN *see* cervical intraepithelial neoplasia
cisplatin 242
clinical breast examination (CBE), described 158, 325
"Clinical Guidelines on the Identification, Evaluation, and Treatment of Overweight and Obesity in Adults: Glossary of Terms" (NHLBI) **110**
clinical psychologists, described 198
clinical trials
  defined **312**
  lung cancer 59, 61
  recurrent cancer 316–18
  versus standard therapy 237–39

Index

CNS *see* central nervous system
co-carcinogen, defined **135**
coenzyme Q10
   cancer treatment 230–31
   defined **230**
Coenzyme Q10 (PDQ): Treatment-Patient (NCI) 227n
colon, described 54
colon cancer *see* colorectal cancer
Colon Cancer Alliance (CCA), contact information 381
"Colon Cancer (PDQ): Treatment-Patient" (NCI) 49n
colonoscopy
   colon cancer 57, 162
   virtual **160–61**
colony stimulating factors, described 212, **212**
colorectal cancer
   exercise 113
   overview 54–57
   risk factors **55**, **56**
   tests 57, 159–62
"Colorectal Cancer (PDQ): Screening-Patient" (NCI) 157n
colposcopy
   cervical cancer 102–3
   defined **100**
combined small cell carcinoma 59
Compazine (prochlorperazine) 224
compensating, described 70
complementary and alternative medicine (CAM)
   defined **312**
   overview 227–36
computed tomography (CAT scan; CT scan)
   cancer diagnosis 183
   colonoscopy **160–61**
   defined **188**
   Paget's disease of the breast **173**
   recurrent cancer 311
consolidation therapy, leukemia 26
constipation, cancer treatment 259–60
Cooke, David A. 3n, 87n, 125n, 307n
coping strategies
   described **360**
   family issues **348**, **358**
   family members 349–58

coping strategies, continued
   friends with cancer 331–48
   living each day **356**
   quick tips **354**
   traumatic events 359–70, **370**
"Coping With Loss And Grief Through Online Support Groups" (ERIC Counseling and Student Services Clearinghouse) 359n
"Coping With Loss - Bereavement and Grief" (NMHA) 359n
Co Q10 *see* coenzyme Q10
core biopsy, described 51, 53
counseling
   anxiety 285–86
   depression 284
   emotional concerns 283–86
   family coping strategies 352
   post-traumatic stress disorder (PTSD) 284–85
creatine, defined **106**
crocinic acid *see* cancell/entelev
Crohn's disease, colon cancer 55
cryosurgery, defined **100**
CT scan *see* computed tomography
cyanogenic glucoside **233**
cyclamate, cancer risk 133–34
cyclophosphamide 243
cytarabine 243
cytokines, described 211, **212**
Cytosar (cytarabine) 243
Cytoxan (cyclophosphamide) 243

D

dacarbazine 243
dating, cancer treatment 297–302
Daunomycin (daunorubicin) 243
daunorubicin 243
"Dealing with Others: Back To School" (Teens Living with Cancer) 275n
"Dealing With Others: People Who Stare" (Teens Living with Cancer) 287n
DEET
   cancer **152**
   cancer concerns 151–54
   safety measures **154**
"DEET: General Fact Sheet" (NPIC) **152**
DEHA *see* diethylhexyl adipate

delta-9-tetrahydrocannabinol (THC) 223–25
dental caries, defined **135**
deodorants, breast cancer 142, 145
depression, cancer side effects 271–72
developmental toxicants, defined **85**
dexamethasone 224
diarrhea, cancer treatment 257–59
diet and nutrition
  cachexia 224–25
  cancer 9
  cancer research 113
  cancer treatment 222
  colon cancer **56**
  recurrent cancer 320, 325
diethylhexyl adipate (DEHA) 150–51
differential, described 191–93
digital rectal examination
  colon cancer 57, 161–62
  prostate cancer 62, 164
dioxin, cancer concerns 148–49
diphenhydramine 224
distant recurrence, described 309
doctors *see* oncologists; physicians
"Do It Yourself: Monthly Breast Self-Exam" (University of Iowa) 169n
doxorubicin 244
dronabinol 223
droperidol 224
DSV **236**
DTIC-Dome (dacarbazine) 243
ductal carcinoma 50
ductal carcinoma in situ, described 52
dysplasia, defined **100**

E

ECG *see* electrocardiogram
echocardiogram, cancer diagnosis 185
EKG *see* electrocardiogram
electric and magnetic fields (EMF)
  defined **129**
  described 131
electrocardiogram (ECG; EKG), cancer diagnosis 185
electronic devices, cancer risk 125–31
elevated body temperature *see* fever
EMF *see* electric and magnetic fields
EMLA *see* eutectic mixture of local anesthetics

emotional concerns
  cancer side effects 271–72
  coping strategies **364**
  counseling 283–86
  family coping strategies 351–55
  isolation 303–6
  loneliness 306
  recurrent cancer 320–22, 326–27
emphysema 68
endometrial cancer, oral contraceptives 121–22
environmental conditions, cancer 10
Environmental Protection Agency (EPA)
  see US Environmental Protection Agency
environmental tobacco smoke (ETS)
  health effects **84**
  health risks **83**
  overview 79–86
"Environmental Tobacco Smoke" (NCI) 67n
enzymes, defined **85**
EPA *see* US Environmental Protection Agency
ependymal tumors, defined **18**
ependymomas, described 15
epididymis
  defined **177**
  described 178–79
epithelial carcinoma, defined **18**
ERIC Counseling and Student Services Clearinghouse, online support groups publication 359n
esophageal cancer
  obesity 113
  tobacco use 71
essiac
  cancer treatment 231
  defined **231**
Essiac/Flor-Essence (PDQ): Treatment-Patient (NCI) 227n
estrogen
  defined **120**
  oral contraceptives 117–18
estrogen receptor test, described 52
etoposide 244
ETS *see* environmental tobacco smoke
eurixor *see* mistletoe
eutectic mixture of local anesthetics (EMLA) cream 218

Index

Ewing, James **39**
Ewing's sarcoma
  defined **38**
  described 13, **39**
  overview 37–39
"Ewing's Sarcoma" (Teens Living with Cancer) 37n
excisional biopsy, described 51, 53
exercise
  cancer prevention 113
  recurrent cancer 326
extra-osseous, Ewing's sarcoma 37

F

"Facts and Statistics about Skin Cancer" (CDC) 45n
false-negative test results, described 166, 167
false-positive test results, described 166, 167
familial adenomatous polyposis, colon cancer **55**
family issues
  cancer **348**, 349–58
  common cancers 49–63
  coping strategies **350**, 356, **358**
FDA *see* US Food and Drug Administration
fecal occult blood test
  colon cancer 57, 159–60
  defined **313**
  described 311
Federal Trade Commission (FTC)
  contact information 397
  described **394**
fertility
  cancer side effects 270
  testicular cancer **178**
fever
  cancer diagnosis 192
  cancer treatment 262–64
  leukemia 25–26
fine needle aspiration biopsy
  breast cancer 52
  lung cancer 61
5-fluorouracil 244
flor-essence
  cancer treatment 231
  defined **231**
Fludara (fludarabine) 244
fludarabine 244

"Fluoridated Water" (NCI) 133n
fluoridated water, cancer risk 135–37
fluorouracil cream 103
Food and Drug Administration (FDA) *see* US Food and Drug Administration
"Four-Step Breast Self-Exam" (Planned Parenthood Federation of America, Inc.) 169n
freeze-dried SV **236**
Frozen SV **236**
FSV **236**
FTC *see* Federal Trade Commission

G

Gale Encyclopedia of Medicine 3n, 227n
gallium scanning, cancer diagnosis 184
gastrointestinal tract, defined **313**
G-CSF *see* growth colony stimulating factor
gender factor
  breast cancer 52–54
  cigar use **75**
  Hodgkin's disease **34**
  leukemia 14
  lung cancer 68
  non-Hodgkin's lymphoma 34
  osteosarcoma 11
genital warts, treatment 103
germ cell tumors
  defined **44**
  described 43–44
  statistics **44**
Getting Ready To Go Back To School (Suite 101.com, Inc.), Web site address 406
girls *versus* boys *see* gender factor
Gleason score, described 63
"Glossary" (FDA) **129**
Go Ask Alice! (Columbia University), Web site address 406
graft-*versus*-host disease, described 218
granisetron 224
grief, described 359–70
Grief During Childhood (ACS), Web site address 406
grieving process, described **362**
growth colony stimulating factor (G-CSF), described 218

"Guide to National Cancer Institute Information Resources for Patients and the Public" (NCI) 373n
gum disease, smokeless tobacco 77
Gurney, J.G. 20
"The Gynecological Visit and Exam: Your Key to Good Health" (Planned Parenthood Federation of America, Inc.) 169n

H

hair loss, cancer treatment 287–90
Hamilton, Scott 175, 179
HCA *see* heterocyclic amines
health care team
 cancer 39
 members **196**
"Health Effects of Overexposure to the Sun" (EPA) 87n
"Health Effects of Smoking Among Young People" (National Center for Chronic Disease Prevention and Health Promotion) 67n
Healthfinder, described 401
heart disease
 cancer treatment 268, 269
 obesity 110
 oral contraceptives 117
 secondhand smoke 68
helical CT scan, described 163
helixor *see* mistletoe
hematocrit, cancer diagnosis 191
hemoglobin, cancer diagnosis 191
hepatic adenoma 123–24
hepatoblastoma, defined **18**
hereditary nonpolyposis colon cancer (HNPCC) **55**
heredity
 breast cancer 51, 141–42
 cancer 9
 colon cancer **55**
 male breast cancer **53**
 skin cancer 46
heterocyclic amines (HCA)
 defined **106**
 described 105–7
"Heterocyclic Amines in Cooked Meats" (NCI) 105n
Hippocrates **4**

histology, described 35
History of Cancer (ACS), Web site addres 407
HNPCC *see* hereditary nonpolyposis colon cancer
Hodgkin's disease
 defined **32**
 described 14–15
 overview 33–34
 statistics **34**
Home Care Guide - Helping Brothers and Sisters Cope (Penn State University Children's Hospital), Web site address 407
homocysteine **268**
hormone therapy
 cancer side effects 269–70
 defined **313**
hormone therapy, breast cancer 143
hospitalizations, cancer treatment 201–3
"How to Evaluate Health Information on the Internet" (NCI) 393n
How You Can Help A Family Who Has A Child With Cancer (National Children's Cancer Society), Web site address 407
Hudson, Melissa **268**
human papillomaviruses (HPV)
 cervical cancer 9, 99–104, **104**, 122–23
 defined **100**, **120**
"Human Papillomaviruses and Cancer" (NCI) 99n
hydrazine sulfate, cancer treatmtent 232–33
Hydrazine Sulfate (PDQ): Treatment-Patient (NCI) 227n
Hydrea (hydroxyruea) 244
hydroxyruea 244
hyperalimentation, cancer treatment 222–23
hypoallergenic, defined **292**

I

I Can Cope, described 378
Idamycin (idarubicin) 245
idarubicin 245
Ifex (ifosfamide) 245
ifosfamide 245
"If You Or Someone You Know Has Cancer" (TeensHealth) 331n
IMF *see* International Myeloma Foundation
imiquimod 103

Index

immune suppression, sun overexposure 89, 90
immune system, body issues 299
immunotherapy *see* biological therapy
"Immunotherapy" (NCI) 205n
implant radiation, defined **206**
Inapsine (droperidol) 224
incidence risk, described 19
incisional biopsy, described 51
Indian rhubarb root **231**
induction chemotherapy
  defined **206**
  leukemia 26
  see also chemotherapy
infectious mononucleosis, Hodgkin's disease **34**
infiltrating ductal carcinoma, described 52
inflammatory breast cancer, described 50, 52
intensification therapy, leukemia 26
Interactions With Friends (Childhood Leukemia Center), Web site address 407
interferon alpha 103
interleukins, described 211, **212**
internal radiation therapy, defined **206**
International Myeloma Foundation (IMF), contact information 382
Internet
  cancer information 393–401
  online support groups 366–3707
interstitial radiation, defined **206**
intrathecal chemotherapy, leukemia 26
intravenous line, described 7
ionizing radiation, defined **129**
irradiation, defined **206**
iscador *see* mistletoe
Iscar *see* mistletoe
isorel *see* mistletoe

J

Jims Juice *see* cancell/entelev
JS-101 *see* cancell/entelev
JS-114 *see* cancell/entelev

K

kelp **231**
Susan G. Komen Breast Cancer Foundation, contact information 390
Kytril (granisetron) 224

L

lactate dehydrogenase (LDH), described 61
laetrile
  cancer treatment 233
  defined **233**
Laetrile/Amygdalin (PDQ): Treatment-Patient (NCI) 227n
LAF *see* Lance Armstrong Foundation
LaMont, J. Thomas **161**
Lance Armstrong Foundation (LAF), contact information 382
  see also Armstrong, Lance
large bowel *see* colon
large cell carcinoma, described 58
large cell lymphoma, described 35
laryngeal cancer, cigar smokers 73
"Late Effects of Childhood Cancer" (CancerSource) 267n
LBBC *see* Living Beyond Breast Cancer
LDH *see* lactate dehydrogenase
learning disabilities, cancer side effects 270–71
Lektinol *see* mistletoe
leukemia
  bone marrow transplantation 214
  described 13–14
  overview 23–29
The Leukemia and Lymphoma Society, contact information 383
leukocytes, leukemia 13
lifetime risk, described 19
light cigarettes
  described **70**
  overview 69–71
  see also tobacco use
limb-salvage surgery, defined **12**
Linet, M. **20**
Lipshultz, Steven **268**
liver tumors, oral contraceptives 123–24
Living Beyond Breast Cancer (LBBC), contact information 383
lobes, described 58
lobular carcinoma 50
lobular carcinoma in situ 53
local recurrence, described 309
local therapy, defined **313**
Locks of Love, contact information 384
Loecher, Barbara 139n, **141**

lomustine 245
Look Good ... Feel Better, described 378
low dose radiation therapy *see* radiation therapy
LRF *see* Lymphoma Research Foundation
lumbar puncture (spinal tap), cancer diagnosis 186–87
lung cancer
  cigar smokers 73
  overview 58–61
  screening tests 162–63, 167
  tests 162–63
  tobacco use 68
"Lung Cancer (PDQ): Screening-Patient" (NCI) 157n
lungs, described 58
lymphatic system, defined **12**
lymph nodes
  breast cancer 49–50
  defined **188**
lymphoblastic lymphoma, described 35
lymphocytes, defined **12**
lymphocytic, pronunciation guide **26**
lymphoma
  bone marrow transplantation 214
  described 14–15
  overview 31–36
  treatment **36**
Lymphoma Research Foundation (LRF), contact information 384
lymph system, described 31–32
Lynch syndrome *see* hereditary nonpolyposis colon cancer
lytic, defined **235**

M

Machuga, Edward 150–51
"Magnetic Field Exposure and Cancer Studies at NCI" (NCI) 125n
magnetic resonance imaging (MRI)
  breast cancer tests 159
  cancer diagnosis 182–83
  defined **188**
  Paget's disease of the breast **173**
  recurrent cancer 312
mainstream smoke, described 80
maintenance therapy, leukemia 27
male breast cancer, heredity **53**

"Male Breast Cancer (PDQ): Treatment-Patient" (NCI) 49n
malignant, defined **6**
malignant melanoma 45
mammary Paget's disease *see* Paget's disease of the breast
mammograms
  breast cancer 144–45, 325
  defined 51
  described 159
  oral contraceptives 124
  radiation exposure 166–67
marijuana, cancer treatment 223–25
"Marijuana Use in Supportive Care for Cancer Patients" (NCI) 219n
Marinol (dronabinol) 223
Matulane (procarbazine) 246
Meadows, Michelle 139n
mean average, described 17–18
mechlorethamine 245
median, described 18–21
Medina, Daniel **144**
MEDLINE, described 400–401
medulloblastoma, bone marrow transplantation 214
melanoma
  defined **88**
  described 45, 87–88, 165
melphalan 245
mercaptopurine 245
metastasis
  defined **6, 12**
  described 4, 308
methotrexate 246
methylprednisolone 224
metoclopramide 224
microwaves, cancer concerns 150–51
Miller, Robin 11n
"Mirror Mirror on the Wall" (Teens Living with Cancer) 287n
"Missed Diagnoses: What Young Women Need to Know" (Loecher) **141**
mistletoe
  cancer treatment 233–34
  described **234**
Mistletoe Extracts (PDQ): Treatment-Patient (NCI) 227n
mitoxantrone 246
mixed small cell/large cell carcinoma 59

Index

MMRF *see* Multiple Myeloma Research Foundation
moles, skin cancer 46–47
monoclonal antibodies
  described 212, **212**
  radiation therapy **206**
Morrin, Martina M. **161**
mortality rates
  described 21
  tobacco use 68
The Mountain You Have Climbed: A Young Adult's Guide to Childhood Cancer Survivorship (National Children's Cancer Society, Inc.) 283n, 297n
mourning, described 361–63
mouth sores, cancer treatment 260–62
MRI *see* magnetic resonance imaging
Multiple Myeloma Research Foundation (MMRF), contact information 385
myelodysplasia, bone marrow transplantation 214
myelogenous, pronunciation guide **27**
Myleran (busulfan) 242
Mysliwiec, Pauline A. **160**

N

NABCO *see* National Alliance of Breast Cancer Organizations
National Alliance of Breast Cancer Organizations (NABCO), contact information 385
National Asian Women's Health Organization (NAWHO), contact information 385
National Bone Marrow Transplant Link (nbmtLink), contact information 386
National Cancer Institute (NCI)
  Cancer Information Service, described **374**
  contact information **238**
  PDQ database, described **374**
  publications
    antiperspirants 139n
    artificial sweeteners 133n
    back to school **276**, **278**, **279**, **280**
    breast cancer 49n, 157n
    cancell/entelev 227n
    cancer information 49n
    cancer information on Internet 393n

National Cancer Institute (NCI), continued
  publications, continued
    cartilage 227n
    cellular telephones 125n
    childhood cancer **20**
    clinical trials 237n
    coenzyme Q10 227n
    colon cancer 49n, 157n
    deodorants 139n
    dictionary **6**, **18**, **24**, **32**, **38**, **44**, **88**, **112**, **189**, **202**, **214**, **230**, **254**
    essiac/flor-essence 227n
    family members with cancer 331n
    fluoridated water 133n
    heterocyclic amines 105n
    hospitalizations 201n
    human papillomaviruses 99n
    hydrazine sulfate 227n
    immunotherapy 205n
    laetrile/amygdalin 227n
    lung cancer 49n, 157n
    magnetic field exposure 125n
    male breast cancer 49n
    medical marijuana 219n
    mistletoe extracts 227n
    Newcastle disease virus 227n
    obesity 109n
    oral cancer 157n
    oral contraceptives 117n
    Paget's disease of the breast **173**
    prostate cancer 49n, 157n
    recurring cancer **189**, 307n
    resource information 373n
    selected vegetables/Sun's soup 227n
    714-X 227n
    skin cancer 157n
    support for cancer patients 303n, 349n
    tobacco use 67n
  Web site, described **374**
National Center for Chronic Disease Prevention and Health Promotion, tobacco use publication 67n
National Childhood Cancer Foundation (NCCF), contact information 386
National Children's Cancer Society
  contact information 386
  publications
    cancer survivors 283n
    dating 297n

National Heart, Lung, and Blood Institute (NHLBI)
  contact information 114
  glossary **110**
National Institute of Dental and Craniofacial Research, described 78
National Institute of Diabetes and Digestive and Kidney Diseases (NIDDK), contact information 114
National Institute of Environmental Health Sciences (NIEHS), magnetic fields information **130**
National Institutes of Health (NIH), contact information 376
National Library of Medicine, described **398**, 400–401
National Marrow Donor Program (NMDP), contact information 387
National Mental Health Association (NMHA)
  contact information 387
  coping strategies publication 359n
"National Organizations That Offer Services to People With Cancer and Their Families" (NCI) 373n
National Patient Travel Center (NPTC), contact information 388
National Pesticide Information Center (NPIC), DEET publication **152**
National Spit Tobacco Education Program (NSTEP), described 79
nausea, cancer treatment 254–57
NAWHO see National Asian Women's Health Organization
nbmtLink see National Bone Marrow Transplant Link
NCCF see National Childhood Cancer Foundation
NCI see National Cancer Institute
needle biopsy, described 52, 53
neuroblastomas, bone marrow transplantation 214
neutropenia
  antibiotic medications 221
  defined **299**
  sexuality 299
neutrophils, cancer diagnosis 192
Newcastle disease virus
  defined **235**
  described 234–35
Newcastle Disease Virus (PDQ): Treatment-Patient (NCI) 227n
NHLBI see National Heart, Lung, and Blood Institute
nicotine
  cigarettes 69–70
  cigars 74
  smokeless tobacco 76
NIDDK see National Institute of Diabetes and Digestive and Kidney Diseases
NIEHS see National Institute of Environmental Health Sciences
Nitrogen Mustard (mechlorethamine) 245
NMDP see National Marrow Donor Program
NMHA see National Mental Health Association
NMRI see nuclear magnetic resonance imaging
non-Burkitt's lymphoma, described 35
non-Hodgkin's lymphoma
  defined **32**
  described 14–15
  overview 34–36
non-ionizing radiofrequency (RF) radiation, defined **129**
nonlytic, defined **235**
nonmelanoma skin cancers, described 88–89, 164
non-small cell lung cancer 58–59
"Non-Small Cell Lung Cancer (PDQ): Treatment-Patient" (NCI) 49n
Novantrone (mitoxantrone) 246
NPIC see National Pesticide Information Center
NPTC see National Patient Travel Center
NSTEP see National Spit Tobacco Education Program
nuclear magnetic resonance imaging (NMRI), defined **188–89**
  see also magnetic resonance imaging
nuclear scan
  cancer diagnosis 183–84
  recurrent cancer 312–13
nurses, described 197–98

Index

nutrition *see* diet and nutrition
nutritionists, described 199

O

oat cell cancer 59
obesity
  cancer 9
  cancer risk 109–16
  cancer risk factor **111**
  defined **110**
  statistics 109
"Obesity and Cancer" (NCI) 109n
occupational hazards, cancer 9–10
occupational therapists, described 199
Oncolink (Abramson Cancer Center), Web site address 407
oncologists
  described 5, 195–96
  osteosarcoma 40
oncology fellow, described 196
Oncovin (vincristine) 247
ondansetron 224
126-F *see* cancell/entelev
The Oral Cancer Foundation, contact information 388
oral cancers
  screening tests 163
  smokeless tobacco 76–77
  tobacco use 71
"Oral Cancer (PDQ: Screening-Patient" (NCI) 157n
oral contraceptives, cancer risk 117–24, **118**
"Oral Contraceptives and Cancer Risk" (NCI) 117n
oral leukoplakia
  defined **78**
  smokeless tobacco 77
osteosarcoma
  defined **38**
  overview 11–13, 40–42
  survival rates **42**
"Osteosarcoma" (Teens Living with Cancer) 37n
ovarian cancer, oral contraceptives 121–22
overweight
  defined **110**
  described 109, 110–11
oxidation, defined **230**

P

packed cell volume (PCV), described 191
paclitaxel 246
PAF *see* Patient Advocate Foundation
Paget, James **172**
Paget's disease of the breast, described 172–73
"Paget's Disease of the Breast: Questions and Answers" (NCI) **173**
Paget's disease of the nipple, described 53
pain management, cancer treatment 249–50
Pap test
  cervical cancer 102
  follow-up care 325
  oral contraceptives 124
Paraplatin (carboplatin) 242
Patient Advocate Foundation (PAF), contact information 388
PCP *see Pneumocystis* pneumonia
PCV *see* packed cell volume
"PDQ Cancer Information Summary" (NCI) 49n, 157n
Pediatric Cancer Care: For Teens Only, Web site address 407
"Peer Relationships and Dating" (National Children's Cancer Society, Inc.) 297n
peripheral neuroepithelioma, described 37
peripheral stem cell transplantation
  defined **214**
  described 216
pesticides, cancer studies **152**
phlebotomists, described 199
physical therapy
  cancer treatment 13
  described 199
physicians, described 195–96
Piccolo, Brian 175–76, 179
piercings, immune system 299
the pill *see* oral contraceptives
Planned Parenthood Federation of America, Inc., publications
  breast self-examination 169n
  gynecological examination 169n
plasma, described 190
plastics, cancer concerns 150–51
"Plastics and the Microwave" (Meadows) 139n

platelets
  cancer diagnosis **190**, 192–93
  defined **12**
  leukemia 14, 23
Platinol (cisplatin) 242
plenosol *see* mistletoe
pleura, described 58
PNET *see* primitive neuroectodermal tumor
Pneumocystis pneumonia (PCP) 221
Podofilox (podophyllotoxin) 103
podophyllin 103
podophyllotoxin 103
pollution, cancer 10
polyps
  colon cancer 55
  colonoscopy **160–61**, 162
post-traumatic stress disorder (PTSD)
  cancer side effects 272
  counseling 284–85
precancerous cervical conditions, described 101–2
premature skin aging, sun overexposure 89
primitive neuroectodermal tumor (PNET), Ewing's sarcoma 37–38
procarbazine 246
prochlorperazine 224
progesterone
  defined **120**
  oral contraceptives 117–18
progesterone receptor test, described 52
progestin
  defined **120**
  described 118
progestogen
  defined **120**
  described 118
prostate cancer
  overview 61–63
  screening tests **163**, 163–64
"Prostate Cancer (PDQ): Screening-Patient" (NCI) 157n
"Prostate Cancer (PDQ): Treatment-Patient" (NCI) 49n
prostate gland, described 61–62
prostate-specific antigen (PSA) test 62–63, 164
prosthesis, defined **12**
PSA *see* prostate-specific antigen
psychiatrists, described 197

PTSD *see* post-traumatic stress disorder
pulmonary function test, cancer diagnosis 186
Purinethol (mercaptopurine) 245

Q

Q10 *see* coenzyme Q10
"Questions and Answers about Cigar Smoking and Cancer" (NCI) 67n

R

racial factor
  breast cancer 50
  Ewing's sarcoma 39
radiation
  cellular telephones 126–27
  described **128**
radiation recall, defined **292**
radiation therapy
  cancer treatment 7–8
  defined **206**
  Hodgkin's disease 34
  leukemia 25
  lymphoma 32, **36**
  non-Hodgkin's lymphoma 36
  overview 208–11
radioisotopes **206**
radiologists, described 197
rayon, cancer concerns 148–49
Reach to Rediscovery, described 378
recurrence, defined **313**
recurrent cancer
  classification 309
  coping strategies 319
  diagnosis 310
  overview 307–22
  treatment plans 314
red blood cells
  cancer diagnosis **190**, 191
  defined **12**
  leukemia 14, 23
red clover **231**
"Reducing Cancer Risk" (TeenHealthFX) 48
reflux disease 112–13
regional recurrence, described 309
Reglan (metoclopramide) 224

Index

relative risk, described 19
relative survival rate, described 21
remission
 defined **6, 313**
 described 8
 leukemia 28–29
reproductive behavior
 cancer 9
 cancer treatment 300–301
reproductive sex organs, germ cell tumors 43
"Reregistration of the Insect Repellent DEET" (EPA) 139n
respiratory therapists, described 199
retinoblastoma
 defined **18**
 described 11
RF *see* non-ionizing radiofrequency
rhabdomyosarcomas, described 15–16
Ries, L.A.G. 20
risk, described 19
risk factors
 breast cancer **50**
 cervical cancer 102
 colon cancer **55**
 human papillomaviruses **101, 102, 103**
 male breast cancer **53**
 skin cancer 46
 stomach cancer 105–8

S

saccharin, cancer risk 134
sarcomas, bone marrow transplantation 214
Sayers, Gayle 175
school coping strategies, cancer treatment 275–82
Science News **144, 268**
screening tests *see* tests
secondhand smoke
 defined **85**
 lung cancer 68
 see also environmental tobacco smoke
selected vegetables
 cancer treatment 235–36
 defined **236**
Selected Vegetables/Sun's Soup (PDQ): Treatment-Patient (NCI) 227n
Septra 221
serotonin antagonists 224

714-X, cancer treatment 228
714-X (PDQ): Treatment-Patient (NCI) 227n
sexual behavior
 cancer 9
 cancer treatment 297–301
 recurrent cancer 326
sexually transmitted diseases (STD)
 described 298–99, 300–301
 human papillomaviruses 99–100
 recurrent cancer 326
shaking chills, cancer treatment 264–66
shark cartilage, cancer treatment 229
sheep sorrel **231**
Sheridan's formula *see* cancell/entelev
sidestream smoke, described 80
sigmoidoscopy, colon cancer 57, 160–61
SIL *see* squamous intraepithelial lesions
Sisters Network, Inc., contact information 389
6-thioguanine 247
skin cancer
 overview 45–48, 87–98
 screening tests 164–65
 types **47, 165**
The Skin Cancer Foundation, contact information 389
"Skin Cancer (PDQ): Screening-Patient" (NCI) 157n
skin problems, cancer treatment 290–92
slippery elm **231**
small cell carcinoma 59
small cell lung cancer 58–61
"Small Cell Lung Cancer (PDQ): Treatment-Patient" (NCI) 49n
small non-cleaved cell lymphoma, described 35
Smith, M.A. 20
smokeless tobacco
 overview 76–79
 statistics 78
"Smokeless Tobacco and Cancer: Questions and Answers" (NCI) 67n
smoking cessation, benefits **86**
Smoking Quitline, contact information **68**
snuff, defined **78**
 see also smokeless tobacco
social workers, described 198
sodium laureth sulfate **146–47**

sodium lauryl sulfate **146–47**
soft tissue sarcomas *see* rhabdomyosarcomas
sonogram, described **173**
speech therapists, described 199
SPF *see* sun protection factor
spinal tap *see* lumbar puncture
spiral CT scan, lung cancer screening 162–63
spit tobacco *see* smokeless tobacco
sputum cytology
   described 60
   lung cancer screening 162
squamous cell carcinomas
   defined **88**
   described 45, 58, 89, 164
squamous intraepithelial lesions (SIL)
   defined **100**
   described 101–2
staging, defined **6**
STARBRIGHT Foundation, contact information 390
steroids, cancer treatment 251, 293–95
stevia, cancer risk 135
stomach cancer, uncooked meats 105–7
stool sample *see* fecal occult blood test
students, cancer treatment 275–82
"The Sun, UV, and You: A Guide to Sunwise Behavior" (EPA) **94, 97**
sunburn, skin types 92
sun protection, action steps **94**
sun protection factor (SPF), skin cancer 48, 92–93
sunscreen
   described 90–98
   ingredients 93–95, *95*
   missed areas **46**
   recurrent cancer 325
   sun protection **94**
"Sunscreen: The Burning Facts" (EPA) 87n
Sun's soup
   cancer treatment 235–36
   defined **236**
supplemental nutrition, types **222**
support systems
   cancer patients 336
   cancer treatment 286
   online support groups 368
   osteosarcoma **42**
   recurrent cancer 321–22
   religion 355

surgeons, described 196
"Surgery" (Teens Living with Cancer) 201n
surgery, defined **313**
surgical procedures
   cancer treatment 7, 203–4
   Ewing's sarcoma 13
   germ cell tumors 44
   osteosarcoma 12, 40–41
survival rates, described 21
SV/DSV **236**
syngeneic transplant, described 215
systemic therapy, defined **313**

T

"Taking Time: Support for People with Cancer and the People Who Care About Them" (NCI) 303n, 349n
"Tampons" (FDA) 139n
tampons, cancer concerns 146, 148–50
Tamra, T. **20**
tanning lotion safety 96–97
tanning salons, recommendations **94**
Taxol (paclitaxel) 246
teachers, cancer treatment 279–81
"A Teen Asks About A Mole" (TeenHealthFX) 45n
TeenHealthFX, publications
   moles 45n
   reducing cancer risk **48**
   Web site address 407
"Teen Opinions on Smoking" (CDC) 67n
TeensHealth
   cancer publication 331n
   contact information 391
Teens Living with Cancer
   publications
      back to school **276, 278, 279, 280**
      cancer affect on appearance 287n
      cancer medications 241n
      cancer treatment side effects 253n
      chemotherapy 205n
      dating 297n
      Ewing's sarcoma 37n
      osteosarcoma 37n
      radiation 205n
      sexuality 297n
      surgery 201n
   Web site address 407

Index

"10 Biggest Breast Cancer Myths" (Weiss; Loecher) 139n
teniposide 247
testicles
  defined **177**
  described 178
testicular cancer
  described 15–16
  diagnosis **176**
  overview 175–79
  self examination 177–79, 324
"Testicular Cancer: Questions and Answers" (NCI) **176, 178**
tests
  breast cancer **158,** 158–59, 165–66
  cancer 157–67
  cancer diagnosis 5
  cervical cancer 102–3
  colon cancer 57, 159–62
  follow-up care 324–25
  lung cancer 60–61, 162–63, 167
  prostate cancer **163,** 163–64
  recurrent cancer 310–14
  skin cancer 164–65
  testicular cancer **176**
THC *see* delta-9-tetrahydrocannabinol
thoracentesis, described 61
Tips 4 Youth, Web site address 407
"TIPS 4 Youth: Facts You Should Know" (CDC) 67n
Tobacco Information and Prevention Source (TIPS) (National Center for Chronic Disease Prevention and Health Promotion) 67n
tobacco-specific nitrosamines (TSNA), described 76
tobacco use
  cancer 8
  cancer risk 67–79
  colon cancer **56**
  health risks **72**
  recurrent cancer 325
  teen opinions **80**
  see also environmental tobacco smoke
total parenteral nutrition (TPN), cancer treatment 222–23
toxic shock syndrome (TSS) 149–50
TPN *see* total parenteral nutrition
trachea (windpipe), described 58

transperineal biopsy, described 63
transrectal biopsy, described 63
transrectal ultrasound, prostate cancer 63, 164
traumatic events, coping strategies 359–70, **370**
trichloroacetic acid 103
"The Truth about 'Light' Cigarettes: Questions and Answers" (NCI) 67n
TSNA *see* tobacco-specific nitrosamines
TSS *see* toxic shock syndrome
tumor markers, defined **189**
tumors
  brain 15
  defined **6**
  described 4
  staging **6**
2bME, Web site address 406

U

ubidecarenone *see* coenzyme Q10
ubiquinone *see* coenzyme Q10
ulcerative colitis, colon cancer **55**
ultrasonography, defined **189**
ultrasound
  cancer diagnosis 185
  Paget's disease of the breast **173**
  recurrent cancer 313–14
ultraviolet (UV) radiation
  overexposure prevention **94**
  skin cancer 46, 87, 90–95
umbilical cord blood transplant, described 216
undifferentiated carcinoma, described 58
University of Iowa, breast self-examination publication 169n
urethra, described 62
US Environmental Protection Agency (EPA)
  contact information 375
  publications
    DEET 139n
    skin cancer 87n
    sun protection **94, 97**
US Food and Drug Administration (FDA)
  artificial sweeteners regulation **136**
  contact information 376, 397
  described **394**
  publications
    glossary **129**
    tampons 139n

US TOO! International, Inc., contact information 391
UV *see* ultraviolet
UV index, described **94, 97**

V

VCR (vincristine) 247
Velban (vinblastine) 247
vinblastine 247
vincristine 247
Vital Options International TeleSupport Cancer Network, contact information 391
vital signs, described 193–94
vitamin D, sun exposure 96
vitamin Q10 *see* coenzyme Q10
vomiting, cancer treatment 254–57
VP-16 (etoposide) 244
Vumon (teniposide) 247
Vysorel *see* mistletoe

W

watercress **231**
Weiss, Marisa 139n
The Wellness Community, contact information 392
"What About Hospitalization?" (NCI) 201n
"What Is a Standard Therapy Versus a Clinical Trial?" (NCI) 237n
"When Cancer Recurs: Meeting the Challenge" (NCI) **189**, 307n
"When Someone in Your Family Has Cancer" (NCI) 331n

When Your Child Goes Back To School (ACS), Web site address 408
white blood cells
  cancer diagnosis **190**, 191
  leukemia 23–24
"Wierd Body Issues" (Teens Living with Cancer) 253n
windpipe *see* trachea
wireless telephones *see* cellular telephones

X

X-rays
  cancer diagnosis 181–82
  defined **189**
  lung cancer 60
  lung cancer screening 162
  radiation exposure 167
  recurrent cancer 311
X-ray therapy, defined **206**

Y

Young, J.L. **20**
Young People With Cancer: A Handbook for Parents (NCI) 201n, 205n, 237n, **276**
  Web site address 408
"Your Treatment Plan: Chemotherapy" (Teens Living with Cancer) 205n
"Your Treatment Plan: Radiation" (Teens Living with Cancer) 205n

Z

Zofran (ondansetron) 224